T0338410

Mapping the Risks and Risk Management Practices in Islamic Banking

Founded in 1807, John Wiley & Sons is the oldest independent publishing company in the United States. With offices in North America, Europe, Australia and Asia, Wiley is globally committed to developing and marketing print and electronic products and services for our customers' professional and personal knowledge and understanding.

The Wiley Finance series contains books written specifically for finance and investment professionals as well as sophisticated individual investors and their financial advisors. Book topics range from portfolio management to e-commerce, risk management, financial engineering, valuation and financial instrument analysis, as well as much more.

For a list of available titles, visit our Web site at www.WileyFinance.com.

Mapping the Risks and Risk Management Practices in Islamic Banking

WAEL KAMAL EID
MEHMET ASUTAY

WILEY

Other Wiley Editorial Offices
John Wiley & Sons, 111 River Street, Hoboken, NJ 07030, USA
John Wiley & Sons, The Atrium, Southern Gate, Chichester, West Sussex, P019 8SQ, United Kingdom
John Wiley& Sons (Canada) Ltd., 5353 Dundas Street West, Suite 400, Toronto, Ontario, M9B 6HB, Canada
John Wiley& Sons Australia Ltd., 42 McDougall Street, Milton, Queensland 4064, Australia
Wiley-VCH, Boschstrasse 12, D-69469 Weinheim, Germany

Library of Congress Cataloging-in-Publication Data
Names: Eid, Wael Kamal, 1977- author. | Asutay, Mehmet, author.
Title: Mapping the risks and risk management practices in Islamic banking / Wael Kamal Eid, Mehmet Asutay.
Description: First Edition. | Hoboken : Wiley, 2019. | Series: The Wiley finance | Includes bibliographical references and index. |
Identifiers: LCCN 2019005871 (print) | LCCN 2019006632 (ebook) | ISBN 9781119077800 (Adobe PDF) | ISBN 9781119077824 (ePub) | ISBN 9781119077817 (hardback)
Subjects: LCSH: Banks and banking—Religious aspects—Islam. | Risk management. | BISAC: BUSINESS & ECONOMICS / Banks & Banking.
Classification: LCC HG3368.A6 (ebook) | LCC HG3368.A6 E393 2019 (print) | DDC 332.1068/1—dc23
LC record available at https://lccn.loc.gov/2019005871

Cover Design: Wiley
Cover Image: © Abdolhamid Ebrahimi/iStock.com

Typeset in 10/12pt, TimesLTStd by SPi Global, Chennai, India.

Printed and bound in Singapore by Markono Print Media Pte Ltd

10 9 8 7 6 5 4 3 2 1

For my mother and father who showed unconditional love and taught me the values of hard work and integrity. And for the light of my life: Pinar, Fares, and Kamal

—Wael Kamal Eid

To the dedication and diligence of the intellectual workers of Islamic finance industry

—Mehmet Asutay

Contents

Foreword

This study is a welcome addition to the literature on risk management in Islamic banking. The financial institutions survived the global financial crisis of 2007–2009 relatively unscathed and the more benign financial environment since has witnessed the stabilisation of Islamic finance. However, its market penetration has remained disappointing during the last decade – a likely explanation for this being the failure of the industry to get the message across to potential clients of the significance of risk-sharing for Islamic finance. There remains a widespread perception that Islamic banking is very similar to its conventional counterpart, which discourages clients from switching their accounts and applying for Islamic financing.

Financial regulators, with some notable exceptions such as Bank Negara in Malaysia, often have the same requirements for all banks, including Islamic banks. This, regulators argue, creates a level playing field; but it makes no allowance for the inherent differences of Islamic banks. Regulators must take some of the blame for Islamic banks not distinguishing themselves as there is a disincentive to introduce more innovative financial products that might thrive more in a more liberal regulatory environment. At present Islamic banks are subject to the same requirements for managing risk, whereas light touch regulation of the sector could facilitate its development.

Dr Eid and Professor Asutay examine the different types of risks banks face including credit risk, concentration risk, market risk, liquidity risk and operational risk. Asset–liability management (ALM) and displaced commercial risk are also covered as well as *Shari'ah* risk. This book therefore provides a very comprehensive approach to risk exposure and how it can be managed. The core of the research was a questionnaire survey completed by participants from 18 countries. The data from the survey was analysed using non-parametric statistical techniques including factor and multivariate analysis. In addition, semi-structured interviews were held with 37 leading Islamic bank professionals; of which 33 comprised the final sample. This provided greater depth to the study and gives the reader a better understanding of the underlying issues.

The book serves as an essential guide to risk management in Islamic banking and is a "must read" for researchers working in this area, including university faculty and postgraduate students of Islamic finance. Although primarily an academic study, the book should prove worthwhile reading for financial regulators and professional bankers working in the Islamic finance industry. The findings from the surveys are clearly explained and there is a useful chapter that provides an interpretative discussion. Overall the work is an insightful and useful piece of research.

Professor Rodney Wilson
Emeritus Professor, Durham University

About the Authors

Wael Kamal Eid, PhD is the Chief Risk Officer at SEDCO Holding and the Chairman of the Audit and Risk Committee of Al Nahdi Medical Company, and Member of AutoWorld Audit Committee. He is a risk specialist in Islamic banking who holds an MBA with Distinction from Warwick Business School, and a PhD in risk management from Durham University.

Dr. Eid has extensive experience in risk management and Islamic banking in the Middle East and Europe. He is also a guest lecturer on Risk Management and Islamic Finance at distinguished universities and speaks regularly at international risk management events and conferences. Dr. Eid is the winner of the 2015 Golden Peacock Award for Risk Management by the prestigious Institute of Directors (IoD).

Mehmet Asutay is a Professor of Middle Eastern and Islamic Political Economy and Finance at the Durham University Business School; Director of the Durham Centre in Islamic Economics and Finance; and Programme Director for the MSc in Islamic Finance and the MSc in Islamic Finance and Management programmes and the Durham Islamic Finance Summer School. Mehmet's teaching, research, publication and supervision of research all falls within Islamic moral economy/Islamic economics, Islamic political economy, Islamic finance and banking, Islamic governance and management and the Middle Eastern political economies. His articles on his research interests have been published in various international academic journals and professional magazines. He has also published and edited books on aspects of Islamic moral economy and Islamic finance.

CHAPTER 1

Introduction

Research Background and Motivation

Risk knows no religion
—Michael Ainley, Head of Wholesale Banking, FSA (2007)

Was Michael Ainley right when he assumed that risk management is similar across different cultures and religions, in this case Islamic and conventional banks? Are Islamic banks just like any other bank that provides financial services, and hence have similar risk management requirements?

The subject of risk management in Islamic banking has many facets. On the surface, the frequently repeated story that Islamic banks are more resilient than conventional ones is attractive in a world torn by a financial tsunami. Unfortunately, at least in the current form in which Islamic banking is practised, this is not entirely true. The assumption at one point early in the crisis was that the Islamic market would be entirely unaffected and would sail through the crunch; and people thought that the financial crisis would be the lift-off platform for Islamic banks. On the contrary, the crisis exposed a number of areas in Islamic banking that needed to be dealt with.

This study examines different aspects of risk management issues in Islamic banking. At the heart of this book is the question of whether Islamic banks are more or less risky than their conventional peers. A review of the existing literature does not provide a clear-cut answer to this question. The majority of the relevant literature gives conflicting views using theoretical arguments rather than a formal empirical analysis. The question is clearly an empirical one, the answer to which requires feedback from the market place. The study thus attempts to fill this gap in the empirical literature on risk management in Islamic banking through a survey-based questionnaire and in-depth interviews.

The difficulties afflicting conventional financial markets since mid-2007 have led to more attention being paid to Islamic alternatives. While the modern Islamic finance industry is still young, it has been growing rapidly for several years, largely on the back of an oil-fuelled economic boom in the Middle East. Much demand came from non-Islamic investors who were simply attracted by good investment opportunities. With awareness of the industry rising, Islamic banks have expanded their operations, especially in the core markets of the Middle East and South Asia, but also in newer markets with substantial Muslim populations, including Sub-Saharan Africa and parts of Europe.

At the same time, risk management is receiving increased attention everywhere due to the financial crisis, and risk management products and methods for Islamic banking and finance (IBF) are certainly a hot issue. The market turmoil of the past few years has triggered a wide-ranging reassessment of the global financial system and a need to understand the causes that led to a financial crisis of a severity not seen since the Great Depression. One of the main areas of attention has been the failure of many financial institutions to manage their risks adequately. In most cases, the industry debate has focused on pure risk management failures, particularly the shortcomings of risk models in measuring risks accurately, without addressing the broader issue of how risk is managed at the highest macroeconomic levels and how the whole financial system is based on greed and lack of morality. Since then the credit crunch has afforded advocates of Islamic finance an opportunity to emphasise *Shari'ah* principles relating to debt and risk, finding a receptive audience beyond the Muslim world. For Islamic financiers, highly complex structured products such as subprime and toxic assets were seen as unacceptable because they were so far removed from their underlying assets.

There appears to be great potential for further growth in Islamic banking, which is still at a relatively early stage. However, there are also a number of challenges associated with developing a new industry with a different approach to risk management. It is notable that although Islamic banks were unscathed by the subprime crisis, many have since suffered from the negative effects of the broader recession, including a collapse in property prices in Dubai, where many Gulf Islamic banks had substantial exposure. The first *sukuk* defaults occurred in 2009 from two Gulf-based corporate institutions: Kuwait's Investment Dar and Saudi Arabia's Saad Group; others followed shortly after.

This research provides an up-to-date overview of current market practices, issues and trends in risk management for Islamic banks. It focuses on practical applications and discusses a wide range of unique risks faced by Islamic banks from the perspective of different ranges of practitioners. The book asserts that the weaknesses of many financial firms in managing their risks have to be looked at in a comprehensive fashion. The root drivers of the prevailing financial system have to be challenged and replaced by a more transparent and ethical alternative.

This research combines conceptual frameworks with 'hands-on' practical perceptions of risk management in Islamic banking in a pioneering piece of research that *Shari'ah* scholars, policy-makers, practitioners, academics and researchers will find of relevance and a motivation to conduct further research in this vital but under-researched area. Although a few *Shari'ah* opinions are included in the book, religious and *Shari'ah* discussions are beyond the scope of this research.

SYSTEMIC IMPORTANCE OF ISLAMIC BANKING AND FINANCE

Islamic finance is the fastest-growing sector in the financial industry at present. Launched to reconcile the financial with the theological needs of a global community of 1.5 billion Muslims, Islamic finance today offers a broad and sophisticated range of products and services. Double-digit growth rates for *Shari'ah*-compliant assets over the past decade have naturally driven Islamic financiers to look beyond historical boundaries to explore new territories, both within and outside the Muslim world.

The increasing international interest in Islamic finance is a reflection of the success that this industry has achieved during its short history. Moreover, *Shari'ah* principles that place emphasis on providing economic added-value to stakeholders, and aim to create equivalence in benefits and costs, free from harmful speculation, are gaining more attention and better understanding globally. Several Western supervisory bodies are incorporating amendments to their supervisory and regulatory legislation to allow for Islamic institutions and *Shari'ah*-compliant products, which will reinforce the role of Islamic finance globally. Nowadays, in European, American and most Western markets, financial institutions are offering more products and services to cater for Islamic finance. Moreover, a great number of financial institutions in Gulf Cooperation Council (GCC) countries and in Asia are managing funds of over USD 300 billion and are encouraged by their markets to provide Islamic financial services (Moody's, 2011a).

Islamic banking, being the main sub-sector within the Islamic finance industry, has been pioneering this exponential growth. According to Moody's (2011a), the total assets held by Islamic banks globally amounted to more than USD 1 trillion by the end of 2010. While Islamic banks have been hit by the economic downturn, they have been considerably less affected than most conventional banks. This is mainly because, unlike conventional banks, the Islamic banks have not been exposed to losses from investment in toxic assets, nor have they been highly dependent on wholesale funds. Furthermore, Islamic instruments are highly useful alternative investments for the diversification of portfolios, as they have low correlation to other market segments, allow the selective underweighting of particular sectors, and seem to be relatively independent of even market turbulences like the subprime crisis. As a consequence, the increasing standardisation of derivatives and *sukuk*, as well as the growing liquidity and organisation of the Islamic capital market, offers many opportunities to innovative investors.

With such a background, it is obvious that Islamic banks have come a long way. The future of these institutions, however, will depend on how they cope with the rapidly changing financial world. With globalisation and the information technology revolution, the scope of different financial institutions has expanded beyond national jurisdictions, particularly for investment and wholesale banks. As a result, the financial sector in particular has become more dynamic, competitive and complex. There has been unprecedented development in computing, mathematical finance and innovation of risk management techniques. Moreover, the financial crisis is likely to challenge the global risk management foundations. All these developments are expected to magnify the challenges that Islamic financial institutions (IFIs) face, particularly as more well-established conventional institutions have begun to provide Islamic financial products. IFIs need to equip themselves with the up-to-date management skills and operational systems to cope with this environment. One major factor that will determine the survival and growth of the industry is how well these institutions manage the risks generated in providing Islamic financial services.

The last three decades have witnessed a shift of focus in the development of Islamic banking. The original objective of the 1960s and 1970s of developing an interest-free financial system is no longer the primary objective for Islamic bankers. The current core issue is to develop an Islamic financial industry which does not suffer from the weaknesses of the conventional banking system, particularly after the current credit crisis. Thus, the focus has shifted to risk management and mitigation, financial engineering, innovation and providing common standards in Islamic finance.

Banking, in all its forms, contains risks that pose a challenge to all stakeholders. Islamic banks, like their conventional counterparts, are financial institutions which provide services to depositors and investors on the one hand and offer financing to companies, the public sector and individuals on the other. They are therefore subject to many risks that are similar to those confronted by conventional banks. There is a growing concern that the risk management practices of Islamic banking are not keeping pace with the global financial market. The rapid growth of Islamic banking on all fronts calls for proactive responses to risk management issues. In addition, *Shari'ah*-compliant banks have their own unique set of risks that differ from those borne by conventional banks. In principle, there is a range of activities through which Islamic banks can work in different ways that enable them to provide funds. These activities are adapted to meet the *Shari'ah* principles that govern Islamic banking, the most important of which is the principle of risk sharing.

Managing risk especially in the current perilous times is no easy task. The events of mid-September 2008 challenged financial institutions' preconceived ideas of how to view risk. Until 15 September 2008, few bankers would have thought a systematically important and highly rated financial institution such as Lehman Brothers could have failed, let alone failed as quickly as it did. Risk management in Islamic banking is a hot issue as little is yet understood on many aspects, with IFIs facing significant challenges in measuring and managing risks. Effective risk management in Islamic banking therefore deserves priority attention because the future of Islamic banks will largely depend on how they manage their unique set of risks. So far, Islamic banking has been free-riding on financial theories and instruments developed within the context of the conventional debt- and interest-based system. Unless the Islamic banking industry develops its own genuine risk management architecture, it cannot achieve the dynamism of the Islamic finance system, which provides the security and viability needed for a more resilient financial system than the debunked Wall Street model.

RESEARCH AIMS, OBJECTIVES AND QUESTIONS

This research attempts to fill the gap in the empirical literature on risk management in Islamic banking. It recognises upfront that Islamic banking offers its own unique approach to risk management. Following a structured approach, first, the research aim and objectives were identified, and then research questions were developed within the context of the broader objectives.

The aim of this research is to explore and analyse the risk and risk management practices in the Islamic banking industry through the perceptions and opinions of participants drawn from the banking and finance industry. In doing so, this research maps out attitudes toward risk in the IBF industry and locates perceptions of the various stakeholders on risk management-related practices in the industry.

In fulfilling the identified research aim, the following specific objectives are developed:

(i) To ascertain the fundamental principles underlying risk management in Islamic banking and the unique risks facing IFIs;
(ii) To investigate the effect of different control variables like region, country, respondent's position, nature of financial institution, nature of operations, and accounting standards on the participant's perception of the nature of risks, risk measurement, and risk management and mitigation approaches of IFIs in comparison to those of conventional banks and with reference to the market conditions in which IFIs operate;
(iii) To evaluate the applicability of Islamic Financial Services Board (IFSB) Standards and Guidelines with respect to risk management and capital

adequacy, and how the Guidelines could operate in a Basel II (and potentially Basel III) era;

(iv) To investigate the real roots of the recent crisis with a view to drawing some lessons for IFIs;

(v) To examine the dichotomy between the theory and practice of Islamic banking; and

(vi) To explore the next chapter for risk management in Islamic banking.

The following specific research questions are developed to address and investigate the broader research objectives:

(i) What are the top risks facing IFIs?

(ii) What is the risk appetite associated with each Islamic finance contract?

(iii) Does risk management in Islamic banking differ from conventional banking?

(iv) Are Islamic banks more or less risky than their conventional peers?

(v) Are Basel II (and potentially Basel III) standards suitable for Islamic banking?

(vi) What are the appropriate capital requirement levels for IFIs?

(vii) Is Islamic banking actually more resilient than conventional banking?

(viii) Could the recent crisis have occurred under an Islamic banking system?

(ix) How developed and significant is hedging to Islamic banking?

(x) Is there divergence between the current practice and moral principles of Islamic banking?

(xi) How does the future look for Islamic banking? What strategies should IFIs follow?

In answering the research questions, the impact of various categories of respondents and their profile indicators on risk perception are also investigated.

RESEARCH HYPOTHESES

Based on the dichotomy that exists between theory and practice in analysing risk management in Islamic banking, this research aims to explore and study the opinions and risk perceptions of various groups of Islamic banking professionals with the aim of answering the identified research questions.

The following research hypotheses were formulated to determine the parameters of the research questions:

(i) The main risks facing Islamic banks are reputational risk, *Shari'ah*-non-compliance risk, asset–liability management risk, liquidity risk and concentration risk.

(ii) Islamic bankers prefer mark-up-based contracts and shy away from profit-sharing contracts.

(iii) Profit-sharing contracts are perceived as more risky than mark-up-based contracts.

(iv) There is no substantial difference between risk management in Islamic banking and conventional banking.

(v) Capital requirement levels should be lower in IFIs than in conventional banks.

(vi) Basel II was drafted with conventional banking very much in mind. IFIs should follow their own standards, e.g. IFSB Principles on capital adequacy.

(vii) Islamic banking is more resilient to economic shocks than is conventional banking, but is not recession proof.

(viii) Not many Islamic banks use the more technically advanced risk measurement and reporting techniques.

(ix) The use of risk measurement techniques is less advanced among Islamic banks than among their conventional peers.

(x) Islamic banks use a number of risk mitigation tools that are intended to be *Shari'ah*-compliant and that are less advanced than those utilised by conventional banks.

(xi) Most IFIs abandoned conservative risk management *Shari'ah* principles in favour of copying conventional structures.

(xii) There is strong potential for Islamic banking provided that it goes back to its roots.

(xiii) Perceptions of Islamic and conventional bankers differ significantly, as Islamic bankers are more biased toward their business model, and vice versa.

The above hypotheses are further broken down into more refined sub-hypotheses for testing purposes later in this research; these are presented in the research methodology chapter (Chapter 6).

SIGNIFICANCE OF THE STUDY

This book has a particular significance as it attempts to provide a complete overview of risk management in Islamic banking. This makes it a valuable resource for both conventional and Islamic investors, as well as for IFIs, researchers, consultants and policy-makers who are faced with the increasing complexity of Islamic instruments. Risk management is receiving more attention all over the world due to the subprime crisis, and for most IFIs, risk management presents specific challenges.

The existing body of knowledge demonstrates that research on risk management in Islamic banking is still scarce. Globally there has been a significant increase in the literature on risk management over the past decade, especially during the past two years. This has emerged largely because of a combination of developments: first, there has been greater reflection on risk mitigation and management in the wake of frequent episodes of financial crisis; second, financial diversification and product innovation have brought new dimensions and types of risks to the forefront; third, the endeavours of the financial community to develop and innovate financial architecture have resulted in financial institutions facing different types of risk. Cross-segment mergers, acquisitions and financial consolidation have blurred the risks of various segments in the industry. However, these developments have revolved around the conventional banking system, benefiting incrementally from the financial engineering and innovation of esoteric products and structures. While Islamic banking has grown substantively in the last few years, appreciation of its risk architecture and profile is still evolving (Greuning and Iqbal, 2008).

Reflecting the increased role of Islamic finance, the literature on Islamic banking has also grown in the last decade. There is now a considerable amount of research on the topic of IBF; nevertheless there are still large gaps in the coverage of topics related to risk management. A large part of the literature focuses on Islamic finance contracts, structures, roots of Islamic finance, comparisons of the instruments used in Islamic and conventional banking, and the regulatory and supervisory challenges related to Islamic banking. This is to be expected because the initial focus of the whole Islamic finance industry was to create awareness of Islamic finance and its basic concepts among a *riba*-dominated financial world. Nevertheless, the last few years have witnessed a shift of focus in the literature on Islamic banking toward more specialised areas like capital markets, mergers and acquisitions, asset management, *sukuk*, structuring and product development, innovation and standardisation. There is, however, relatively little research conducted on risk management and capital requirements for Islamic banking; such research includes studies by Haron and Hin Hock (2007), Iqbal and Mirarkor (2007), Akkizidis and Khandelwal (2007), Grais and Kulathunga (2007), Greuning and Iqbal (2007), Mahlknecht, M (2009), Sundararajan (2007), and others as explored in Chapter 3.

Given the lack of sufficient research about risk management in Islamic banking, there is even less empirical research available in this vital area. A limited number of papers discuss risks in IFIs but they do so in academic terms instead of pragmatic analysis of data. On the other hand, empirical papers on Islamic banks focus on issues related to efficiency and financial stability, such as Yudistira (2004), Moktar et al., (2006) and Heiko and Cihak (2008). But risk management in Islamic banking has not been thoroughly analysed in an empirical fashion, with the exception of a handful of sources like the profound work done by Khan and Ahmed (2001), Noraini et al. (2009) and Mahlknecht (2009).

In addition, the previous studies on risk management in Islamic banking only highlight the issues without offering any feasible solutions. Therefore, this book is considered distinct, and departs from previous studies by offering practical and feasible recommendations to improve risk management architectures within Islamic banking. Moreover, this study provides a larger sample size within the wider populations in the Islamic banking industry, and includes a very well diversified sample of respondents (geographically, by background, by the nature of activities of their organisations, as well as by other control variables) to enable the researcher to obtain better findings by conducting significance tests on the differences between various groups. The survey findings are further enhanced by in-depth interviews with senior Islamic banking professionals, which allow more room for interviewees to express their views in a less formal and more open way than in the structured questionnaire. The interview sample is also well diversified.

Finally, while a few scholars have researched the practical implementation of risk management in Islamic banking, this book is the first of its kind to do so after the recent credit crisis. The book extracts empirical evidence from the perceptions of Islamic banking professionals and from the recent crisis to substantiate the research process and the findings of the research.

OVERVIEW OF THE RESEARCH METHODOLOGY

In responding to the research questions outlined above, this book undertakes a combination of two research methods: firstly, a comprehensive review of the existing literature and theory, and secondly, an empirical study to elicit opinions and perceptions in response to the theory which is discussed in the literature. Both quantitative and qualitative data analyses are used for this part.

In the first part of the research, the theoretical framework of this study was constructed through the literature review, which is presented in a series of chapters. The main literature sources were journals, conference proceedings, books, reports, theses and bank regulators' papers. Due to the fact that literature on risk management in Islamic banking is scant, information and quotations from interviews are used in the literature review to substantiate the argument. This may not accord with convention; however, this strategy helped to provide a better understanding by combining primary and secondary material on the subject matter.

The second part of the book is concerned with an empirical study which investigates the respondents' perceptions of risk management issues in Islamic banking. A survey technique using questionnaires is used in this context to obtain primary data from the target sample of bankers, financiers and *Shari'ah* scholars. The data was analysed using Statistical Package for Social Science (SPSS) software. In addition, semi-structured interviews are used to substantiate and compare the questionnaire findings. A detailed description of the research process is presented in Chapter 6.

OVERVIEW OF THE RESEARCH

This study consists of two major sections, namely background and empirical work. Chapters 2 to 6 are the foundational chapters for the following five; these latter form the empirical part of the book.

Following this brief introduction, the book continues with 10 closely interrelated chapters. There is unavoidably some overlap of discussion and cross-referencing. The overview of Chapters 2 to 11 is as follows:

Chapter 2 Principles of Islamic Banking and Finance reviews the existing literature, texts and other relevant reference materials. In order to understand the risks that IFIs face, this chapter first briefly discusses the nature of these institutions with the objective of providing an introduction to Islamic banking and its instruments; however, this is not intended to provide a detailed description of how Islamic financial products are structured. This chapter is divided into three sections: the first explains the basic tenets of Islamic finance and the most commonly used terms and contracts, the second discusses the important financial instruments available and the market size, and the third looks at the international standardisation bodies.

Chapter 3 Risk Management in Islamic Banks: A Theoretical Perspective commences with an overview of risk management in general. After defining and identifying different risks, specific issues related to risk management and mitigation in Islamic banking are discussed. Risks are classified into two main categories: risks which Islamic banks have in common with traditional banks as financial intermediaries, and risks which are unique to Islamic banks due to their compliance with the *Shari'ah* principles. The risk characteristics of Islamic products and the complexities of some of these are rigorously examined. This chapter is based on both academic desk research and practical views form the open interviews conducted.

As for **Chapter 4 Capital Adequacy for Islamic Banks: A Survey**, realising the significance of capital in today's Basel-dominated era, a designated chapter is allocated to analysing capital adequacy for Islamic banks. This chapter examines the need for capital and provides the rational and historical background of the Basel I, II and III frameworks. It then highlights the detailed analysis of credit, market and operational risks that has been given by the Basel II Accord. Proposed amendments to the Accord after the recent crisis and the proposed Basel III standards are discussed. The chapter then examines the applicability of the three Pillars of Basel II to Islamic banking. The chapter also signifies the link between the role of social responsibility of Islamic finance and market disclosure. This chapter further identifies the key role the Islamic Financial Services Board (IFSB) plays in the development of standards for risk management in the Islamic financial industry.

Chapter 5 focuses on **Islamic Banking and the Financial Crisis**. In theory, Islamic banks are more resilient to economic shocks than conventional banks. Sadly, close mimicry of Western products in the pursuit of easy profits caused Islamic banking to divert from the basic principles laid down more than 1400 years ago. Hence, Islamic banks are currently feeling the effects of the recession despite their limited exposure to higher-risk financial products. The recent crisis acts as a wake-up call; if Islamic banks learn the right lessons, they could bounce back strongly. This chapter combines evidence from the recent crisis with the principles discussed in the previous chapters to prove that the Islamic financial system, specifically with its different approach to risk, can act as panacea for economic woes.

Chapter 6 Research Framework and Methodology discusses the research strategy and methodology adopted for the data collection process. It presents in great detail the recommended research procedures by making reference to the various research methodology textbooks on the appropriate research process and technique to be used. The rationale and justifications for each of the tools and techniques used throughout this study are also presented. In addition, the chapter also presents more closely the refined research sub-hypothesis which is to be tested in the analysis chapter.

Chapter 7 Profiling Perspectives on Risk Dimensions in Islamic Finance: Descriptive Questionnaire Data Analysis takes the research to the market place by analysing data and presenting the results from a survey on risk management issues in IFIs. It includes a demographic profile analysis and also the core variables for the research. The purpose of this chapter is to give an overview analysis of the findings from the survey. The descriptive analysis benefited from a frequency analysis, which also includes the frequency percentage, mean and standard deviations value for each of the variables; this provides readers with grounding knowledge for the overall results.

Chapter 8 Analysing Perceptions of Risk and Risk Management Dimensions and Issues: Inferential Statistical Analysis presents further analysis of the views and risk perceptions of respondents using inferential statistical tools such as the Kruskal-Wallis test, factor analysis, MANOVA multivariate analysis of variance and the Chi-Square tests. The results of the analysis are discussed, interpreted and justified in great detail. The aim is to explore the results in as much detail as possible from the data in order to respond to the research questions.

Chapter 9 Exploring Perceptions of Risk and Risk Management Practices in Islamic Banking: Interview Data Analysis is an analysis of the semi-structured interviews conducted with a number of Islamic banking professionals from banking institutions, consulting and law firms, academia and rating agencies. A focused coding technique is used to analyse and sort the findings. This chapter represents the findings of the qualitative analysis.

Chapter 10 Contextualising the Findings: An Interpretative Discussion presents the overall discussion of the findings in Chapters 7, 8 and 9 by responding to each of the research hypotheses. The chapter provides an in-depth discussion of each of the hypotheses, and also makes cross-references to the theory and findings of previous studies in order to link together all the pertinent main findings in this study. The outcome of this chapter helps to derive the overall conclusions of the study.

The last chapter, **Chapter 11 Conclusion and Research Recommendations**, presents a summary of the major findings, recommendations and limitations, and offers suggestions for future research.

CHAPTER 2

Principles of Islamic Banking and Finance

Until the global credit crunch hit the capital and financial markets in the middle of 2008, Islamic finance had enjoyed uninterrupted growth since the start of the decade to become an industry with about USD 1 trillion in assets (Moody's, 2011a). In terms of the size of the world's finance industry as a whole, this is still very small, less than a 1% share; but with nearly 25% of the world's population being Muslim, it is obvious that the potential for growth is enormous (Eedle, 2009). The global potential market for Islamic finance is conservatively estimated at USD 4 trillion, whereas the actual size of the market is USD 1 trillion, or a market share of 25%, which means that there is still around 75% of the market to capture (Moody's, 2011a).

Despite being presented as a new phenomenon, Islamic finance has been practised since the Middle Ages. It has risen in prominence over the last 30 years. This is largely due to the growing financial resources of oil-producing countries where Islam is the main religion, an increase in wealth and financial sophistication, and an increasing demand for financial services. In recent times, the emerging Islamic banking sector has achieved acceptance in the Western world where there is increasing interest in ethical finance, and funds managed by Islamic institutions continue to grow.

In order to understand the risks that Islamic banks face, this chapter first discusses the nature of Islamic banking. It also provides a brief introduction to Islamic banking and its basic contracts, defines default in Islamic finance, and distinguishes the elements of an Islamic bank's risk profile that need to be evaluated differently as compared to conventional banking. As an initial foundational chapter, it paves the way for the following chapters analysing risk management in Islamic banking. This chapter, however, is not designed to provide a detailed history of the origins and evolution of the industry, nor an in-depth analysis of how Islamic financial products are structured.

HISTORICAL BACKGROUND OF ISLAMIC BANKING AND FINANCE

In Western and Central Europe, modern financial institutions in both banking and insurance started to evolve during the 17th century, notably in Britain, as a response to the development of capitalism, and in part due to the development of mathematical techniques in finance. The industrial revolution in the late 18th and early 19th centuries provided the basis for their further growth. With the dissolution of the Ottoman Empire, Britain and France established settlements in a number of Arab countries that had formerly been part of the Empire, and Western-style financial institutions were introduced. In the absence of Islamic financial institutions (IFIs), those in need of financial services in these countries turned to the Western-style or conventional banks and insurance companies, without paying too much attention to their non-compliance with *Shari'ah* rules and principles. In the case of savings, an alternative was simply to hold them in the form of cash (AbdelKarim and Archer, 2005).

This institutionally passive financial behaviour began to change in the 1950s and 1960s after these countries achieved political independence; which also put the development of Muslim identity on the agenda. In fact, the initiation of modern Islamic finance dates back to 1962 with the establishment of *Tabung Haji* in Malaysia, and the *Mit Ghamr* bank in Egypt in 1963 (Iqbal and Molyneux, 2005). However, the institutionalisation of Islamic banking was not achieved until the 1970s, when a global network of Islamic banks started to emerge.

In the post-independence period changes took place in the political climate of most Muslim nations and many Arab oil-exporting countries, which experienced tremendous economic growth following the sharp rise in oil prices in 1973. Most of the earnings from the sale of crude oil were surplus to the immediate needs of these countries, leading to an increase in the circulated currency and commercial activity. This increased wealth gave rise to a major need for financial intermediation for the investment of petrodollars, mainly outside the Middle Eastern and Muslim countries, which had limited capacity to absorb such a volume of investment. The situation constituted a major impetus for the development of Islamic banking institutions (AbdelKarim and Archer, 2005). This coincided with the growth in Muslim identity construction which emerged from religious passion in several Muslim countries calling for reform and for a return to basic Islamic principles. Recent examples of such a search for Muslim identity through the medium of various Islamic movements include Egypt, Iran, Syria, Sudan, Algeria, Jordan and Palestine. In line with the Muslim search for identity, the substantial Muslim populations increasingly sought to direct their financial surpluses and businesses into *Shari'ah*-compliant or Islamic banks and financial institutions (Lewis and

Algaoud, 2001). Thus, although the principles of Islamic finance have had roots in the Holy *Qur'an* for the last 1400 years, modern Islamic banking emerged only in the 1970s.

Islamic banking grew rapidly throughout the 1990s, and during the past few years there have been significant developments in the world of Islamic banking and finance (IBF). As a result, the industry has evolved from a regional business into one of global scale. As part of this process, Islamic and Western financial institutions (such as HSBC, BNP-Paribas, Citibank, Standard Chartered Bank, etc.) have focused their attention on the growing customer demand for *Shari'ah*-compliant financing, investments and insurance products. It is a fact that international banks and other service providers are aware of the significant liquidity available in the Middle East. The choice of *Shari'ah*-compliant investments has also broadened and includes structured products, mutual funds, direct investments in initial public offerings, leasing and real estate projects, discretionary portfolios and alternative investment strategies like hedge funds, private equity, venture capital and Islamic insurance (*Takaful*). Development in consumer financing has also been unprecedented, and consumer financing products today include Islamic mortgages, credit cards, car finance, personal loans and lease finance.

Islamic banking today is viewed as one of the fastest-growing segments of the Islamic financial industry. It has experienced double-digit growth, spurred by the licensing of new banks, largely in local markets, the establishment of Islamic windows and subsidiaries by major international banks, and partial or full conversion of conventional banks into Islamic banks. Table 2.1 summarises the considerable progress that has been made in almost all aspects of Islamic finance over the past three decades.

With the internationalisation of Islamic finance, further progress was made in developing capital markets. The pace of product innovation has increased, and Islamic banking is currently the fastest-growing segment of the credit market in Muslim countries. Recently IFIs have started moving toward equity funds, *sukuk*, advanced treasury services, balance sheet management, and innovative asset management.

Of notice is the recent rash of new Islamic bank start-ups, even during the current market turbulence. In fact, there are many reasons why new IFIs have been mushrooming across the board:

(i) Financial theory states that a booming and profitable market naturally attracts new entrants because excess demand needs to be met by additional supply; the Islamic finance market is driven by demand.

(ii) Financing needs in the retail sector are far from optimally served by the banking industry, especially in the Arab countries of the Muslim universe: retail

TABLE 2.1   Modern history of developments in Islamic finance

Time Period	Development
Pre-1950s	Barclays Bank opens its Cairo branch to process financial transactions related to construction of the Suez Canal in the 1890s. Islamic scholars challenge the operations of the bank, criticising it for charging interest. This criticism spreads to other Arab regions and to the Indian subcontinent, where there is a sizable Muslim community. The majority of *Shari'ah* scholars declare that interest in all its forms amounts to the prohibited element of *riba*.
1950s–60s	Initial theoretical work on Islamic economics begins. By 1953, Islamic economists offer the first description of an interest-free bank based on either two-tier *mudarabah* or *wakala*. *Mitghamr* Bank in Egypt and Pilgrimage Fund in Malaysia start operations.
1970s	The first Islamic commercial bank, Dubai Islamic Bank, opens in 1974. The Islamic Development Bank (IDB) is established in 1975. The accumulation of oil revenues and petrodollars increases the demand for *Shari'ah*-compliant products.
1980s	The Islamic Research and Training Institute (IRTI) is established by the IDB in 1981. Banking systems are converted to interest-free banking systems in the Islamic Republic of Iran, in Pakistan and in the Sudan. Increased demand attracts Western intermediation and institutions. Countries like Bahrain and Malaysia promote Islamic banking parallel to the conventional banking system.
1990s	Attention is paid to the need for accounting standards and a regulatory framework. A self-regulating agency, the Accounting and Auditing Organization for Islamic Financial Institutions (AAOIFI), is established in Bahrain. Islamic insurance (*Takaful*) is introduced. Islamic equity funds are established. The Dow Jones Islamic Index and the FTSE Index of *Shari'ah*-compatible stock are developed.
2000–the present	The Islamic Financial Services Board (IFSB) is established to deal with regulatory, supervisory and corporate governance issues of the Islamic finance industry. *Sukuk* are launched and the Islamic capital market has emerged. Islamic mortgages are offered in the US and UK.

Source: Based on data from Greuning and Iqbal (2008, p. 13)

banking in the Middle East was discovered in the 1990s and there is still a lot to do, especially in the mortgage sub-sector, where IFIs can offer attractive solutions.

(iii) Governments have been very supportive of the Islamic financial industry, mainly for two reasons: one is symbolic and consists of sponsoring one or more institutions to show some form of state proselytism, and the other is purely economic, as IFIs are a powerful means to fund large infrastructure needs. Asset-backed, infrastructure and project finance is naturally in line with the principle of Islamic finance, just like mortgage lending (Moody's, 2009a).

As part of the developments, conventional banks that have been offering *Shari'ah*-compliant products for years through Islamic windows in Asia, especially in Malaysia, are now establishing specialised Islamic subsidiaries. This provides more visibility and clarity to the whole banking market, while doubtless contributing to the success of Islamic finance in the country, following more than two decades of government support for the alternative financial model, which now controls more than 15% of the country's banking assets (Moody's, 2009a).

SIZE OF THE INDUSTRY

One of the most visible gaps in the infrastructure of the Islamic financial services industry is the limited availability of systematic and reliable statistical information (IFSB, 2007). Most resources, like Bloomberg (2009), Oliver Wyman (2009), Standard & Poor's (2010a) and recently IFSB (2018) agree that Islamic finance represents 1% of global assets. These resources suggest that half of the 1.4 billion Muslims worldwide would opt for Islamic finance if given a competitive alternative to conventional services, indicating economies of scope and scale for the development of the Islamic finance industry.

According to Moody's (2011a), the Islamic finance market has been growing at over 30% annually since 2000 and is set for continued strong growth. At the end of 2010, Islamic finance totalled USD 1 trillion in assets, which increased to USD 2,050.2 trillion in 2017 (IFSB, 2018), implying over 100% growth in Islamic financing activity including Islamic banking assets, *sukuk* outstanding, Islamic funds, *takaful* contributions and USD 53 billion in revenues. It is expected to double over the next five years. The opportunity is commanding attention beyond Islamic incumbents, as witnessed by the spurt in Islamic start-ups and conventional players opening Islamic windows. Due to such impressive developments, interest in Islamic finance has spread beyond Muslim countries, and leading financial centres such as London and Luxembourg have been pushing to position themselves as major Islamic finance hubs.

In recent years, the growth of Islamic banking assets has outstripped that of conventional banking assets, even given the rapid system-wide asset growth. According to Standard & Poor's (2009), conventional banking assets had nearly tripled between 2003 and 2008, while Islamic banking assets multiplied by seven, albeit starting from a much lower base. Demand for Islamic banking products has increased not only from retail customers, deemed to be those most interested in *Shari'ah*-compliant products, but also from private sector corporate and government-related entities. At the same time, financial innovation has contributed to facilitating the supply of financial products and services, from retail products, like housing or car financing programs, to more sophisticated products like *sukuk* or mutual funds. On the supply side, some banks have opted to be converted from conventional to Islamic banking, either through a full transformation or following a business diversification strategy. In fact, the most dynamic growth in Islamic banking comes from conventional banks. It appears that they have enlarged or transformed their product suite to attract new customers or avoid losing existing ones. In addition, several governments of non-Muslim countries, in particular the UK, have announced plans to issue *sukuk* in the past, but issues have yet to materialise.

That said, the sort of asset growth witnessed prior to the financial crisis in 2007 and even in 2008, of around 25%, will not be repeated during the coming few years. As detailed by IFSB (2018:12), the compound asset growth rate in the Islamic banking sector was 8.8% between 2014 and 2017, while financing grew by 8.8% and deposit growth rate was 9.4% As part of this slowdown, liquidity ratios of Islamic banks are deteriorating, because banks are using their own excess liquidity accumulated in the past to fund their incremental business volumes. The developments demonstrate that funding is becoming increasingly costly; retail depositors are more cautious and savvy corporate depositors are asking for better returns to compensate for their perception of mounting credit risk. On the other side of the balance sheet, defaults of corporate and retail borrowers are expected to rise sharply, which will trigger more conservative credit policies, lower credit volumes, and more provisioning charges. Asset classes like real estate, *sukuk*, equity and private equity are expected to under-perform relative to historical returns.

As Figure 2.1 and Table 2.2 show, the Gulf Cooperation Council (GCC) is the largest market for IBF. It accounts for 42% of global Islamic finance assets but its population remains a very small fraction of the global Muslim population. While the share of the Middle East and North Africa (MENA) region in the global Islamic finance industry was 29.1% in 2017, with the largest share being Iran, the share of Asian countries remained at 24.4% with the largest share claimed by Malaysia.

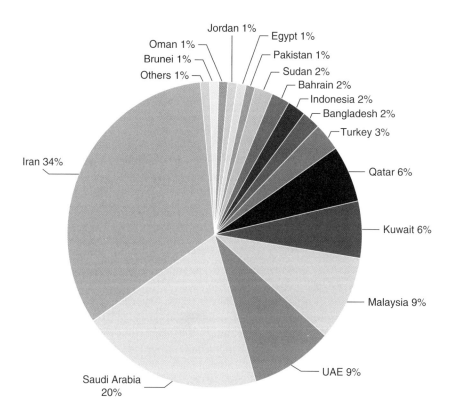

FIGURE 2.1 Global Islamic banking assets by country

Source: IFSB (2018). Reproduced with permission from Islamic Financial Services Board

TABLE 2.2 Size of the Islamic finance industry (USD billion)

Region	Banking Assets	*Sukuk* Out-standing	Islamic Funds Assets	*Takaful* Contri-butions	Total	Share (%)
Asia	232.0	239.5	24.8	3.3	499.6	24.4
GCC	683.0	139.2	26.8	12.6	861.6	42.0
MENA (ex. GCC)	569.0	17.8	0.1	9.5	596.4	29.1
Africa (ex. North Africa)	27.1	2.0	1.6	0.7	31.4	1.5
Others	46.4	1.5	13.3	0.0	61.3	3.0
Total	1,557.5	399.9	66.7	26.1	2,050.2	100

Source: IFSB (2018). Reproduced with permission from Islamic Financial Services Board

PRINCIPLES OF ISLAMIC BANKING AND FINANCE

After providing a general introduction to the developments and trends in the Islamic finance industry, it is essential to present the foundational principles of IBF. These principles can be summarised by five core rules, three being prohibition-related principles and two being positive measures (KPMG, 2006):

(i) **The prohibition of interest (*riba*):** No financial transaction should be based on the payment or receipt of interest; hence, fixed return is prohibited in the Islamic tradition. Therefore, profit from indebtedness or the trading of debts is seen to be unethical. Instead, the investor and investee should share in the risks and profits generated from a venture, an asset or a project.

(ii) **The prohibition of uncertainty (*gharar*):** Uncertainty in terms of a financial contract is considered unlawful, but not risk per se. Consequently, speculation (*maysir*) is forbidden. Therefore, financial derivatives are usually not permissible under *Shari'ah*-compliant finance despite the possible application for risk mitigation or risk transfer.

(iii) **The prohibition of unlawful (*haram*) assets:** No financial transaction should be directed toward economic and financial sectors considered unlawful according to the *Shari'ah*, such as arms dealing or the tobacco or gambling industries, as well as all enterprises for which financial leverage (indebtedness) would be deemed excessive (including conventional banks).

(iv) **The risk and profit and loss sharing (PLS) obligation:** Parties to a financial contract should share in the risks and rewards derived from such financing or investment transactions. PLS converts the relationship from borrower and lender to that of partners.

(v) **The asset-backing obligation:** Any financial transaction should be based on a tangible, identifiable underlying asset. Thus, Islamic teaching encourages financing economic activity through asset-based mechanisms as opposed to the financialisation of the economy.

BASIC ISLAMIC FINANCING CONTRACTS

Based on the principles identified in the previous section, over many years a number of financial contracts have been developed and used within Muslim societies as *Shari'ah*-compliant contracts. However, in recent years, with the financial developments in IBF, new products have also been engineered. Figure 2.2 presents a brief overview of the main Islamic financial instruments; it is not the intention of this section to explain those contracts in detail but rather to briefly explain the basic foundations.

Debt-Based Contracts	Customer undertakes a debt obligation to the bank backed by an asset, e.g., *Murabahah, Salam, Istisna'a*
Fee-Based Contracts	Bank charges a fixed fee in exchange for a service provided to the customer, e.g. *Wakala, Ijara, Wadia*
Participatory Contracts	Bank and customer co-invest in a partnership agreement, e.g. *Mudarabah, Musharakah* and Diminishing *Mushraka*

FIGURE 2.2 Overview of Islamic financial instruments
Source: Based on data from Oliver Wyman (2009)

Most contracts in Islamic banking are primarily based on (or are a combination of) the instruments identified in Figure 2.2.

Murabahah

According to *murabahah* contracts, one party (the seller) purchases commodities from a supplier and sells the commodities to the other (the buyer) at an agreed mark-up price. The profit generated by the on-sale is derived as a profit resulting from a sale and is not treated as interest. Accordingly, buyers requiring cash will immediately sell the commodities in the market to generate cash. *Murabahah* is also commonly known as 'cost-plus financing' or 'mark-up'.

The term *murabahah* contracts refers to a cost-plus transaction in which a bank purchases a tangible asset required by a customer, and then re-sells it to the customer at a predetermined profit. It involves three parties: the purchaser/importer, the seller/exporter and the financier. The Islamic financier provides finance by purchasing the desired commodity from a third party and reselling it to the purchaser at a predetermined higher price (mark-up), payable in instalments (Sundararajan and Errico, 2002). The key is that the financier must have a title to the goods at some point in the transaction.

To date, commodity *murabahah* has been the backbone of IBF; it is a vital product in Islamic finance, and it has been intensively used by IFIs for money market transactions, investment and retail activities. While no accurate figures exist for commodity *murabahah* volumes, industry experts estimate that at least USD 3 billion worth of commodities are traded daily off the London Metal Exchange (Over The Counter (OTC) Contracts). In 2013 it was stated that USD 8–11 billion commodity transactions took place in the GCC region (*Islamic Finance News*, 2013:4). This figure is likely to increase with the mounting interest in Islamic finance.

Commodity *murabahah* has been heavily used as a mechanism for cash generation; some refer to the transaction as *tawarruq*, which lexically means 'generating cash' in Arabic. However, this is not the purpose *murabahah* was initially designed for. *Shari'ah* scholars are not pleased with this practice (pure *tawarruq*). They are pushing more toward genuine *murabahah* through which the bank buys the actual commodity (a car, furniture, appliances, etc.) and re-sells it to the customer at a cost-plus margin (Consumer Finance).

Mudarabah (Profit-Sharing Agreement)

Mudarabah as an Islamic finance instrument is arranged between a bank (acting as a silent partner) and one or more entrepreneurs. The bank provides the entrepreneur with the funding for a specific commercial activity. However, the entrepreneur does not contribute any funding themselves, but contributes management expertise. The entrepreneur earns an agreed portion of the profits ('management fee' or '*mudarib* fee'). In turn, the financial institution is guaranteed a percentage of the profits (agreed upon beforehand) and assumes all of the risk in terms of financial loss. This is accompanied by considerable risk, and therefore the financial institution involved performs careful risk and credit analysis. On the whole, *mudarabah* transactions account for less than 10% of worldwide Islamic banking operations; it is similar to a Western-style limited partnership, with one party contributing capital while the other runs the business, and profit is distributed based on a negotiated percentage of ownership. Many banks use *mudarabah* to mobilise funds through savings and investment accounts (Usmani, 2002).

Musharakah (Equity Participation)

Musharakah as an essential IBF instrument involves a partnership between the bank and the entrepreneur: both contribute to the capital of the enterprise. An equity financing arrangement is widely regarded as the purest form of Islamic financing, where partners contribute capital to a project and share in both its risks and rewards. In a *musharakah* contract, a formal contract is normally in place, outlining the obligations and rights of both parties: profits can be allocated in any pre-agreed ratio, and losses are borne in proportion to the capital of each partner (Sundararajan and Errico, 2002). *Musharakah* conforms to the principle of PLS and is suitable for long-term project financing; hence it is considered to be the purest form of Islamic finance.

Ijarah and *Ijarah wa-Iqtinah*

Ijarah and *ijarah wa-Iqtinah* are Islamic leasing concepts similar to Western operating and financial leases. *Ijarah* is similar to a conventional operating lease whereby an Islamic bank (lessor) leases the asset to a client (lessee) for agreed-upon payments and period of time, but with no option for ownership by the lessee. The lessor takes the responsibility of maintaining and insuring the asset.

Ijarha wa-Iqtinah, on the other hand, is comparable to a financial/capital lease where the lessee has the option of owning the asset at the termination of the lease (Akkizidis and Khandelwal, 2007). The conditions governing both types of leasing are that assets must have a long secure productive life, and lease payments must be agreed on in advance to avoid any speculation. The price of the asset at the end of the contract period cannot be predetermined, and can only be determined when the lease contract is terminated.

Under Islamic leasing the lessee is obliged to start making lease payments only after the leased asset has actually been delivered. If that asset were destroyed, the lessee would cease making payments to the lessor, a practice that is contrary to most Western lease financing.

Istisna'a

Istisna'a as a concept offers a number of future structuring possibilities used mostly to finance long-term large-scale facilities. It is basically a contractual agreement whereby a party undertakes to produce a specific thing according to certain agreed-upon specifications at a determined price and for a fixed date of delivery. This undertaking of production includes any process of manufacturing, construction, assembly or packaging. In *istisna'a*, the work is not conditioned to be accomplished by the undertaking party and this work or part of it can be done by others under their control and responsibility. The price may be paid in advance or in instalments, according to the preference of the parties (Iqbal and Llewellyn, 2002). *Istisna'a* is thus a certain form of futures market which enables an entrepreneur to sell their output to the bank at a predetermined price. It is a profit-mark-up contract similar to a *murabahah*; however, the *istisna'a* deal can relate to something not in existence at the time of signing the contract, while *murabahah* is an order to buy commodities which are in existence, in hand or available in the market.

Wakala

Wakala is a financial relationship between principal and agent. The contract of *wakala* means designating a person or legal entity to act on one's behalf or as one's representative. It has been a common practice to appoint an agent (*wakil*) to facilitate trade operations.

A *wakala* contract gives a power of attorney or an agency assignment to a financial intermediary to perform a certain task. On the surface, there does not appear to be much difference between a *mudarabah* and a *wakala* contract, since both are principal–agent contracts. However, the main difference is that in the case of *mudarabah* the *mudarib* has full control and freedom to utilise funds according to their professional knowledge, as opposed to the case of *wakala* where the *wakil* does not have similar freedom (Siddiqi, 1983). A *wakil* acts only as a representative to execute a particular task according to the instructions given. Recently, more banks have been using *walaka* for money market transactions to replace the commodity *murabahah*, which involve more complications and raise *Shari'ah* concerns when used for generating cash (*tawarruq*), as previously discussed. An Islamic bank can accept or place *wakala*, whereas a conventional bank can only use *wakala* placements to deposit with an Islamic counterparty.

Bai' Salam

Salam is also known as 'forward sale'. It was originally allowed to meet the needs of small farmers who required money during the harvesting period to meet expenses. In this transaction the bank pays the seller in advance the full agreed price of a specified quality and quantity of a commodity that the latter promises to deliver in the future. The entire price has to be paid in advance.

This form of finance is similar to forward purchase, and it has been applied in the case of agricultural products as their seasonality signifies the need for such finance. It should be noted that *salam* exposes banks to market risk, especially fluctuations in commodity prices. To avoid this, modern bankers are using the '*parallel salam*', where a bank enters into two simultaneous agreements for the same future date, one as a buyer and the other as a seller; this takes care of commodity price fluctuations to a certain extent, but still requires managing the risk of non-delivery of the commodity on the due date (Usmani, 2002).

Other Islamic Financial Products

Other than the main Islamic finance contracts discussed above, there are several variants of different instruments available in the market. Some of the popular ones are briefly described below. However, *sukuk* as a financial instrument is discussed in detail in the following section.

(i) **Hibah:** *Hibah* is a form of gift used to repay account holders in an Islamic bank. Current account and savings account holders in an Islamic bank do not get any interest; however, at the end of the year the bank, at its discretion, can give some *hibah* as a part of its compensation to the account holders (Iqbal and Mirakhor, 2007).

(ii) **Musawama:** *Musawama* is very similar to *murabahah*, except that the seller does not need to disclose the cost of goods (Moody's, 2009a).

(iii) **Qard Hassan:** *Qard hassan* is a loan on a goodwill basis which is totally free of any extra cost. The debtor is required to return only the principal borrowed amount, although they may return anything extra, whatever they feel appropriate. This is a true *riba*-free loan (Usmani, 2002).

(iv) Wadiah: In the case of *wadiah*, the bank works as the trustee for funds of customers. However, the bank does not guarantee any interest but can give some *hibah*, which can compensate customers (Iqbal and Mirakhor, 2007).

SUKUK: A STEP TOWARD SECURITISATION

As an extensively used financial instrument in recent years, *sukuk* is not a contract on its own, but rather is a product based on one or more Islamic finance contracts that was introduced in order to address the asset/liability dichotomy in Islamic banking. Prior to 2000, this particular market was virtually non-existent, but in the past few years it has experienced tremendous growth.

What is *Sukuk*?

Sukuk is an Arabic term meaning 'certificate'. In a financial sense, *sukuk* may be understood as a *Shari'ah*-compliant 'bond'. In its simplest form *sukuk* represents ownership of an asset or its usufruct. The claim embodied in *sukuk* is not simply a claim to cash flow but an ownership claim. This also differentiates *sukuk* from conventional bonds as the latter proceed over interest-bearing securities, whereas *sukuk* are basically investment certificates consisting of ownership claims in a pool of assets (Dar Al Istithmar, 2006).

Sukuk (plural of *sak*) were extensively used by Muslims in the Middle Ages as papers representing financial obligations originating from trade and other commercial activities. However, the present structures of *sukuk* are different from the *sukuk* originally used and are akin to the conventional concept of securitisation: a process in which ownership of the underlying assets is transferred to a large number of investors through certificates representing proportionate value of the relevant assets (Askari et al., 2009).

Types of *Sukuk*

Sukuk can be of many types (14 eligible *sukuk* types have been identified by the AAOIFI), depending upon the type of Islamic modes of financing and trades used in its structuring. However, the most common category in the market is *ijara sukuk*, which are backed by leases and often guaranteed by sovereign or regional governments. Because of the predominance of *ijara sukuk*, these transactions are commonly viewed as the *de facto* benchmarks in the Islamic marketplace.

Ijara sukuk are structured around a specific asset, such as a building, property or infrastructure facility. The asset itself is sold to a special-purpose entity that then issues the *sukuk* to fund the asset's purchase price. The special-purpose entity then leases the asset and receives periodic lease payments. At maturity, or in the event of dissolution, the special-purpose entity sells the asset back to the original seller at a predetermined price that includes any outstanding amounts still owed under the terms of the *ijara sukuk* (Standard & Poor's, 2010a).

Developments in the *Sukuk* Market

Sukuk growth has been a factor in local debt capital markets, which were also virtually non-existent before 2000. Taking advantage of *sukuk* was a much-needed solution to the problem of increasing Islamic banks' funding options. *Sukuk* allow Islamic banks to allocate excess funds to alternative classes of instruments; they have, thus, helped banks to move away from conventional strategies related to equity and property alone. Similarly, *sukuk* varieties have been used by Islamic banks as tools in their investment portfolios to hedge against their more volatile credit exposures.

After two turbulent years, Standard & Poor's (2011) stated that the *sukuk* market was back on track. Issuance reached a record high of USD 51.2 billion in 2010, including those issued and maturing that same year. This represented about 26% of the cumulative amount of issuances since 1996 and beats the previous peak in 2007 by 34%. The revival of *sukuk* issuance in 2011 indicated that the depth and breadth of *sukuk* issuance will continue to hinge on the extent of the global economic recovery. This is notably crucial for the return of corporate *sukuk* issuers, including financial institutions, which fell from an average of about 65% over 2001–2007 to a mere 12% of issuance in 2010. In geographic terms, the regional economic slowdown since mid-2008 curtailed the financing needs of Gulf issuers. In doing so, it re-centred the *sukuk* market growth on its historical engine and mainstay, Malaysia, which accounted for 78% of *sukuk* in 2010. As can be seen in Figure 2.2, *sukuk* issuance reached its peak in 2012 with about USD 130 billion, and later experienced gradual decreases in 2013 and 2014 due to the liquidity shortage caused by the sharp decline in oil revenues in the Gulf region. In 2015, *sukuk* issuance sharply decreased to about USD 65 billion, which remains the lowest level since the recovery in 2011. As stated by IFSB (2018:25), *sukuk* issuance demonstrated a gradual increase in 2016 and 2017, reaching about USD 92 billion in 2017. This indicates a robust approximately 23% increase over the USD 75 billion *sukuk* issuance in 2016. Figure 2.3 depicts the developments and trends in the *sukuk* issuance over the years.

Standard & Poor's (2011) does not foresee that non-Muslim countries will change the shape of the market over the medium term. During the crisis, Western

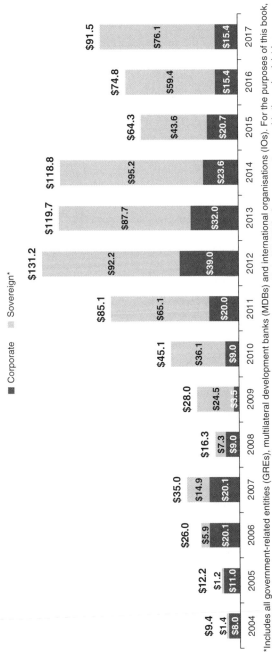

Global *sukuk* issuance historical trend

Global *sukuk* issuance 2004-2017 in bn

■ Corporate ■ Sovereign*

*Includes all government-related entities (GREs), multilateral development banks (MDBs) and international organisations (IOs). For the purposes of this book, 'GREs' refers to *sukuk* obligors with a shareholding structure representing more than two-thirds (66.67%) of government ownership through ministries, authorities, etc. or other GREs such as sovereign wealth funds.

FIGURE 2.3 Global *sukuk* issuance 2004–2017
Source: IFSB (2018:25). Reproduced with permission from Islamic Financial Services Board

investors showed a marked interest in *sukuk*, partly because their average yield had been slightly higher than that available on a 'plain vanilla' comparable conventional instrument, owing to the structured nature and lower liquidity of *sukuk*. However, it is believed that this trend will slow down once rates begin to rise, which will increase the average yield of conventional bonds.

In addition, Moody's (2011a) expect that the complex web of socioeconomic, political and religious issues in many non-Muslim countries is holding back any swift uptake of *sukuk*. Instead, it is argued that the market's future lies with countries whose economies have been less affected by the crisis, namely the GCC and South East Asia. The broader global demand for *sukuk* still depends on increasing their liquidity and standardising *Shari'ah* interpretation. The developments, however, indicate that the market needs leaders to provide vision and direction, to take the domestic and compartmentalised initiatives of various countries toward clear international and standardised market principles (Standard & Poor's, 2011).

The market is yet to witness the first convincing and sizable *sukuk* issuance from a European or non-Muslim Asian country since the debut involving the five-year €100 million German State of Saxony Anhalt *sukuk* in 2004. The UK, which has been the most likely, active and vocal candidate since its announcement in 2007 of a planned Sterling-denominated *sukuk*, backtracked in January 2011, citing lack of value for money. In June 2014, the UK government issued £200 million sovereign *sukuk*, which made the UK the first non-Muslim-majority country to issue sovereign *sukuk*. The South Korean government, meanwhile, failed in December 2010 to pass an amendment that would remove the tax disadvantage of *sukuk* compared with conventional bonds, but it will try again in the near future. The effect of these international setbacks to the *sukuk* may reverberate on other prospective issuers. Most of these non-Muslim countries have announced their intention to enter the *sukuk* market for opportunistic reasons, such as to tap the much-coveted liquidity available in the GCC countries or Asia; but it remains doubtful that they would do this at any cost (Standard & Poor's, 2011). However, in recent years, Luxembourg, South Africa and Hong Kong have issued sovereign *sukuk*, which has given a new momentum for the expansion of Islamic capital markets beyond the traditional jurisdictions.

Furthermore, one of the interviewees in this research, Qaedi (2010), explains that the market is now moving toward listed instruments, both in international markets and in local markets such as Dubai, Malaysia or Saudi Arabia. The majority of *sukuk* to date have been issued in the form of over-the-counter instruments that investment bankers developed to fit the specific needs of issuers, and then privately placed to meet the needs of investors. Listing *sukuk* on organised markets is important for the liquidity of the instrument itself, and also makes it easier for investors to manage, both in terms of liquidity and price discovery.

The main uncertainty within *sukuk* lies in current market conditions. The default of some *sukuk* has raised questions about this relatively young market. These *sukuk* were issued by East Cameron Partners (ECP), The Investment Dar (TID) and Saad Group. *Sukuk* issued by Nakheel PJSC avoided default thanks to a last-minute support package. Once investors have a clearer view of the possible outcome of the two recent defaults, the *sukuk* market is likely to grow more strongly, perhaps after making some adjustments reflecting lessons learned. Beyond 2010, a major impediment to the emergence of an integrated, global *sukuk* market remains in the lack of standardisation, especially regarding *Shari'ah* compliance and the legal environment. Another major problem is the liquidity squeeze in the Gulf region, which was considered a potential adverse impact. However, the trends demonstrate that after the initial impact, the *sukuk* market is again on the rise, in particular with new entrants such as Indonesia, Nigeria, Pakistan and Turkey among others.

Abdul-Ghani (2009) explains that despite enormous success, the *sukuk* market is not as deep or liquid as a regular bond market. Regardless of growing demand fuelled by banks, corporations and governments in the GCC region, there is a shortage of supply. Additionally, the *sukuk* market is still stagnant: holders keep their bonds to maturity and there is relatively little secondary market trading. The ability to trade their bond portfolios gives banks the flexibility to adjust their asset–liability management process to their liking and to hedge themselves against sudden movements in asset prices by matching durations on both sides.

So far, IBF institutions have preferred an originate-and-hold business model due to the lack of a secondary market for loans and *sukuk*; however, in the longer term, IBF institutions with limited capital resources might be more inclined to adopt an originate-and-distribute business approach, provided disintermediation picks up, market depth and liquidity improves, and growth in Islamic assets continues unabated.

As depicted by Figure 2.4, the Malaysian ringgit (MYR) has been the currency of choice every year since the inception of the market, with ringgit-denominated *sukuk* representing about 59% of total issuance over the period from 1996 to 2010 or more than twice the US dollar-denominated ones. Malaysia has notably funded infrastructure projects with ringgit-denominated *sukuk*, since Islamic investors tend to prefer asset-backed projects. But ringgit-denominated issuance is not limited to Malaysian issuers. The National Bank of Abu Dhabi issued the equivalent of a combined $325 million in the Malaysian currency in June and December 2010 to tap a deeper *sukuk* market (Standard & Poor's, 2011). US dollar-denominated *sukuk* made up only about 8% of *sukuk* issued in 2010, which has demonstrated some significant change since then. Any pickup in dollar-denominated issuances would likely follow a pickup in the GCC region, which has most of its currencies fully or partially pegged to the US dollar.

Global *sukuk* issuance by country

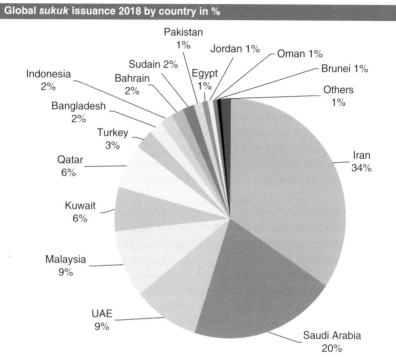

FIGURE 2.4 Global *sukuk* issuance by country 2018
Source: IFSB (2018). Reproduced with permission from Islamic Financial Services Board

While *mudarabah, musharakah* and *ijara* are widely applied, the actual legal structure behind the *sukuk* risk characteristics can vary significantly, even within a single 'type'. According to Zawya (2011), *ijara* and *murabahah* structures accounted for about three-quarters of total *sukuk* issued in 2010, and this trend is expected to continue for the next few years. The remainder was in the form of *istithmar, wakala, musharakah* and *salam* structures. Thus, until there is some broad consensual standardisation in *sukuk*, investors will need to look at each structure individually to understand the cash flow, risk and return profile, irrespective of the type of *sukuk* structure used.

Due to the availability of a large variety of *sukuk* structures in the market, detailed discussion of the *sukuk* is beyond the scope of this book and hence has not been dealt with. Chapter 3 looks at *sukuk* from a risk management perspective, while Chapter 5 discusses a new phenomenon in *sukuk*: default.

ISLAMIC BANKING VERSUS CONVENTIONAL BANKING

The previous sections aimed to provide information regarding the foundational principles and salient futures of IBF as well as developments and trends in the IBF sector. As has been mentioned, the overarching principle of Islamic banking is that all forms of interest are prohibited. The Islamic financial model works on the basis of risk-sharing (Mirakhor and Zaidi, 2007), as explained by Khandelwal (FRSGlobal, 2009): "because interest is prohibited under *Shari'ah* law, suppliers of funds become investors instead of creditors. The provider of financial capital and the entrepreneur share business risk in return for shares of the profits, and this has an impact on risk management". However, the use of profit-sharing modes in Islamic banks changes the nature of the risks that these institutions face, as shown in Figure 2.5.

Islamic finance is based on the concept of profit- and risk-sharing and avoidance of the concept of interest. This means that the finance provider is not automatically entitled to payment in full of principal and periodic distributions, but that risk needs to be taken by the finance provider, along with the borrower. This contrasts with the conventional/Western concept of lending, which results in a number of considerations that need to be taken into account when assessing the risk profile of an Islamic bank. Table 2.3 summarises on high level the main differences between Islamic finance and conventional finance.

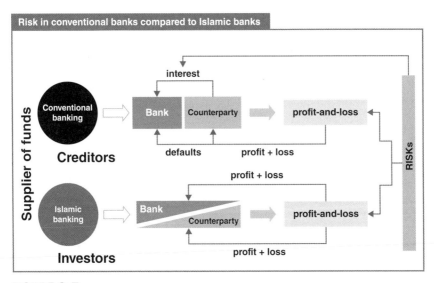

FIGURE 2.5   Risks in conventional banks versus those in Islamic banks
Source: Adapted from FRSGlobal (2009)

TABLE 2.3   Differences between Islamic finance and conventional finance

Conventional Finance	Islamic Finance
Primarily based on interest rate	Interest is prohibited
Facilitates financial activities	Facilitates social, economic and financial activities
Structured and formalised	Unstructured and still informal in many ways
Stress on financial efficiency	Stress on social, ethical and financial efficiency
Restricted moral dimension	Strong moral dimension
Highly systematised in terms of risk management, accounting and other standards	Standards for risk management, accounting and other activities are still developing
Existing set of legislation to deal with legal issues	Legal support still in development with several legal areas under doubt
Highly developed banking and financial product market	Developing banking and financial product market
Existence of conventional money market	Non-existence of significant Islamic money market
Availability of interbank funds	Non-availability of interbank funds
Strong and developed secondary market for securities	Non-existing secondary market for securities
Existence of short-term money market	Non-existence of short-term money market

Source: Adapted from Akkizidis and Khandelwal (2007:3)

It is also critical to develop an understanding of the spectrum of the risk and return profiles of different Islamic financial instruments. Often the Islamic financial system is equated with an all-equity-based system, which ignores the fact that the system also has several other types of contract which are not based on PLS. Contracts such as sales, trade financing and leasing constitute a large portion of the system, but these contracts are not based on equity (Iqbal and Mirakhor, 2007). The existence of such non-equity-based instruments has an important implication: these instruments have a risk/return profile that is very similar to a conventional fixed-income security.

In addition, Islamic banking, despite having been in existence in its modern form for over three decades, is still in many respects an infant industry, as depicted in Figure 2.6. Islamic banks are striving to build their reputation by exploiting 'blind spots' in the market and by trying to develop competitive advantage. They are in serious rivalry for customers' loyalty and face high levels of

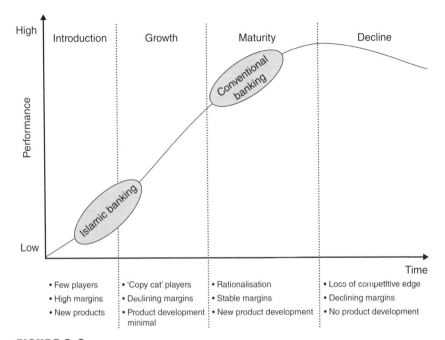

FIGURE 2.6   Development stages of Islamic banking

uncertainty. Conventional banking, on the other hand, is at a mature stage. The market is dominated by powerful players, and entrepreneurial actions continue but are greatly de-emphasised.

As discussed, the core principles of Islamic finance, especially the PLS characteristic, have unique risk management implications. In conventional banking, if the payment of outstanding commitments is not timely or not in accordance with the terms and conditions of the obligations then default has occurred. However, in Islamic banking, if PLS obligations were in fact to absorb losses, this would not in itself be viewed, at least in theory, as a default event, as investors have contractually agreed to share in losses (Chowdhury, 2010).

It should be noted that Chapter 3 explores these risk management implications in detail.

INSTITUTIONAL DEVELOPMENTS IN ISLAMIC BANKING AND FINANCE INDUSTRY

The private sector has been much more active than the public sector in the growth of Islamic finance, as development in Islamic finance is mainly due to economic liberalisation and hence the private sector. However, a number of governments, such as those of Bahrain and Malaysia, have made serious efforts to establish financial centres for IFIs. An institutional infrastructure to support the development of the financial sector is slowly emerging with collaboration between the private and public sectors. Such developments include institutions to deal with accounting and regulatory standards, corporate governance, credit ratings and capital markets. These efforts to develop institutions are also supported by several stakeholders such as the International Monetary Fund (IMF), central banks of leading Muslim countries, international standard-setting bodies and financial centres (Askari et al., 2009). These institutions are depicted in Table 2.4 with their functional roles.

Al-Ghamrawy (2010), one of the interviewees for this research, stated, however, that "there are several fine organizations dedicated to the promotion of Islamic finance across various jurisdictions. The problem is that they do not well-co-ordinate with each other." Figure 2.7 lays out the institutional developments in IBF. The degree of maturity of Islamic institutions is much lower than that of the conventional system. However, driven by industry research and inspired by international linkages, these institutions are continuously evolving.

The main institutions in the institutionalisation of IBF are explained in brief as follows:

Islamic Development Bank (IDB): The IDB was established in 1975 as a regional development institution to promote economic development in Muslim countries through Islamic finance. Since its creation, the IDB has established several sister institutions to develop private sector insurance facilities and trade and export financing. Additionally, the IDB has played a key role in developing institutional infrastructure to promote Islamic financial systems. Some notable contributions of the IDB are institutions to enhance the regulatory framework and standardisation of the Islamic banking industry, such as: the AAOIFI; the IFSB; the General Council of Islamic Banks and Financial Institutions (GCIBFI); the International Islamic Financial Market (IIFM); the Islamic International Rating Agency (IIRA); the Liquidity Management Centre (LMC); and the International Islamic Centre for Reconciliation and Commercial Arbitration (IICRA) (Askari et al., 2009).

Islamic Research and Training Institute (IRTI): The IRTI, the research arm of IDB, was established in 1981 to undertake research, training and knowledge-generation activities in Islamic finance. The IRTI has become a centre of knowledge dissemination by developing a rich resource centre for research through collections of in-house research papers, seminar proceedings, lectures, translations, journals and articles (Askari et al., 2009).

Accounting and Auditing Organization for Islamic Financial Institutions (AAOIFI): In 1991 the AAOIFI was established in Bahrain as a self-regulation

TABLE 2.4 Key institutions in the Islamic financial industry

Acronym	Organisation	Function
IDB	Islamic Development Bank	Development institution formed in 1975 to promote Islamic finance and economic development *Member/ sister organisations*: **ICD** – Islamic Corporation for the Development of the Private Sector **ICIEC** – Islamic Corporation for the Insurance of Investment and Export Credit; Islamic insurance company, providing insurance products for investments and export credits **IRTI** – Islamic Research and Training Institute; Research and training arm **ITFC** – International Islamic Trade Finance Corporation **Solidarity Fund** – To reduce poverty in Organisation of Islamic Cooperation (OIC) countries **ARCIFI** – Arbitration and Reconciliation Centre for Islamic Financial Institutions
AAOIFI	Accounting & Auditing Organization for Islamic Financial Institutions	Accounting and *Shari'ah* standard-setting body
IFSB	Islamic Financial Services Board	Standard-setting institution to ensure best practices and help member countries with regulating Islamic financial institutions
IIFM	International Islamic Financial Markets	Trade association to promote capital markets
IIRA	Islamic International Rating Agency	Rating agency
LMC	Liquidity Management Centre	Institution to provide liquidity enhancement to the financial system
CIBAFI	General Council of Islamic Banks and Financial Institutions	Trade association of Islamic banks to enhance member institutions' ability to better service customers around the world through transparent banking practices

Source: Askari et al. (2009:39). © John Wiley & Sons, Inc. Reproduced with permission

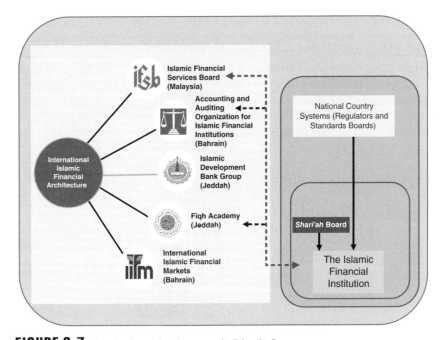

FIGURE 2.7   Institutional developments in Islamic finance
Notes: The dashed arrow depicts advisory roles; the solid arrow depicts supervisory roles.

agency for the industry to tackle the problem of *Shari'ah* compliance and gaps in applying conventional financial reporting standards to Islamic banks. The AAOIFI's membership consists of about 97 institutions spanning over 24 countries, and it has issued around 50 standards on accounting, auditing, governance, ethical and *Shari'ah* standards. The AAOIFI's *Shari'ah* board is paving the way toward *Shari'ah* harmonisation of banking practices throughout the world. The banking supervisors in a number of countries, such as Bahrain, Jordan and Sudan, require Islamic banks to comply with the AAOIFI standards or, as in the case of Qatar and Saudi Arabia, are specifying these standards as guidelines (Greuning and Iqbal, 2008).

Islamic Financial Services Board (IFSB): The AAOIFI was successful in defining accounting and *Shari'ah* standards, while the IFSB was officially inaugurated in November 2002 in Kuala Lumpur, Malaysia, with the help of the IMF, to address systemic stability and various regulatory issues relating to the Islamic financial services industry. As of June 2011, the 195 members of the IFSB included 49 regulatory and supervisory authorities as well as the IMF, World Bank, BIS, IDB, Asian Development Bank, Islamic Corporation for the Development of

Private Sector, Saudi Arabia, and 138 market players and professional firms operating in 39 jurisdictions (IFSB, 2011). The government of Malaysia has enacted the IFSB Act 2002, which gives the IFSB the immunities and privileges usually granted to international organisations and diplomatic missions (Greuning and Iqbal, 2008). The primary objective of the IFSB is to develop uniform regulatory and transparency standards to address characteristics specific to IFIs, keeping in mind the national financial environment, international standards, core principles and good practices. The IFSB has made significant contributions in the areas of corporate governance, risk management and regulation. The IFSB issued a number of guiding principles on risk management, capital adequacy, corporate governance and transparency in IBF. Archer and Abdul Karim (2007) highlight that in spite of the high quality of these standards, they have been adopted in only a handful of countries, which are listed and depicted in Table 2.5.

General Council of Islamic Banks and Financial Institutions (CIBAFI): Formed in 2001, CIBAFI is a non-profit organisation based in Manama, Bahrain, which provides information and services to the Islamic financial services industry. CIBAFI focuses on media and awareness, information and research, and strategic planning in relation to the IBF industry (IFSB, 2007).

Liquidity Management Centre (LMC): The LMC was founded in 2002 in Bahrain to facilitate the investment of surplus funds of IFIs into financial instruments structured in accordance with *Shari'ah* principles. The key objective of the LMC is to facilitate the creation of an interbank money market that will allow IFIs to more effectively manage their asset/liability mismatch through participation as both investors and borrowers (Mahlknecht, 2009). In addition, the Centre attracts assets from governments, financial institutions and corporates in both the private and public sectors in many countries. The assets are securitised into readily transferable securities or structured into other innovative investment instruments (Greuning and Iqbal, 2008). The equal shareholders include Bahrain Islamic Bank, Dubai Islamic Bank, IDB and Kuwait Finance House.

International Islamic Financial Market (IIFM): The Bahrain-based IIFM was created in 2002 as cooperation between various supervisory authorities of Islamic countries. The major objectives of the IIFM are (a) to address the liquidity problem by expanding the maturity structure of instruments, and (b) to help in the creation of secondary market activity with designated market makers where such instruments can be actively traded. The IIFM focuses on standardisation and harmonisation within the industry. Its primary focus is the advancement and unification of Islamic financial documents, structures and contracts (Wilson, 2009). It signed a Memorandum of Understanding with the International Capital Market Association (ICMA) to develop a master repurchase (repo) agreement to help

TABLE 2.5 IFSB Standards

Publication	Year
Published Standards:	
IFSB-1: Guiding Principles of Risk Management for Institutions (other than Insurance Institutions) offering only Islamic Financial Services (IIFS)	December 2005
IFSB-2: Capital Adequacy Standard for Institutions (other than Insurance Institutions) offering only Islamic Financial Services (IIFS)	December 2005
IFSB-3: Guiding Principles on Corporate Governance for Institutions Offering Only Islamic Financial Services (Excluding Islamic Insurance (*Takaful*) Institutions and Islamic Mutual Funds)	December 2006
IFSB-4: Disclosures to Promote Transparency and Market Discipline for Institutions offering Islamic Financial Services (excluding Islamic Insurance (*Takaful*) Institutions and Islamic Mutual Funds)	December 2007
IFSB-5: Guidance on Key Elements in the Supervisory Review Process of Institutions offering Islamic Financial Services (excluding Islamic Insurance (*Takaful*) Institutions and Islamic Mutual Funds)	December 2007
GN-1: Guidance Note in Connection with the Capital Adequacy Standard: Recognition of Ratings by External Credit Assessment Institutions (ECAIs) on *Shari'ah*-Compliant Financial Instruments	March 2008
IFSB-6: Guiding Principles on Governance for Islamic Collective Investment Schemes	January 2009
IFSB-7: Capital Adequacy Requirements for *Sukuk*, Securitisations and Real Estate Investment	January 2009
IFSB-8: Guiding Principles on Governance for *Takaful* (Islamic Insurance) Undertakings	December 2009
IFSB-9: Guiding Principles on Conduct of Business	December 2009
IFSB-10: Guiding Principles on *Shari'ah* Governance Systems for Institutions Offering Islamic Financial Services	December 2009
IFSB-11: Standard on Solvency Requirements for *Takaful* (Islamic Insurance) Undertakings	December 2010
Other Documents:	
Issues in Regulation and Supervision of *Takaful* (Islamic Insurance) by IFSB and International Association of Insurance Supervisors	August 2006

TABLE 2.5 (*Continued*)

Publication	Year
Islamic Financial Services Industry Development: Ten-Year Framework and Strategies	May 2007
Compilation Guide on Prudential and Structural Islamic Finance Indicators: Guidance on the Compilation and Dissemination of Prudential and Structural Islamic Finance Indicators for Banking and Near-Banking Institutions Offering Islamic Financial Services	November 2007
TN-1: Technical Note on Issues in Strengthening Liquidity Management of Institutions Offering Islamic Financial Services: The Development of Islamic Money Markets	March 2008

Source: Compiled by the author from http://www.ifsb.org. Access date: 14 June 2011

central banks manage liquidity in the *sukuk* market, and with the International Swaps and Derivatives Association (ISDA) to develop a *Tahawwut* (Hedging) Master Agreement (Mahlknecht, 2009). In October 2008, IIFM marked a milestone with the launch of the first-ever universal Master Agreement in Islamic finance: the Master Agreement for Treasury Placement (MATP). The MATP, which is to cater for global commodity *murabahah* trades, is a perfect example of how standardisation can take place (IIFM, 2009).

Islamic International Rating Agency (IIRA): The IIRA aims to assist in the development of regional financial markets by providing an assessment of the risk profiles of entities and instruments that can be used for investment decisions. The organisation has a board of directors and *Shari'ah* boards as well as an independent rating committee. The IIRA also provides a unique service for rating the quality of the *Shari'ah* compliance of a financial institution (Askari et al., 2009).

International Islamic Liquidity Management Corporation (IILM): Finally, October 2010 saw the signing and launch of the IILM, the latest transnational body to serve the global Islamic finance industry. The ultimate aim of the IILM is to enhance international integration of the Islamic money market and capital markets and to better equip them to face any liquidity crises.

CONCLUSION

This chapter provided an overview of Islamic financial principles. The development of IBF was introduced and the market size was explored. Additionally, major differences between conventional and Islamic banking were also presented. Islamic banks, similar to their conventional counterparts, act as financial intermediaries; they transform the characteristics of the financial inflows they capture, as part of their funding strategies, into *Shari'ah*-compliant placement, financing and investment instruments. However, asset classes managed by IFIs may differ from those of conventional banks, not so much in their economic substance, but more in their financial form (Iqbal and Mirakhor, 2007).

Financial contracts in Islamic finance are not archetypal. They have special relationships between the contracting parties, which sometimes change during the different stages of the contract. The origin, intensity and spread of risks are unique for IFIs, mainly because of the participatory risk relationship by the investor.

It should be noted that using the PLS principle to reward depositors is a unique feature of Islamic banks. This feature, along with the different modes of financing and the *Shari'ah*-compliant set of business activities, changes the nature of risks that Islamic banks face. Hence, risk management for Islamic banks is a far more complex issue as compared to that of conventional banking.

CHAPTER 3

Risk Management in Islamic Banks

A Theoretical Perspective

The fact that people are full of greed, fear, or folly is predictable.
The sequence is not predictable.

—Warren Buffett

It has been argued by proponents of Islamic finance that most Islamic banking products are less risky than conventional banking products because they are based on real assets. These advocates strongly argue that Islamic banks are recession-proof and are more resilient to economic shocks than their conventional peers. On the other hand, opponents of Islamic finance believe that most of the conventional risks are also present in Islamic banking in addition to further risks that are quite specific to the Islamic structure. They strongly argue that Islamic banking is more risky and less developed than the Western Wall Street banking model. Who is right? Where does the truth reside?

These are challenging questions, the answer to which requires careful examination of the associated risks within Islamic finance in general as well as other areas of Islamic operations and the macro environment that could have an impact on the risk culture, risk tolerance and risk management of Islamic banks. A review of the existing literature does not provide a clear answer to these grey areas in Islamic banking, as the existing body of knowledge is still limited.

Risk management is at the heart of banks' financial intermediation process, and has assumed the utmost importance amid the recession, which has witnessed the worst complexity and volatility in financial markets in living memory. Basel II and widespread write-downs have highlighted the importance of sufficient capital adequacy and, more importantly, set a framework for improving the overall risk management architecture in banks. Appropriate risk management has become a differentiating factor in building competitive advantages for financial institutions.

Today, regulators, creditors and rating agencies place great emphasis on risk management frameworks and corporate governance, particularly in fast-growing emerging markets where such factors tend to attract lower scores than in more mature economic and business environments.

Islamic financial institutions (IFIs) are no exception. Similarly to conventional banks, they face many challenges in adequately defining, identifying, measuring, selecting, pricing and mitigating risks across business lines and asset classes. Unfortunately, risk management is an ignored area of research in Islamic finance. Therefore, a number of challenges are still being confronted in this field. These challenges stem from different sources. First, a number of risk management techniques are not available to IFIs due to *Shari'ah*-compliance requirements. Islamic alternatives to several hedging and risk mitigation techniques that are widely used in conventional banking have not yet been explored. Second, there are a number of *Shari'ah* positions which affect risk management processes directly. Some of these are lack of effective means to deal with wilful default, prohibition of sale of debt, prohibition of currency forwards and futures, among others. Third, lack of standardisation of Islamic financial contracts is also an important source of the challenges in this regard.

The majority of the risks faced by conventional financial institutions (such as credit risk, market risk, operational risk, liquidity risk, macroeconomic risk, etc.) are also faced by Islamic banks. However, the magnitude of some of these risks is different for Islamic banks due to their unique business model. In addition, IFIs face further risks that stem from the different characteristics of assets and liabilities, balance sheet structure and compliance with *Shari'ah* principles. Furthermore, the profit-sharing feature of Islamic banking introduces some additional risks. For example, paying the investment depositors a share of the bank's profits introduces withdrawal risk, fiduciary risk and displaced commercial risk. In addition, the various Islamic modes of finance have their own unique risk characteristics. Thus, the nature of some risks that IFIs face is different from those of their conventional counterparts.

In Islamic finance, the importance of risk management is clearly acknowledged. While conventional finance, with its roots in neo-classical economic theory, has developed instruments to identify and trade risks, in Islam risk cannot be sold in any matter. Risk management in Islamic finance is therefore built on the foundation that risk must be shared between parties as opposed to being assumed by one party or the other.

Realising the significance of risk management, the Islamic Finance Services Board (IFSB) issued a comprehensive standards document on risk management in December 2005: *IFSB-1*: Guiding Principles of Risk Management for Institutions (other than Insurance Institutions) Offering only Islamic Financial Services (IFS). This complements the Basel Committee on Banking Supervision (BCBS) standards to address the specificity of Islamic products. Islamic banks' balance sheet structures indicate that there is a great diversity of classifications on both the asset and liability sides. Such variety affects the ease of comparison both between differing Islamic institutions and between Islamic institutions and their conventional peers, making it difficult to apply just one appropriate risk management approach. Therefore, the IFSB has prudently adopted a principles-based approach. The IFSB standard lists 15 guiding principles for risk management in IFIs. There is a general requirement followed by requirements covering credit, equity investment, market, liquidity, rate-of-return and operational risks (IFSB, 2005a). Overall, the main differences between these principles and those appropriate for a conventional bank relate to five key areas:

(i) The range of asset classes found in Islamic banks;
(ii) The relatively weak position of investment account holders (IAHs);
(iii) The importance of the *Shari'ah* supervisory board and the bank's ability to provide the board with adequate information as well as to abide by its rulings;
(iv) Rate-of-return risk; and
(v) New operational risks.

Notwithstanding the IFSB's endeavour to provide the Islamic banking industry with a set of guidelines toward best-practice risk management, a number of additional risk issues at IFIs deserve further examination as detailed in this chapter.

The aim of this chapter is to define what differentiates IFIs in terms of their risk profiles, and to highlight the potential implications that such differences may make to IFIs' financial strength and risk identification, management and mitigation. Thus, this chapter maps the risk structure in IFIs but also discusses the risk management strategies developed and utilised by IFIs.

This chapter attempts to answer the long-debated question of whether Islamic banking is less or more risky than conventional banking. In doing so it reviews the existing literature on risks in Islamic banking with reference to risks in conventional banking. The theoretical literature review is intermingled within the discussion about each risk type. It commences by researching risks that are common to both Islamic and conventional banks, and asserts that Islamic banks face similar risks to different degrees. It then explores other risk areas which are unique to Islamic banks due to their unique business model and contracts. Furthermore, specific issues related to risk management and mitigation in Islamic banking are also discussed. The last section draws some conclusions.

RISK MANAGEMENT: BASIC CONCEPTS AND TECHNIQUES

What is Risk Management?

Risk is generally the possibility of an unplanned event that, if allowed to develop, could adversely affect all or part of the institution's business, leading to loss of revenue, failure to meet key strategic goals or objectives, reduced company reputation or missed opportunities to increase or improve any of these. Risk can be defined as the variability or volatility of unexpected outcomes. It is usually measured by the standard deviation of historic outcomes (Das, 2006).

Risk management is the term applied to the process adopted by the business for identifying, analysing, evaluating, treating, monitoring and communicating risks associated with all the activities of the business in a way that will enable the institution to minimise its losses, maximise opportunities and achieve its stated strategic objectives (Jorion and Khoury, 1996). The risk management process is a comprehensive system that includes creating an appropriate risk management environment; maintaining an efficient risk measurement, mitigation and monitoring process; and establishing an adequate internal control arrangement (Khan and Ahmed, 2001).

Risk management is a continuous and vigilant process; it is an activity more than an action. The goal of an effective risk management system is not only to avoid losses, but also to ensure that the bank achieves its targeted financial results with a high degree of reliability and consistency. Taking risks is an integral part of any financial business. Risk arises when there is a possibility of more than one outcome and the ultimate outcome is unknown (Schroeck, 2002). Though all businesses face uncertainty, financial institutions face some special kinds of risks, given their nature of activities.

Risk management, in a broad sense, is not only a discipline for specialised professionals, but permeates every activity of a financial institution. It starts with a clear definition of the chosen risk tolerance for the bank at all levels of the organisation, and includes management actions aimed at ensuring that its risk profile remains within the agreed risk tolerance. In addition, it is not limited to a narrow consideration of the risks undertaken by the institution, but evaluates these in the context of the external environment and how this can affect the bank The recent financial crisis, with the near collapse of the financial system in September–October 2008, provides a striking example of what can happen when risk is poorly managed, as is shown in Chapter 5.

Since all financial entities are directly or indirectly interwoven and interlinked, they create a complicated web of uncertainties which makes up the mass of the financial risk. Risk in a banking context arises from any transaction or business decision that contains uncertainty related to the result. Because virtually every bank transaction is associated with some level of uncertainty, nearly every trans-action contributes to the overall risk of a bank (Schroeck, 2002). Risks are part of financial intermediation; undertaking a business transaction or an investment decision involves some degree of risk-taking regarding the future performance or outcome of the activity. The survival and success of a financial organisation depends on the efficiency with which it can manage its risks. According to Engel (2010) (Head of Risk Management at the European Islamic Investment Bank and one of the interviewees), "banks are in the risk business, they got to take risks. Once money has gone out of the door, the bank has taken a whole array of risks . . . The most insidious and dangerous risk is zero risk. This arises when a risk manager always says 'no' and comes up with many reasons not to do a deal."

History of Risk Management

The appreciation of risk was the important building block in the development of modern financial systems. In the 20th century, the economist Irving Fisher was the first to appreciate the importance of risk in the functioning of financial mar-kets (Bessis, 1999). In the 1930s a number of renowned economists, most notably John Maynard Keynes, saw the importance of risk in the selection of portfolios. However, in their analysis the role of risk was largely limited to affecting expected gains and speculative and hedging activities. This strain of analysis led to results covering the relationship of futures prices and expected spot prices, the impact of risk on assessing the value of future streams of income, and eventually to the development of the portfolio theory (Askari et al., 2009).

However, risk management as an independent topic is a fairly new field; although financial institutions have been always exposed to risks, the formal study of managing risk started in the second half of the last century. Markowitz's (1959) decisive paper initiated the risk-return trade-off discussion; it first indicated that portfolio selection was a problem of maximising expected return and minimising risks. A higher-than-expected return from a portfolio (measured by the mean) can result only from taking more risks. Thus, the problem for investors was to find the optimal risk–return combination. Markowitz's analysis also points out the systematic and unsystematic components of risk. While the unsystematic component, known as idiosyncratic risk, can be mitigated by diversification of assets, the systematic component has to be borne by the investor. Markowitz's approach, however, faces operational problems when a large number of assets are involved (Khan and Ahmed, 2001).

Sharpe's Capital Asset Pricing Model (CAPM) introduced the concepts of systematic and residual risks in 1964 (Stremme, 2005). Advances in this model include Single-Factor Models of Risk that estimate the beta of an asset. While residual (firm-specific) risk can be diversified, beta measures the sensitivity of the portfolio to business cycles (an aggregate index). The dependence of CAPM on a single index to explain the risks inherent in assets is too simplistic. Arbitrage Pricing Theory proposed by Ross in 1976 suggests that multiple factors affect the expected return of an asset. The implication of the Multiple Factor Model is that the total risk is the sum of the various factor-related risks and residual risk. According to Stremme (2005), the CAPM paved the way for more advanced capital-structuring models like the Weighted Average Cost of Capital (WACC), the Modigliani and Miller Theorem on optimal capital structure in 1959 and 1963, the Myers' Trade-off Theory (1977), the Black-Scholes-Merton option pricing, the Efficient Market Hypothesis and the renowned Pecking Order Theory, which was granted the Nobel Prize in Economics in 2001.

Modern risk management frameworks and processes have developed over the past three decades. Traditionally, risk management was engrained in management practices. Like Islamic finance, risk management has come a long way during its short history. "If you mentioned the title Risk Manager 25 years ago, people would laugh at you … Bankers only realised credit risk, all other risks including corporate governance, liquidity, money laundering, and even market risk were merely responsibilities of senior management and board members" says Lowe (2010), Head of Risk Management at Qatar Islamic Bank (UK) and one of the interviewees for this research. It was only when financial products started becoming complicated that risk management evolved as an independent integrated framework. The development of derivatives, pricing models, portfolios and sophisticated international financial trading required independent risk management teams and advanced models to identify, measure, monitor and control different risks.

It was in the mid-1990s, when JP Morgan started developing Value at Risk (VaR) models, that risk management began gaining prominence among banking executives. Gradually risk management started shifting to the hands of mathematicians and physicists, who developed sophisticated models that tempted management to take decisions based on statistical modelling rather than credit fundamentals. During the past two decades, there has been an unprecedented development in the mathematical and quantitative treatment of financial variables with critical implications for banks. An important impact of this development has been decomposing risk through financial engineering and product development, which has made risk management a serious scientific process. These innovations have led to significant cost reductions for most financial institutions. However, at the same time, additional uncertainties have been created, which could have serious consequences for risk management (IFSB, 2007). For example, executives at UBS and Merrill Lynch in some instances took decisions that relied on models that they did not fully understand. However, this wave is coming to an end and there will be a shift in power again to the basics, together with the help of mathematical models. It is a fact, however, that realising a fine balance remains a key challenge.

Systemic Importance of Risk Management

Over the last few decades, risk management has gained prominence in the global banking industry. The significant changes to the banking business have changed the nature of risks faced by financial institutions. Whereas two decades ago a financial institution was primarily faced with credit and market risk only, today's financial institution is exposed to a whole array of new risks, and this list is expanding. Risk management is today at the heart of banks' financial intermediation process, and plays a major role in determining a bank's rating and financial strength.

It should be noted that current risks can become tomorrow's potential losses unless they are managed efficiently. However, although most risks cannot be eliminated, they can be managed. The element of risk also brings opportunities, and to gain from these opportunities, the risk should be managed properly. For a bank, some of the risks can turn into losses and may even cause liquidation. A risk is in many cases hidden before it is visible as a loss. Risk and return are usually correlated: the higher the risk, the higher the return. A bank with a conservative approach may not fully utilise its funds and thus have a higher cost of capital, whereas a bank with high-risk appetite can over-lend, thereby increasing the chances of a failure. Currently, pricing of loans is largely based on risk. A risky loan which is under-priced may prove to be a drag on profitability, whereas a sound loan which is over-priced may deter good customers.

In the financial world, therefore, risk and return are two sides of the same coin. It is easy to lend and to obtain attractive returns from risky borrowers. The price to pay is a risk that is higher than the prudent bank's risk. The prudent bank limits risk, and therefore both future losses and expected revenues, by restricting business volume and screening out risky borrowers. The prudent bank avoids losses but it might suffer from lower market share and lower revenues. However, after a while, the risk-taker might find that higher losses materialise and obtain an end performance lower than that of the prudent lender. Who performs best? Unless some measure of risk is assigned to income, it is impossible to compare policies driven by different risk appetites. Comparing performances without risk adjustment is akin to comparing apples and oranges. The rationale of risk adjustment is in making comparable different performances attached to different risk levels (PwC, 2008).

Sundararajan (2007) provides four reasons for the importance of the application of modern approaches to risk measurement and management in Islamic banking:

(i) To properly recognise the unique mix of risks in Islamic finance contracts;
(ii) To ensure proper pricing of Islamic finance facilities, including returns to IAHs;

(iii) To manage and control various types of risks; and

(iv) To ensure adequacy of capital and its effective allocation, according to the risk profile of the Islamic bank.

It is important to state that risk management is one of the critical factors in providing better returns to shareholders, as it is an important source of value creation in banks (Schroeck, 2002). Risk management is also a necessity for stability of the overall financial system.

Risk Management Versus Risk Measurement

There is a difference between risk measurement and risk management. While risk measurement deals with quantification of risk exposures, risk management refers to "the overall process that a financial institution follows to define a business strategy, to identify the risks to which it is exposed, to quantify those risks, and to understand and control the nature of risks it faces" (Khan and Ahmed, 2001). As the definition identifies, risk management is strictly linked to risk measurement; it is difficult to manage risk if the risk measurements are not robust (McKenzie, 2007).

Risk Management Framework

There are several risk management structures available worldwide, as has been explained in different studies; however, the most commonly used framework in today's modern world is based on four key domains: (i) risk culture and governance, (ii) risk management, (iii) risk measurement, and (iv) infrastructure and information systems (EIIB, 2010b).

These four pillars of risk management should not be considered in isolation. Rather, the dynamic interaction between them is at the core of risk management, as illustrated in Figure 3.1. They are discussed in detail in the following sections.

Risk culture and governance A strong risk culture and tone from the top management are vital for effective risk management. The board of directors and the executive committee are responsible for choosing the appropriate level of risk appetite for the bank and for ensuring that its risk profile remains within the bank's risk tolerance. The board of directors is key to providing effective checks and balances to a bank's management and ensuring that compensation policies are designed to avoid excessive risk-taking (McKenzie, 2007). At the same time, concrete support from senior management and the board is essential to ensuring that the risk function has the necessary authority, is appropriately staffed, and has the required infrastructure to measure and analyse risk in a timely manner.

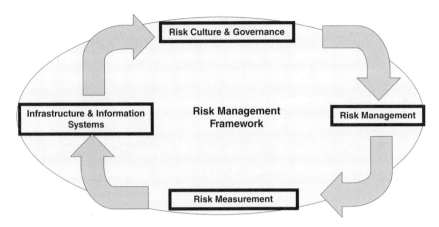

FIGURE 3.1 Risk management framework

As discussed in the available body of knowledge, culture, strategy and competitive position all influence risk appetite. Different banks will have different tolerances for different risks. A bank's risk appetite for credit risk in consumer lending might be quite different from its appetite for market risk in its investment banking operation. A major benefit of defining risk appetite is that it helps to ensure that the risk culture is made explicit (PwC, 2008).

The headwind that chief risk officers and risk management staff typically face, in particular in boom times, was effectively summarised by the Bank for International Settlements (BIS) in its 79th Annual Report. The BIS (2009) noted: "Without support from top management, it did not matter much what the chief risk officer said or to whom he or she said it. The structural problem was compounded by the behavioural response to a risk officer whose job is to tell people to limit or stop what they are doing. If what they are doing is profitable, it is going to be difficult to get managers and directors to listen."

Engel (2010), one of the interviewees for this research, adds, "I keep reminding everyone at my bank to 'Think Capital, Think Risk'; everybody has got to engage in the risk culture if you want to implement a successful risk management framework."

Risk management Once the risk tolerance for the financial institution has been agreed, this has to be translated into a coherent risk limitation system for different types of risks as well as for the different business activities of the bank. In addition, risk mitigation will be needed to ensure that the risk profile of specific portfolios or activities does not exceed the allocated limit – hence the link between risk

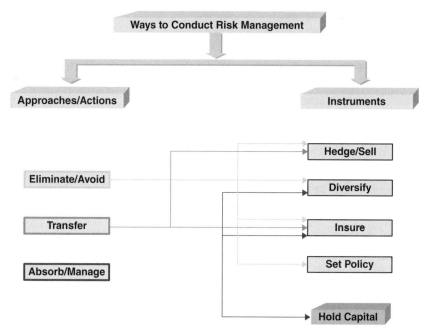

FIGURE 3.2 Ways to conduct risk management
Source: Schroeck (2002:79). © John Wiley & Sons, Inc. Reproduced with permission

governance and risk management. Figure 3.2 illustrates that a sound risk management process requires appropriate linkage between approaches and actions that enable eliminating, transferring or managing risk, and instruments that facilitate the hedging and diversifying of those risks that the organisation cannot manage.

Risk measurement Risk cannot be managed without being measured. The crisis has made apparent that further work is required to enable banks to measure their risks with some degree of accuracy, particularly in relation to complex financial instruments, as well as to capture the interrelationship across different types of risk. In measuring and managing risk, the adoption of multiple risk measures is necessary to prevent important dimensions of risk being overlooked. For example, statistical measures, such as VaR, need to be complemented by stress-testing analysis. The results of models can be a valuable input into the decision-making process of a bank, but they cannot replace judgement. Lowe (2010) asserts that models and formulas should support a sound fundamental analysis, but never replace it.

Infrastructure and information systems A robust risk infrastructure and good data quality are the essential elements for a bank to be able to measure in an accurate and timely manner the risks that it is taking. It is also a key element for effective risk reporting, which, as discussed above, is essential for the board of directors and the executives to make informed decisions (EIIB, 2010b). So, the risk infrastructure and information systems pillar links to risk culture and governance. Consequently, with this process the circle is closed.

RISK MANAGEMENT AND THE CREDIT CRUNCH

Since 2008, the financial crisis has uncovered significant deficiencies in the way in which financial institutions manage risk. It has become clear that risk management has lacked the necessary authority to exert an appropriate influence over profit centres. The tools used to manage risk have also been found deficient, from stress-testing and scenario analysis to the reliance on external rating agencies.

While it is too early to count the ultimate survivors, or reach conclusions about whether (or to what extent) risk management may have contributed to some banks' ability to endure stress, it is noted that effective or ineffective risk management is often cited as the root of success or failure. However, as the dust starts to settle from the financial crisis, a consensus around what needs to be fixed is begining to form. Consequently, many Western institutions are subjecting their risk management policies and processes to a significant overhaul, and are investigating a wide range of tools and techniques to give them a better overall picture of risk.

While efforts to upgrade risk management techniques are commendable, there is a more fundamental point to address around the risk culture of the organisation. It has become apparent that, during the boom, the concerns of risk managers were all too often swept aside in the quest for profit and competitive advantage. As the banking industry seeks to rebuild itself, the balance of power needs to shift back toward risk management. Armed with appropriate authority, clear visibility into lines of business, and the ear of senior executives, risk management will become an integral part of any future recovery (Economist Intelligence Unit, 2009).

CLASSIFICATION OF RISKS

There are several ways in which risks are classified. One way is to distinguish between business risk and financial risks. Business risk arises from the nature of a firm's business; it relates to factors affecting the product market. Financial risk arises from possible losses in financial markets due to movements in financial variables (Jorion and Khoury, 1996).

Khan and Ahmed (2001) present another way of decomposing risk between systematic and unsystematic components. While systematic risk is associated with the overall market or the economy, unsystematic risk is linked to a specific asset or firm. Asset-specific unsystematic risk can be mitigated in a large diversified portfolio, but systematic risk is non-diversifiable. Parts of systematic risk, however, can be reduced through risk mitigation and transferring techniques.

While Santomero (1997) classifies risks faced by financial institutions into three types (risks that can be eliminated, risks that can be transferred to others, and risks that can be managed by the institution), financial intermediaries would avoid certain risks by implementing simple business practices and not taking up activities that impose risks upon them. Risk avoidance techniques would include the standardisation of all business-related activities and processes, construction of diversified portfolios, and implementation of an incentive-compatible scheme with accountability of actions. Some risks that banks face can be reduced or eliminated by transferring or selling these in well-defined markets. Risk-transferring techniques include use of derivatives for hedging, selling or buying of financial claims; changing borrowing terms, etc. Iqbal and Llewellyn (2002) differentiate between two types of risk: 'uncontrollable risk' or chance, over which the bank, as the decision maker, has no control whatsoever; and 'controllable' or responsive risk, which can be controlled and affected by the bank.

Nonetheless, as previously discussed, most risks cannot be eliminated or transferred and must be absorbed by the financial institution, either due to the complexity of the risk and difficulty in separating it from the asset, or because the risk is accepted by the financial institutions as being central to their business. These risks are accepted because banks specialise in dealing with them and get rewarded accordingly.

Akkizidis and Khandelwal (2007) group risks into three major categories: financial, business and operational risks. Financial risk will generally include credit, market and liquidity risks. Business risk is a combination of management risk and strategic risk. Operational risk can arise due to people, process and systems, as well as several other factors. Some of the other relevant risks for the financial industry can be commodity risk, country and political risk, reputational risk, legal risk, concentration risk, regulatory risk and systemic risk related to interconnected unfavourable events across the industry.

Greuning and Iqbal (2008) classify risks into four major categories as depicted by Table 3.1. Financial risks are subject to complex interdependencies that may significantly increase a bank's overall risk profile. For example, a bank engaged in foreign currency business is normally exposed to currency risk, but it is also exposed to credit, liquidity and re-pricing risks if it carries open positions or mismatches in its forward book. Operational risks are related to a bank's organisation and functioning, including technologies, compliance with bank policies and

TABLE 3.1   Banking risk exposures

Financial Risks	Operational Risks	Business Risks	Event Risks
Balance sheet structure	Internal fraud	Macro policy	Political
Income statement structure and profitability	External fraud	Financial infrastructure	Contagion
Capital adequacy	Employment practices and workplace safety	Legal infrastructure	Banking crisis
Credit	Clients, products and business services	Legal liability	Other exogenous risks
Liquidity	Damage to physical assets	Regulatory compliance	
Market	Business disruption and system failures (technology risk)	Reputational and fiduciary	
Interest rate	Execution, delivery and process management	Country risks	

Source: Based on data from Greuning and Iqbal (2008:65)

procedures, and measures against mismanagement and fraud. Business risks are associated with a bank's business environment, including macroeconomic and policy concerns, legal and regulatory factors, and the financial sector's infrastructure, such as payment systems and the auditing profession. Event risks include all types of exogenous risks that, if they were to materialise, would jeopardise a bank's operations or undermine its financial condition.

Iqbal and Mirakhor (2007) divide the risk profile of a financial institution into four groups: financial, business, treasury and governance risks. They define financial risk as the exposures that result in a direct financial loss to the assets or the liabilities of a bank, including credit, market and equity risks. Business risks are associated with a bank's business environment, including macroeconomic and policy concerns, legal and regulatory factors, and the overall banking sector infrastructure such as payment systems and the auditing profession. Treasury risks include risks arising from the management of the financial resources of the financial institution in terms of cash management, equity management, liquidity management, and asset and liability management (ALM). Finally, governance risk refers to the risk arising from a failure in governance of the institution, from negligence in conducting business and meeting contractual obligations, and from a weak internal and external institutional environment, including legal risk, whereby a bank is unable to enforce its contracts.

It is important to note another dimension of risk – the interaction and mutation of risks. Usually risks combine with each other, creating new risks. For example, the risk on investments consists of credit risk and market risk, as well as an element of operational risk. A change in the value of the investment is a market risk, downgrading of the investment by a rating agency will involve credit risk, whereas an error in documenting the guarantees will be classified as operational risk. Similarly, the inability to manage market risk can be considered operational risk rather than pure market risk. To what extent this needs to be allocated using market risk methodology and operational risk methodology is complicated to determine. When allocating capital to manage risks, this merging of risks can cause duplicate allocations and thus increase the capital allocation (Akkizidis and Khandelwal, 2007). This is a grey area of risk management requiring further probing.

For the purpose of this research, risks will be classified into two main categories: risks which Islamic banks have in common with traditional banks and risks which are unique to Islamic banks due to their compliance with *Shari'ah*. Although Islamic banks share many of the same types of risk as their conventional counterparts, they find these risks complex and difficult to mitigate for various reasons. First, unlike conventional banks, given trading-based instruments and equity financing, there are significant market risks along with credit risk in the banking book of Islamic banks. Second, risks intermingle and change from one type to another at different stages of a transaction. For example, during the transaction period of a *salam* contract, the bank is exposed to credit risk, and at the conclusion of the contract it is exposed to commodity price risk. Third, Islamic banks are constrained in using some of the risk mitigation instruments that their conventional counterparts use, as these are not yet generally allowed under *Shari'ah* principles. Finally, the profit-and-loss-sharing (PLS) modes in Islamic banks change the nature of the risks these institutions face.

RISKS COMMON TO BOTH ISLAMIC AND CONVENTIONAL BANKS

The majority of the risks faced by conventional financial institutions such as credit risk, market risk, liquidity risk, operational risk, etc. are also faced by the IFIs. However, the magnitude of some of these risks is different for Islamic banks due to their unique business model and compliance with the *Shari'ah* principles. Thus, the nature of some risks that IFIs face is different from those of their conventional counterparts. Special attention must be paid to the contractual role of Islamic banks because the relationship between parties during the lifetime of the contract gives Islamic finance a different orientation toward risk. Even when risk management techniques in conventional finance are applicable to Islamic products, the implementation of risk management, especially in hedging market, price, foreign exchange (FX) and commodity risks, is problematic. The following sections present an introduction to particular risk areas.

Credit Risk

Credit risk is generally defined as the risk of loss arising from default or failure to perform (EIIB, 2010b). It is also referred to as 'default risk', which is one of the earliest recognised risks in the financial industry. Traditionally, a large part of a bank's profit came from the lending business, and the majority of bank losses were also related to this aspect of risk management; hence the focus was primarily on credit risk.

Banks have always monitored and mitigated credit risk actively, through a number of mechanisms such as country limits, counterparty limits, large exposure limits, diversification, covenants, delegations, internal and external ratings, watch lists, etc. However, credit risk assessment remains judgement-based because it cannot be precisely calculated ahead of time since the likelihood of default is highly uncertain and thus difficult to predict accurately. Credit applications, referred to as credit scoring models, play an important role in combining qualitative and quantitative risk aspects of clients including, but not limited to, operating experience, management expertise, asset quality, leverage and liquidity ratios, earnings, debt service, etc. (Akkizidis and Khandelwal, 2007).

Credit risk in Islamic banks   The IFSB Principles of Credit Risk can help to develop an understanding of the nature of credit risks in Islamic banks, as in Box 3.1.

BOX 3.1: IFSB PRINCIPLES OF CREDIT RISK MANAGEMENT

Principle 2.1:   IIFS shall have in place a strategy for financing, using various instruments in compliance with *Sharī'ah*, whereby it recognises the potential credit exposures that may arise at different stages of the various financing agreements.

Principle 2.2:   IIFS shall carry out a due diligence review in respect of counterparties prior to deciding on the choice of an appropriate Islamic financing instrument.

Principle 2.3:   IIFS shall have in place appropriate methodologies for measuring and reporting the credit risk exposures arising under each Islamic financing instrument.

(Continued)

> **Principle 2.4:** IIFS shall have in place *Sharī'ah*-compliant credit risk mitigating techniques appropriate for each Islamic financing instrument.
>
> Source: Based on data from IFSB (2005a)

The unique characteristics of the financial instruments offered by Islamic banks result in the following special credit risks:

(i) First, access to collateral and foreclosure are difficult. One of the five key pillars of modern Islamic finance is the obligation to back any transaction by a tangible, identifiable, underlying asset. This means that IFIs – at least in theory – back their transactions with collateral. Consequently, collateral coverage is usually higher for IFIs than for conventional banks. In short, IFIs naturally have a high level of collateralisation on their credit portfolios, and thus are in a position to somewhat reduce their economic, if not regulatory, exposures at default.

Contrary to conventional banks, whose customers are not always obliged to disclose the purpose of their borrowings, Islamic banks finance the acquisition of identifiable assets of which they have legal ownership, in most cases until maturity and final repayment. This is notably the case for *ijarah* and diminishing *musharakah* operations, in which the bank acquires the asset and leases it to the customer, with ownership transfer taking place only at maturity. The bank, as the legal owner of the asset, is therefore in a favourable position to foreclose on this asset (in the case of a default), and sell it on a secondary market (Moody's, 2008a).

In practice, however, collateral foreclosure can be much more difficult, especially for residential real estate. Given the take-off in residential real estate lending in Gulf Cooperation Council (GCC) countries, this question of foreclosure is set to become critical. Although an Islamic bank is in theory in a position to evict a customer from a property and resell it in the case of a default on the loan backed by the property, this would be unlikely to happen in practice, owing to the bank's 'social responsibility'. According to Chowdhury (2010), one of the interviewees for this research, there are, however, instances when such a decision may be taken by a bank and authorised by its *Shari'ah* board – notably when specific conditions were set out and agreed upon before the conclusion of the transaction. In such cases, foreclosure may be easier than for conventional banks, as the property belongs to the Islamic bank. As a matter of fact, this type of structuring is sometimes used by conventional banks, as it is a strong way of reducing the problem of foreclosure. In addition, there are other problems with posting collaterals as securities, especially in developing countries, where most Islamic banks operate, or in declining times like the recent recession. Typical problems include illiquidity of the collateral or inability of the bank to sell it, difficulties in determining the fair market value on a periodic basis, and legal obstacles in taking possession of the collateral. Diminishing *musharakah* contracts are increasingly used as a financing mechanism for *Shari'ah*-compliant home purchase, particularly in Dubai (Moody's, 2008b).

However, when the financing is based on other *Shari'ah*-compliant schemes where the property is not registered in the bank's name, the IFI will find itself in the same position as its conventional peers.

(ii) *Murabahah* is the most predominantly used Islamic financial contract. Based on the contract's similarity in risk characteristics with those of interest-based contracts, *murabahah* is approved as an acceptable mode of finance in a number of regulatory jurisdictions. However, such a standardised contract may not be acceptable to all *fiqh* scholars. Moreover, as the contract stands at present, there is a lack of complete uniformity in *fiqh* viewpoints. The different views among scholars can be a source of counterparty risk as a result of the atmosphere of ineffective litigation (Khan and Ahmed, 2001). The main point in this regard stems from the fact that financial *murabahah* is a contemporary contract which has been designed by combining a number of different contracts. There is a complete consensus among all *fiqh* scholars that this new contract has been approved as a form of deferred trading. The condition of its validity is based on the fact that the bank must buy (become owner) and afterwards transfer the ownership direct to the client. The order placed by the client is not a sale contract but merely a promise to buy. According to the OIC *Fiqh* Academy Resolution, a promise can be binding on one party only. The OIC *Fiqh* Academy, AAOIFI and most Islamic banks treat the promise to buy as binding on the client. Some other scholars, however, are of the opinion that the promise is not binding on the client; the client, even after placing an order and paying the commitment fee, can rescind the contract. The most important counterparty risk specific to *murabahah* arises due to the unsettled nature of the contract (Iqbal and Mirakhor, 2007).

(iii) In the case of *mudarabah* investments, where the Islamic bank enters into the *mudarabah* contract as *rab al-mal* (principal) with an external *mudarib* (agent), the Islamic bank is exposed to an enhanced credit risk on the amounts advanced to the *mudarib* in addition to the typical principal–agent problems. The nature of the *mudarabah* contract is such that it does not give the bank appropriate rights to monitor the *mudarib* or to participate in management of the project, which makes it difficult to assess and manage credit risk. The bank is not in a position to know or decide how the activities of the *mudarib* can be monitored accurately, especially if losses are claimed. This risk is especially present in markets where information asymmetry is high and transparency in financial disclosure by the *mudarib* is low (Greuning and Iqbal, 2008).

(iv) In *bay' al-salam* contracts, the bank is exposed to the risk of failure to provide goods on time, or supply of a different quality of goods from that contractually specified. Such failures could result in a delay or default in payment, and hence to financial losses to the Islamic bank. *Salam* is an agricultural-based contract and hence the counterparty risks may be due to factors beyond the normal credit quality of the client. The credit quality of the client may be very good but the supply may not come as contractually agreed due to natural calamities. Since agriculture is exposed to catastrophic risks, the counterparty risks are expected to be above-average in *bay' al-salam* (Iqbal and Mirakhor, 2007).

(v) The counterparty risks under *istisna'a* contracts are similar to the risks faced by Islamic banks under *bay' al-salam* contracts. However, the object of *istisna'a* is more within the control of the counterparty and less exposed to natural calamities as compared to the object of *salam*. Therefore, it can be expected that the counterparty risk of the sub-contractor of *istisna'a*, although fairly high, is less severe than that of the *salam* (Akkizidis and Khandelwal, 2007). In addition, under the *istisna'a* agreement IFIs are deemed to remain the beneficial owners of financed assets until the borrower pays back the final instalment. In the case where the borrower defaults before maturity, the IFI is entitled to dispose of the financed assets, which are generally illiquid because they are specific to the nature of the plant, the industry or the enterprise to which the IFI's funds were initially allocated. In the case of default, the IFI – more so than any conventional bank – becomes a merchant, acting in the field of commerce rather than in that of pure financial intermediation. This puts additional pressure on IFIs to equip themselves with the correct technical and professional expertise for both credit assessment and the management of underlying asset valuation, trading and liquidity, should loan foreclosure and collateral realisation occur (Mahlknecht, 2009).

(vi) Credit risk management for Islamic banks is further complicated by additional externalities. For example, in the case of default by the counterparty, Islamic banks are prohibited from charging any accrued interest or imposing any penalty, except in the case of deliberate procrastination (Greuning and

Iqbal, 2008). Clients may take advantage by delaying payment, knowing that the Islamic bank will not charge a penalty or require extra payments. During the delay, the bank's capital is stuck in non-productive activity. To mitigate this risk, Islamic banks tend to charge defaulting customers (who prove to be negligent) a penalty for late payments, which the banks donate to charity and do not include in their income. This helps to prevent potential similar situations.

(vii) Islamic banks have less sophisticated credit risk management practices, mostly because of the lack of databases and insufficient track record. Conventional banks use these tools to reduce their credit risk, a luxury not yet available to Islamic banks. For example, the calculation of probability of default (PD), loss given default (LGD), expected losses (EL), exposure at default (EAD) and credit VaR do not generally exist in Islamic banking. There are endeavours by Moody's and Standard & Poor's to develop such models for Islamic banks, or to adjust some of the existing models like CreditEdge, RiskCalc and Risk Tracker to accommodate Islamic banking. These models are still work in progress and are faced by huge difficulties stemming from the fact that there is limited systematic data available in the Islamic banking world to date.

Concentration Risk

Islamic banks tend to have a concentration base of assets and/or deposits; they face high concentration by name and sector, as well as high geographical concentration. The limited scope of eligible asset classes for IFIs increases concentration in investment portfolios, which tends to be mitigated by a lower appetite for speculative transactions. Since Islam forbids *gharar* and speculation, IFIs are naturally crowded out from the high-risk/high-return leveraged and/or structured investment asset classes. As such instruments tend to be, in one form or another, based either on interest (*riba*) or derivatives (not commonly allowed by *Shari'ah* supervisory boards, although Islamic 'equivalents' are appearing), their technical eligibility is in most cases difficult to justify. IFIs thus limit the scope of their investment strategies to 'plain vanilla' asset classes such as stocks, *sukuk* and real estate, notwithstanding their cash reserves in the form of short-term international *murabahahs* for liquidity purposes. A limited range of permissible asset allocations leads to concentration risks in IFIs' investment portfolios, by asset class, sector and usually also by name. This led some IFIs to suffer severe losses during the recession. For example, IFIs that invested heavily in stock markets were exposed to swings in equity prices. Moreover, IFIs are usually significantly exposed to the real estate sector, as it is compliant with *Shari'ah* principles. Some Islamic banks in the GCC have significant exposure to this sector (directly or indirectly through collateral or *sukuk*), which magnifies the market risk especially during bearish market conditions.

Because most Islamic financial transactions have an underlying asset at their centre, Islamic banks tend to own more physical assets than conventional banks, and "what is a better asset than real estate?", wonders Marx (2010), one of the interviewees for this research.

There has been a build-up of these assets during a benign period of credit risk and rising asset values; a time when the market has seen ample liquidity (Moore, 2009). The recent straitened times that impacted on markets around the globe have still to be felt in many of the countries where Islamic banks operate; Dubai was a clear example. The particular concentrations seen in Islamic banks and the similarity of many of their operations are causes for concern.

In addition, the immaturity of securitisation in the industry means that this financial technology has not been widely used to remove such excess concentrations from the balance sheet, although 2007 did see the first few transactions of commercial property loans and residential *ijarah* mortgages. In particular, *sukuk* are scarce and constitute an illiquid market where investors tend to stick to a buy-and-hold approach rather than move toward more active bond trading (Moody's, 2011a).

Moreover, concentration risks arise from the banks' limited geographic reach, as most IFIs are domestic players and only a few have material operations outside their home country. One interesting exception is the Al Baraka Banking Group, which has a material presence in more than a dozen jurisdictions across the Muslim world that brings a good amount of de-correlation between the Group's sub-portfolios.

Islamic banks also suffer from concentration on the liability side, leading to poor asset–liability management (ALM), as discussed in the section 'Asset–Liability Management'. At present, IFIs rely heavily on maintaining good relationships with depositors. However, these relationships can be tested during times of distress or changing market conditions, when depositors tend to change loyalties and shift to large financial institutions which they perceive to be safer. By diversifying their base of depositors, Islamic banks could reduce their exposure to displacement or withdrawal risks. According to Askari et al. (2009), with the changing face of banking and the introduction of internet-based banking, achieving a high degree of geographic diversity on the liabilities side is conceivable and should be encouraged.

Concentration and potential volatility in the credit quality of portfolios have made it necessary for IFIs to maintain strong capitalisation despite rapid growth. This has in turn put pressure on dividend payouts, and sometimes also on shareholders to inject fresh capital.

Market Risk

Market risk is generally defined as the risk of loss arising from changes in market prices and profit rates, which will result in a change in earnings or fair value of a financial obligation resulting in a capital gain or loss upon realisation of the asset (EIIB, 2010d). The losses can be in on and off balance sheet positions arising from adverse movements in market prices, i.e. fluctuations in yields and profit rates (rate-of-return risk), foreign exchange rates (FX risk), equity and commodity prices (price risk). The price volatility of most assets held in investment and trading portfolios is often significant. Volatility prevails even in mature markets, although it is much higher in emerging or illiquid markets.

Market risk was recognised in the late 1980s, after the increase in the importance of stock markets, when banks started investing heavily in securities (Davis, 2009a). Market risk is difficult to measure due to diversified portfolios, since it will consist of several markets, currencies, indexes and instruments. The larger the diversification of the portfolio, the more difficult it is to accurately estimate market risks due to the correlation between risks.

Market risk management By its very nature, market risk requires constant management attention and adequate analysis. Although there are several ways to measure and manage market risks, which vary among banks, most banks have limits and triggers for portfolios, individual transactions, sectors and even traders. Banks also use marking to market, stop-loss provisions, gap analysis, back-testing and stress-testing for the daily risk management of banking and trading books. Stress-testing is gaining more popularity to help predict expected losses.

Factor sensitivities and VaR can be used for marked-to-market trading. VaR is the most well-known methodology to quantify and evaluate market risk in a systematic fashion. It is one of the newer risk management tools that indicates how much a firm can lose or make with a certain probability in a given time horizon. VaR summarises financial risk inherent in portfolios into a simple number. It is the value of potential losses that will not be exceeded in more than a given fraction of possible events. This fraction, expressed as a percentage, is called the 'tolerance level'. For example, stating that VaR is 100 at the tolerance level of 5% means that the chances that futures losses exceed 100 are equal to 5% (Bessis, 1999). Though VaR is used to measure market risk in general, it incorporates many other risks like foreign currency, commodities and equities. In fact, VaR applies to all levels of risk management, including credit risk, although it is often associated with market risk only (Bessis, 1999). It has many variations and can be estimated in different ways like the Monte Carlo approach, the Parametric approach and the Historical approach. However, VaR models possess some latent weaknesses arising from the fact that they are tailor-made models. As a risk indicator, VaR works best for smaller positions in liquid markets. In the most recent crisis (like many in the past), the biggest losses occurred when several firms built up concentrations, sometimes unknown to their managers and often unknown to each other. Then, when liquidity evaporated, firms were stuck with big positions or were forced to liquidate at the same time, exacerbating the trend in falling values. In either case, increases in observed market volatility caused the VaR attributed to remaining positions to rise. Thus, VaR has also been criticised for being a pro-cyclical risk measure. The use of other measures to supplement VaR, such as Expected Shortfall (the average of all the hypothetical losses beyond daily VaR), can help provide better market risk management (Moody's, 2009c). Therefore, data inputs should be carefully assessed before the appropriate model is applied. In addition, the conventional market is full of complex derivative products for hedging the positions to manage market risk.

Market risk in Islamic banks The IFSB Principles of Market Risk Management, as illustrated in Box 3.2, introduce the risk management strategy for market risk.

BOX 3.2: IFSB PRINCIPLES OF MARKET RISK MANAGEMENT

Principle 4.1: IIFS shall have in place an appropriate framework for market risk management (including reporting) in respect of all assets held, including those that do not have a ready market and/or are exposed to high price volatility.

Source: Based on data from IFSB (2005a)

Market risk in Islamic financial markets inherently exists within the lifetime of Islamic contracts. The management of market risks is made more difficult for Islamic banks due to the limited number of risk management tools/instruments available to them. For example, it is difficult for an IFI to use hedging instruments, such as derivatives, as these are generally forbidden. On a positive note, the prohibition of *gharar* usually tempers the risk profile of Islamic banks simply by limiting the size of their trading operations. Market risk for IFIs can be divided into six categories as follows:

Rate-of-return risk (profit rate risk) The IFSB Principles of Rate-of-Return Risk Management, as in Box 3.3, introduce the risk management strategy for rate-of-return risk.

BOX 3.3: IFSB PRINCIPLES OF RATE-OF-RETURN RISK MANAGEMENT

Principle 6.1: IIFS shall establish a comprehensive risk management and reporting process to assess the potential impacts of market factors affecting rates of return on assets in comparison with the expected rates of return for IAHs.

Principle 6.2: IIFS shall have in place an appropriate framework for managing displaced commercial risk, where applicable.

Source: Based on data from IFSB (2005a)

Islamic banks are not exposed to an 'interest rate risk', as interest is not compliant with the *Shari'ah*. However, they potentially face even more complex rate-of-return risks and benchmark risks. Lee (2008) explains that Islamic banks do not operate in a closed economy; if interest rates rise sharply in relation to mark-up rates, deposits will flow from Islamic banks into conventional banks and vice versa.

This results from a mismatch between the yield earned on the bank's assets and that served on its liabilities. Controlling margin rates is at the heart of IFIs' ALM. The management of interest rate risk is one of the fundamental tasks of the ALM committees of conventional banks. Similarly, IFIs face the same issue of identifying, measuring and controlling the risk exposure stemming from the expected cash inflows and outflows of assets and liabilities according to their economic maturities. Like conventional banks, IFIs have both a portfolio yielding fixed income over the duration of contracts and a portfolio generating floating rates of profit.

However, unlike conventional banks, the charge attached to funding costs is supposed to be a function of asset yields, as per the core principle of profit-sharing underlying Islamic banking and finance (IBF), which is at the heart of Profit-Sharing Investment Accounts (PSIAs). Should there be no smoothing of returns to PSIA holders, those IFIs that resort materially to PSIAs for funding would in theory be less profitable than conventional banks when the interest- or profit-rate cycle is at its peak, because when conventional banks face a predetermined cost of funds, IFIs would on the contrary be in a position to share more returns with PSIA holders (Thun, 2010).

The opposite scenario would also be true: when the interest- or profit-rate cycle trends down toward its trough, IFIs would buffer the decline by distributing less profit to PSIA holders, whereas conventional banks would have to absorb the same cost of funds at a time when net asset yields had shrunk, therefore reducing more substantially their margins. If PSIA principles are applied, a lower income on outstanding loans and participations goes hand in hand with lower payments to depositors and the bank's solvency is not endangered (Visser, 2009). In practice, however, the losses of Islamic banks are not shared with PSIA holders and often a minimum yield on deposits is 'implicitly' guaranteed. As a result, the potential benefits of PLS finance cannot be realised. There is often an implicit promise of some minimal return on deposits, or a *de facto* guarantee of non-negative returns (Turen, 1995).

Another difference between Islamic and conventional banks is their respective capacity to use derivatives to hedge their loan books against adverse interest-/profit-rate scenarios. IFIs have a natural preference for short-term exposures or contractual credit terms that would allow for quick re-pricing schemes, such as *ijarah* or diminishing *musharakah*, which typically re-price every quarter, behaving like floating profit rate loans. These mechanisms make it less necessary for Islamic banks to resort to (expensive) profit rate swaps for hedging purposes. Less than a handful of IFIs to date have had access to such hedging instruments for *Shari'ah* related reasons and because so far these instruments are still very scarce, illiquid, based on over-the-counter arrangements, and thus still quite costly (Askari et al., 2009).

In the longer term, IFIs are expected to be increasingly exposed to project finance and mortgage lending, two of the most likely and powerful engines for the future momentum of Gulf banking markets. In both lines of business, an IFI's capacity to supply long-term fixed-rate financing would be viewed as a key competitive advantage. From a balance sheet management perspective, the IFI's corresponding capacity to manage the derived profit rate risk would be critical, particularly under Basel II's Pillar 2.

In some cases, IFIs can employ nascent *Shari'ah*-compliant hedging techniques. Dubai Islamic Bank and Deutsche Bank AG have stated that they have established the first ever *Shari'ah*-compliant profit rate collar (Ayub, 2007). For less sophisticated IFIs, the matching of floating and fixed yields can be used as a natural way to cover these risks. An *ijara* portfolio – with a floating margin or re-pricing characteristics – could be used to reduce an IFI's exposure to margin risk resulting from the use of PSIAs as a funding source. As IFIs usually benefit from a large portion of unremunerated deposits, as is the case for Saudi Arabia-based Al Rajhi Bank, this can also be a good mitigating factor for margin-related risks.

The core opportunity comes from developing products to manage profit rate risks and FX risks using fixed/floating profit swaps and currency swaps. Profit rate swaps rely mostly on the double *murabahah* approach, referred to as the 'dual *murabahah*' agreement (Marx, 2010). Although straightforward FX contracts are not permissible, there are several alternative solutions, which all have their respective challenges, such as: back-to-back *qard al-hasan*, dual commodity *murabahah* contracts, *waad*, *arboun* and others as discussed under the 'Risk Mitigation in Islamic Banking' section.

Equity investment risk   The IFSB Principles, as in Box 3.4, introduce the risk management strategy for equity investment risk management.

BOX 3.4: IFSB PRINCIPLES OF RATE OF EQUITY INVESTMENT RISK MANAGEMENT

Principle 3.1:   IIFS shall have in place appropriate strategies, risk management and reporting processes in respect of the risk characteristics of equity investments, including *Muḍārabah* and *Mushārakah* investments.

Principle 3.2:   IIFS shall ensure that their valuation methodologies are appropriate and consistent, and shall assess the potential impacts of their methods on profit calculations and allocations. The methods shall be mutually agreed between the IIFS and the *Muḍārib* and/or *Mushārakah* partners.

Principle 3.3:   IIFS shall define and establish the exit strategies in respect of their equity investment activities, including extension and redemption conditions for *Muḍārabah* and *Mushārakah* investments, subject to the approval of the institution's *Sharī'ah* Board.

Source: Based on data from IFSB (2005a)

Most banks, whether conventional or Islamic, deal in quoted and non-quoted equities all over the world. Typical examples of equity investments are holdings of shares in the stock market, private equity investments, syndications, management buyouts, etc. However, the nature of Islamic finance contracts, particularly the *musharakah* and *mudarabah* contracts, may result in specific equity risks to IFIs. This is mainly because one of their main characteristics lies in the sharing between the IFI and the partner of profit and loss that is driven by the share in the investment's equity (Grais and Kulathunga, 2007). Therefore, the degree of risk under those contracts is relatively higher than that of other investments.

Mudarabah can expose the IFI to moral hazard and to principal–agent problems when the bank enters as *rab al-mal* and the *mudarib* is the agent. While the bank bears all the losses in case of negative outcome, it cannot oblige the *mudarib* to take appropriate action or exert the required level of effort needed to generate the expected level returns. Such situations might be exploited by the *mudarib* (Greuning and Iqbal, 2008).

This moral hazard problem would be reduced in *musharakah*, where the capital of the partner is always at stake. Furthermore, the bank's position as an equity partner would minimise the problem of information asymmetry, as it would have the right to participate in management of the project in which it is investing. However, the *musharakah* asset class has an associated cost in the form of adverse selection and therefore requires extensive due diligence in terms of screening, information gathering and enhanced monitoring afterwards. Each *musharakah* contract requires careful analysis and negotiation of PLS arrangements, leading to higher costs of intermediation.

In addition, equity investments may not generate steady income, and capital gain might be the only source of return. The unscheduled nature of cash flows makes it difficult to forecast and manage them.

As a result of the additional equity problems associated with both types of contracts, IFIs in practice tend to allocate limited funds to these asset classes. This implies an increased reliance on asset-backed securities, which limits the choice of investments and ultimately might hamper the bank's ability to manage risks and diversify its portfolio (Greuning and Iqbal, 2008). A few IFIs also tend to build portfolios of participations in the capital of a set of financial and industrial companies held for strategic purposes. Usually, *mudarabah* contracts are used, as is the case for *Shari'ah*-compliant investment and/or private equity firms such as Arcapita Bank and Gulf Finance House in Bahrain.

Mark-up risk Islamic banks are exposed to mark-up risk, as the mark-up rate used in *murabahah* or other trade-financing contracts is fixed for the duration of the contract, while the general 'market mark-up rate' used in the financial market may rise or fall over that time period (FRSGlobal, 2009). This means that the prevailing market mark-up rate may rise beyond the rate the bank has locked into a contract, making the bank unable to benefit from higher rates. Very often the mark-up rate (or benchmark rate) will be an international one such as the London Interbank Offered Rate (LIBOR), which gives rise also to a so-called 'benchmark risk'.

Benchmark risk Benchmark risk is the risk of loss due to a change in the margin between domestic rates of return and the benchmark rates of return, which may not be linked closely to domestic returns. For instance, Islamic products issued in Malaysia can be linked to the Kuala Lumpur Interbank Offered Rate (KLibor), the national variant of LIBOR, but this is certainly not the case for all countries and contracts (Mahlknecht, 2009). In the absence of an Islamic benchmark or reference rate, a questionable but common practice has been to use the LIBOR as a proxy which aligns the market risk closely with the movement in LIBOR rates.

According to an interview with Yaccubi (2010), the practice of using LIBOR as the reference benchmark was originally considered an exception allowed by *Shari'ah* scholars under the law of necessity. This exception has become a general rule and the practice is so prevailing that most practitioners do not even question it. Yet, using LIBOR as a benchmark has its proponents and opponents.

The proponents of the practice argue that it is simply a reference point of the current capital market indicating the opportunity cost of capital, which should not be different in global markets where Islamic and conventional banking coexist (Askari et al., 2009). If the opportunity cost of capital is not the same, arbitrage opportunities will arise. They also argue that using a non-*Shari'ah*-compliant reference point does not invalidate a *Shari'ah*-compliant transaction, as the index is just used as a reference. Moreover, an Islamic benchmark is not expected in the near term. According to the *Shari'ah* scholar Aznan Hasan, "A dual system which has both Islamic and conventional benchmark financing rates could throw markets into disarray ... People will arbitrage. Once they see conventional financing is much better, they will go for conventional. Once they see Islamic is much better, they will go for Islamic. In that situation, it will give a big turbulence to a country. The subject has to be treated very delicately" (Y-Sing, 2009).

On the other hand, opponents of this practice argue that in an Islamic economic system, the rate of return on a financial asset should be derived from the rate of return in the real sector and using LIBOR as a benchmark does precisely the opposite, and thus violates the foundation of an Islamic financial system (Askari et al., 2009).

Currency risk Currency risk is of a 'speculative' nature and could result in a gain or loss depending on the direction of exchange rate shifts and whether a bank is net long or net short in the foreign currency. For example, in the case of a net long position in the foreign currency, domestic currency depreciation will result in a net gain for a bank, and a currency appreciation will produce a loss, and vice versa, explains Fochler (2010), who was interviewed for this research.

As for conventional banks, IFIs' exposure to foreign exchange risk can be harmful. While conventional banks can easily hedge themselves through swaps or other hedging instruments, these are generally forbidden in Islamic finance, making the situation more challenging for IFIs. However, most Islamic banks are active in the GCC, where local currencies are pegged either to the US dollar or to a basket of international currencies, reducing tremendously their volatility. In the longer run, GCC economies might converge toward a single regional currency, the anchor of which might not be the US dollar or the euro, but potentially a wider mix of internationally recognised currencies. This would in turn allow for some discrepancy between the reporting currency of GCC-based IFIs and the various cash flows they generate from multiples geographies. This will become even more obvious as IFIs such as Kuwait Finance House, Al Rajhi Bank and Qatar Islamic Bank are expanding abroad in a more ordered and ambitious manner, sometimes in other emerging markets including the relatively volatile economies of Pakistan, Turkey, Sudan and even Yemen. These jurisdictions are increasingly the key to the future growth of IFIs as they have far larger Muslim populations and are comparatively underbanked (Standard & Poor's, 2010b).

Commodity and price risks   In the case of *salam* contracts, IFIs are exposed to commodity price volatility during the period between delivery of the commodity and its sale at the prevailing market price. This risk is similar to the market risk of a forward contract if it is not hedged properly. In order to hedge its position, an Islamic bank may enter into a parallel (off-setting) *bay' al-salam* contract (Greuning and Iqbal, 2008). Similarly, when the *istisna'a* contract is used, the delivery of the commodity is at a specific time in the future, where its price may differ from the set one.

In addition, *salam* contracts are neither exchange traded nor traded over the counter. Thus, all the *salam* contracts end up in physical deliveries and ownership of commodities. These commodities require inventories exposing the IFI to storage costs and other related price risk. Such costs and risks are unique to Islamic banks (Greuning and Iqbal, 2008).

In *murabahah* contracts the bank is financing the contract on a certain profit added to the initial commodity price. The difference between the agreed and the future market price of the commodity is the actual exposure of the corresponding risk that banks take, at least in theory. In practice, the bank takes the commodity risk for a few seconds as it purchases and sells the commodities to commodity brokers – like Dawnay Day, Richmond, Aston commodities and others – who enter into a purchase undertaking with the bank. This practice, referred to as *tawarruq*, has been criticised by many *Shari'ah* scholars. It was approved initially as an interim solution until IFIs move to genuine commodity *murabahah*, but it seems that several banks took advantage from this interim approval and prefer to stick to *tawarruq* as it bears minimal commodity risks to the bank.

In addition, in the case of an operating *ijarah*, the IFI is exposed to market risk in the case of a fall in the residual value of the leased asset at the maturity of the lease term (Ahmed and Khan, 2007).

Finally, IFIs have been investing heavily in the *sukuk* market. However, given that the secondary market for *sukuk* is very limited, the prices of such instruments are highly distorted. Thus, IFIs holding such securities are exposed to volatility in yield, unless they hold the *sukuk* until maturity.

Managing market risk for IFIs   In order to manage market risk, first Islamic banks must be able to measure it accurately. To date, there is not a single Islamic banking system that is capable of measuring market risk properly (Marx, 2010).

According to Bhat, one of the interviewees for this research (from InfrasoftTech, a specialised IT company for developing technology solutions and systems for Islamic banks): "I am confident Islamic banks will get there, it is a matter of time. One has to remember that conventional banking has mega banks that are capable of spending millions on developing sophisticated systems, something that Islamic banking is missing, given its relative nascent state." His interview was not included in the final sample, however.

In the absence of *Shari'ah*-compliant hedging tools and liquid secondary markets, managing market risk is more expensive in Islamic banking than it is in conventional banking. Marx (2010), one of the interviewees for this research, adds "for example, to carry a profit rate swap in the Islamic banking market, I have to pay around 30 bps higher than what this would usually cost in the conventional market. This is because very few banks have the capability, systems and credit lines available to write Islamic profit rate swaps and they exploit this position."

Most advanced market risk management tools, such as VaR, and simulation models require huge trading volumes, a long history of price changes and volatility in order to be able to perform back-testing and stress-testing. This is simply unavailable for Islamic banking given its relatively new state and the limited market liquidity. VaR does not work well for illiquid markets with high concentrations; unfortunately this is the current state of most Islamic banking operators. In addition, issuers in Islamic finance tend to have a relatively small number of issues with short-term maturities. Furthermore, there tends to be a wide gap between the bid/offer spreads on Islamic instruments due to limited liquidity. All these factors indirectly distort the applicability of conventional market risk management tools in Islamic banking. "Islamic banking is not mature enough to apply existing conventional market risk mitigation and hedging techniques. It needs to develop its own set of risk management tools" adds Qaedi (2010), one of the interviewees for this research.

In the absence of sophisticated tools, Islamic banks tend to use traditional risk management techniques to manage their market risk. Simple stress-testing, marking to market, stop-loss provisions, position limits, duration methodologies, scenario analysis, price sensitivity and profit rate analysis are the most commonly used practices, mainly carried out using spreadsheets rather than sophisticated IT systems. "Very simple models, but currently adequate given the complexity of Islamic banking" comments Lowe (2010), one of the interviewees for this research.

Liquidity Risk

Liquidity is necessary for banks to compensate for expected and unexpected balance sheet fluctuations and to provide funds for growth. It represents a bank's ability to accommodate the redemption of deposits and other liabilities and to cover the demand for funding in the loan and investment portfolio (Iqbal and Mirakhor, 2007). Liquidity needs usually are determined by the construction of a maturity ladder that comprises expected cash inflows and outflows over a series of specific time bands; liquidity management is related to a net funding requirement.

Liquidity risk results when the bank's ability to match the maturity of assets and liabilities is impaired. In other words, the risk arises due to insufficient liquidity for normal operating requirements reducing the bank's ability to meet its liabilities when they fall due. This risk may result from either difficulties in obtaining cash at reasonable cost from borrowings (funding risk) or sale of assets (asset liquidity risk). While funding risk can be controlled by proper planning of cash flow needs and seeking newer sources of funds to finance cash shortfalls, the asset liquidity risk can be mitigated by diversification of assets and setting limits of certain illiquid products (Khan and Ahmed, 2001).

The market turmoil that began in mid-2007 has highlighted the crucial importance of market liquidity to the banking sector. The contraction of liquidity in certain structured product and interbank markets, as well as an increased probability of off balance sheet commitments coming onto banks' balance sheets, led to severe funding liquidity strains for some banks and central bank intervention in some cases. These events emphasised the interrelationship between funding, liquidity and credit risks, and the fact that liquidity is a key determinant of the soundness of the banking sector (BCBS, 2008). Financial innovation and global market developments have transformed the nature of liquidity risk in recent years. The funding of some banks has shifted toward a greater reliance on the capital markets, which are potentially a more volatile source of funding than traditional retail deposits. In addition, the growth and product range of the securitisation market has broadened as the originate-to-distribute business model has become more widespread. Northern Rock is a classic example of a bank that was brought down due to lack of liquidity rather than any credit or solvency risk. The bank simply borrowed for the short term from the capital markets and lent for the long term to residential mortgages.

Inspired by international drive from the Basel Committee on Banking Supervision (BCBS) and the Committee of European Banking Supervisors on liquidity management, regulators around the globe have been working on introducing a series of new rules outlining features of a new liquidity regime which proposes much higher levels of stress-testing and stricter liquidity management approaches. Basel III is the most obvious example.

Liquidity risk in Islamic banks IFSB Principles, as in Box 3.5, introduce the risk management strategy for liquidity risk management.

BOX 3.5: IFSB PRINCIPLES OF LIQUIDITY RISK MANAGEMENT

Principle 5.1: IIFS shall have in place a liquidity management framework (including reporting) taking into account separately and on an overall basis their liquidity exposures in respect of each category of current accounts, unrestricted and restricted investment accounts.

Principle 5.2: IIFS shall assume liquidity risk commensurate with their ability to have sufficient recourse to *Sharī'ah*-compliant funds to mitigate such risk.

Source: Based on data from IFSB (2005a)

Islamic banks have traditionally held high levels of cash/liquid assets, ideally to safeguard the interests of their depositors, investors and shareholders against credit upheavals and liquidity crunch. This reduces liquidity risks in an economic downturn. In addition, from a leverage perspective, IFIs' operational models are built upon conservative fundamental values that discourage the use of disproportionate levels of debt to finance assets, as well as speculative and doubtful investments, a position which has inhibited the industry in terms of its use of leverage. As a result, IFIs' funding portfolios are highly concentrated in a few liquid assets and are deficient in terms of a securitised asset base (IFSB, 2008a).

At the same time, underutilised surplus liquidity on most IFIs' books has led to weak asset–liability management, which translates into liquidity risk. This risk arises from the scarcity of medium- and long-term funds to reduce the gap between assets and liabilities. The analysis in Figure 3.3 categorises the assets and liabilities of a sample of 20 leading Islamic banks into short term, medium term and long term. IFIs use short- and medium-term liabilities to finance long-term assets. Currently, IFIs are highly dependent on short-term funds to manage their longer-tenure liabilities. This issue has become even more crucial in today's capital market environment because the frequency of asset write-downs is on the rise. In the wake of global financial developments, liquidity has become one of the most critical risks for IFIs for the following reasons:

(i) Limited availability of *Shari'ah*-compliant liquidity management instruments because most instruments used for liquidity management purposes are interest-based and *Shari'ah* does not allow the sale of debt, other than at its face value. Thus, to raise funds by selling debt-based assets is not an option for IFIs;

Balance sheet breakdown

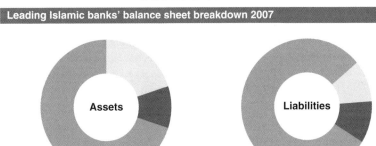

Short term
■ Medium term
▨ Long term

Sample of 20 leading Islamic banks
Note: Asset/liability tenure defined as follows: Short term 0 to 3 months; Medium term 3+ months
to 2 years; Long term 2+ years and beyond

FIGURE 3.3 Breakdown analysis of leading Islamic banks' balance sheets
Source: Based on data from Zawya and Oliver Wyman Analysis (2009)

(ii) Shallow secondary market exists to enable IFIs to manage their liquidity (Qaedi, 2010);

(iii) Absence of lender of last resort (central bank), which is vital for meeting the bank's need for short-term cash flow;

(iv) Wide maturity mismatches between assets and liabilities as funding is still dominated by short-term customer deposits, whereas credit portfolios (namely in the retail, mortgage and project finance segments) tend to witness longer tenors and duration (Moody's, 2009c); and

(v) Certain characteristics of some Islamic finance instruments give rise to liquidity risks. For instance, liquidity becomes a problem given the cancellation risks in *murabahah* or the inability to trade *murabahah* or *salam* contracts (Alvi, 2009a).

Despite the efforts of the Central Bank of Bahrain (CBB) and others to provide a range of liquid instruments in which Islamic banks can place their surplus cash, there is still a great shortage of liquid instruments, which means IFIs tend to have more non-earning assets on their books. Typically, Islamic banks would place their excess cash reserves into short-term interbank *murabahahs*, at a cost compared to conventional banks. Indeed, short-term *murabahahs* resemble money market interbank placements, but as *murabahah* contracts make it necessary for commodity brokers to be involved, costs for managing liquidity might be high. As a consequence, IFIs are truly – and often more visibly – subject to the constant trade-off between profitability and liquidity in a binary way (Moody's, 2009c).

Contrary to conventional banks, which benefit from a range of asset classes displaying different characteristics in terms of liquidity and profitability, IFIs at this stage of the development of the Islamic financial industry barely have an alternative – profitable but highly illiquid asset classes (such as credit exposures and *sukuk*); or highly liquid short-term *murabahahs* with international investment-grade banks, but at a cost. Even before the present crisis, liquidity on the secondary *sukuk* markets was quite limited. The fact that most *sukuk* investors have always adopted a buy-and-hold strategy only exacerbates the normal problems associated with a relatively new market. Critically in the current environment, such a situation could also continue to slow the efforts of central banks to boost *sukuk* liquidity.

The assets side of the balance sheet will typically show investments in securities, leased assets and real estate. It will also show equity investments in joint ventures or capital ventures and sales receivables, and also inventories of assets held for sale. Most of these assets are illiquid and it is unlikely that any could be sold in a short space of time.

Fortunately, yields on Islamic assets in many markets are still sufficient for the cost of managing liquidity, because 'borrowers' are often willing to pay a premium for the Islamic nature of the banking relationship they build with the IFI. In the future, however, as the industry matures, margins might come under pressure and the trade-off between liquidity and profitability might lead to an increase in IFIs' risk appetite, provided that instruments for liquidity management purposes are not designed for the benefit of IFIs (Moody's, 2009c).

Figure 3.4, extracted from a typical credit application for an anonymous counterparty at the European Islamic Investment Bank, illustrates a typical liquidity structure of many Islamic banks with an imbalanced funding continuum heavily reliant on short-term customer deposits. IFIs normally have a high volume of assets, which are generally of longer term than most deposits. Islamic banks have to manage this funding gap carefully: if there were a liquidity freeze like the one that struck Western banks, the damage among Islamic banks would be greater.

Islamic banks use cash from deposits and short-term liquid assets to finance long-term liabilities. As a result, the liability makeup affects their funding structures differently and reflects an institution's specific asset–liability management policies. In comparison with conventional banks, asset-backed transactions (depending on the character of the asset) can expose an IFI both as an investor with high credit risk and also as an owner when dealing with long-term assets such as property and/or infrastructure. In order to mitigate this long-term liability-related risk, an IFI should have a vast pool of assets with a maturity range

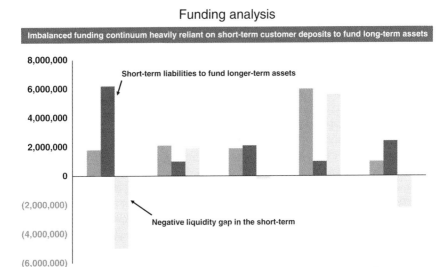

FIGURE 3.4 Example of imbalanced funding continuum at an Islamic bank
Source: Based on data from a credit application for an anonymous counterparty at the European Islamic Investment Bank (2010)

at its disposal to close the asset–liability gap (Lowe, 2010; Lowe was interviewed for this research).

As a result, the Islamic banking industry is faced with a conundrum: its institutions maintain high concentrations in current/short-term liabilities, but, at the same time, they are exposed to highly profitable, but illiquid, long-term assets (e.g. property and infrastructure, and *sukuk*), and they have limited access to long-term funding solutions. The nature of the Islamic banking model and *Shari'ah*-compliant laws applicable to the available asset classes means that these banks are persistently faced with a swap between liquidity and profitability (Moody's, 2009c).

According to McKinsey & Company (2009), on the liquidity front, as depicted in Figure 3.5, Islamic banks have a more pronounced maturity mismatch than conventional banks. However, Islamic Banks source more funds from deposits.

Attempts to reduce liquidity risk for Islamic banks The abovementioned factors made liquidity risk management far from an easy task for IFIs, which need to weather possible liquidity shortages in light of unforeseen events. For instance, during the financial crisis in Turkey during the period 2000–2001, IFIs faced severe liquidity problems and one, Ihlas Finance, collapsed (Standard &

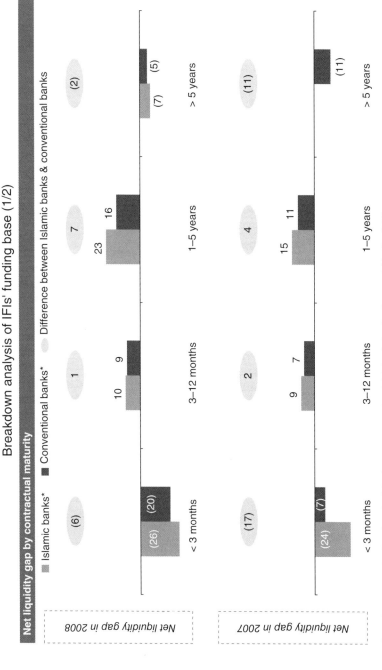

Breakdown analysis of IFIs' funding base (1/2)

Net liquidity gap by contractual maturity

■ Islamic banks*   ■ Conventional banks*   ● Difference between Islamic banks & conventional banks

Net liquidity gap in 2008

(6)   1   7   (2)

(26)   10   23
(20)   9   16   (7)   (5)

< 3 months   3–12 months   1–5 years   > 5 years

Net liquidity gap in 2007

(17)   2   4   (11)

(24)   9   15
(7)   7   11   (11)

< 3 months   3–12 months   1–5 years   > 5 years

*Based on a sample of 7 of each of the largest conventional & Islamic banks (by assets) in the GCC

FIGURE 3.5 Breakdown analysis of IFIs' funding base

Source: Authors' analysis based on figures from McKinsey & Company (2009)

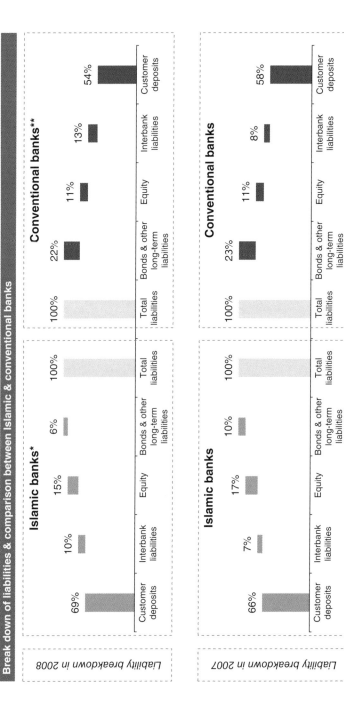

FIGURE 3.5 (Continued)

*Includes all pure Islamic banks in the UAE , KSA, Kuwait & Qatar
** Includes all conventional banks in the UAE , KSA, Kuwait & Qatar

Poor's, 2010a). Market participants hope that the greater use of innovative asset classes will complement the currently variety-starved asset section on the balance sheet and help IFIs deal with liquidity concerns more efficiently. Several developments have taken place with a view to meeting this challenge.

In Saudi Arabia, the Saudi Arabian Monetary Agency (SAMA) has developed an ad hoc instrument called *mutajara*, which behaves like a repurchase agreement, known as 'repo' in the banking world. Contractually, it is a term deposit with SAMA or other financial institutions, but 75% of this deposit can be 'repoed' at SAMA at any point in time for liquidity purposes. This is notably the case for Al Rajhi Bank, which has an investment portfolio that can be repoed with SAMA (Moody's, 2009c).

In Bahrain, the CBB is also working on developing a *Shari'ah*-compliant repo scheme. In addition, the Liquidity Management Centre (LMC) was founded in 2002 in Bahrain to facilitate the investment of surplus funds of IFIs into financial instruments structured in accordance with *Shari'ah* principles. It also aims to assist the International Islamic Financial Markets (IIFM) in the creation of secondary market activity with designated market makers where such instruments can be actively traded. Early in 2009, the IIFM announced that it has plans to cooperate with the International Capital Market Association (ICMA) to develop a repo-type liquidity management tool in order to manage overnight liquidity more efficiently in the future (Mahlknecht, 2009).

Similarly, the Central Bank of Sudan has introduced *Shari'ah*-compatible securities to provide liquidity in the market (Greuning and Iqbal, 2008).

Malaysia had also taken steps to reduce liquidity risk among Islamic banks. The central bank, Bank Negara Malaysia, introduced the Islamic Interbank Money Market (IIMM) in early 1994. The activities of the IIMM include the purchase and sale of Islamic financial instruments among market participants, interbank investment activities through *mudarabah* interbank investment scheme, and a cheque clearing and settlement system. The Islamic financial instruments that are currently being traded in the market on the basis of *bay' al-dayn* (sale of debt) are bankers' acceptances, Islamic bills, Islamic mortgage bonds and Islamic private securities. In addition, IFIs can sell government investment issues to the central bank, as and when required, to meet their liquidity needs. In turn, IFIs can buy *Shari'ah*-compliant investment issues from the central bank (Greuning and Iqbal, 2008).

Whereas the contract of *bay' al-dayn* is commonly accepted and practised in the Malaysian financial markets, it is not accepted by the majority of *Shari'ah* scholars outside of Malaysia, who maintain that debt can be traded only *at par*. According to one of the interviewees for this research, Kailani (2010), if trade is not at par, they feel that the practice opens the door to *riba*.

Mahlknecht (2009) suggests creating a common pool to which all IFIs contribute a specific percentage of their deposits in exchange for the right to receive interest-free loans overnight or for up to three days. He adds that an exceptionally promising route would be to integrate the IDB into such structures in order to encourage cross-border participation by Islamic banks.

Finally, the introduction of *sukuk* is a good development that can provide the foundation for the development of secondary markets. A *sukuk* structured on *murabahah*, *salam* and *istisn'a* should be held to maturity, while *sukuk* structured on equity basis (*musharakah* and *mudarabah*) or *ijarah sukuk* can be traded on the secondary market (Dar Al Istithmar, 2006). Legislative steps, including the creation of Saudi *sukuk* and bond market under the *Tadawul* (the Saudi stock exchange), are improving the prospects of *sukuk* becoming an attractive liquid instrument. Recent similar reforms in South Korea and Indonesia should also support the longer-term viability of the primary *sukuk* market and the establishment of an active secondary market, which will benefit the longer-term prospects of *sukuk* as an investment instrument among issuers and investors alike. According to Standard & Poor's (2009), such developments are timely steps that should both diversify Islamic finance assets and address investor needs, as well as adding depth to the market and enhancing transparency and efficiency among market participants.

Sukuk offer a longer-term and more stable source of funding. In addition, governments and government-related institutions have made it clear on several occasions that their role on the *sukuk* market would not be limited to that of a benchmark-setter; issuing sovereign and public sector *sukuk* would also contribute to enhancing the overall liquidity of the market. However, *sukuk* still constitute a very small proportion of the balance sheet despite the recent rapid growth in this funding source. Still illiquid, dominated by local issuances and hardly traded globally, *sukuk* cannot be considered an effective fixed-income instrument for active management of balance sheets and liquidity. According to one of the interviewees for this research, Marx (2010), most repurchase agreements (repos) with bank counterparts or central banks are *riba*-based, so *sukuk* can hardly be used as repo collateral and very seldom serves as the basis for raising emergency liquidity in the event of need.

The gradual introduction of *sukuk* funds will help create a secondary market for *sukuk*, whereby investors, including banks, can price their *sukuk* fairly, enhancing both liquidity and secondary market tradability (Moody's, 2009d).

Market observers have pointed out that the lack of *sukuk* liquidity is still a primary weakness compared with conventional bonds. Another interviewee in this research, Masri (2010), argues that central banks and major international institutions do not accept any of the currently issued *sukuk* for repos: (i) because of the lack of secondary market for *sukuk*; (ii) because of the non-convertibility to other currencies; and (iii) because most *sukuk* issues are not rated by international rating agencies. The first *sukuk* that is expected to be internationally accepted for repos is the long-anticipated *sukuk* to be issued by the UK government. Masri believes that, until a sophisticated repos market is developed for Islamic finance, the liquidity problem will persist. "There are initiatives to develop a *Shari'ah*-compliant repo market but for the time being Islamic banks have only limited scope for getting hold of money in a quick way. The lack of *Shari'ah*-compliant assets and a tendency for Islamic investors to buy and hold their investments have stunted the secondary market", as identified by Qaedi (2010), one of the interviewees for this research.

So far, IFIs have preferred an originate-and-hold business model due to the lack of a secondary market for loans and *sukuk*. However, in the longer term, IFIs with limited capital resources might be more inclined to adopt an originate-and-distribute business approach, provided disintermediation picks up, market depth and liquidity improves, and growth in Islamic assets continues unabated.

The effect of the credit crisis on the *sukuk* market and the emergence of defaults are thoroughly discussed in Chapter 5.

Furthermore, Marx (2010), who was interviewed for this research, explains that traditionally Islamic banks have circumvented the lack of an Islamic money market by entering into bilateral commodity trades with Western banks that produce a return very close to the equivalent money market instruments. Although this is a valuable source of liquidity, it is an inadequate and fragmented solution to a problem that is perceived to be one of the greatest hindrances to a fully integrated Islamic financial system. One of the aims of the LMC is to provide instruments that have greater *Shari'ah* credibility and are more competitively priced than the commodity *murabahah* transactions currently undertaken in the market.

Because of the lack of adequate *Shari'ah*-compliant money market instruments for liquidity management and the underdevelopment of Islamic money markets, the studies by IFSB in March 2008 provide suggestions for the development of the Islamic money market. Among the suggestions are to design a low-risk Islamic money market and Islamic government financing instruments and to incorporate Islamic government financing instruments as an integral part of the overall public debt and financing programme and foster its development (IFSB, 2008a).

Finally, October 2010 saw the signing and launch of the International Islamic Liquidity Management Corporation (IILM), the latest transnational body to serve the global Islamic finance industry. The ultimate aim of the IILM is to enhance international integration of the Islamic money market and capital markets and to better equip them to face any liquidity crises. This breakthrough will surely help take Islamic finance to a higher level of development. It was proposed by the IILM to include only AAA-rated *Shari'ah*-compliant *sukuk* issued by sovereigns, quasi-sovereigns and a selected number of major corporates. However, critics have suggested that the pool of AAA-rated papers is not sufficient. Governor Zeti, Bank

Negara Malaysia, stated, "we inject or withdraw liquidity from the system. There are very strict criteria for the eligibility of assets, as it is not the shareholders themselves that would allocate assets. Central banks can nominate entities to donate assets, which can be monetised. They will issue Islamic commercial papers against these assets through special purpose vehicles. They will be the primary dealers and they will create the markets" (IFSB, 2011).

Asset–Liability Management

Asset–liability management (ALM) is closely correlated with liquidity risk management. It is simply the practice of managing risks that arise due to mismatches between the assets and liabilities of a bank. ALM is a management tool that involves the raising and use of funds in terms of strategic planning, implementation and control processes that affect the volume, mix, maturity, profit rate sensitivity, quality and liquidity of a bank's assets and liabilities. The primary goal of ALM is to produce a high-quality, stable, large and growing flow of net interest/profit rate income (Greuning and Iqbal, 2008). This goal is accomplished by achieving the optimum combination and level of assets, liabilities and financial risk.

Funding sources for IFIs Table 3.2 shows that the limited range of possible funding sources for IFIs leads to concentrated liabilities, imbalanced funding mixes and stretched capital management strategies. IFIs' wholesale liabilities tend to be concentrated as they are generally well entrenched in retail banking, which gives them access to a large, and increasing, pool of relatively cheap deposits. When these are not in the form of Profit-Sharing Investment Accounts (PSIAs), Islamic banks benefit from the fact that a portion of Islamic deposits tend to be non-interest-bearing. This lowers their cost of funding compared with conventional banks, increases their margins and improves their profitability. In addition, Islamic depositors tend to display a strong sense of loyalty as they are less rate-sensitive. This results in a longer-term behavioural nature of deposits. However, as in most cases the contractual tenor of those deposits is short term: the banks remain exposed to maturity/liquidity risk. In other words, in times of crisis the bank may witness substantial withdrawals.

There are two types of PSIAs: restricted and unrestricted. For unrestricted PSIAs there is no identified asset allocation, while for restricted accounts the bank acts in a fiduciary capacity, with the investor choosing the nature of the investment to be made. In some cases these are accounted for as off balance sheet. For these accounts, banks maintain two types of reserves: a profit equalisation reserve to smooth returns and Investment Risk Reserves (IRRs) to absorb capital losses. While contractually investors are expected to absorb losses (the bank being

TABLE 3.2 Simplified balance sheet of an IFI

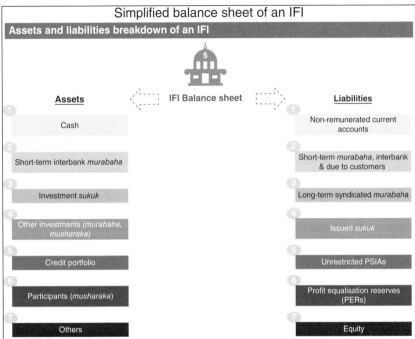

liable only if there is negligence or fraud), the reality may be very different. Banks are under pressure to offer competitive returns and repay in full on the due date to ensure these assets continue to be funded. PSIAs in general have maturities of 12 months, and the assets financed tend to be fungible (Moody's, 2008a).

Apart from retail accounts, which are in most cases both granular and stable across business cycles, IFIs also resort to wholesale creditors for funding. So far, *sukuk* have not served as the main term funding source: only a handful of IFIs have issued medium-term *sukuk* so far, or are expected to do so in the near future, such as Sharjah Islamic Bank, Abu Dhabi Islamic Bank and Al Baraka Banking Group. For asset-backed *sukuk*, an Islamic bank needs to originate enough income-generating contracts, the underlying assets of which are owned by the bank (like in *ijarah* and/or *musharakah*), for the *sukuk* to be possible. However, the majority of *sukuk* issued so far, particularly in the Gulf region, have been asset-based rather than asset-backed, with 'par value repurchase undertaking' structures whereby the market value of the underlying assets bears little or no relation to the funding amounts raised, argues Qaedi (2010), one of the interviewees for this research. Also, as these are not true-sale structures, any non-liquid

TABLE 3.3 Sources of funds: Islamic versus traditional banks

Islamic Banks	Traditional Banks
Tier 1 — Capital (equity)	Tier 1 — Capital (equity)
Tier 2 — Capital	Tier 2 — Capital (subordinated loans)
Current accounts	Current accounts
Saving accounts	Interest-based saving accounts
Unrestricted Profit-Sharing Investment Accounts (PSIAs)	Time and certificates of deposits
Profit Equalisation Reserves (PERs)	Reserves
Investment Risk Reserves (IRRs)	
Shareholders' equity protects these liabilities only in case of fiduciary risks (theory); PERs and IRRs	Shareholders' equity and subordinated loans protect these liabilities against all risks
Cost of funds: variable	Cost of funds: fixed

Source: Based on data from Khan (2004)

assets can be used. Therefore, IFIs typically raise short- to long-term funds from bank and non-bank customers, who tend to be price sensitive, relatively unstable (except those from the public sector) and concentrated, as depicted by Table 3.3. Deposit concentration is generally a significant risk factor for IFIs.

It should be noted that IFIs' funding bands remain imbalanced. Between deposits in their various forms (*qard hasan*, PSIAs, *murabahah*, etc.) and Tier 1 capital, IFIs have so far had access to a limited number of alternative funding sources with different features in terms of priority of claims and thus cost. Only very few subordinated *sukuk* have been issued so far. Malayan Banking Berhad in Malaysia, for example, issued a junior *sukuk* eligible as Tier 2 debt under Bank Negara Malaysia's regulation. According to Marx (2010), who was interviewed for this research, bank securitisation, other Tier 2 instruments, Tier 3 short-term debt to cover the regulatory capital charge of market risk, as well as plain vanilla and innovative hybrid capital notes, are non-existent in the Islamic financial industry. One of the reasons behind such a vacuum in the wide – but often grey – area between deposit and core capital of IFIs lies in the fact that a number of *Shari'ah* supervisory boards have been uncomfortable so far with the concept of differentiating between priorities of claims of various classes of stakeholders in the case of liquidation, adds another interviewee, Chowdhury (2010).

IFIs' capital management strategies therefore tend to be stretched. Allocation of economic capital to business units using risk-adjusted return-on-capital methodologies, for example, is barely applied, except in a handful of well-advanced institutions globally. However, even in the conventional universe, the allocation of economic capital to business units is still limited to a relatively small number of institutions that adopt more sophisticated risk management techniques. Therefore, it is not surprising that advanced approaches for economic capital computation have not so far been widely adopted by IFIs in emerging markets. Capital allocation tends to be inefficient at this stage, although this is not disadvantageous to a large extent as: (i) capitalisation ratios are high, and capital is not scarce in the geographies where IFIs are most active (typically in the Gulf region); (ii) asset yields are wide enough to serve record Return on Equity; and (iii) actual yields on equity far exceed shareholders' required rates of return (Moody's, 2008b).

In the longer run, and after the current financial tsunami, competitive pressure and massive losses will drive margins down. In addition, customers will become more educated about the concepts and principles underlying IBF and will tend to be less willing to accept lower returns on their deposits and switch more naturally to PSIAs, driving IFIs' funding costs up. Finally, capital has become scarcer given the recent losses and bailouts in the banking sector. All of these elements could easily change the nature of the IFIs' profitability equation, with lower net returns directed toward more demanding shareholders. A solution to the conundrum would be to let capitalisation ratios dwindle gradually to protect returns to shareholders while building assets more efficiently above targeted hurdle rates (Visser, 2009). Another option is to look for alternative financing vehicles like hybrid instruments, various classes of PSIAs and securitisation. Although debt obligations can be traded only at face value under *Shari'ah* law, this does not apply to the trading of assets, which opens the potential for the use of securitisation of assets such as leases (Visser, 2009). However, significant legal hurdles need to be overcome before securitisation can become a feasible source of funding for Islamic banks.

As a fact, capital is a very expensive way of funding. Islamic banks, particularly in the GCC, therefore engage in higher-risk/high-yield transactions to make up for the expensive funding via capital and consequently keep shareholders satisfied with high returns. Those IFIs forced themselves, unintentionally, up the risk curve instead of diversifying their risks. This makes the balance sheet of Islamic banks quite polarised, with high real estate assets. This led Islamic banks to a high concentration risk, on both sides of the balance sheet. A typical balance sheet structure of many Islamic banks displays high exposure to properties on the assets side; and limited funding sources with high reliance on short-term liabilities and capital on the other side. This is a very unfavourable funding continuum that has led Islamic banks to a vicious circle of risks: one risk creating the next.

ALM in Islamic banking: theory versus practice In theory, IFIs should be less exposed to asset–liability mismatch than their conventional counterparts. This comparative advantage is rooted in the 'pass through' nature of Islamic banks, which act as agents for investors/depositors and pass all profits and losses through to them (Greuning and Iqbal, 2008). In addition, the risk-sharing feature of Islamic finance plays a critical role. Following the theoretical model, any negative shock to an Islamic bank is absorbed by both shareholders and investors/depositors. On the other hand, depositors in the conventional system have a fixed claim on the returns of the bank's assets, irrespective of the bank's profitability on its assets side. In other words, holders of PSIAs in the Islamic system should share in the bank's profits and losses alongside shareholders, and are exposed to the risk of losing all or part of their initial investment. This contractual agreement between the IFI and the PSIA holders should be based on a 'pass through' mechanism in which all profits and losses are passed to the investors. Thus, the problem of asset–liability mismatch should not exist. Some regulators have recognised this and require these assets (generally 50% risk-weighting) to be included in capital adequacy calculations and the reserves as Tier 2 capital (FRSGlobal, 2009). Greuning and Iqbal (2008) argue that this type of financial intermediation contributes to the stability of the financial system. Because of the nature of contracts both on the assets and liabilities sides on the balance sheet, IFIs are often less vulnerable to external shocks and less susceptible to insolvency. Chapter 5 covers in detail how the Islamic financial system could act as a panacea for economic woes if its fundamentals are genuinely applied.

The challenge to Islamic banks is to determine the rights and obligations of PSIA holders vis-à-vis shareholders, especially when various types of *Shari'ah*-compliant deposit accounts are offered, so as to ensure the required disclosures and transparency in the distribution of profits and the sharing of risks (IFSB, 2007).

Lowe (2010), one of the interviewees in this study, explains that from an analytical perspective, PSIAs should not be classified as equity-like liabilities, despite their (theoretical) loss-absorbing characteristics. PSIAs are rather considered as more debt-like liabilities. The rationale behind this treatment of PSIAs as liabilities with no capital benefits is that, from an economic and practical perspective, PSIAs:

(i) Are not permanent capital, as they tend to be very short-dated (with maturities typically below one year);

(ii) Can be withdrawn before maturity, provided that the PSIA holder gives up their contractual return to be earned at maturity;

(iii) Have no voting rights; and

(iv) In practice, are very rarely allowed to absorb losses.

However, in practice the challenge is where there is a clear differentiation between PSIA holders and equity holders. Can IFIs avoid combining shareholders' and PSIA holders' funds, as the theory would suggest? The liabilities of Islamic banks may – in common with assets – have very different profiles and need careful management. The biggest issue remains the position of PSIA. Juristically, PSIA are a form of limited term equity rather than debt claims on the bank, and therefore losses relating to the assets they fund should not affect the bank's own capital. However, Islamic banks are not immune from runs or panic withdrawals, and PSIA holders typically have the right to withdraw their funds at short notice, forgoing their share of the profit for the most recent period and also their share of any losses that might have arisen, explains Kailani (2010), who was interviewed for this research.

Visser (2009) strongly opposes PSIAs by arguing that they involve a moral hazard problem, as they might give the bank an incentive for risk-taking and for operating with very little of their own funds. Depositors will have to take the brunt if investments go sour, just like equity investors in a conventional investment company, only they have no say in the appointment of management. They only thing depositors can do is to shift their funds to other banks, but they may not always have sufficient information to do so in time. He adds that this moral hazard problem was cited as one reason by the Rector of Al-Azhar University in Cairo in his 2002 *fatwa* for declaring interest-bearing banking deposits *halal*. Visser (2009) obviously misses the point that regulators and *Shari'ah* boards will not allow IFIs to misuse PSIAs, and that IFIs put the utmost importance on avoiding any jeopardy to their reputation.

Engel (2010), one of the interviewees for this research, adds that unrestricted PSIA funds will generally be combined with those of the bank's shareholders who may have quite different risk appetites, as PSIA holders are generally looking for a safe investment, similar to deposit account holders in conventional banks. In practice, the treatment of the fund-combining issue is handled differently. Shamil Bank of Bahrain has so far applied a strict distinction, for management account and return computation purposes, between assets financed by shareholders' funds and what the bank calls 'unrestricted investment accounts'. Conversely, Kuwait Finance House – like most IFIs – does not explicitly segregate classes of liabilities and prefers a more flexible and convenient way of computing a total gross return on assets, and then applying both a *musharakah* and *mudarabah* fee to isolate returns to PSIA holders (Moody's, 2008a).

The practice is therefore different from the theory, and the means of determining shareholder's share is not always transparent. Notwithstanding such practical differences among IFIs in both combining funding sources and computing returns, 'displaced commercial risk' is always at stake, giving birth to various mechanisms of smoothing returns. Although displaced commercial risk is a unique risk to IFIs, it is discussed in this section because it forms an essential part of ALM for Islamic banks.

Displaced commercial risk Displaced commercial risk is indeed a term reflecting the risk of liquidity suddenly drying up as a consequence of massive withdrawals should the IFI's assets yield returns for PSIA holders lower than expected, or worse, negative rates of profits. It is the transfer of the risk associated with deposits to equity holders. This arises when under commercial pressure banks forgo a part of profit to pay the depositors to prevent withdrawals due to a lower return (AAOIFI, 1999). Displaced commercial risk implies that the bank, although it may operate in full compliance with the *Shari'ah* requirements, may not be able to pay competitive rates of return as compared to its peer group Islamic banks and other competitors. Depositors will again have the incentive to seek withdrawal. To prevent withdrawal, the shareholders will need to apportion part of their own share in profits or even equity to the PSIA holders.

As demonstrated below, the practice of smoothing investment returns through profit equalisation reserves (PERs), IRRs and active management of *mudarib* fees is a very common feature of IFIs to avoid random, business and confidence-driven liquidity crises. As a matter of fact, a negative return on PSIAs would not constitute a breach of contractual obligations, as PSIAs are supposed to absorb losses other than those triggered by misconduct or negligence, and therefore this would not be considered a default. Nevertheless, default might be subsequently triggered by the very tight liquidity conditions the IFI would face in the case of massive runs on deposits. While this is in keeping with the risk-sharing principles encouraged by Islam, it remains to be seen how such account holders would react to losses on their accounts.

Some banking regulators have taken the view that this practice of smoothing returns results in a modification of the legal attributes of the PSIA such that Islamic banks have a 'constructive obligation' to continue smoothing returns. This means that the practice of smoothing becomes obligatory, and unrestricted PSIA holders effectively have the same rights as conventional depositors according to Chowdhury (2010; Chowdhury was interviewed for this research). Kailani (2010) explained, during the interview for this research, that a typical problem in Western countries with highly developed markets is the legal definition of a 'bank' as a 'deposit-taking institution' – deposits having the legal status of debt contracts and being 'capital certain' – whereas Islamic banks accept deposits as PSIAs, which cannot be capital certain as the *Shari'ah* does not permit this.

Unfortunately, insofar as both Islamic banks and their supervisory authorities in some countries consider unrestricted investment accounts to be a product designed to compete with, and to be an acceptable substitute for, conventional deposits, profit smoothing in such an environment may be considered an inherent attribute of the product rather than a means of deliberately avoiding transparency and market discipline, especially if it is combined with in-substance capital certainty (Archer and Karim, 2007). This undermines an important inherent characteristic of risk mitigation within Islamic banking, as discussed in Chapter 5.

Managing displaced commercial risk efficiently is a dynamic exercise

Thun (2010), one of the interviewees for this research, explains that traditionally there are a number of lines of defence against displaced commercial risk: IRRs and the bank's *mudarib* fee tend to absorb expected losses; PERs are used to cover unexpected losses of manageable magnitude; and, ultimately, shareholders' funds stand against unexpected losses with a higher net impact. Figure 3.6 shows how Islamic banks use these lines of defence to ensure stability.

IRRs are built from periodic provisions for expected statistical losses, which come as a deduction from the asset portfolio, in the same way that loan-loss reserves are deducted from conventional banks' loan books. IRRs are gradually built from the periodic provision charge equivalent to the expected losses attached to IFIs' investment portfolios, transiting through the IFI's income statement. Should actual losses be in line with IRRs, there is limited likelihood that displaced commercial risk would materialise into a bank run and thus into a liquidity crisis. Indeed, returns to PSIA holders would not be negatively affected. IRRs are

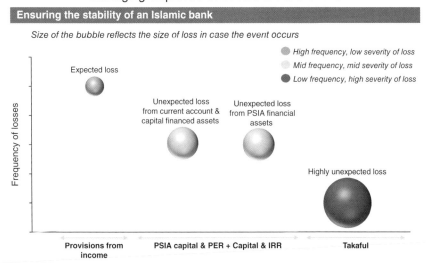

FIGURE 3.6 Managing displaced commercial risk in IFIs
Source: Khan, T. (2004)

generally deducted from income distributable to PSIA holders after the PERs are accounted for, and after the *mudarib* fee is captured by the IFI (Thun, 2010).

Reducing *mudarib* fees to protect returns to PSIA holders remains a management decision. PSIAs are the combination of a *musharakah* contract (whereby PSIA holders and shareholders bring funds to the banking venture) and a *mudarabah* contract (whereby the IFI's managers allocate PSIA holders' funds to various asset classes on their behalf). Therefore, the IFI is eligible, under the *mudarabah* contract, for a *mudarib* (management) fee, which typically constitutes 20–40% of asset yields net of PERs. In case asset yields deteriorate beyond levels absorbable by IRRs, the IFI's management team, in line with the board's formal approval, could reduce management fees ex post, which it can do contractually (although unilateral increases of *mudarib* fees are strictly forbidden). This is viewed as a gift of the bank to PSIA holders to earn their loyalty across the cycle (Chowdhury, 2010). Typically, *mudarib* fee reductions tend to apply when unexpected losses (beyond expected losses handled by IRRs) are manageable one-offs. When exceeding a certain threshold, losses would be covered by PERs (Thun, 2010).

PERs, a grey area in the capital continuum, collectively belong to PSIA holders for smoothing their returns. PERs are accounted for before any computation of the *mudarib* fee or IRRs. PERs are extracted from gross asset yields. Their purpose is to provide an excess return to PSIA holders in periods where assets have performed worse than expected, and therefore when yields on PSIAs might be lower for a given IFI than for its Islamic and conventional peers. PERs collectively belong to present and future PSIA holders, although past PSIA holders (who might not be current or future customers of the IFI) may have contributed to building them (Putz, 2010; one of the interviewees). This is in line with the principle according to which the various stakeholders of an IFI are subject to collective solidarity. PERs, being a future claim of PSIA holders on the bank, are not part of capital in accounting terms, and thus are not subject to distribution to shareholders (Greuning and Iqbal, 2008). From a regulatory perspective, however, the treatment suggested by the IFSB is very subtle, particularly in Western jurisdictions; just like the treatment of PSIAs for the computation of capital adequacy ratios of IFIs under Basel II, which is explained in detail in Chapter 4.

Smith (2010), Senior Analyst–Financial Institutions at Fitch Ratings and one of the interviewees for this research, explains that shareholders' funds constitute the ultimate line of defence against displaced commercial risk. Ultimately, should IRRs, *mudarib* fee cuts and PERs be insufficient to protect depositors from excessive volatility regarding PSIA returns, shareholders can lawfully use their own capital to compensate for possible losses or PSIA holders' opportunity costs. Shareholders' funds have in the past been used to compensate holders of investment accounts, such as in 1998 for Dubai Islamic Bank PJSC and in 1990 for Kuwait Finance House. In both cases, PSIA holders suffered no losses.

Mahlknecht (2009) argues that an extreme example of displaced commercial risk is the International Islamic Bank for Investment and Development in Egypt, which distributed all of its profits to IAHs and nothing to shareholders from the middle to late 1980s. In 1988 the bank distributed to its depositors an amount exceeding its profits, and the difference appeared in the bank's accounts a 'loss carried forward'. The practice of forgoing part or all of the shareholder's profits may adversely affect the bank's own capital, which can lead to insolvency in extreme cases.

In short, although in theory there should be no mismatch between assets and liabilities of an Islamic bank, current practices have introduced distortions that expose banks to asset–liability mismatch risk, especially when they have no liquid assets with which they can hedge such risks. Greuning and Iqbal (2008) believe that IFIs should standardise how to deal with displaced commercial risk, and that the rights of PSIAs should be clearly stated and explained to all depositors. They suggest that the profits should be deducted only from long-term depositors, who are more likely to be exposed to such risk, and not from short-term depositors, who are not exposed to it.

Operational Risk

Historically, operational risk has been defined as all risks other than market, credit and liquidity risk. However, the BCBS (2006) has narrowed this definition within Basel II by stating that operational risk is "The risk of loss resulting from inadequate or failed internal processes, people or systems or from external events." This definition includes legal risk, but excludes strategic and reputational risk.

Operational risk has been recently recognised and has been gaining prominence in risk-related research. It is now part of the integrated risk management framework of all financial institutions, which typically increases with the scope and size of activities of a bank but can be mitigated by a sophisticated risk management function and systems. The major components of operational risk are people, processes, technology and external events (usually catastrophic). People risk includes human error, lack of expertise and compliance, and fraud. Process risk includes risks related to different aspects of running a business, which may include regular business processes, risk related to new products and services, inadequate controls, etc. (Akkizidis and Khandelwal, 2007).

Lowe (2010) argues that operational risks are rather difficult to measure and manage because these risks become apparent only once a problem arises. He stated that risks associated with operational risk could include:

(i) *Internal fraud.* For example, intentional misreporting of positions, employee theft, and insider trading on an employee's own account;

(ii) *External fraud.* For example, robbery, forgery, cheque kiting and damage from computer hacking;

(iii) *Employment practices and workplace safety*. For example, workers' compensation claims, violation of employee health and safety rules, organised labour activities, discrimination claims and general liability;

(iv) *Clients, products and business practices*. For example, fiduciary breaches, misuse of confidential customer information, improper trading activities on the bank's account, money laundering and sale of unauthorised products;

(v) *Damage to physical assets*. For example, terrorism, vandalism, earthquakes, fires and floods;

(vi) *Business disruption and system failures*. For example, hardware and software failures, telecommunication problems and utility outages; and

(vii) *Execution, delivery and process management*. For example, data entry errors, collateral management failures, incomplete legal documentation, unapproved access given to client accounts, non-client counterparty misperformance and vendor disputes.

The wide range of activities included in operational risks make it difficult to apply a standard model to all organisations and hence there is a lack of universally accepted standard models. Banks often use internal audit ratings, quality self-assessments, operational risk indicators or Key Risk Indicators (KRIs) such as volume, turnover, rate of errors, income and loss volatilities, etc.

Operational risk in Islamic banks   IFSB Principles, as in Box 3.6, introduce the risk management strategy for operational risk management.

BOX 3.6: IFSB PRINCIPLES OF OPERATIONAL RISK MANAGEMENT

Principle 7.1:   IIFS shall have in place adequate systems and controls, including *Sharī'ah* Board/Advisor, to ensure compliance with *Sharī'ah* rules and principles.

Principle 7.2:   IIFS shall have in place appropriate mechanisms to safeguard the interests of all fund providers. Where IAH funds are commingled with the IIFS's own funds, the IIFS shall ensure that the bases for asset, revenue, expense and profit allocations are established, applied and reported in a manner consistent with the IIFS's fiduciary responsibilities.

Source: Based on data from IFSB (2005a)

Operational risk is considered high on the list of risk exposures for Islamic banks. A survey by Khan and Ahmed (2001) shows that the managers of Islamic banks perceive operational risk as the most critical risk after mark-up risk. The survey found that operational risk is lower in the fixed-income contracts of *murabahah* and *ijarah*, and higher in the deferred sales contracts of *salam* and *istisna'a*. The relatively higher rankings of these instruments indicate that banks find them complex and difficult to implement.

An internal control problem cost Dubai Islamic Bank USD 50 million in 1998 when a bank official did not conform to the bank's credit terms. This resulted in a one-day run on the bank's deposits to the tune of USD 138 million, representing around 7% of the bank's total deposits at that time (Greuning and Iqbal, 2008).

It is argued that operational risks are likely to be significant for IFIs due to their specific contractual features. Moreover, Islamic products are less commoditised and require more tailoring and oversight, and this leads to substantial overheads and higher operational risk. One of the interviewees in this research, Lowe (2010), asserts that a number of small IFIs have allowed their businesses to grow rapidly without a proper organisational infrastructure in place. He listed some specific aspects of Islamic banking that could raise the operational risk of Islamic banks:

(i) Cancellation risks in the nonbinding *murabahah* and *istisna'a* contracts;
(ii) Failure of the internal control system to detect and manage potential problems in the operational process and back-office;
(iii) Potential difficulties in enforcing Islamic contracts in a broader legal environment;
(iv) Need to maintain and manage commodity inventories often in illiquid markets;
(v) The monitoring of PLS arrangements cannot easily be standardised; and
(vi) Potential costs and risk of monitoring equity-type contracts and the associated legal risk.

People risk and the scarcity of qualified human resources is the most striking weakness of the whole industry (Brown et al., 2007). In fact, scarcity of talent might impede, for a while, the growth dynamics of Islamic banks. There is a clear, identifiable and sometimes quantifiable shortage of skilled managers, officers and clerks in the *Shari'ah*-compliant financial universe. Not only is the industry growing fast, triggering pressure on existing staff to absorb increasing volumes, but a number of new entrants are also entering the arena: markets like Bahrain, Qatar, Saudi Arabia, the UAE, Malaysia and Singapore, among others, have witnessed the incorporation of a large number of new IFIs announcing authorised capital of unprecedented size. Newcomers must be staffed and newly trained employees are scarce because education, training and experience take time to build exploitable competences (Mahlknecht, 2009). The easiest and most effective way to quickly staff freshly instituted organisations is to acquire them from existing banks, creating visible pressure on the labour market in the entire industry. Risks including management discontinuity, excessive growth of personnel expenses, innovation disincentives and lack of experienced staff might all damage an IFI's capacity to build competitive advantages, and ultimately its market position, reputation and business model.

On a positive note, several professional qualifications in Islamic finance have been created in different regions over the last few years. This should ease the pressure on the industry in the medium term. It is necessary to create a pool of highly qualified professionals with in-depth knowledge of not only the *Shari'ah* and its objectives, but also Islamic and conventional finance and financial engineering. Directors and senior management of Islamic banks too should be required to attend such courses.

Technology risk is another type of operational risk that is specifically high for Islamic banks. It is associated with the use of software and telecommunications systems that are not tailored specifically to the needs of Islamic banks. Like any other business, Islamic banks require bespoke software; given the nature of business the computer software available in the market for conventional banks may not be appropriate for IFIs. Compliance with *Shari'ah* rules requires management information systems that are scarce and expensive to develop. The currently available systems are less robust than those in conventional banks; they are either bespoke systems or ones that have been modified to handle Islamic products. There are few systems that have been specifically designed for the use of Islamic banks and are in widespread use (Brown et al., 2007). Santhosh Bhat, one of the interviewees for this research but whose interview was not included in the final sample, stated that "the most critical features of any Islamic banking software is the automation of profit pooling, which is the calculation of weighting and distribution of profit to the depositors according to the *Shari'ah*-compliant distribution method". The latest systems and technologies as used in conventional banks are often not used by Islamic banks.

Documentation risk is higher for Islamic banks than for conventional banks partly as a result of the lack of standardisation in the contracts and also because any deficiencies in the documentation could make the contract unenforceable (Moore, 2009).

In short, given the newness of Islamic banks and their unique business model, operational risk can be acute in these institutions. Therefore, the three methods of measuring operational risk proposed by the Basel II Accord have to be adapted considerably if they are to be applied to Islamic banks. This is explored in detail in Chapter 4.

FURTHER RISK AREAS SPECIFIC TO ISLAMIC BANKS

In addition to the traditional risk that Islamic banks share with their conventional counterparts as financial intermediaries, Islamic banks are also exposed to several risks that are very specific to their business model. Such specific risks are equally important and stem from the nature of their contracts, business environment, competition and certain prevailing practices.

Displaced Commercial Risk

As discussed in the section 'Asset–Liability Management', Displaced Commercial Risk is a risk unique to Islamic banks that stems from their ALM practices.

Shari'ah Non-Compliance Risk

Shari'ah non-compliance risk is related to the structure and functioning of *Shari'ah* boards at the institutional and systemic level. This risk could be of four types, which are strongly correlated and linked:

Lack of standardisation risk The *Shari'ah* is subject to interpretation, particularly in the field of economic and financial transactions known as the *fiqh al-muaamalat*. Therefore, from one market to another, from one school of thought (*madhab*) to another, and even from one *Shari'ah* scholar to another, the fine line between what is considered lawful at any point in time and what is not considered lawful can be so thin that *fatawa* may differ substantially. This difference in the interpretation of *Shari'ah* rules results in differences in financial reporting, auditing and accounting treatment. For instance, while some *Shari'ah* scholars consider the terms of a *murabahah* or *istisna'a* contract to be binding on the buyer, others argue that the buyer has the option to decline even after placing an order and paying the commitment fee, explains Al-Ghamrawy (2010), Managing Director at Al Baraka Bank-Egypt and one of the interviewees for this research. Differing attitudes toward hedging techniques such as forwards, futures and options provide another example of a large divergence of opinion that does not benefit the industry (IFSB, 2007).

These differences can be partly attributed to the presence of the *Shari'ah* board, which governs and guides the banks regarding the conduct of Islamic banking. The *Shari'ah* board interprets various products and situations based on the *Qur'an*, *Sunnah* and *fiqh* (Islamic jurisprudence). There are four classical schools of Islamic thought, namely *Hanafi*, *Maliki*, *Shafi'i* and *Hanbali*, which have specific presences in different parts of the world, and hence the *Shari'ah* rulings differ based on the different schools. China and Turkey are more influenced by the *Hanafi*; in a large part of Africa *Maliki* is followed; Indonesia and Malaysia have large numbers of followers of the *Shafi'i* school; and *Hanbali* appears to be followed in Saudi Arabia (Akkizidis and Khandelwal, 2007). These four schools represent most of the commonly accepted rulings of Islamic jurisprudence. The interpretations of *Shari'ah* scholars can be based on one or more schools of though and hence can have impact on the conduct of the Islamic banking.

Multiple factors are considered before the *Shari'ah* board provides a ruling on a particular case. This multiplicity of methods of financing has been a prime reason for the lack of standardisation of products, processes and policies. It did not hamper the growth and development of Islamic banking, but has resulted in some confusion among the followers of Islamic banking. This has direct effect on risk management for Islamic banking. Also, due to the multiplicity of interpretations of situations, progress in developing specific legislation for Islamic banking has been slow. Malaysia, Pakistan and Bahrain have developed specific legislation dealing with Islamic banking, whereas most of the other countries offering Islamic banking are using conventional banking legislation with some modifications for Islamic banking along with *Shari'ah* rulings (Akkizidis and Khandelwal, 2007).

This variation is not only time-consuming and costly but it also leads to confusion about what Islamic banking really encompasses and therefore hinders its widespread acceptance. It also makes it difficult for regulators – especially in non-Muslim countries – to understand the idea of Islamic banking. Consequently, regulators tend to be restrictive in granting licences for Islamic banks. The same applies to investors and customers, who sometimes find themselves reluctant to invest in Islamic banks because of their confusion about the concept and its specific products.

The curious case of *Investment Dar Company ('TID')* v. *Blom Development Bank* may have some significant implications for the Islamic finance industry. Blom Development Bank of Lebanon had placed various 'funds' with TID of Kuwait, pursuant to a *wakala* arrangement. TID became distressed during the course of 2008/09 with the onset of the credit crunch and announced a restructuring. In May 2009, it defaulted on the profit/coupon of its USD 100 million *sukuk* issue, and since then there has been much confusion regarding the status and progress of the restructuring. TID then argued that the previously executed *wakala* arrangements with Blom Development Bank did not actually comply with *Shari'ah* principles; hence, all related agreements should therefore be considered *ultra vires* (or void). The court issued a summary judgment ordering payment of the capital amount but not the anticipated profit required, which necessitated consideration at a full trial. Chowdhury (2010) hence states that "It is widely felt that the application of *Shari'ah* compliance as a commercial and defensive legal tool undermines the credibility and ethical ethos that underpins Islamic finance."

Shari'ah arbitrage risk The competitive dynamics of IFIs, together with lack of standardisation, could enhance *Shari'ah* arbitrage, itself a component of *Shari'ah*-compliance risk. IFIs compete head on with conventional banks, but they also position themselves as contenders within the Islamic financial industry, sometimes internationally, if not globally. The different *Shari'ah* interpretations give rise to *Shari'ah* arbitrage, which is the risk of resort to the most liberal interpretation of financial Islam for business purposes (Visser, 2009). Therefore, Muslim investors and originators might be tempted by *Shari'ah* arbitrage. *Shari'ah* arbitrage might also lead an IFI to crowd itself out of the market because it may not be considered sufficiently *Shari'ah*-compliant by its constituency, the final decision-making body as to *Shari'ah* compliance, which is beyond the reach of any *fatwa*. This could be damaging from a macro-industrial perspective, should the whole Islamic financial industry be overly heterogeneous to the point where fragmentation becomes unavoidable and durable (Yaccubi, 2010).

Non-compliance risk Chowdhury (2010) argues that the relationship between an Islamic bank and its customers is not only that of an agent and principal; it is also based on implicit trust that the bank will respect the desires of its customers to comply fully with *Shari'ah*. This relationship is what really distinguishes Islamic banks from their conventional counterparts and it is the sole justification of their existence. If the bank is unable to maintain this trust, by not being *Shari'ah*-compliant, it risks losing the confidence of its customers. This could severely damage the creditworthiness of an IFI. For instance, Muslim depositors might withdraw their funds from a bank, triggering a liquidity crisis. Retail customers that are mainly attracted by the Islamic nature of a bank might also stop requesting loans from this institution, triggering a downturn in profitability.

Wilson (2002) argues that what distinguishes IFIs from their conventional counterparts is not only the unique products they have on offer but also the commonality of their client base, who all have been attracted to IFIs because they provide products compatible with *Shari'ah*, which the clients themselves respect and believe in. The high level of trust between IFIs and their clients reduces the risks of moral hazard. Therefore, IFIs should ensure transparency in compliance *Shari'ah* and place this issue at the top of their priorities.

Shortfall of scholars This is an industry-related rather than an organisation-specific risk. There are few *Shari'ah* experts in commercial law and finance law. Most scholars who go on to specialise as academics do so in fields such as theology or history, while those who specialise in practical subjects become experts on the laws of *zakah*, marriage and divorce, or inheritance (Selvam, 2008). The industry is no longer able to produce qualified scholars at the required rate, particularly due to the long and arduous process involved, which includes learning the finer points of modern capital markets. It could take up to anywhere between 10 and 15 years for a person to qualify as a *Shari'ah* scholar and sign off on a *fatwa* due to the extensive training and guidance required to become an established scholar, according to Chowdhury (2010). He also stated, "There are only a few scholars who combine knowledge of the *Shari'ah* with an understanding of the working of modern finance... I personally know several scholars who have written advanced academic dissertations on subjects dealing with the classical jurisprudence of commerce and transacting." However, as Sheikh Yusuf Talal DeLorenzo (cited by Selvam, 2008) states "their knowledge is theoretical, these scholars are of no practical use to modern Islamic finance."

Another obstacle is mastering the language of communication needed in the financial realm. *Shari'ah* scholars need to be conversant in both Arabic, the language of the *Shari'ah*, and English, the main language of modern finance. "Most scholars are not fluent in English and the Islamic finance industry in dominated in the English language at the moment," adds Kailani (2010), another interviewee.

The strategy consultant firm Funds@Work (2009) carried out research on the landscape of *Shari'ah* scholars. The results, as depicted in Figure 3.7, show that among 271 organisations researched (including banks, mutual funds, insurance companies and private equity funds), there were 180 scholars with 956 positions; this remains an important challenge with various risk implications. If this shortage of *Shari'ah* scholars is not reversed, Islamic finance may not grow as quickly as it could.

It should also be noted that the shortage of skills applies not only at the scholarly level, but also in the wider industry as discussed earlier.

Reputational Risk

It takes 20 years to build a reputation and five minutes to destroy it.
—Warren Buffet as quoted in Askari et al. (2009)

Historically, reputational risk used to be considered a subset of operational risk; however, convincing arguments have been put forth over time to distinguish reputational risk from operational risk and to highlight the sole significance of the former. According to Askari et al. (2009), a survey conducted by Pricewater-houseCooper (PwC) in early 2004, showed that of 1400 CEOs taking part in the study 35% identified reputational risk as either 'one of the biggest threats' (10%) or 'a significant threat' (25%) to their business growth prospects. Reputational risk is the most critical risk for IFIs, because the total loss caused by reputational damage can well extend beyond the bank's liquidation value and affect the whole industry for generations, regionally, internationally and even globally. Once a bank's reputations has been damaged or tainted, restoring market confidence

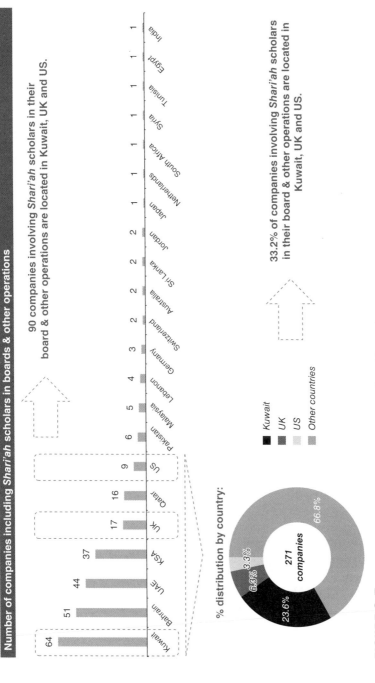

FIGURE 3.7 *Shari'ah* scholars' involvement in boards and beyond

Source: Authors' analysis based on figures provided by Funds@Work (2009:4)

is extremely challenging. Nevertheless, all Islamic banks in a given market are exposed to such risk. Close collaboration among financial institutions, standardisation of contracts and practices, self-examination, investing in customer awareness, and establishment of industry associations are some of the steps needed to mitigate reputational risk. "Reputational risk is certainly a major issue for a growing industry like Islamic banking and finance" said Richard Thomas (2009), Managing Director of Global Securities House.

Reputational risk for IFIs can occur at different levels. First, as a matter of image, loan foreclosure and security realisation, described as a relative strength of Islamic banks, are double-edged swords. Taking into account the expected take-off in mortgage lending especially in the GCC countries, the question of loan foreclosure and collateral seizing may be critical going forward. An IFI can hardly feel comfortable in the case of a Muslim family defaulting on the financial obligation pertaining to its primary residential property. In a number of jurisdictions, such a scenario would immediately trigger legal action leading the (conventional) bank to take full ownership of the collateralised property, at the expense of the borrower, who would be forced to relocate to an alternative, often smaller, home. According to Smith (2010), one of the interviewees for this research, in the context of the Muslim societies where IFIs are most active, it would be quite damaging for the IFI's 'ethical' reputation to leave a Muslim family homeless for the sake of profit, and then to sell the seized property post-foreclosure on the secondary market, since real estate Islamic finance presents itself as an ethical alternative to conventional banking. Therefore, should mortgage financing pick up in a number of Islamic jurisdictions, reputational risk management would call for a number of mitigating mechanisms like mutual *takaful* attached to housing loans.

Reputational risk can also arise from the fact that Islamic finance is a relatively young industry, and a single failed institution could trigger negative publicity for other banks in the industry, affecting their market share, profitability and liquidity. For example, Islamic Bank of Britain (IBB) has been suffering since its inception in 2004 from the negative publicity about Islamic banking among British customers caused by the collapse of the Bank of Credit and Commerce International (BCCI) in 1991 and the withdrawal of Al Baraka Bank from the UK market in 1993.[1] It took IBB's management tremendous effort to overcome the damage caused to trust in Islamic banking in the Western world.

More broadly, reputational risk might stem from the misconception that IFIs, through *zakat* and other charitable donations, might be close to violent militant groups. In order to avoid even the perception of such involvement, IFIs, particularly in the aftermath of 9/11, have materially invested in know-your-customers (KYC) and anti-money laundering (AML) systems in order to enhance their processes and procedures for the early detection and reporting of doubtful and fraudulent transactions, sometimes at a heavy cost. For example, in

2006 there was US state enforcement action against Doha Bank's Islamic banking arm in its New York branch relating to insufficient anti-money-laundering controls and systems. In April 2009, Doha Bank paid a fine of USD 5 million, which was imposed by two US government agencies: the Financial Crimes Enforcement Network and the Office of the Comptroller of the Currency. The post 9/11 environment necessitates the attention of IFIs to reputational risk due to the increased scrutiny and regulations to which they are subject.

Finally, if an Islamic bank is viewed as non-*Shari'ah*-compliant this could break the trust of its retail, corporate and even money market customers. This could trigger a liquidity crisis as devout Muslim depositors might withdraw their funds.

Askari et al. (2009) highlight that, although there has not been a major failure of an Islamic bank in more than 30 years, there have been instances of failures of financial institutions claiming to offer Islamic financial products, for example, Ihlas Finans of Turkey in early 2001, The Islamic Bank of South Africa in 1997, and Islamic investment companies in Egypt in the 1980s.

Accounting Standards

In a relatively immature and fragmented Islamic banking industry, there is a need to establish an adequate infrastructure, including the setting up of uniform accounting standards. Until recently, IFIs had developed their own standards in cooperation with their domestic regulators. However, this resulted in a lack of comparability between the financial statements of different institutions in different countries. The need is now widely recognised to provide users of financial statements with more meaningful, transparent and comparable information on the financial performance of the reporting entity.

AAOIFI has made some progress in developing a level playing field among Islamic banks, preparing a common set of accounting standards and developing consistent auditing standards and banking practices for those institutions, as well as starting to create a benchmark for *Shari'ah* compliance. Accounting standards issued to date reflect the adoption of conventional accounting practice, amended to reflect the nature of Islamic banking and incorporating compliance with *Shari'ah* doctrines (Mahlknecht, 2009).

AAOIFI and IFSB have played pioneering roles in designing key accounting, risk management, auditing and reporting standards for IFIs. They have complemented these with *Shari'ah* standards for contracts and governance, and have built awareness of major risk and prudential issues in Islamic finance. However, the pace of adoption of standards is slow. Also, considerable challenges remain to upgrade the standards and develop new ones in order to support the rapid innovations in the industry, and to align the accounting and auditing standards more closely with the evolving regulatory standards. AAOIFI and IFSB standards are still under refinement and are not mandatory; and hence are still not used by several IFIs.

Eglinton (2010), Director of Banking and Capital Markets at Ernest & Young and one of the interviewees for this research, adds that consistency is of great importance and significantly different treatments of the same item can and do occur; this makes it difficult and potential confusion arises relating to the treatment of investment accounts. Should these be on or off balance sheet? Are they with or without recourse? Differing treatment of investment accounts can have significant implications for capital adequacy calculations and liquidity requirements. Income recognition (cash or accrual) at inception, receipt or ultimate repayment and expense recognition (deducted from profit apportionment) are also important issues as different treatments can have a significant impact on reported profitability.

Despite AAOIFI's efforts, its standards are not mandatory because of the overriding need to comply with domestic regulatory requirements, with the exception of a handful of countries, such as Bahrain and Sudan, where banking supervisors require Islamic banks to comply with the AAOIFI standards.

Most countries use the International Financial Reporting Standards (IFRS) or US GAAP standards for their accounting, or some close local adaptation. These have limitations for good transparency of the operations of Islamic institutions and may lead to very poor disclosure of important aspects of their operations. However, many regulators believe that they need one set of accounting rules to be applied by all banks in their jurisdiction and so they are reluctant to depart from this practice.

AAOIFI has, however, continued working closely with regulators and the International Accounting Standards Committee in order to encourage adoption of its standards. An increasing number of institutions produce financial statements that conform to both IFRS and AAOIFI standards (Moore, 2009). Eglinton (2010) adds that "This may be the way to go, especially as AAOIFI has never wanted to reinvent the wheel but has stated that its standards should be used to give more appropriate presentation only when IFRS is not suitable."

Fiduciary Risk

Fiduciary risk is derived directly from the PLS feature of Islamic finance, and is closely interlinked with corporate governance risk. AAOIFI defines fiduciary risk as "being legally liable for a breach of the investment contract either for non-compliance with *Shari'ah* rules or for mismanagement of investors' funds" (Moore, 2009). As fiduciary agents, IFIs are expected to act in the best interests of investors, depositors and shareholders. If and when these objectives diverge from the actions of the bank, the bank is exposed to fiduciary risk.

Fiduciary risk can lead to dire consequences. First, it can cause reputational risk, creating panic among depositors, who may rush to withdraw their funds. Second, it may require the IFI to pay a penalty or compensation, which may result in a financial loss. Third, it can have a negative impact on the market price of shareholders' equity. Fourth, it can affect the bank's cost of and access to liquidity. Finally, it may lead to insolvency if the IFI is unable to meet the demands of current IAHs (Greuning and Iqbal, 2008).

In this context, information disclosure facilitates market discipline and enables different stakeholders to protect their own interests by allowing depositors to withdraw their funds, shareholders to sell their shares, and regulators to take necessary actions in case of mismanagement or misconduct (Greuning and Iqbal, 2008).

In its Exposure Draft on Risk Management, the IFSB gave some examples of how fiduciary risks may arise; these do not appear in the final standard but give a useful indication of the sort of risks that can arise (Moore, 2009):

(i) A critical aspect of IFIs' activities relates to the potentially large availability of funds available by current account holders, whereby, as a result of the inappropriate management decision, IFIs may increase disproportionately their investment portfolios' returns by excessively leveraging these funds without due regard to risks arising from sudden and unexpectedly high levels of withdrawals from current accounts.

(ii) Where IFIs manage and invest various funds in longer-term investment projects, investment funds received over a more prolonged period may be commingled inappropriately. For example, if funds provided by more longstanding investors are invested in a troubled project, there is a risk that the IFI could use other IAH funds received later on to invest in the same project in the hope that the project may be salvaged. Distortions may arise when the IFI reports an attractive return to longer standing fund providers when they are in fact being paid out of funds paid in by more recent investors.

(iii) The reinvestment of profits (rather than their distribution to investors) may give rise to unfair advantages to the IFI, which may thereby extend the period of a poorly performing investment. This may unfairly increase the exposure of incoming IAHs to losses, which may have already existed prior to their investment.

(iv) The risk of conflicts of interest exists where poorly performing assets and/or restructured assets of the IFI may be transferred by the IFI's management from on balance sheet to off balance sheet accounts where the restricted IAH would bear the risk of loss. Such misapplications of funds could result in the investment risk being removed from the IFI's balance sheet but, based on an agency contract, the IFI may earn fees inappropriately on the investment management and would not share in any eventual losses recorded after the transfer.

(v) When purchasing assets at a very low price, IFIs may 'park' them in a subsidiary or related company and, when the opportunity arises, sell them to the IAH at a higher price.

(vi) Other internal and operational issues may not be directly related to IAHs' investments but may give rise to exposure to losses for IAHs. For example, the risks derived from such elements as an excessive allocation of expenses and the hiring of less experienced staff affect the quality of investment performance and oversight.

Moore (2009) argues that these indicate some of the ways in which a less than scrupulous management could manipulate returns to suit their purposes. There appear to be many ways management might conceal their errors, and lack of transparency means that their actions would be hard to discover.

Corporate Governance Risk

Corporate governance has a particular importance for Islamic banks because of the unique nature of their stakeholders. All banks, as a result of their role in national and local economies and financial systems, have a broader group of stakeholders than other institutions have. But in the case of IFIs, the group is even wider as PSIA holders and *Shari'ah* boards must be added (Moore, 2009).

Deposits in conventional banks are, by definition, capital protected. Depositors also often have the comfort of deposit insurance schemes and the comfort that banks can turn to the lender of last resort to fend off any temporary problems. Regulators and supervisors do not want to see depositors lose money as it could have dire consequences for the whole financial system. However, the same protection is not offered to PSIA holders, particularly unrestricted PSIAs. Here, not only do the account holders have no say in how their money is invested, it is often also commingled with the bank's own funds. It is easy to see that situations could arise where there is a conflict of interest between shareholders and PSIA holders, while management may have a third agenda. This might be in the area of risk appetite or in the share of profits that would be allocated to the different parties. While shareholders can make their wishes heard through the board of directors, PSIA holders have no such voice. Assets can be transferred between unrestricted PSIAs, shareholders' equity and other funds; and as disclosure requirements have stood, only management need to know what happened or why it happened (Moore, 2009).

The IFSB produced its standard on corporate governance in December 2006. One of its proposals is that each IFI should establish a governance committee of its board, one of whose responsibilities should be to ensure that the interests of its PSIA holders are looked after (IFSB, 2006). In addition, AAOIFI has set governance standards for Islamic institutions that cover the appointment, composition and responsibilities of the *Shari'ah* board, one of which is to protect the interests of depositors and PSIA holders (Kailani, 2010). As such, this board is a critical governance body within the bank.

It has been suggested by many that the governance process would be significantly enhanced by allowing PSIA holders some representation on the board of directors and by an improvement in the transparency of financial reporting. Another proposal that has been put into practice by the Al Baraka Group is to have a separate investors' committee (Moore, 2009). However, the practicality of both proposals is questionable.

Corporate governance practices can have a material impact on the bank's risk profile, particularly in countries where such practices are weak. Islamic banks do not generally have robust corporate governance frameworks in place. However, in this they are no different from some of their local conventional peers. For instance, family ownership/majority ownership by a core shareholder group is seen in both segments of an Islamic country's banking system. Their prevalence weakens the rights of minority shareholders, may lead to unmerited appointments or promotion of family members, and could give rise to conflicts of interest between different stakeholders. The lack of genuinely independent directors is a shortcoming of emerging markets in general and impairs a board's ability to maintain accountability and provide strategic guidance.

The exposure of big family businesses is among the most important risks for Islamic banks and the GCC business environment in general. Saudi Arabia is a clear example: Ahmad Hamad Algosaibi & Brothers owes money to more than 100 banks. This family-owned company owned a Bahraini bank, the International Banking Corporation (TIBC), which defaulted on USD 2.2 billion of debt in early May 2009. In addition, Algosaibi had defaulted on some USD 1 billion of foreign exchange, trade finance and swap agreements, and was seeking restructuring of all its group obligations, which are reported to include about USD 2.5 billion owed to Saudi banks and hundreds of millions of dollars owed elsewhere. Closely connected with family ties, the Saad Group and its subsidiary Awal Bank, owned by Maan Al Sanea, were also restructuring debt: the Group owes banks at least USD 5.5 billion. The ripples from the Saad and Algosaibi defaults also extend into international waters, weakly in concrete financial terms but perhaps more lastingly in terms of sentiment. Both groups borrowed from foreign banks: Algosaibi took out a USD 700 million syndicated loan in May 2007 arranged by BNP Paribas and WestLB, while a USD 150 million borrowing in 2006 by Awal was arranged by Arab Bank, Gulf International Bank and Hypovereinsbank. *The Financial Times* reported on 11 June 2009 that several of the international banks with a relationship with Saad and Mr Al Sanea had closed down credit lines. It is hard to find an Islamic bank in the GCC or Europe without significant exposure to these entities. According to Damak (2010), who was interviewed for this research, gross loan exposure within the GCC to the Saad and Algosaibi Groups amounts to USD 9.6 billion for 30 banks in the six GCC countries. Such developments and incidents have resulted in questioning of the nature of corporate governance, if any, in the Middle East, as the two conglomerates were controlled by family members. This Saudi banking scandal is, on one level, a family affair.

The GCC Board Directors Institute, a Dubai-based non-profit that seeks to improve corporate governance standards, issued a report in 2009 highlighting the need for corporate governance reform in the six GCC member states – Bahrain, Kuwait, Oman, Qatar, Saudi Arabia and the UAE. The report *Building Better Boards* notes that only 55% of GCC companies disclose the main executive positions of board members, compared with 100% in Europe, and only 32% of companies disclose other positions held by board members, compared with 97% in Europe. It urges a reduction in the number of boards on which directors serve; the appointment of strong audit, nomination and remuneration committees; efforts to attract more international directors to the boards of Gulf companies; and the promotion of greater corporate transparency (Townsend, 2009).

Thus, corporate governance risk in the GCC, where most Islamic banks reside, has become publicly exposed. Poor corporate governance imposes heavy costs. The need for additional efforts toward improved corporate transparency is paramount. As long as Gulf companies and banks restricted their activities largely within the region, there was little pressure to change those opaque practices. However, growing links with international markets and financial institutions are generating greater demands for reform. Changing corporate practices, however, will not be easy. Governance reform needs to be addressed against the cultural backdrop in the Gulf, which places great emphasis on reputation and discretion. Nevertheless, in recent years Bahrain, Dubai and Qatar have created financial centres that promote high standards of regulation and corporate disclosure, including the requirement to publish regular results under IFRS.

Regulatory and Tax Issues

As the nature of their operations is different, IFIs face different problems in respect of legal, regulatory and taxation rules. In order to foster stability in Islamic banking, there is a need to develop uniform regulatory and transparency standards that are tailored to the specific characteristics of Islamic financial products and institutions. This task, while taking into consideration the financial environment in each country, also needs adaptation of the international standards, core principles and good practices to the specific needs of IFIs. For example, IFIs have to purchase assets for onward sale or lease to their clients. As such, the levy of taxation and fees on their purchases leads to an uneven playing field for them compared with their conventional counterparts. To avoid such costs, IFIs in some jurisdictions resort to practices creating doubts with respect to *Shari'ah* compliance (Ayub, 2007).

Some regulations need to be amended before an Islamic bank can operate within a particular economy; an example is stamp duties in mortgaging transactions in Western markets. Since the Islamic bank purchases a product on behalf of a client and then resells it, double stamp duties should not be charged in such circumstances. Regulators in countries where both systems operate side by side should recognise the need to set up flexible regulatory and tax frameworks that could facilitate banking operations in line with the *Shari'ah* principles. Flexibilities granted by the Financial Services Authority (FSA) in Britain to accommodate the specific needs of Islamic banking are a welcome move; it is hoped that the process of adaptation of laws will continue in order to make London an international hub for the Islamic finance industry in coming years.

Legal Risk

Given the different nature of financial contracts, Islamic banks face risks related to their documentation and enforcement. As there are no standard forms of contracts for various financial instruments, Islamic banks prepare documentation according to their understanding of the *Shari'ah*, the local laws and their needs and concerns. Lack of standardised contracts along with the fact that there are no litigation systems to resolve problems associated with enforceability of contracts by the counterparty increases the legal risks associated with the Islamic contractual agreements (Khan and Ahmed, 2001).

There are special concerns for Islamic banks over the enforceability of contracts. Conventional banks use well-established products for which standard documentation has been developed over the years that is accepted globally. This gives comfort, despite any limitations that may exist in the legal systems of the countries where the banks operate. This is not the case for Islamic products as yet. If problems arise and cases go to court, there is considerable uncertainty as to the court's decision (Moore, 2009).

Furthermore, the legal environment in some Islamic countries tends to be ambiguous and has never been tested, which constrains the ability to enforce a contract, recover bad debts or realise collateral. For example, Chowdhury (2010) states that "in the GCC, the rule of precedent does not apply to court cases, and insolvency rules have not been tested before". Dey and Holder (2008) explain that courts in the UAE and Saudi Arabia will generally not honour any provisions of a foreign legal system which are contrary to *Shari'ah,* public order, morals or any mandatory provisions of the local law.

A number of recent court decisions have proven that when it comes to resolving disputes arising from Islamic finance contracts, *Shari'ah* rules and principles do not necessarily apply. This is simply because, most often, the issues in dispute are not *Shari'ah* in nature, but rather specific to the civil and commercial rights and obligations as contracted by the parties. The precedent here is the case of *Shamil Bank of Bahrain* v. *Beximco Pharmaceuticals Ltd* in 2004, when the Court of Appeal ruled that it was not possible for the case to be considered based on principles of *Shari'ah* law (HMCS, 2009). There were two main reasons. First, there is no provision for the choice or application of a non-national system of law, such as *Shari'ah*. Second, because the application of *Shari'ah* principles was a matter of debate, even in a Muslim country.

To mitigate this risk, contracts have to be written very carefully to minimise potential disputes and state the governing law. At present, most Islamic finance contracts are governed by English law, and a few under New York law. There are also advantages in standardisation of documentation. However, local courts may not enforce an English legal judgment without re-examining the merits of the claim and may not recognise English law as the law of the contract, or only to the extent that it is not incompatible with local law and public policy. This would mean that the local courts could seek to reinterpret documents governed by English law as if they were governed by local law. They could therefore give effect to the documents in a manner not intended by the parties (Miller, 2008). For instance, around 110 banks from all over the world are currently struggling in courts trying to retrieve their money from the defaulting Ahmed Hamad Algosaibi & Brothers Group and the Golden Belt *sukuk* issued by Saad Group in Saudi Arabia. The ongoing litigation has proved that the ability to enforce English judgments in Saudi Arabia is almost non-existent, and that liquidation rules in the GCC are lagging behind.

Short Track Record

Modern Islamic banking has been in existence for only three decades and many products are less than a decade old. This is in addition to the fact that most Islamic banks are active in the developing world where transparency, corporate governance and risk management at large are still work in progress, or non-existent.

RISK CATEGORIES ARE ENTANGLED

In a large number of Islamic finance contracts it is often challenging to distinguish between risks because risk categories of a different nature are entangled, along with the changing relationship of parties during the lifetime of the contract. Also, the nature of risks contained in Islamic instruments is likely to change significantly over time.

This is referred to as 'conglomeration of risks', whereby each mode of finance carries various risks bundled together (Khan, 2004). For example, in an *ijarah* contract, which resembles a financial lease, the IFI buys an asset that is subsequently leased or rented to a customer against periodic rental payments. The IFI remains the owner of the leased asset throughout the duration of the lease contract, leaving the bank exposed to the residual value of the asset at maturity or should the lessee be willing to terminate the *ijarah* relationship prior to maturity. The management of leased assets' residual value is a feature that differs materially from credit risk management and assumes access to robust and reliable market data as to asset-price volatility and behaviour across economic cycles and business conditions; all the more so as IFIs tend to run a portfolio of asset inventories that they buy and then sell or lease (FRSGlobal, 2009).

Inventory management is another aspect that separates IFIs, from a risk management perspective, from their conventional peers. Similar issues arise when it comes to diminishing *musharakah* contracts (co-ownership contracts whereby the customer's ownership share in a financed asset increases as principal is incrementally repaid to the bank). Should the customer default, the IFI's share in the financed asset is used as collateral, the value of which might be volatile and naturally subject to scrutiny and management independently of the customer's perceived creditworthiness (Moody's, 2009a).

In addition, given trading-based instruments and equity financing, there are significant market risks along with credit risk in the banking book of Islamic banks. For example, trade-based contracts (*murabahah, salam* and *istisna'a*) and *ijarah* are exposed to both credit and market risks. During the transaction period of a *salam* contract the bank is exposed to credit risk, and at the conclusion of the contract it is exposed to commodity price risk, the liquidity risk of its conversion into cash, the operational risk of its storage and movement, etc. (Ahmed and Khan, 2007).

RISK MANAGEMENT ISSUES IN *SUKUK*

Sukuk present specific market and credit risks, particularly with regard to pricing, delays in scheduled payments, events of default, asset protection, structural issues and reporting standards. The risk and return in *sukuk* are linked to the underlying assets. The key distinction when looking at *sukuk* from a risk-management perspective is whether they are asset-backed or asset-based via a repurchase undertaking. In other words, do *sukuk* holders rely on the assets themselves or on the ultimate originator for repayment? Due to the nature of *sukuk*, all transactions are likely to involve a set of underlying assets. Both parties – the issuer and the investors – share the risks in the transaction. Where investors enjoy asset-backing, they benefit from some form of security or lien over the assets, and are therefore in a preferential position over other, unsecured creditors. In other words, in the event that the issuer were to default or become insolvent, the *sukuk* holders would be able to recover their exposure by taking control of and ultimately realising the value from the underlying asset(s) (Moody's, 2008a). There have been a couple of notable issues where the assets were 'truly' sold, like Tamweel and Sorouh PJSC, both UAE transactions. They still account for the minority of overall global *sukuk* issuance.

Where the transaction is asset-based (which has been the case for the vast majority of *sukuk* so far), the originator undertakes to repurchase the assets from the issuer at maturity of the *sukuk*, or upon a pre-defined early termination event, for an amount equal to the principal repayment. In such a repurchase undertaking, the true market value of the underlying asset (or asset portfolio) is irrelevant to the *sukuk* holders, as the amount is defined to be equivalent to the notes. In this case, investors in *sukuk* rely wholly on the originator's creditworthiness for repayment. Box 3.7 depicts the practical case of default of East Cameron Partners (ECP) *sukuk* and the legal complication associated with recovering the assets by investors. This class of *sukuk* is identical to unsecured lending from a risk perspective. The vast majority of *sukuk* structures to date fall into this category; they do not aim to complete an off balance sheet transfer of the assets from the originator. In this sense, from a risk profile, the investors bear similar risk to unsecured lending (Dey and Holder, 2008), and their credit risk will be identical to a conventional unsecured bond.

"There is no scope in the courts for such vagaries – either the investors have a legally enforceable claim on assets or they do not. So when crunch time comes, those investors in asset-based structures are left with nothing: no assets, no security, just an unsecured claim in substance like a debt of the company", explains Engel (2010). Most *sukuk* are currently asset-based rather than asset-backed, with a few exceptions. Many investors – Islamic and non-Islamic alike – simply want a fixed-income bond, and it is this powerful investor demand that primarily drives the shape of market. Therefore, securitisation has not really taken off in Islamic finance. Thomas (2009) hence states, "The way forward is to revert to the asset-backed *sukuk*."

It should also be mentioned that there is no track record of *sukuk* enforcement to date, and the issue of effective legal ownership of assets between a company and its related sovereign have yet to be tested.

BOX 3.7: PRACTICAL DEFAULT CASE OF ASSET-BASED *SUKUK*

East Cameron Asset-Backed *Sukuk*: Who owns the assets?

The East Cameron Partners L.P. (ECP) *sukuk* was relatively small one at USD 165.67 million and was issued in July 2006. It was the first issued by a US company and was a genuine effort at an asset-backed *musharakah*. It was secured by an interest in the oil and gas royalty rights on two gas fields in the Gulf of Mexico. On 16 October 2008, ECP (the originating company) filed for Chapter 11 / bankruptcy in the US courts.

A *sukuk* enforcement event was then triggered on 3 September 2008 due to a shortfall in the stressed oil and gas reserves. As an asset-backed structure *sukuk* investors already have legal rights over the oil and gas assets but ECP requested a ruling that the transaction was not a 'true sale' but a 'secured loan'. In the former, *sukuk* investors have sole rights to the assets; in the latter they would lose their rights and share the assets with the other creditors should ECP enter Chapter 7 (liquidation).

Ultimately providing asset security for investors is a legal issue that impacts conventional and *sukuk* structures equally. The concept is well tested in the US so investors' rights should be preserved if structured correctly. In the Middle East, legal systems are less tested and secured *sukuk* are the minority. Investors in asset-based *sukuk* have no senior claim or lien over the *sukuk* assets – but this is deliberate and clear to most parties.

Source: Based on data from Denton Wilde Sapte (2009)

Transparency is another issue with *sukuk*. Some of the *sukuk* had a huge lack of transparency and the complexities were beyond the comprehension of some scholars and market participants alike. The absence of disclosure and the very weak transparency standards make a clear assessment almost impossible. Going forward, transparency guidelines will be an important part of *sukuk* issue; it will affect not only the risk management but also the pricing of the *sukuk* (Abdul-Ghani, 2009).

Moreover, *sukuk* tend to be document intensive and relatively complex compared to conventional bonds because of the underlying asset structure. They also involve a complex relationship between *Shari'ah* and local (very often secular) legal systems, and the scope for conflict is great (Miller, 2008).

RISK MITIGATION IN ISLAMIC BANKING

Hedging can be one of the most contentious issues in Islamic banking. Conventional futures and short positions, which are often vital ingredients in risk mitigation, can be difficult to achieve under *Shari'ah* principles (KPMG, 2006). By the late 1990s and early 2000s, there began discussion on the scope of financial engineering and derivatives in Islamic finance. This did not receive much attention in the literature, primarily because most of transactions were designed by lawyers and *Shari'ah* experts and were executed in private by financial institutions who did not discuss the structure in a transparent manner (Askari et al., 2009).

The unique nature of risks faced by Islamic banks, combined with the restrictions added by *Shari'ah*, makes risk mitigation for Islamic banks a difficult and complex process. There are risks that Islamic banks, like their conventional counterparts, can manage and control through appropriate risk policies and controls, and traditional risk management tools like risk diversification, credit ratings, on balance sheet netting, GAP analysis, stress-testing, etc. Such traditional tools do not conflict with the *Shari'ah* principles. However, there are other risks that banks cannot eliminate and that can be reduced only by transferring or selling those risks in well-defined markets. These risks can generate unexpected losses that need capital insulation, and hedging can help to restrict the impact of unexpected loss. Traditionally, in the conventional world risk-transfer techniques include the use of derivatives for hedging, selling or buying of financial claims, and changing borrowing terms. The challenge is, however, that most of the conventional hedging tools do not so far comply with the *Shari'ah* requirements.

Until recently, it had been the opinion of most *Shari'ah* scholars that hedging would fall into the category of speculation and uncertainty. In the last few years, however, the increasing sophistication of Islamic banking products has led some scholars to take the view that Islamic banks may be able to enter into hedging arrangements provided that the hedging tool is in itself structured in a *Shari'ah*-compliant manner, and that the trade is being entered into to protect against a genuine exposure or liability, rather than solely for speculative purposes. According to Khan (2010), "there is growing demand for hedging and *Shari'ah*-compliant derivatives which would be used merely for hedging and not speculation".

In fact, hedging techniques and derivatives have drawn a lot of debate with regard to their permissibility. There are two schools of thought when it comes to hedging in Islamic finance: a very conservative view that prohibits hedging in all its forms, and a more liberal view that is looking to develop *Shari'ah*-compliant hedging tools. This conservative school of thought accuses derivatives of causing volatility in the market through speculation without being involved in real economic transactions. Nonetheless, another viewpoint is that some derivatives are permissible because they involve the full transaction price and do not cause injustice to anyone.

There are two approaches that can be adopted in the product development of hedging tools for Islamic banks: first, through replicating a conventional product. For example, a swap, repo or future could be used as a starting point, followed by transformation into a *Shari'ah*-compliant instrument. However, this is not the most efficient method of product development because there will be additional costs involved to fulfil *Shari'ah* requirements; it is also less creative. The second approach would be to focus on the function of the instrument and design tools suitable for that purpose. That is what is known as financial engineering. Much research is needed before those techniques can be adapted to Islamic banking. But things are certainly moving in the world of Islamic hedging. In September 2006, the IIFM signed a Memorandum of Understanding with the International Swaps and Derivatives Association (ISDA), with an eye to developing a master agreement for documenting privately negotiated *Shari'ah*-compliant derivatives transactions (Visser, 2009). The ISDA may prove crucial in helping to lift Islamic risk management to a point at which basic- to medium-level hedging instruments can be introduced, as it has expertise in developing derivatives. In addition, the IIFM is currently working on developing a *Tahawwut* (Hedging) Master Agreement, which will lead the way in risk minimisation of Islamic economic activity.

Afaq Khan, CEO Standard Chartered Saadiq and Director of IIFM, said: "Risk management solutions are the need of the Islamic industry with particular focus on treasury risk management. Islamic financial institutions (FIs) continue to grow within their home markets and are increasingly adopting regional and international expansion strategies. It is imperative that they have adequate risk management tools to allow them to play a responsible role in their local economy and also in their expansion plans. *Tahawwut* Master Agreement is another important initiative from IIFM to help the industry in developing a mutually agreed standardised document. This will make it easy for banks to trade with each other" (IIFM, 2009).

This will play a critical role in the development of risk mitigation tools in Islamic banking.

Another challenge for Islamic hedging tools is the lack of liquidity in the secondary market. Derivatives and hedging tools in conventional banking thrive on trading in the liquid secondary market. This is an obstacle for IFIs as liquidity is simply not there yet. Most Islamic banks, as previously discussed, have large balance sheet mismatches, which are difficult to bridge given the lack of long-duration liabilities.

There has been substantial development in finding ways to apply derivatives to reduce certain risks such as currency and commodity risks: in Malaysia, for example, some *Shari'ah*-compliant hedging instruments, such as profit rate swaps, have been introduced. However, much of this progress remains localised with limited scope for cross-border application and further work is still needed.

Credit Derivatives

In recent years derivatives have been increasingly taking an important role not only as instruments to mitigate risks but also as sources of income generation. They are one of the newest tools for managing credit risks. A derivative is an instrument whose value depends on the value of something else. In these instruments the underlying risk of a credit is separated from the credit itself and sold to possible investors whose individual risk profile may be such that the default risk attracts their investment decision (Ahmed and Khan, 2007). This can be done by packaging, securitisation and marketing credit risk exposures with a variety of credit risk features. Derivatives come in many guises, for example, futures, options and swap contracts (Davis, 2009b).

Futures are forward contracts of standardised amounts that are traded in organised markets. Like futures, options are financial contracts of standardised amounts that give buyers/sellers the right to buy/sell without any obligation to do so. A swap involves agreement between two or more parties to exchange a set of cash flows in the future according to predetermined specifications (Stremme, 2005).

Shari'ah and Islamic Derivatives

Discussion on Islamic derivative products is rare, and even what is available in the literature is not very favourable. In general, it is argued by many *Shari'ah* scholars that conventional derivatives are not compliant with the precepts of *Shari'ah* for various reasons.

First, they entail *gharar* (uncertainty in a contract or sale in which the goods may or may not be available or exist) and *maysir* (the forbidden act of gambling or playing games of chance with the intention of making an easy or unearned profit) and are therefore viewed in a similar way to gambling. For example, the argument is often put forward that the huge trading volume of derivative markets is indicative of extensive speculation, that the market attracts and accentuates speculative behaviour.

A second issue that causes uneasiness among *fiqh* scholars is the fact that a large portion of those trading in derivative markets have no intention of either making or taking delivery of the underlying asset; they are based on a system of margin calls without real movement of goods. Third, standard options, swaps and futures contracts stem from debt and are connected to the sale and purchase of debts and liabilities (Yaccubi, 2010). *Shari'ah* permits taking on risk only proportionate to the real value of the asset and not beyond the value of the real asset (Usmani, 2009). As a result, the scope for risk-transfer techniques in Islamic finance is limited at the present.

Derivatives also introduce a serious moral hazard to the financial matrix due to the nature of their structures. In some situations, a bank could benefit from the customer's default, as the bank makes profit from the Credit Default Swaps (CDS) it bought on this customer. In a creditor's meeting to help the customer, for example, this particular bank will have a hidden agenda of trying to make the customer default. This goes against the core principles of Islamic finance that promote the wellbeing of society.

While the OIC *Fiqh* Council has endorsed *arbun* under the condition that a time limit is specified for the option, the concept of *arbun* is merely acceptable to the extent of part payment after finalisation of the deal. Its legality as a separate sale (i.e. *bai'al-arbun*), detached from real transactions, is in general not approved by the *Shari'ah* scholars. Of the main schools of Islamic *fiqh*, only the *Hanbali* considers *bai' al-arbun* to be a valid legal contract (Ayub, 2007).

Kamali (2005) argues that commodity derivatives should be viewed under the broad scope of public interest or *maslahah*. In addition, Chapra (2007) debates that hedging has become an important instrument for the management of risks in the present international economic and financial environment where there is a great deal of instability in exchange rates as well as other market prices. He makes a suggestion to the *fiqh* jurists to review their position on currency hedging contracts. To explain his view, he assumes that a Saudi businessman places an order for Japanese goods worth a million dollars (Rls 3.75 million) to be delivered three months from now. If the exchange rate is 117 Yen per dollar, and if the exchange rate remains stable, Yen 117 million will become due at the time of delivery of goods. Since exchange rates are not stable, and consequently if the Yen appreciates over these three months by say 5%, the Saudi importer will have to pay Rls 3.94 million for the goods instead of Rls 3.75 million. The Saudi businessman will therefore incur an unforeseen loss of Rls 190,000.

Although recognising that the verdict so far is that hedging is not permissible, Chapra (2007) argues that this opinion is based on three objections: hedging involves *gharar*, interest payment and receipt, and forward sale of currencies. All three of these are prohibited by the *Shari'ah*. However, as far as *gharar* is concerned, the objection is not valid because hedging in fact helps eliminate *gharar* by enabling the importer to buy the needed foreign exchange at the current exchange rate. The bank, which sells forward Yen, also does not get involved in *gharar* because it purchases the Yen spot and invests them until the time of delivery. The bank therefore earns a return on the Yen that it invests for three months but also loses the return it would have earned on the Riyals or the dollars that were used to purchase the Yen. The differential in the two rates of return determines the premium or the discount on the forward contract. The second objection with regard to interest can be handled by requiring the Islamic banks to invest the Yen or other foreign currencies purchased in a manner permitted by Islam. There would not have been any interest, but rather profit earned on the investments. The third objection is, of course, very serious. Chapra (2007) argues that although Islam prohibits forward transactions in currencies, we live in a world where instability in the foreign exchange markets has become an unavoidable reality. It is very risky for businessmen as well as Islamic banks to carry unhedged foreign exchange positions on their balance sheets, particularly in crisis situations when exchange rates are very volatile. "If they do not resort to hedging, they actually get involved in *gharar* more intensively. In addition, one of the important objectives of the *Shari'ah*, which is the protection of wealth, is compromised unnecessarily" (Chapra, 2007).

Engel (2010) explains that derivatives will come for Islamic banks; it is just a matter of time. Today the closest structure is *sukuk*, with lease agreements and the transfer of ownership rights, but still a lot of work is needed. The Malaysian market is more liberal than the GCC market and the Islamic financiers in Malaysia are working hard on developing Islamic derivatives that would have a wide acceptance among *Shari'ah* scholars. Lowe (2010) adds that "if the scholars rule all derivatives *haram*, this would make hedging very difficult for Islamic banks".

It is said that a wise man learns from others' mistakes; Islamic banking should learn from the painful experience of conventional banking in the over-use of derivatives. Derivatives should be used for hedging to reduce risks rather than for profit-generating purposes. The use should also be carefully controlled and audited by the individual banks and regulators. Judging derivatives should be made within context.

Islamic Hedging Tools

Islamic banking needs to move quickly toward viable hedging alternatives if it is to sustain the growth that it has enjoyed so far. However, Islamic banks are not using any equivalent of credit derivatives, as sale of debt is prohibited, almost by all scholars, except in Malaysia. With the dramatic improvement in financial innovation in Islamic finance, some endeavours have been successful in providing that a number of contracts exist in Islamic banking that could be considered a basis for derivative instruments within an Islamic framework. These are *bai'salam*, *arbun*, *khiyar al-shart*, *wa'ad* and dual *murabahah*.

Bai' salam   *Bai' salam* is similar to the conventional forward contract. However, the major difference is that in a *bai' salam* contract the buyer pays the entire amount in full at the time the contract is initiated. The contract also stipulates that this payment must be in the form of cash. The buyer in a contract therefore is an Islamic bank. Because there is full prepayment, this potential contract is beneficial to the seller. As such, the predetermined price is normally lower than the potential price. The price behaviour is certainly different from that of conventional forward contracts, where the forward price is typically higher than the spot price by the amount of the carrying cost. Credit or counterparty risks of forward and *bai' salam* contracts are therefore different. In a *bai' salam* contract, the risk would be one-sided because the buyer has fully paid, and therefore only the buyer faces the seller's default risk as opposed to both parties facing risk, as in a forward contract. In order to overcome the potential for default on the part of the seller, the *Shari'ah* allows the buyer to require security, which may be in the form of a guarantee or pledge (Noraini et al., 2009).

Visser (2009) adds that, instead of using forward contacts for swaps, as they have been traditionally utilised, one could also hedge price risks with the help of futures. Since the buyer of a future really wants to take delivery of a good and thus there is no speculation, futures contracts should be met with less disapproval. It should be noted that the *Maliki* school allows futures contracts to be traded, like they have always done for *bai' salam* contracts, but the *Hanafi*, *Shafii* and *Hanbali* schools do not.

Ahmed and Khan (2007) assert that by virtue of a number of *fiqh* resolutions, conventions and new research, the scope for commodity futures in Islamic finance is widening; the potential of futures contracts is tremendous in risk management and control. Kamali (2005) argues that if new technology can eliminate *gharar* in the contract, then it may be reconsidered by *Shari'ah* scholars. Futures contracts should not be branded as *maysir* as they serve an economic purpose – to reduce price risk. The implementation of a contemporary futures contract removes *gharar*, which is the basis on which these contracts are forbidden, and in the future they may prove to be instrumental in managing risks in Islamic banking, particularly commodity risks. He adds that *Shari'ah* scholars' requirement for the possession of assets prior to sale is in principle in order to avoid *gharar*, but this argument against futures does not hold water as delivery is guaranteed by the futures clearing house. Kamali concludes that futures contracts are Islamically permissible provided that they steer clear of *haram* commodities and of interest elements.

It should be mentioned that there are a few Muslim countries with futures markets: Indonesia (coffee and crude palm oil), Kazakhstan (wheat), Malaysia (crude palm oil, stick index and government debt), and Turkey (currency). In addition, there is some over-the-counter trading based on *bai'salam* in a number of Islamic countries, including Iran (Visser, 2009).

Arbun *Arbun* is a contract whereby a buyer of goods makes an immediate down-payment of part of the price against future delivery. The buyer has the option to pay the balance, being the purchase price less the down-payment, at any time until a specified final purchase date. However, should the buyer choose not to buy the goods by the final purchase date, the down-payment will be forfeited. It is very similar to the call option in conventional finance. The main difference is that a call option is purchased by paying a premium which is not offset against the purchase price should the option be exercised, whereas the down-payment on an *arbun* purchase is part payment for the good or asset if the sale is effectuated (Visser, 2009). Islamic funds have successfully utilised *arbun* to minimise portfolio risks in what are now popularly known in the Islamic financial markets as the Principal Protected Funds (PPFs) (Ahmed and Khan, 2007). Further development should move toward credit risk mitigation by way of Islamic credit default swaps and the development of options under the *arbun* structure.

It should be noted that the *Hanbali* school is the most liberal in allowing *arbun*; other schools, in particular the *Hanafi* school, tend to be opposed to it (Yaccubi, 2010). They argue that the retention of a down-payment by the seller is akin to misappropriation of the property of others and hence is not permissible (Visser, 2009).

Khiyar al-shart *Khiyar al-Shart* (option of condition) is a contract in which one or both parties to a contract (or even a third party) holds an option (embedded within the contract) to confirm or rescind the contract within a specified time contingent on the fulfilment of a stipulated condition. The contract has embedded options that could be triggered if the underlying asset's price exceeds certain bounds. The features of this contract in relation to its exercise are similar to a conventional put option. What differentiates the *khiyar al-shart* option from conventional options is that there can be no separate fee paid at the start of the contract in respect of granting the option right. Therefore, it is the delivery price of the underlying asset which includes an element that recognises the economic value awarded to the option holder in the contract. Ahmed and Khan (2007) argue that there are no *fiqh* objections to using non-detachable embedded options and that in Sudan such a contractual agreement has become a regular feature of the *salam* contract.

Wa'ad *Bai' salam*, *arbun* and *khiyar al-shart* all involve bilateral binding contracts, whereas the rules are less stringent with a *wa'ad* contract. It is a promise whereby the party looking to hedge provides a unilateral binding undertaking to buy currency from a third party at a given price in the future. The third party is not under any obligation to act on the transaction when the offer to purchase is submitted, resulting in significant counterparty risk (Wyman, 2009).

Dual murabahah In conventional terms a Dual Currency Deposit is a fixed deposit with variable terms for the currency of payment. Deposits are made in one currency, but repayment at maturity occurs either in the currency of the initial deposit or in another agreed-upon currency, depending on the occurrence of a trigger event. The 'optionality' is typically created by buying an option from the client. Rather than return the option premium to the client as a flat payment, it is embedded in the deposit and returned to the client as an enhancement to the deposit yield. This deposit creates foreign exchange rate risk for the investor and is therefore only suitable for clients with a specific view or risk appetite.

To replicate the above payoff and risk profile in an Islamic environment, Islamic banks combine commodity *murabahah* and *wa'ad* technology, enabling the bank to pay the customer an increased profit on the *murabahah* and settle the principal amount of the deferred price in a pre-specified different currency. Figure 3.8 provides a detailed explanation of how the dual currency *murabahah* can be used as a risk mitigation tool.

Further Risk Mitigation Provisions Inherent in Islamic Banking

IFIs have to absorb the risks that they cannot transfer or mitigate. This is done through the use of collateral, guarantees, loss reserves and provisions, allocation of capital through the Risk-Adjusted Return-On-Capital (RAROC) exercise, risk weightings, etc. Sundararajan and Errico (2002) argue that in addition to the traditional risk mitigants, the management of the risk-return mix, particularly of unrestricted PSIAs, could be used as a key tool of risk management. Appropriate policies toward PERs (and possibly IRRs), coupled with appropriate pricing of investment accounts to match the underlying risks, would improve the extent of overall risk-sharing by these accounts.

Also, under a PLS system the Islamic bank is subject to higher screening and monitoring, making the danger of insolvency lower, provided that PLS principles are rigorously applied. Managing the risk-sharing of IAHs through proper pricing, reserving and disclosure policies would greatly enhance risk management in Islamic banks.

Chapra (2007) argues that PLS might go a long way toward preventing financial crises, as it would substantially reduce the moral hazard problems associated with prudential supervision of banking, in particular the incentive given by deposit guarantees for high-risk lending and investment. In addition, it is argued that under PLS there would be more discipline in the system. Depositors would be more interested in the soundness of the banks and in the quality of the banks' assets, in order to prevent having to accept negative returns. Banks would also have a better incentive to be careful in selecting borrowers and projects.

The PLS feature of Islamic banking therefore provides an inherent risk management tool that could be of great help to banks and the whole system if properly

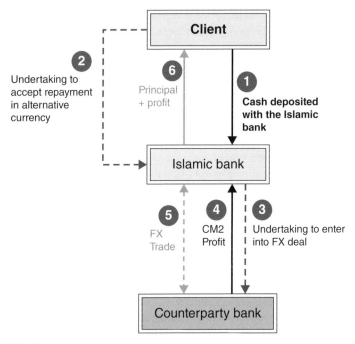

FIGURE 3.8 Dual currency *murabahah* structure

1. Client (as seller) undertakes a commodity *murabahah* with the Islamic bank (as purchaser) in a specified original currency (e.g. USD);

2. Contemporaneously, but separately, the Client issues an undertaking to the Islamic bank to buy a specified amount of alternative currency (e.g. EUR) in exchange for a specified amount of the original currency (e.g. USD);

3. The Islamic bank will give an undertaking to a Counterparty bank to enter into an FX trade which mirrors the undertaking given by the Client to the Islamic bank;

4. The Islamic bank completes a contemporaneous but separate *murabahah* transaction (CM2) with the Counterparty bank and receives the *murabahah* price. This transaction will be concluded for spot settlement with no deferred payment;

5. At maturity, subject to the prevailing FX rates, the Islamic bank may enter into an FX trade with the Counterparty bank pursuant to the Islamic bank's undertaking;

6. At maturity, subject to the prevailing FX rates, the Islamic bank may enter into an FX trade with the Client pursuant to the Client's undertaking. The Islamic bank pays the *murabahah* principal to the client in the original currency and (if appropriate) completes the FX trade with the client to exchange the original currency with the alternative currency. The profit is paid in the original currency.

implemented. Under capital allocation, the IFSB supervisory discretion formula is a step in the right direction as it acknowledges the risks assumed by PSIA holders and incentivise banks – through lower capital requirements – to adopt more PLS financing modes, as explained in Chapter 4.

In practice, however, the losses of Islamic banks are not shared with PSIA holders, and often a minimum yield on deposits is 'implicitly' guaranteed. As a result the potential benefits of PLS finance cannot be realised. According to Sundararajan (2007), available empirical evidence shows that in practice, because Islamic banks try to provide *Shari'ah*-compliant alternatives to conventional products, there is considerable smoothing of the profits paid out to the unrestricted IAHs, and correspondingly reduced sharing of risk between the bank and the holders of such investment accounts, with banks bearing the majority of the risk. The extent of this *de facto* departure from the risk-sharing principle for unrestricted IAHs varies between countries; in some countries banks are expected – though not legally bound – to bear virtually all of the asset risk, while in others it is simply a matter of competitive pressure. Under current practices, reserves are passively adjusted to provide a stable return to unrestricted IAHs, effectively not allowing any risk mitigation through investment account management. For example, many banks with sharply divergent risk profiles and returns on assets seem to be offering almost identical returns on unrestricted IAHs, and these are broadly in line with the general rate of return on deposits in conventional banks.

Moreover, most Islamic banks realise the risk management gaps in their current business models especially in the areas of liquidity and hedging. Therefore, Islamic banks traditionally have been holding a comparatively larger proportion of their assets in reserve accounts, resulting in higher buffers than conventional banks.

Finally, some constraints attached to the status of IFIs, as sellers and buyers of tangible goods – as opposed to conventional banks intermediating between cash inflows and outflows with different maturities – also have risk-mitigating benefits. One rule of the key principles of modern Islamic finance states that any financial transaction should be backed by a tangible, identifiable underlying asset. This is a powerful way for the IFI to secure, at least in principle, strong access to the collateral backing the transaction. In short, IFIs naturally have a high level of collateralisation on their credit portfolios, and thus are in a position to somewhat reduce their economic, if not regulatory, exposures at default. In addition, IFIs have in principle greater visibility in terms of the economic allocation of the funds they supply to borrowers. Indeed, contrary to a conventional financial institution where a customer is not obliged to disclose the purpose of its loan, the IFI finances the acquisition of an identifiable asset legal ownership of which belongs, in most cases, to the bank until full repayment is made.

SURVEYING RISK MANAGEMENT PRACTICES IN ISLAMIC BANKS: A REVIEW OF EMPIRICAL RESEARCH

Given the importance of risk management for the survival of financial institutions, it is no surprise that there are numerous conceptual studies about risk management frameworks and techniques for conventional banks. Also, there are many empirical findings that examine different aspects of risk management practices by various financial institutions.

In the context of Islamic banking, however, risk management is an under-researched area. A few studies have been carried out on the theoretical side of risk management in Islamic banking, including the work of Haron and Hin Hock (2007) on market and credit risk; they explain the inherent risk, i.e. credit and market risk exposures in IFIs. They also illustrate the importance of displaced commercial risk in Islamic banking. They conclude that certain risks may be considered as being inherent in the operations of both Islamic and conventional banks. Although the risk exposures of IFIs differ and may be more complex than those of conventional financial institutions, the principles of credit and market risk management are applicable to both.

Apart from those two risks, Archer and Haron (2007) show that IFIs are exposed to a number of operational risks that are different from those faced by conventional banks. They argue that the complexities of a number of their products, as well as their relative novelty in the contemporary financial services market, combined with the fiduciary obligations of an Islamic bank when it acts as a *mudarib*, imply that for IFIs operational risk is a very important consideration.

Other conceptual research about risk management in Islamic finance includes Iqbal and Mirarkor (2007), Akkizidis and Khandelwal (2008), Grais and Kulathunga (2007), Greuning and Iqbal (2007) and Sundararajan (2007).

On the empirical side, research about risk management in Islamic finance is limited. An earlier study by Khan and Ahmed (2001) is still the most profound empirical research, which examined different aspects of risk management issues in IFIs. They sent out questionnaires to 68 IFIs in 28 countries and also visited Bahrain, Egypt, Malaysia and the UAE to discuss issues related to risk management with the officials of the IFIs. A total of 17 questionnaires were received from 10 countries in their study, which touched on different aspects of risk management in IFIs. Their study first identified the severity of different risks and then examined the risk management process in Islamic banks. Among the traditional risks facing Islamic banks, mark-up risk was ranked the highest, followed by operational risk. The results show that IFIs face some risks that are different from those faced by conventional financial institutions. These banks reveal that some of these risks are considered more serious than the conventional risks faced by financial institutions. Profit-sharing modes of financing (diminishing *musharakah*, *musharakah* and *mudarabah*) and product-deferred sale (*salam* and *istisna'a*) are considered more risky than *murababah* and *ijarah*. Other risks arise in Islamic banks, as they pay depositors a share of the profit that is not fixed ex ante. The results of the survey of risk perception in different modes of financing by Khan and Ahmed (2001) thus show that the risk level is considered elevated as depicted by Table 3.4.

Their research also indicates that Islamic banks have been able to establish better risk-management policies and procedures in measuring, mitigating and monitoring risks, with internal controls somewhere in the middle. The results also point out that the lack of some instruments (like short-term financial assets and derivatives) and of a money market hampers risk management in IFIs. There is a need for research in these areas to develop instruments and markets for these instruments that are compatible with the *Shari'ah*. At government level, the legal system and regulatory framework of the Islamic financial system need to be understood and appropriate policies should be undertaken to cater to the needs of IFIs.

Furthermore, Khan and Prodhan (1992) carried out a survey that focused on the integration of Islamic banks with conventional banking and the problems arising from the potential conflict, such as the need for convertible instruments, proper accounting procedures, etc. They concluded that with an Islamic banking system it becomes more important for the government to take an active position in terms of enforcing regulations and overseeing economic activity. "If policy measures are piecemeal and fiscal intervention uncoordinated, then an inefficient conventional banking and fiscal sector is replaced by an equally inefficient Islamic system" (Khan and Prodhan, 1992:20)

TABLE 3.4   Risk perception in different modes of financing

Contract	Credit Risk	Mark-up Risk	Liquidity Risk	Operational Risk
Murabahah	2.56	2.87	2.67	2.93
Mudarabah	3.25	3.00	2.46	3.08
Musharakah	3.69	3.40	2.92	3.18
Ijarah	2.64	3.92	3.10	2.90
Istisna'a	3.13	3.57	3.00	3.29
Salam	3.20	3.50	3.20	3.25
Diminishing Musharakah	3.33	3.40	3.33	3.40

Note: The rank has a scale of 1 to 5, with 1 indicating 'Not Serious' and 5 denoting 'Critically Serious'
Source: Based on data from Khan and Ahmed (2001:64)

Moreover, Samad (2004) empirically studied the performance differences between conventional and Bahraini Islamic banks by t-testing nine accounting ratios by studying 21 banks, out of which six were Islamic, over the period 1991–2001. He concluded that both types of bank performed equally well in terms of profitability and liquidity. However, Islamic banks seem to be less exposed to credit risk.

In recent International Monetary Fund (IMF) research, Heiko and Cihak (2008) used data from 77 Islamic banks and 397 commercial banks across 18 jurisdictions with a substantial presence of *Shari'ah*-compliant banks to provide a cross-country empirical analysis of the role of these banks in financial stability using their so-called z-scores. The z-score combines a bank's capitalisation, profitability and a measure of risk faced by the bank into a single index. The interpretation of the z-score is straightforward: the lower the score, the more likely it is that a bank will run out of capital. Defining large banks as those with total assets of more than USD 1 billion and small banks as all others, the study found that:

(i) Small Islamic banks tend to be financially stronger (that is, have higher z-scores) than small and large conventional banks;

(ii) Large conventional banks tend to be financially stronger than large Islamic banks; and

(iii) Small Islamic banks tend to be financially stronger than large Islamic banks.

A plausible explanation of the contrast between the high stability in small Islamic banks and the relatively lower stability in larger ones is that it is significantly more complex for Islamic banks to adjust their credit risk monitoring system as they become bigger. For example, the PLS modes used by Islamic banks are more diverse and more difficult to standardise than loans used by conventional banks. As a result, as the scale of the banking operation grows, monitoring of credit risk rapidly becomes much more complex, which results in greater prominence of problems relating to adverse selection and moral hazard. Another explanation is that small banks concentrate on low-risk investments and fee income, while large banks do more PLS business. The authors also found that as the presence of Islamic banks grows in a country's financial system, there is no significant impact on the soundness of other banks. This suggests that Islamic and conventional banks can coexist in the same system without substantial 'crowding out' effects through competition and deteriorating soundness.

More recently, Shaikh and Jalbani (2009) also provided a differential analysis of risk management procedures in Islamic banking. Studying a sample of four banks, this research used Return on Equity (ROE) as the benchmark for the comparative performance of Islamic banks and conventional banks. The study concluded that there is a strong relationship between the *ROE* of both Islamic and conventional banks, and that the risk management procedures in Islamic banks are adequate to mitigate their largely equity-based investments and give their customers adequate returns which are comparable with conventional banks. The paper optimistically concluded that the issue of equity-based business of Islamic banks posing slightly more risk than conventional banks is well mitigated by Islamic banks through their effective and adequate distinct risk management procedures. However, the research behind this book does not agree with the research methodology and the findings of that study.

More relevant to this study is the work of Rosman and Abdul Rahman's (2010), which found that the lack of effective risk management practices for both liquidity risks and rate-of-return risk/displaced commercial risk will be the prime concern for Islamic banks and regulatory agencies. They argue that the inadequacy of risk management practices by Islamic banks may threaten their sustainability especially during financial crises. They assert that Islamic banks are still lacking in the use of technically advanced risk measurement approaches. Hence, IFIs need to further enhance risk measurement approaches to measure complex risks such as liquidity risk and rate-of-return risk/displaced commercial risk. Islamic banks are also found to be mostly complacent in their risk mitigation approaches as they continue to utilise risk mitigation techniques that are widely used by the conventional banks. These findings lead to the need to develop the unique *Shari'ah*-compliant risk mitigation techniques

Finally, Noraini et al. (2009) attempted to ascertain the perceptions of Islamic bankers about the nature of risks, risk measurement, and risk management techniques in their banks. The study covered 28 Islamic banks in 14 countries, using a questionnaire survey. The results indicated that Islamic banks are mostly exposed to similar types of risk to those in conventional banks, but that there are differences in the level of the risks. However, the study found no evidence that Islamic bankers in different countries perceived risks differently. The study recommends that each risk be assessed separately for each financial instrument in order to facilitate appropriate risk management. The findings also suggest that Islamic banks are perceived to use less technically advanced risk measurement techniques, of which the most commonly used are maturity matching, gap analysis and credit ratings. In addition, Noraini et al.'s research shows that Islamic banks are not fully using *Shari'ah*-compliant risk mitigation methods, which are different from the ones used by conventional banks. The findings of their study have both theoretical and policy implications for the issue of transparency, with particular reference to risk reporting in Islamic banks.

CONCLUSION

Islamic banks are, for the most part, still small and in the start-up phase of development in an industry which is itself relatively young. Whereas risk management is practised widely in conventional financial markets, it is underdeveloped in Islamic finance. This gives rise to an array of risks which are not yet well comprehended. Moreover, risks unique to Islamic banks arise from the specific features of Islamic contracts and the overall legal, governance and liquidity infrastructure of Islamic finance. Literature review reveals that the infrastructural environment of most Islamic banks is characterised by weak transparency, high concentration risks, lack of commonly accepted *Shari'ah*-compliance and accounting standards, and shortage of liquidity and hedging products. To solve these problems Islamic finance institutions like the AAOIFI, IFSB, LMC, IILM, IIFM and others have developed a core set of accounting, liquidity, governance, risk management, auditing and *Shari'ah* standards. Nevertheless, IFIs still face risks connected to the enforceability of promises, efficient management of funding and asset liquidity, and many other limitations. Several areas such as asset pricing, hedging and risk mitigation therefore require further research. For example, in the absence of a risk-free asset, how will the CAPM behave? Or using Black's zero-beta model, how will the model behave with restrictions on short selling? Several such issues have not been researched yet (Askari et al., 2009). Adopting accepted risk models from the conventional banking practice or making suitable adjustments to best practices pose major challenges.

The future of Islamic banking will depend to a large extent on innovation. The immediate need is to develop instruments that enhance liquidity; to develop secondary money and interbank markets; to perform asset–liability and risk management; and to develop Islamically acceptable risk hedging tools.

In some ways, Islamic banking could be less risky than the conventional banking industry because there are several features that could make IFIs less vulnerable to risk. For instance, Islamic banks are able, in theory, to pass through a negative shock on the asset side to the PSIA depositors. The risk-sharing arrangements on the deposit side provide another layer of protection to the bank. In addition, it could be argued that the need to provide stable and competitive returns to investors, the shareholders' responsibility for negligence or misconduct, and the more difficult access to liquidity put pressures on Islamic banks to be more conservative (Heiko and Cihak, 2008) and to keep liquidity buffers. Furthermore, because depositors share in the risks (and typically do not have deposit guarantee) they have more incentives to exercise tight oversight over bank management. Finally, Islamic banks have traditionally held a comparatively larger proportion of their assets than commercial banks in reserve accounts. So, even though Islamic investments are more risky than conventional instruments, these higher risks have traditionally been compensated for by higher buffers.

In 2007, Michael Ainley, Head of Wholesale Banking at the FSA, stated at the Islamic Finance Summit in London that "Risk knows no religion" (Ainley, 2007). He obviously did not get it fully right when he thought that risks are similar for

Islamic and conventional banks. Although conventional and Islamic markets share similar risks, the level of risk is different and certainly higher in the case of today's Islamic banking. A common perception about Islamic banking is that it is expected to be safer and more resilient than the debunked Wall Street model, a perception which is not entirely correct. Advocates of Islamic banking have recently, especially after the start of the credit crisis, been claiming that Islamic finance is a safe haven. The truth is that Islamic banking in its current state can be riskier than conventional banking because of the additional risk management challenges and constraints the industry faces.

In theory, Islamic banking is safer than conventional banking. The theory is, unfortunately, a long way from fact in current financial practice. Since the risk management needs of Islamic banking are not yet being met, the system is not functioning at its full potential. There is a growing realisation that the long-term sustainable growth of Islamic banking will depend largely on the development of risk-sharing products. Chapter 5 thoroughly explains that Islamic banking could be a safe haven provided that its broader principles on a macro-level are entirely followed by all participants. In other words, when the short-terms risks and the longer-term stability are put together, the outlook for the Islamic banking industry looks less risky than its critics claim.

Having mapped out the risk and the risk management techniques and practices in this chapter, the next chapter continues with discussion of capital adequacy in Islamic banks. This is further explored, like the issues in this chapter, empirically in Chapters 7, 8 and 9.

NOTE

1. Although BCCI – which was incorporated in Luxembourg – was a conventional bank, the fact that it had lots of Muslims on board created the illusion that it was an Islamic bank.

CHAPTER 4

Capital Adequacy for Islamic Banks

A Survey

Capital isn't scarce; vision is

—Sam Walton

Financial liberalisation, as part of globalisation, has been followed keenly by developing countries since the 1990s. Several restrictions were eased, and self-regulation was considered to be the motivating factor. However, developments show that everything did not work well. There were several instances of malpractice, financial frauds and some failures. In responding to this, regulators started looking at the existing set of standards and ways to overcome the issue of balancing control and freedom. From simple capital provisions to comprehensive frameworks for risk management, the practice of risk management, as a result, has undergone wholesale transformation over the past two decades (Akkizidis and Khandelwal, 2007). More systematic transformation has taken place during the current straitened times. It is a fact that each country has its own set of regulations based on several parameters. The most common among them is the requirement to hold minimum capital indexed to the activities of the bank.

Capital adequacy is at the core of supervisory activities all over the world. It is an important benchmark for the soundness of financial institutions. It is gaining more prominence after the recent credit crunch, which saw numerous financial institutions collapsing because their capital was not big enough to absorb the risks they were taking. Developments have shown that the market turmoil turned out to be deeper and more enduring than previously anticipated and that financial markets are failing to sustain the normal flow of capital. Regulators, banks and industry participants realised that capital is a critical factor for the intrinsic strength of banks. Therefore, this chapter is designated to discuss capital adequacy in Islamic banking, which is explored empirically in the following chapters with the opinions of sample bankers, financiers, *Shari'ah* scholars and academics.

The fundamental principle that capital is the currency of risk and that adequate capital protects against distress applies equally to all banks. Therefore, the implementation of Basel II is as critical to Islamic banks as it is to their conventional counterparts. With necessary adjustments, the three Pillars of Basel II could be applicable to Islamic banks. The need for supervisory oversight in Pillar 2 can hardly be overemphasised, as market discipline through disclosure will provide greater transparency and benefit to Islamic banks. The capital treatment of Profit-Sharing Investment Accounts (PSIAs) adds complexity to capital requirements for Islamic banks. Notwithstanding the loss-absorbing features of PSIAs, in practice they behave like normal deposits and most regulators do not treat them as having capital features. Hence, the risk-sharing characteristic of PSIAs requires special capital treatment.

The previous two chapters have dealt with the evolution of Islamic banking and the major types of risks in conventional and Islamic banks. The present chapter provides a brief review of the Basel II Accord and is hence largely based on documents issued by the Basel Committee on Banking Supervision (BCBS). A brief summary of the original Basel I Accord is presented, highlighting the major limitations of the first Accord. A summary of the three Pillars of Basel II and the forthcoming Basel III standards and their applicability for Islamic financial institutions (IFIs) is also presented. The Islamic Financial Services Board (IFSB) has issued capital adequacy standards for the Islamic financial industry, which are discussed in detail. This chapter, however, does not thoroughly discuss Basel II, nor does it examine every single detail of the IFSB papers, as plenty of literature exists about the Basel Accords and other Bank for International Settlements (BIS) guidelines, and the IFSB papers are brief and simple enough to be self-explanatory. This chapter highlights the specifics of capital adequacy requirements for IFIs, explains the differences between the conventional Basel Accords and the Islamic version provided by the IFSB, and illustrates how the capital adequacy requirement can be used as a tool for risk mitigation for Islamic banks.

SIGNIFICANCE OF CAPITAL IN BANKING

Nearly all jurisdictions with active banking markets require banks to maintain a minimum level of capital. Capital plays an important role in any business but it is critically important in the case of banks, as it serves as a foundation for a bank's future growth and as a cushion against its unexpected losses. Adequately capitalised banks as well-managed banks are better able to withstand losses and to provide credit to consumers and businesses alike throughout the business cycle, particularly during downturns. Hence, capital is one of the key determinants and indicators of the soundness of a bank, not only because adequate capital serves as a safety net, but also because it is the ultimate determinant of a bank's lending and investment capacity. Adequate levels of capital thereby help to promote public confidence in the banking system.

Banks by the nature of their business have a lower capital-to-liabilities ratio than other types of business. This low ratio is a reflection of the nature of the intermediation business and acceptance of large amounts of liabilities in the form of deposits. To encourage prudent management of the risks associated with the unique balance sheet structure, regulators require banks to maintain a certain level of capital. The idea behind such a requirement is that a bank's balance sheet should not be expanded beyond the level of risks its capital can absorb. The technical challenge, however, for both banks and supervisors, has been to determine how much capital is necessary to serve as a sufficient buffer against unexpected losses. If capital levels are too low, banks may be unable to absorb high levels of losses. On the other hand, excessively low levels of capital increase the risk of bank failures which, in turn, may put depositors' funds at risk. Under-capitalised banks are highly prone to the risk of insolvency and can also suffer from retarded growth. If capital levels are too high, banks may not be able to make the most efficient use of their resources. A bank which is over-capitalised will have low return on its capital and will not be able to pay decent dividends to its shareholders (Jorion and Khoury, 1996). Thus, arriving at an optimal level of capital is in the best interest of banks and shareholders. Both financial intermediaries and regulators are therefore sensitive to the dual role of capital. Financial intermediaries tend to focus more on the earnings-generating role, while regulators tend to be focused on the stability-cushion role.

CLASSIFICATION OF CAPITAL

Defining what constitutes capital is a long-debated issue. However, there is a wide acceptance of the capital structure that has been stipulated by the BCBS, which segregates capital into three categories as set out in Table 4.1.

In general, according to BCBS (2006), the capital of a bank should have three important characteristics:

(i) It must be permanent;
(ii) It must not impose mandatory fixed charges against earnings; and
(iii) It must allow for legal subordination to the rights of depositors and other creditors.

TABLE 4.1 Classification of capital in the Basel Accords

Classification	Contents
Tier 1 (core capital)	Ordinary paid-up share of capital or common stock, disclosed reserves from post-tax retained earnings, non-cumulative perpetual preferred stock (goodwill to be deducted)
Tier 2 (supplementary capital)	Undisclosed reserves, asset revaluation reserves, general provisions or general loan-loss provisions, hybrid (debt-equity) capital instruments and subordinated term debts
Tier 3	Unsecured debt: subordinated and fully paid up, to have an original maturity of at least two years and not be repayable before the agreed repayment date unless the supervisory authority agrees

Source: Adapted from Greuning and Iqbal (2008:223)

STEPS IN THE BASEL ACCORD

One cannot discuss capital adequacy without mentioning the renowned Basel Accord. The Bank for International Settlements (BIS) was established on 17 May 1930; it is the oldest international financial institution. It provides a platform for consultative cooperation among the central banks. The role of BIS has undergone change as per the needs of the international financial sector. BIS now also acts as an institution for collection, compilation and dissemination of economic and financial statistics. It actively promotes global financial stability, and also performs the traditional banking function for the central bank community (gold and foreign exchange transactions). It has several committees working on different aspects of international financial stability. The BCBS, as part of the BIS structure, was formed at the end of 1974 by the Governors of the G10 nations. The BCBS issued a series of documents beginning in 1975 on banking supervision (Akkizidis and Khandelwal, 2007).

The Basel I Accord

The 1988 Basel Capital Accord set out the first internationally accepted definition of, and minimum measure for, bank capital. The Basel Committee designed the 1988 Accord as a simple standard so that it could be applied to banks in several jurisdictions. It requires banks to divide their exposures up into broad 'classes' reflecting similar types of borrowers. A minimum capital of 8% of risk-weighted assets (RWAs) was given. For example, 0% for cash, 20% for claims on multi-lateral development banks, 50% for residential mortgages and 100% for loans to the private sector. These risk-based capital charges roughly attempted to create a greater penalty for riskier assets (Jorion and Khoury, 1996).

While the 1988 Accord was initially applied only to internationally active banks in the G10 countries, it quickly became acknowledged as a benchmark measure of a bank's solvency and is believed to have been adopted in some form by more than 100 countries (KPMG, 2007).

The 1996 Amendment

The 1988 Basel Accord was soon proved insufficient and rendered obsolete by rapid changes in the financial sector. The 1996 amendment covered the four major risk categories of market risk (Akkizidis and Khandelwal, 2007:82–83):

(i) Interest rate-related instruments;
(ii) Equities;
(iii) Foreign exchange risk; and
(iv) Commodities.

Issues with the Basel I Accord

The world financial system has seen considerable changes since the introduction of the Basel I Accord. Financial markets have become more volatile, and a significant degree of financial innovation has taken place. There have also been incidents of economic turbulence leading to widespread financial crises – for example, in Asia in 1997 and in Eastern Europe in 1998. In addition, advances in risk management practices, technology and banking markets have made the 1988 Accord's simple approach to measuring capital less meaningful for many banking organisations. For example, the 1988 Accord sets capital requirements based on broad classes of exposures and does not distinguish between the relative degrees of creditworthiness among individual borrowers.

In a similar manner, improvements in internal processes, the adoption of more advanced risk measurement techniques, and the increasing use of sophisticated risk management practices, such as securitisation, have changed leading organisations' monitoring and management of exposures and activities – this has been the result of Basel I. However, supervisors and sophisticated banking organisations have found that the static rules set out in the 1988 Accord have not kept pace with advances in sound risk management practices. This suggests that the existing capital regulations did not reflect banks' actual business practices. In other words, it was not sufficiently risk sensitive (KPMG, 2007).

The Basel II Accord

In June 2004, the Basel Committee finalised a comprehensive revision to the Basel Accord. In the European Union, the new Capital Adequacy Directive began to apply to all banks from 2007 onwards, with the most advanced methods being viable from 2008. US regulators decided to apply Basel II to a small number of large banks, with other banks subject to a revised version of Basel I.

How does Basel II differ from the 1988 Basel Capital Accord? The Basel II Framework is more reflective of the underlying risks in banking and provides stronger incentives for improved risk management. It builds on the 1988 Accord's basic structure for setting capital requirements and improves the capital framework's sensitivity to the risks that banks actually face. This will be achieved in part by aligning capital requirements more closely to the risk of credit loss and by introducing a new capital charge for exposures to the risk of loss caused by operational failures (EIIB, 2010c).

The Basel Committee, however, broadly maintained the aggregate level of minimum capital requirements, while providing incentives to adopt the more advanced risk-sensitive approaches of the revised framework. Basel II combines these minimum capital requirements with supervisory review and market discipline to encourage improvements in risk management.

Basel II also covers a wide range of risks which were not previously included in the original Accord, such as operational risk, country risk, legal risk, concentration risk, liquidity risk and reputational risk. Basel II marks a shift from transaction-based supervision to risk-based supervision (KPMG, 2007).

The Three Pillars of Basel II

The overarching goal for the Basel II Framework is to promote the adequate capitalisation of banks and to encourage improvements in risk management, thereby strengthening the stability of the financial system. This goal was accomplished through the introduction of 'three pillars' that mutually reinforce each other and that create incentives for banks to enhance the quality of their control processes. The first pillar represents a significant strengthening of the minimum requirements set out in the 1988 Accord, while the second and third pillars represent innovative additions to capital supervision. Figure 4.1 provides an overall structure of the Basel II Framework and the sub-components of each of its main three pillars.

When estimating the minimum capital requirements, there are two types of capital that can be calculated by financial institutions: economic capital and regulatory capital. As opposed to regulatory capital, which is set by regulators, economic capital is the amount of capital estimated by the bank's management to be maintained. Setting a higher limit for economic capital provides some room for leverage

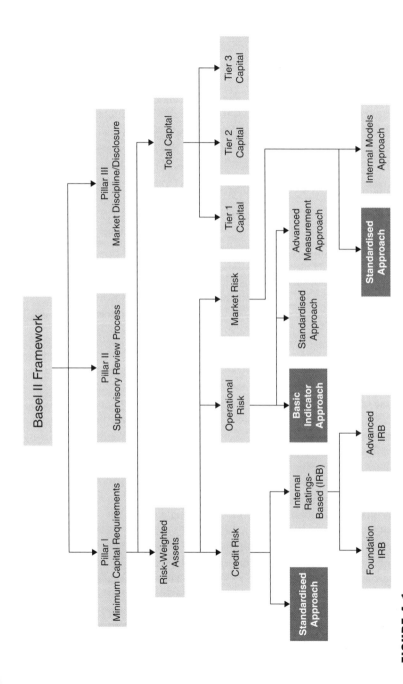

FIGURE 4.1 Structure of the Basel II Accord

Note: The shaded Approaches are the ones most commonly used by Islamic banks

133

for banks. Economic capital is covered by Pillar 2, while regulatory capital is covered by Pillar 1 of the Basel II Accord.

Pillar 1 of the new capital framework revises the 1988 Accord's guidelines by aligning the *minimum capital requirements* more closely to each bank's actual risk of economic loss.

Basel II improves the capital framework's sensitivity to the risk of credit losses generally by requiring higher levels of capital for those borrowers thought to present higher levels of credit risk, and vice versa. The calculation of the minimum capital is presented with the help of the Capital Adequacy Ratio (CAR), which is defined by Equation 4.1:

Equation 4.1 CAR computation according to Basel II Accord

$$\frac{\text{Capital (Tier 1, 2, 3 and deductions)}}{\text{RWA(Credit risk + Market risk + Operational risk charge)}}$$

$$= \text{Bank's capital ratio} \geq 8\%$$

The equation defines the CAR as the ratio of the bank's capital (Tier 1 and Tier 2) to its RWAs, and it should not be lower than 8%. However, the regulators in each jurisdiction are given the discretion to impose a higher percentage if required).

Three options are available to allow banks and supervisors to choose an approach that seems most appropriate for the level of sophistication of a bank's activities and internal controls.

Credit risk capital charge Credit risks are of such great importance to banks from the regulators' perspective that the original 1988 Capital Accord required capital only against credit risks for on and off balance sheet assets. The primary concern of regulators is that banks should be aware of their credit risk and maintain a minimum level of capital to overcome any instability caused by default by a client. Basel II classifies assets into five risk categories (0%, 10%, 20%, 50% and 100%), depending on their rating.

Under the Standardised Approach (SA) to credit risk, banks that engage in less complex forms of lending and credit underwriting and that have simpler control structures may use external measures of credit risk to assess the credit quality of their borrowers for regulatory capital purposes.

Banks that engage in more sophisticated risk-taking and that have developed advanced risk measurement systems may, with the approval of their supervisors, select from one of two Internal Ratings-Based (IRB) approaches to credit risk. Under an IRB approach, banks rely partly on their own measures of a borrower's credit risk to determine their capital requirements, subject to strict data, validation and operational requirements (BCBS, 2006).

Market risk capital charge The BCBS described detailed methods for the calculation of capital charges for (i) foreign exchange risk, (ii) interest rate risk, (iii) equity position risk, (iv) commodities risk, and (v) derivative trading. The capital charge for foreign exchange risk may exclude structured foreign exchange positions. The capital charge for interest rate risk is applied to the current trading book items. The Committee has prescribed two alternative models to measure market risk: the SA and the Internal Model Approach (IMA).

Operational risk capital charge Unlike Basel I, which focused on credit risk, Basel II includes an explicit measure for operational risk. This new capital Accord requires all banks to hold adequate capital against potential operational losses. The new framework establishes an explicit capital charge for a bank's exposures to the risk of losses caused by failures in systems, processes or staff, or to losses that are caused by external events such as natural disasters. Similar to the range of options provided for assessing exposures to credit risk, banks will choose one of three approaches for measuring their exposure to operational risk that they and their supervisors agree reflects the quality and sophistication of their internal controls over this particular risk area. Banks have the option to choose from the Basic Indicator Approach (BIA), the SA or the Advanced Measurement Approach (AMA).

By aligning capital charges more closely to a bank's own measures of its exposures to credit, market and operational risks, the Basel II Framework encourages banks to refine those measures. It also provides explicit incentives in the form of lower capital requirements for banks to adopt more comprehensive and accurate measures of risk, as well as more effective processes for controlling their exposures to risk.

While understanding the risks and the allocation of capital under Pillar 1 is a critical step, the core elements of supervision (Pillar 2) and market discipline (Pillar 3) are equally important. The Basel Committee believes that a well-designed capital requirement standard cannot be made effective in the absence of strong and prudent supervision.

Pillar 2 of the new capital framework recognises the necessity of exercising an effective *supervisory review* of banks' internal assessments of their overall risks to ensure that bank management is exercising sound judgement and has set aside adequate capital for these risks.

Supervisors will evaluate the activities and risk profiles of individual banks to determine whether those organisations should hold higher levels of capital than the minimum requirements in Pillar 1 would specify, and to see whether there is any need for remedial actions.

The Committee expects that, when supervisors engage banks in a dialogue about their internal processes for measuring and managing their risks, they will help to create implicit incentives for organisations to develop sound control structures and to improve those processes.

The Committee cautions that increased capital should not be taken as the only option for addressing risks. It advised the use of other means such as: strengthening risk management, applying internal limits, strengthening the level of provisions and reserves, and improving internal controls. Capital should not be treated as a substitute for adequate control or risk management processes.

Pillar 3 leverages the ability of *market discipline* to motivate prudent management by enhancing the degree of transparency in banks' public reporting. It sets out the public disclosures that banks must make that lend greater insight into the adequacy of their capitalisation. The disclosure requirements are based on the concept of materiality, i.e. banks must include all information where omission or misstatement could change or influence the decisions of information users. The only exception is proprietary or confidential information, the sharing of which could undermine a bank's competitive position.

The Committee believes that, when marketplace participants have a sufficient understanding of a bank's activities and the controls it has in place to manage its exposures, they are better able to distinguish between banking organisations so that they can reward those that manage their risks prudently and penalise those that do not.

Criticism of and Amendments to the Basel II Accord

As previously mentioned, after the Asian and the Eastern European financial crises in the 1990s, there was increasing concern that the Basel I Accord did not provide an effective means to ensure that capital requirements matched a bank's true risk profile. The risk measurement and control aspects of the Basel I Accord needed to be improved, which led to the introduction of the Basel II Accord. Similar concerns are being raised about Basel II after the financial tsunami that engulfed the world from 2008. As a result, voices have been raised criticising Basel II and requesting a new Accord for measuring and controlling capital requirements (British Bankers' Association, 2009).

"Shortcomings in the Basel II Accord will be definitely addressed" stated Engel (2010). This is essential, as the crisis has revealed that, on its own, without a strong liquidity pillar, Basel II is impotent. The Basel regime, which was always meant to be an evolutionary process, will change. The trend – apparent already before the crisis – toward loosening the definition of regulatory capital will be reversed. Definitions of capital will tighten and regulatory capital requirements will increase. Capital must no longer be looked at in isolation. The regulations must recognise the interplay between liquidity and capital and the ability of liquidity problems to become capital problems. In addition to developing a more prescriptive regime for liquidity risk, future capital rules should make excessive leveraging incrementally more expensive and address procyclicality, potentially by requiring banks to maintain larger capital buffers over the cycle (British Bankers' Association, 2009). It is worth mentioning that even before the crisis Basel II was widely criticised for encouraging pro-cyclicality, which dynamic provisioning is designed to offset.

The Basel Committee met in March 2009 to discuss embracing provisioning and higher capital. A statement on the BIS website stated that "This will be achieved by a combination of measures such as introducing standards to promote the build-up of capital buffers that can be drawn down in periods of stress, strengthening the quality of bank capital, improving the risk coverage of the capital framework, and introducing a non-risk supplementary measure." On 13 July 2009, the BCBS announced that proposals for enhancing the Basel II Framework have been finalised. The Committee is strengthening the treatment for certain securitisations in Pillar 1 (minimum capital requirements). It is introducing higher risk weights for resecuritisation exposures to better reflect the risk inherent in these products and is also requiring that banks conduct more rigorous credit analyses of externally rated securitisation exposures.

The supplemental Pillar 2 guidance addresses several notable weaknesses that were revealed in banks' risk management processes during the financial turmoil. The areas addressed include:

 (i) Firm-wide governance and risk management;
 (ii) Capturing the risk of off balance sheet exposures and securitisation activities;
(iii) Managing risk concentrations;
 (iv) Providing incentives for banks to better manage risk and returns over the long term; and
 (v) Sound stress-testing and compensation practices.

The Pillar 3 (market discipline) requirements have been strengthened in several key areas, including:

 (i) Securitisation exposures in the trading book;
 (ii) Sponsorship of off balance sheet vehicles;
(iii) Resecuritisation exposures; and
 (iv) Pipeline and warehousing risks with regard to securitisation exposures.

On 17 December 2009 the BCBS issued two consultative documents, one entitled 'Strengthening the Resilience of the Banking Sector' and the other 'International Framework for Liquidity Risk Measurement, Standards and Monitoring'. These documents contain proposals to strengthen global capital and liquidity regulations with the goal of promoting a more resilient banking sector (BCBS, 2009b). Together with the measures already approved in July 2009, they form the core of the new Basel III Accord. In fact, Basel II is correct in principle but was wrong in implementation. Regulators should focus more on the implementation side.

BASEL II AND ISLAMIC BANKS

Islamic finance has become part of the global financial industry since the early 1990s; it is therefore subject to international standards and regulations. Capital adequacy will hence remain as a core issue for risk management, whether for conventional banks or Islamic banks, as the concept of having sufficient capital cannot be refuted in Islamic finance. Although the risks in Islamic banks are more contract-centric than the conventional product-centric, Basel II standards can still be applied with some adjustments. Thus, application of Basel II is a matter of adoption of the standards to the needs of Islamic banks.

Pillar 1

Unlike depositors of conventional banks, the contractual agreement between Islamic banks and investment account holders (IAHs) is based on the concept of profit and loss sharing (PLS), which makes IAHs a unique class of quasi-liability holders: they are neither depositors nor equity holders. Although they are not part of the bank's capital, they are expected to absorb all losses on the investments made through their funds, unless there is evidence of negligence or misconduct on the part of the bank. This has serious implications for the determination of adequate capital for Islamic banks as highlighted by Grais and Kulathunga (2007:79) in the following points:

(i) PSIAs should not be subject to any capital requirements other than to cover liability for negligence and misconduct by the bank, and to winding-down expenses.

(ii) Investments funded by current accounts carry commercial banking risks and should be subject to adequate risk weights and capital allocation.

(iii) Restricted PSIAs on the liabilities side form a collection of heterogeneous investments funds resembling a fund of funds. Therefore, banks holding such funds should be subject to the same capital requirements as are applicable to fund managers.

(iv) The presence of displaced commercial risk and the practice of income smoothing have indirect implications for Islamic banks' capital adequacy, which a regulator may take into account when determining the CAR.

(v) Islamic banks acting as intermediaries may face a moral hazard issue. Since, as agent, the bank is not liable for losses but shares the profits with the IAHs, it may have an incentive to maximise the investments funded by the account holder and to attract more accounts than it has the capacity to handle. This can lead to investment decisions that are riskier than the IAH is willing to accept. Such 'incentive misalignment' may lead to higher displaced commercial risk, which necessitates higher capital requirements.

Grais and Kulathunga (2007) add that capital as it is classified in conventional banking cannot be used in Islamic banking. To be considered adequately capitalised, banks are required to hold a minimum capital (Tier 1 and Tier 2) equal to 8% of RWAs (in most cases). Tier 1 capital is the same for Islamic and conventional banks. However, in Islamic banks the reserves include the shareholders' portion of the Profit Equalisation Reserves (PERs), which is included in disclosed reserves. In Tier 2 capital, there are no hybrid capital instruments or subordinated debts, as these would bear interest and contravene *Shari'ah* principles. Furthermore, an issue is the treatment of unrestricted PSIAs, which may be viewed as equity investments on a limited term.

In addition, operational risk exposures appear to be higher in Islamic banks. Akkizidis and Khandelwal (2007) argue that the BIA as indicated by Basel II does not appear to be a case of perfect fit for Islamic banks. The 15% provision for operational risk of the average of three years' gross income needs to be examined thoroughly. The use of gross income as the BIA could be misleading in Islamic banks, insofar as the large volume of transactions in commodities and the use of structured finance raise operational exposures that are not captured by gross income. In contrast, the SA, which allows for different business lines, would be more suited, but it would have to be adapted to the needs of Islamic banks as the different risk weights proposed by the SA are not entirely applicable to their needs. In particular, agency services under *mudarabah* and commodity inventory management need to be considered explicitly. The allocation of 18% risk weight for business lines such as corporate finance, trading and sales, and settlements may not represent the true picture of risk exposures of Islamic banks as trading and sales in Islamic finance may include some *murabahah* transactions and some exposure from financing large accounts through *istisna'a*. Also, the SA allocates 12% to retail banking, asset management and retail brokerage, which does not fully apply to Islamic banks. As previously discussed, the risk exposures differ greatly during different stages of the Islamic finance contract and a blanket of 12% does not appear to map the risk exposure completely.

Furthermore, the IRB under credit risk, the IMA under market risk, and the AMA under operational risk are largely not applicable to Islamic banks for several reasons: first, the absence of widespread rating for Islamic finance; second, the changing nature of the relationships during the lifetime of the contract; and third, difficulties in estimating PDs (probability of default), LGDs (loss given default), and EADs (exposure at default) for Islamic finance.

Determination of Risk Weights

Assigning risk weights to different asset classes depends on the contractual relationship between the bank and the borrower. For conventional banks, the majority of assets are debt-based, whereas for IFIs, the assets range from trade financing to equity partnership; this fact changes the nature of risks. In some instruments there are additional risks which are not present in conventional instruments. Therefore, the calculation of risk weights for the assets of IFIs differs from the conventional banks because, according to Iqbal and Mirakhor (2007:126):

(i) Assets based on trade are not truly financial assets and carry risk other than credit and market risks;

(ii) There are non-financial assets such as real estate, commodities, *istisna'a* and *ijara* contracts that have special risk characteristics;

(iii) IFIs carry partnership and PLS assets, which have a higher risk profile; and

(iv) IFIs do not have well-defined risk mitigation and hedging instruments, which raises the overall risk level of assets.

Another complication in risk weightings is explained by Alsayed (2008): as finance provided by Islamic banks is asset-backed, it is connected to the value of tangible assets. These assets are subject to volatility in their values (as distinct from depreciation). Banks are therefore exposed to not only the risk of default by a customer, but also volatility in the amount of credit mitigation available from the asset in the event of the need to realise their value. This means that there are not just RWAs for the book value of the outstanding credit facility, but also so-called 'market risk charges' in respect of the value of the assets collateralising the finance facility, at the start of the life of a facility, sometimes during the life of a facility, and at termination of the facility if the customer returns the assets to the bank and does not take title. The regulatory risk-weighting framework for Islamic banks is therefore more complex than that of conventional banks, and Islamic banks need additional risk management policies and procedures to manage these risks.

Pillar 2

The role of supervisors is more critical due to the evolving nature of the Islamic financial industry. Strong regulatory support in the form of monitoring and assistance is needed for Islamic banks. Some of the recommendations of Pillar 2 can be applied to Islamic banks, such as strengthening risk management systems, applying internal limits, strengthening the level of provisions and reserves, improving internal controls, focusing on concentration risk and business cycle risks, etc. A few of the Pillar 2 recommendations, although very relevant for conventional banks, do not hold ground for Islamic banks (Grais and Kulathunga, 2007). For example, liquidity risk, which is classified as residual risk under Pillar 2, is one of the most important risks in Islamic banks. Liquidity risk management is at the core of risk management in Islamic banking.

Ironically, after the recent financial crisis and the failure of some banks due to liquidity issues, the BCBS declared the need for a special directive to address liquidity. Regulators around the world began to introduce stricter liquidity standards and independent measures to monitor liquidity.

Pillar 3

The absence of comparable information is one of the main issues in Islamic financial reporting. Since Accounting and Auditing Organization for Islamic Financial Institutions (AAOIFI) standards are not mandatory, there have been limited implementations, and the problem of non-comparability remains. Basel II recommendations regarding consistent and comparable information are highly applicable to the Islamic financial industry. Due to the social commitment attached to Islamic finance, there is special need for market disclosure, and therefore transparency is considered to be at the core of Islamic financial contracts, and thus should also be reflected in reporting.

The role of information in risk management in Islamic banking is more critical compared to in conventional banking, as PLS contracts are heavily biased toward availability of information for managing the risks. It is therefore mandatory to report the investment of funds, lines of business, activities and sources of revenue. Due to its nature and ethical foundations, social responsibility is of the utmost importance in Islamic finance. Moreover, direct market discipline is embedded in the risk-sharing principle of Islamic finance because IAHs share in the risk of the IFI and are not offered guarantees; incentives are created for a wider range of stakeholders in the bank to monitor its activities and risk-taking, which reduces the moral hazard problem. Along with this, there is greater emphasis on transparency, and thus Pillar 3 of Basel II has more relevance for the Islamic financial industry (Grais and Kulathunga, 2007).

Several recent studies by the World Bank and the IMF such as Greuning and Iqbal (2008), Hasan and Dridi (2010) and others have highlighted the significance of the appropriate balance of prudential supervision and market discipline in Islamic finance; and the related implications for the industry specifically and wider financial stability in general are also discussed.

BASEL III

The new tougher framework for international banking came into being in September 2010, when the new guidelines for risk management were announced by the BIS. This new set of rules was denominated as Basel III requirements and was accepted two months later in November 2010 during the G20 meeting in Seoul, South Korea. G20 leaders endorsed the Basel III capital and liquidity framework, and committed to fully adopt and implement these standards within the agreed timeframe that is consistent with economic recovery and financial stability – a finely judged balance. The new framework will be translated into national laws and regulations, and will be implemented commencing on 1 January 2013 and fully phased in by 1 January 2019.

As a result of Basel III, the capital ratio requirement has increased; the eligibility of capital has been tightened, thus reducing the amount of capital banks have to meet the required ratio; and the calculation of RWAs has changed leading to an increase for many institutions. Although implementing Basel III has its challenges and may ultimately not be sufficient to help banks globally withstand another financial blow, it is hoped that the new Accord will improve banking confidence and increase competition between banks. To achieve these objectives, the BCBS Basel III proposals are broken down into three main areas, as shown in Figure 4.2, that address:

(i) Capital reform (including quality and quantity of capital, complete risk coverage, leverage ratio and the introduction of capital conservation buffers and a counter-cyclical capital buffer);

(ii) Liquidity reform (short-term and long-term ratios); and

(iii) Other elements relating to general improvements to the stability of the financial system.

The implications of Basel III for capital can be summarised as in Equation 4.2:

Equation 4.2 Implications of Basel III for capital

$$\text{Capital ratio} \uparrow = \frac{\text{Eligible Capital} \downarrow}{\text{Risk-weighted assets} \uparrow}$$

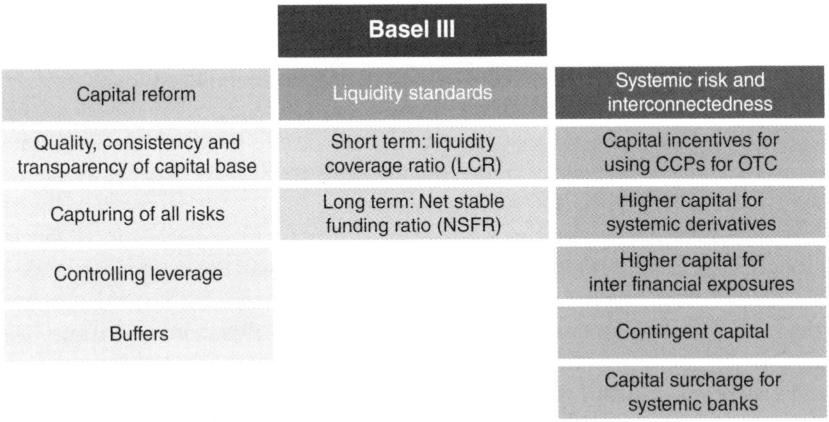

Basel III		
Capital reform	Liquidity standards	Systemic risk and interconnectedness
Quality, consistency and transparency of capital base	Short term: liquidity coverage ratio (LCR)	Capital incentives for using CCPs for OTC
Capturing of all risks	Long term: Net stable funding ratio (NSFR)	Higher capital for systemic derivatives
Controlling leverage		Higher capital for inter financial exposures
Buffers		Contingent capital
		Capital surcharge for systemic banks

FIGURE 4.2   Main components of the Basel III Accord
Source: Authors' analysis based on Basel III Framework from BIS

It should be noted that in general Basel III aims at reducing procyclicality and promoting counter-cyclical buffers through a combination of forward-looking provisioning and capital buffers. While considering Basel III directionally positive, Moody's (2011b) does not expect it to cure the structural challenges banks face from a credit perspective, including illiquidity and high leverage levels, as well as the tension between equity holders and bank managers whose focus is on maximising profits, in contrast to risk-averse bondholders.

IFSB PRINCIPLES ON CAPITAL ADEQUACY

Since Basel II did not answer all the risk management issues for IFIs, there has been a need for alternative and supportive standards, as "Basel II was drafted with conventional banking very much in mind", as observed by Lowe (2010).

With the growing size of IFIs all over the world, there have been efforts to develop prudent supervisory norms. Thinking along the lines of Basel II and recognising the differences in the nature of Islamic banks, AAOIFI drafted a basic standard on capital adequacy of IFIs in 1999. This standard was further enhanced by the IFSB, which in December 2005 released the Guiding Principles of Risk Management for Institutions (Other than Insurance Institutions) Offering Only Islamic Financial Services (IFSB-1). Also in December 2005, the IFSB issued the first Capital Adequacy Standards for Institutions (Other than Insurance Institutions) Offering Only Islamic Financial Services (IFSB-2). This was complemented in March 2008 with the IFSB's Guidance Note in Connection with the Capital Adequacy Standard: Recognition of Ratings by External Credit Assessment Institutions (ECAIs) on *Shari'ah*-Compliant Financial Institutions (GN-1). Finally, in January 2009 the IFSB issued Capital Adequacy Requirements for Sukuk Securitisations and Real Estate Investment (IFSB-7), which deals with aspects relating to regulatory capital requirements for *sukuk* that are not covered in the previous issued standards.

Such intensive documentation is well prepared and addresses the relevant issues that are fundamental for the successful application of Basel II to IFIs. Archer and Karim (2007) highlight that, in spite of their high quality, these standards have been adopted in only a handful of countries. As with most standards, the respective banking regulators need to customise some of their own requirements.

The IFSB Standard on Capital Adequacy (IFSB-2) highlights that Islamic banks carry partnership and PLS assets that have a higher risk profile, and that Islamic banks do not have well-defined instruments for mitigating and hedging risks. In the case of partnership-based contracts such as *mudarabah* and *musharakah*, the bank is exposed to both credit and market risk that need to be analysed in a similar manner to the methodology of the Basel Accords. When such partnership-based assets are acquired in the form of tangible assets, such as commodities, and are held for trading, the only exposure is to market risk because credit risk is minimised by direct ownership of the assets. However, there is significant risk of capital impairment when direct investment takes place in such contracts and the investments will be held until maturity. Treatment of this risk within the Basel Framework is not straightforward and therefore requires special attention.

The key principle underlying the IFSB's approach is that PERs (and PSIAs overall) have a loss-absorbing feature, the intensity of which would not merit inclusion in eligible capital (the numerator of Basel II's capital adequacy ratio), but rather would allow for some deductions from computed RWAs (the denominator of Basel II's capital adequacy ratio), depending on the conservativeness of the regulator in terms of the degree to which PSIAs and PERs would be deemed capital-like instruments. PERs being a future claim of PSIA holders on the bank, they are not part of capital in accounting terms, and thus are not subject to distribution to shareholders. From a regulatory perspective, however, the treatment suggested by the IFSB is very subtle, particularly in Western jurisdictions.

The IFSB-2 Standard covers minimum capital adequacy requirements based predominantly on the SA for credit risk with respect to Pillar 1 of Basel II, and the various applicable measurement methods for market risk set out in the 1996 Market Risk Amendment. The IFSB is aware of the fact that some Islamic banks are progressively improving their risk management practices to the extent that they will be in a position to meet the requirement for applying the Internal Models Approach for measuring their risk exposures.

The IFSB (2005b) states that: "While this Standard stops short of explaining approaches other than the Standardised approach, supervisory authorities are welcome to use other approaches for regulatory capital purposes if they have the ability to address the infrastructure issues adequately. The IFSB will monitor these developments and plans to consult the industry in the future and eventually to make any necessary revisions."

In respect of capital charge for operational risk, the IFSB Standard recommends using either the BIA or the SA given the structure of business lines of Islamic banks at the present stage. The Standard also recommends excluding the share of PSIA holders from gross income in determining capital charge for operational risk. This adjustment is necessary because Islamic banks share these profits with their depositors/investors.

Moreover, the Standard does not address the requirements covered by Pillar 2 (Supervisory Review Process) and Pillar 3 (Market Discipline) of Basel II, as the IFSB intends to cover these two issues in separate standards.

This Standard comprehensively discusses the nature of risks and the appropriate risk weights to be used for different assets. It deals with the minimum capital adequacy requirement for both credit and market risks of seven *Shari'ah*-compliant instruments: (i) *murabahah*, (ii) *salam*, (iii) *istisna'a*, (iv) *ijarah*, (v) *musharakah* and diminishing *musharakah*, (vi) *mudarabah* and (vii) *sukuk*. Discussion of each contract includes risk weights to be assigned to each for market and credit risks.

In calculating the CAR, the regulatory capital as the numerator shall be calculated in relation to the total RWAs as the denominator. The total of RWAs is determined by multiplying the capital requirements for market risk and operational risk by 12.5 (which is the reciprocal of the minimum CAR of 8%) and adding the resulting figures to the sum of RWAs computed for credit risk. The minimum capital adequacy requirements for Islamic banks shall be a CAR of not lower than 8% of its total capital. In this, Tier 2 capital is limited to 100% of Tier 1 capital.

The *Shari'ah* rules and principles, whereby IAHs provide funds to the Islamic bank on the basis of profit-sharing and loss-bearing *mudarabah* contracts instead of debt-based deposits, mean that the IAHs would share in the profits of a successful operation, but could lose all or part of their investments. The liability of the IAHs is limited to the capital provided, and the potential loss of the Islamic bank is restricted to the value or opportunity cost of its work.

In other words, the assets financed by IAHs are excluded from the calculation of the capital ratio, considering that IAHs directly share in the profits and losses

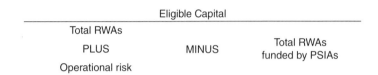

FIGURE 4.3   IFSB standard formula for calculating CAR

of those assets, and the loss to the bank (as *mudarib*) is limited to the time and resources spent on the investments, except in the case of negligence or misconduct.

However, if negligence, mismanagement, fraud or breach of contract conditions can be proven, the Islamic bank will be financially liable for the capital of the IAHs. Therefore, IAHs normally bear the credit and market risks of the investment, while the Islamic bank bears the operational risk.

The IFSB Standard is defined in two formulae: standard and discretionary. In the standard formula, depicted by Figure 4.3, capital is divided by RWAs excluding the assets financed by IAHs, based on the rationale explained earlier. The size of the RWAs is determined for credit risk first then adjusted to accommodate for the market and operational risks. To determine the adjustment, the capital requirements for market risk and operational risk are multiplied by 12.5 (which is the reciprocal of the minimum CAR of 8%).

The second formula, depicted by Figure 4.4, is referred to as the supervisory discretion formula, and is modified to accommodate the existence of reserves maintained by Islamic banks to minimise displaced commercial, withdrawal and systematic risks. In jurisdictions where an Islamic bank has practised the type of income smoothing for IAHs, the supervisory authority has discretion to require the Islamic bank to include a specified percentage of assets financed by PSIA in the denominator of the CAR (represented by α in the Supervisory Discretion Formula). α is simply the percentage of depositors' risk absorbed by the Islamic bank as a percentage of capital required for assets funded by PSIAs. This would apply to RWAs financed by both unrestricted and restricted PSIAs. Further adjustment is made for PER and Investment Risk Reserves (IRRs) in such a manner that a certain fraction of the RWAs funded by the reserves is deducted from the denominator. The rationale given for this adjustment is to allow central banks and supervisors

FIGURE 4.4 IFSB supervisory discretion formula for calculating CAR

to decide on the profit-sharing/loss-bearing risk (displaced commercial risk) that IFIs are exposed to. For instance, the Bahrain Central Bank has ruled α to be 30% for the kingdom (Farook, 2008:19–20). This implies that PSIAs will bear up to 70% of their losses, while the remaining 30% will be borne by the shareholders of the bank.

However, what if an individual IFI is more resistant to shocks in the local economy because it already undertakes pure performance-based PLS with PSIAs, i.e. the IFI has a lower displaced commercial risk? Farook (2008:19) argues that the supervisory discretion formula is applied on a jurisdictional basis, and assumes that all IFIs in that particular jurisdiction fit into the 'one-size-fits-all' category. He adds that most central banks that have applied this regulation did so in such a manner, and there is nothing particularly wrong with this in the absence of a better indicator of individual displaced commercial risk exposure. For example, the Central Bank of Kuwait approved the implementation of the amended capital adequacy ratio on local Islamic banks starting from 30 June 2009, aiming to give Islamic banks incentives to improve their ways of managing risks.

Table 4.2 summarises the main differences in Capital Adequacy Standards between Basel II and IFSB

The following example, depicted by Figure 4.5, demonstrates the difference in calculating CAR between Basel II and IFSB. Let us assume that bank A is an Islamic bank with the following balance sheet structure and that its regulator requires supervisory authority discretion (α) of 25%. The example proves that the risk-sharing characteristic of PSIAs requires special capital treatment. Calculating the bank's capital adequacy requirements according to the IFSB Standard formula

TABLE 4.2   Capital Adequacy Standards: Basel II versus IFSB

Capital Adequacy Standards for Credit Risk		
Criteria	Basel II	IFSB
Risk weight	Calibrated on the basis of external ratings by the Basel Committee	Calibrated on the basis of external ratings by the Basel Committee; varies according to contract stage and financing mode
Treatment of equity in the banking book	>= 150% for venture capital and private equity investments	Simple risk weight method (risk weight 300 or 400%) or supervisory slotting method (risk weight 90–270%)
Credit risk mitigation techniques	Includes financial collateral, credit derivatives, guarantees, netting (on and off balance sheet)	Includes profit-sharing investment accounts (PSIAs), or cash on deposits with Islamic banks, guarantees, financial collateral and pledged assets
Capital Adequacy Standards for Market Risk		
Criteria	Basel II	IFSB
Category	Equity, foreign exchange, interest rate risk in the trading book, commodities	Equity, foreign exchange, interest rate risk in the trading book, commodities, inventories
Measurement	1996 market risk amendments (standardised and internal models)	1996 market risk amendments (standardised measurement method)
Capital Adequacy Standards for Operational Risk		
Criteria	Basel II	IFSB
Gross income	Annual average gross income (previous three years)	Annual average gross income (previous three years), excluding PSIA holders' share of income

Source: Combined analysis based on IFSB (2008b) and BCBS (2006). Reproduced with permission from Islamic Financial Services Board.

lead to a higher CAR than for Basel II, meaning that Islamic banks that invest in partnership and PLS assets will have a better CAR due to the loss-absorbing feature of these asset classes. Figure 4.5 also demonstrates that calculating an Islamic bank's CAR according to the IFSB supervisory discretion formula is more practical, as the supervisory discretion formula is modified to accommodate the existence of reserves maintained by IFIs to minimise displaced

Assets	£ mn	Liabilities & Equity	£ mn
Commodity *murabahah*	£150	Demand deposits	£150
Mudarahah investments	£100	Unrestricted PSIAs	£400
Musharakah investments	£120	Restricted PSIAs	£350
Trade financing	£400	PER	£40
Salam & Istisna'a	£100	IRR	£50
Ijarah	£150	Shareholders' Capital	£30
Total assets	**£1,020**	**Total liab. & equity**	**£1,020**
Total RWAs	£250		
RWAs financed by PSIAs	£150		
RWAs financed by PER and IRR	£15		
Supervisory authority discretion (α)	25%		
Market risk	£4		
Operational risk	£2		
Market and operational risk capital charge	£75		
$(4 \times 12.5 + 2 \times 12.5)$			

FIGURE 4.5   Computation of CAR for an Islamic bank

commercial and withdrawal. When an Islamic bank has practised income smoothing for IAHs, the supervisory authority has discretion to require the Islamic bank to include a specified percentage of assets financed by PSIAs in the denominator of the CAR (represented by α). The IFSB supervisory discretion formula therefore gives a natural incentive to IFIs to engage in providing true economic returns to PSIAs and to stop the smoothing practice.

Equation 4.3 CAR according to Basel II Accord Pillar 1

$$\frac{£30 \text{ mn}}{£250 \text{ mn} + £75 \text{ mn}} = 9.23\%$$

Equation 4.4 CAR according to IFSB Standard Formula

$$\frac{£30 \text{ mn}}{(£250 \text{ mn} + £75 \text{ mn}) - (£150 \text{ mn} + £15 \text{ mn})} = 18.75\%$$

Equation 4.5 CAR according to IFSB Supervisory Discretion Formula

$$\frac{£30 \text{ mn}}{(£250 \text{ mn} + £75 \text{ mn}) - (0.75 \times £150 \text{ mn} - 0.25 \times £15 \text{ mn})} = 13.87\%$$

As Wan Yusuf (2011) states, the capital adequacy framework for Islamic banks in Malaysia was implemented on 1 January 2008 and was developed based on the Capital Adequacy Standard for Institutions (other than Insurance Institutions) Offering Only Islamic Financial Services issued by the IFSB in December 2005. The Malaysia Framework is applicable to all Islamic banks licensed under Section 3 (4) of the Islamic Banking Act 1983. The analysis conducted on 12 Islamic banks shows that all banks follow the Capital Adequacy Framework for Islamic banking in Malaysia. The exception was in 2006, when Bank Islam fell below the requirements due to net loss of RM 1.30 billion. It was attributed to non-performing loans that severely affected the bank. However, the figure was improved to exceed the minimum regulatory requirement after additional capital injection. The analysis showed that banks in the study were over-capitalised. The excess capital could be used to reallocate assets where they could shift to more risky assets such as loans rather than less risky assets such as government bonds. This in turn would increase banks' profitability and thus enhance their efficiency by optimal utilisation of available resources. The study also revealed that domestic Islamic banks in Malaysia hold lower Risk-Weighted Capital Ratio compared to foreign Islamic banks, which can be attributed to familiarity with the local financial environment. It means that foreign Islamic banks are over-capitalised especially in the early years of establishment. The assets that banks hold tend to be under a safer risk category and the bank moves toward riskier assets as it gains a foothold in the industry. Not much difference exists between fully fledged Islamic banks such as Bank Islam Malaysia Berhad and Bank Muamalat Malaysia Berhad, which were established before 2003, and Islamic banks originated from Islamic banking windows, which were established after 2003, with regard to Risk-Weighted Capital Ratio. This could be due to the parent banks' familiarity with the local financial environment and understanding of the Malaysian financial system. Experience and familiarity leads banks to have a wider portfolio of riskier assets in order to fully utilise capital and enhance efficiency.

CAPITAL ADEQUACY AS A TOOL FOR RISK MITIGATION

As discussed in the previous chapter, risk mitigation is a key challenge for Islamic banks. Mimicking conventional risk mitigation techniques is not the best way forward because of the constraints imposed on Islamic banking by *Shari'ah* principles and mainly because the Wall Street conventional banking model has proved to be unstable and unsustainable. Some Islamic hedging tools have been developed; others are still work in progress, opening the door for huge opportunities in financial engineering. However, the risk-sharing characteristic of PSIAs in Islamic banking could greatly enhance risk management and mitigation in IFIs provided that proper pricing, reserving and disclosure are maintained. A measure of the extent to which the risks to shareholders are reduced on account of risk-sharing with IAHs should be the basis of any capital relief or lower risk weights on assets funded by PSIAs. The IFSB supervisory discretion formula is therefore a step in the right direction, with α representing the extent of total risk assumed by the PSIAs, with the remainder absorbed by the shareholders on account of displaced commercial risk. To take the IFSB standards forward, disclosure for IFIs needs to become more comprehensive and transparent, with a focus on disclosure of risk profile, risk-return mix and internal governance. This requires coordination of supervisory disclosure rules and accounting standards. In addition, the regulators should monitor and recognise the actual extent of risk-sharing by IAHs in assessing capital adequacy, and thereby encourage more effective and transparent risk-sharing with IAHs. Adequate disclosure by the IFI of the risks borne by PSIAs and shareholders should be a supervisory requirement for giving a low value to the parameter in the supervisory discretion. Thus, inadequate disclosure would result in a high value being set for α in addition to higher risk weights for profit-sharing assets, and hence granting little or no capital relief to the Islamic bank. In addition, Islamic banks that treat PSIAs as a substitute for conventional deposits should be dealt with by the regulator by treating these IAHs in the same way as liabilities for the purpose of calculating capital adequacy ratio. On the other hand, banks that practically implement the risk-sharing technique will be keen on proper disclosure to enjoy higher capital relief. This would provide the greatest risk mitigation tool for Islamic banks.

CONCLUSION

It should be noted that risks in Islamic banking are more contract-centric than in conventional banking, where risks tend to be more product-centric. Islamic financial contracts are characterised by the changing relationship between the contracting parties during the lifetime of the contract. This has a direct bearing on the risk exposures and relevant capital charges. Soundness and safety for banks depend to a great extent on the capital they hold. Since there is a constant dilemma to find the optimal mix of capital for business and regulatory purposes, the Basel I Accord was the first-ever systematic attempt at a global level to provide a framework for capital adequacy. Due to the rapid changes in the financial world, the original Accord proved to be insufficient to cover increasing complexities in financial markets. Basel II (and potentially Basel III) revolutionised the concept of risk management with the detailed analysis of credit, market and operational risks. The three mutually enforcing Pillars of Basel II have improved the Framework's sensitivity to the risks that banks actually face.

This chapter examined the three Pillars of Basel II and their relevance to Islamic banks. It has become obvious that, although some of the principles of risk management as proposed in Basel II are applicable to the Islamic financial industry, the Accord was developed with the perspective of conventional banks and, hence, does not apply to Islamic banks without suitable modifications.

The IFSB has played a key role in the development of risk management and capital adequacy standards in the Islamic financial industry. The IFSB's efforts should be considered as the first attempt at consolidating the Islamic financial risk management principles under one umbrella. More effort and research is needed in this underresearched area. Moreover, the IFSB standards should be made mandatory for Islamic banks to allow for wider implementation, consistency and standardisation of risk management principles across the IFI. This requires collaboration between regulators, IFSB, AAOIFI, Islamic banks and industry experts.

It should be mentioned that Sam Walton was indeed right, as finding capital is not the biggest challenge. It is the management and control of capital in an optimum way that worries financial institutions and regulators around the world. International standards like those issued by BCBS, AAOIFI and the IFSB act as capital guides that provide industry practitioners with vision for the right direction. It is up to individual banks to make proper use of the compass or lose their way along the hard financial journey.

CHAPTER 5

Islamic Banking and the Financial Crisis

*Clearly, the crisis is dire. The situation is deteriorating, and it demands
urgent and immediate action*
—Barack Obama, on the economic crisis (2009)

There has been great optimism about the resilience of Islamic finance over the
past few years due to the failures witnessed in the conventional financial world;
this is, however, based on prejudice rather than proper analysis. Although this optimism has faded out recently, it still exists to a lesser degree. Immediately following
the outbreak of the credit crisis in the West, advocates of Islamic finance filled
stages and conferences with long emotional speeches on topics like: 'the resilience
of the Islamic financial industry', 'Islamic banking is recession-proof', 'Islamic
finance could have saved the world', etc. In such emotional discourses it is forgotten that modern Islamic financial institutions (IFIs) have been deviating from
the foundational principles and aspirations of Islamic moral economy for some
time now – principles which could, to a certain degree, provide some resilience
against crisis. In theory, the Islamic finance world is definitely more resilient to
economic shocks than the flawed Wall Street model, but unfortunately theory is a
long way from fact in current financial practice, as practitioners of Islamic finance
to date have been mimicking conventional products. This mimicking has resulted
in a close correlation between the two systems.

However, it is evident that Islamic banking has avoided some of the major
causes of the problems in the conventional system, especially in relation to
speculation and trading in derivative instruments that are far removed from
the underlying asset. It is not because IFIs' risk management architecture and
culture were more robust that they avoided carrying toxic products on their
books; structurally, they have simply been banned – so far – from investing
in such asset classes, as per the core principles they abide by. It is true that
most Islamic deals are backed by real assets. There is no doubt that Islamic

banks are more resilient to economic shocks than their conventional peers. This was proven in Malaysia during the 1997 currency crisis and it has been confirmed by the delayed effect of the current financial crisis on Islamic banking and finance (IBF). This has changed the world's perception of this young industry and given it the chance to grow substantially.

It has been argued that if the world had followed the true principles of Islamic finance, the subprime loan crisis and the collapse of some of the world's largest banks could have been avoided. This raises the interesting question of whether Islamic finance can offer solutions to avoid another global financial crisis. Are the risk management characteristics inherent in Islamic finance more resistant to global woes and economic shocks? Since risk management is essential to prevent crisis, raising such questions is imperative in gauging the resilience of a particular financial method. This is the essential research question of this book, which aims to empirically explore whether Islamic banking provides a more resilient model.

The relevant Western literature suggests that, theoretically, Islamic banks are more risky than their conventional counterparts in some respects. Western researchers have been urging Islamic banks to follow the steps of conventional banks in adopting sophisticated risk management and mitigation techniques, which have been the pride of Western financial markets until recently. On the other hand, in most literature by Islamic scholars or economists, Islamic banking is presented as a safe haven and a less risky mode of finance. In such studies, one tends to read about the relative benefits of the Islamic economic system, albeit completely normative statements based on theoretical principles without any substantial empirical evidence. Islamic researchers argue that the lack of evidence is due to the absence of real economy that follows full Islamic principles and where economies do, such as in the case of Iran and Sudan, there have been lapses in governance or modifications in the *Shari'ah* compliance rules that have substantially altered the actual premise of Islamic economics. Hence, researchers were largely unable to empirically detect the impact of following pure Islamic finance principles or to ascertain whether Islamic finance is inherently better than its conventional counterpart. The answer came – paradoxically from the West – in the form of the credit crunch, which has at least shown the shortcomings of the conventional system and has given Islamic finance an opportunity to be marketed as an alternative.

Over the last few years the world economy went into severe recession, starting with the subprime mortgage debt write-downs in the US and the spiralling food and commodity price inflation, followed by quick deflation, all of which have had a crippling effect on world economies. Figure 5.1 shows the bleak economic picture worldwide in September 2009, amid the peak of the crisis. Most world economies were in recession. The cost of debt had increased and therefore access to finance had dried up. So what are the causes of this crisis and where is

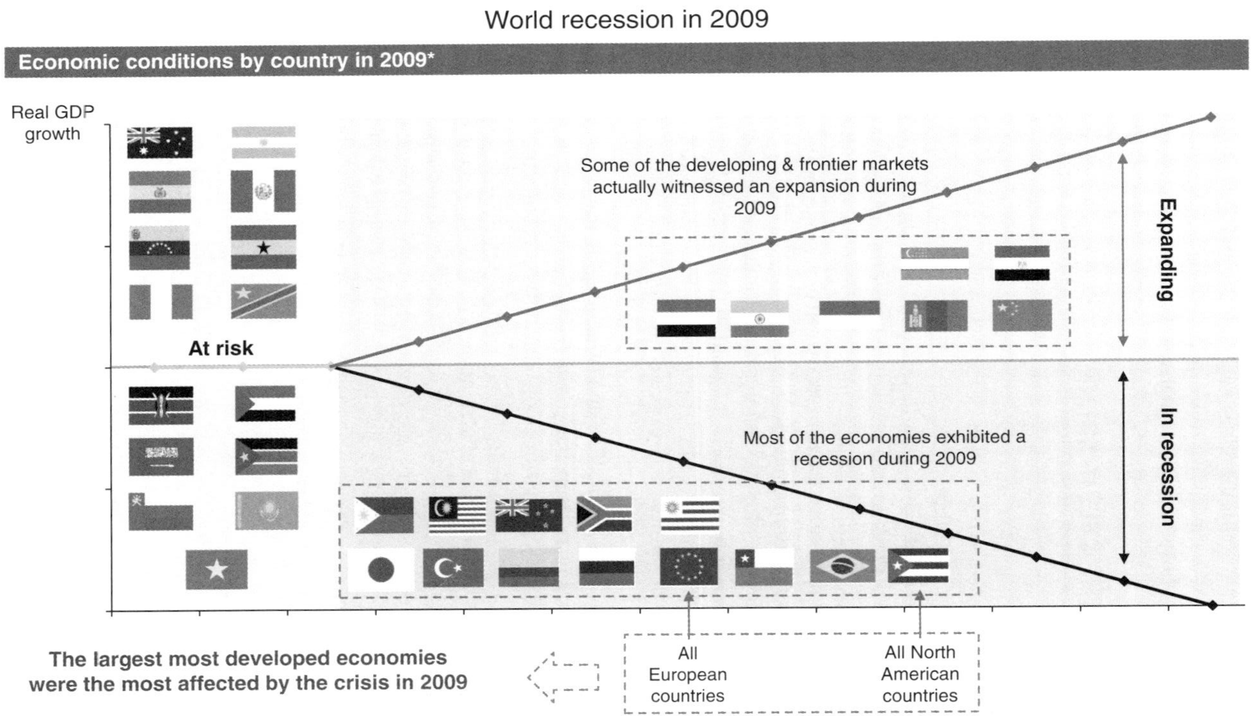

Economic conditions by country in 2009*

World recession in 2009

Real GDP growth

Expanding   In recession

Some of the developing & frontier markets actually witnessed an expansion during 2009

At risk

Most of the economies exhibited a recession during 2009

All European countries

All North American countries

The largest most developed economies were the most affected by the crisis in 2009

FIGURE 5.1   World recession in 2009

*The position of the country's flag within the chart only indicates whether it has witnessed an expansion, recession or was at risk during 2009. Hence, it does not highlight each country's level of real GDP growth.

Source: Authors' analysis based on figures from Moody economy.com Dismal Scientist, status September 2009

the connection to Islamic banking? These are the questions to which this chapter aims to find answers; and building on what has been discussed in the previous chapters, evidence will emerge that Islamic finance has conservative risk management techniques – implicitly bent to it – that could provide a safer alternative.

UNDERSTANDING THE CREDIT CRISIS

The Debt Bubble

The financial crisis started in one corner of the US mortgage market, but the fallout from the collapse of the subprime lending bubble has spread across the globe via the disintermediation of the originate-to-distribute banking model. What began as a crisis for individual markets and institutions has now undermined the foundations of the entire global financial system. Credit markets were the first to be engulfed, but the contagion subsequently reached all asset classes that were reliant on a combination of cheap money and high leverage, bringing the demise of the independent Wall Street investment banking model and sending countries from Iceland to Hungary 'cap-in-hand' to the International Monetary Fund (IMF).

In the period of the run up to the crisis, the US and the global economy displayed robust growth, which was expected to continue. Interest rates were low, liquidity was high and growing, financial innovations were proceeding at a rapid pace (especially in securitisation and structure finance), complacency in the face of growing risk was deepening, and regulation as well as supervision receding and weakening. All of this created an incentive structure that encouraged excessive risk-taking in search of higher yields. By March of 2007, the excesses "came home to roost" (Mirakhor and Krichene, 2009). Easy credit had already created an incentive for home purchases and refinancing of existing mortgages, while prices in the housing market were already increasing, indicating a boom. This provided the primary motivation for the emergence of the subprime market, for, as long as house prices were increasing, the underlying debt obligation would be continuously validated by an increase in value regardless of the size of the down payment, the credit record of the buyer, or the adequacy of documentation.

The liquidity crunch was fundamentally the result of the credit bubble bursting. Too much liquidity and overcapacity in the industry resulted in much lower underwriting standards. Consequently, consumers became overleveraged. With new entrants in both the mortgage lending and bank loan markets, competition led to loan terms that did not compensate for the risks. In this process, the risk management model followed by financial institutions is to be blamed for the crisis, as rising risk and falling returns became a dangerous mix.

It should be mentioned that the economy is always passing through cycles in the long term, or what economists call 'Kondratief cycles', within which there are other small cycles. The current cycle is not new, nor did it occur overnight (Economist Intelligence Unit, 2009). Many commentators recognised the potential consequences long before they became real. Yet the feeling seemed to be that 'as long as the music was playing, lenders had to dance'. Indeed, a financial institution cannot afford to sit out the dance unless it can stomach a significant loss of market share. In a hypercompetitive market, however, banks sometimes have to take the long-term view and refrain from dancing. Some did, as they shunned option adjustable-rate mortgages and high loan-to-value products, and their better performance in the current environment is already beginning to differentiate itself.

Banks around the world have been put under significant pressure; most affected are those that were originally highly leveraged and heavily dependent on wholesale funding. A few years ago, it would have been unthinkable that iconic financial services groups would become so widely distrusted. Regaining this trust is, however, key to worldwide economic recovery. Figure 5.2 depicts how the market value of the world's largest banks had significantly shrunk between mid-2007 and January 2009. Banking giants saw their market value diminishing at an unprecedented pace. For example, Royal Bank of Scotland had its market value shrink from USD 120 billion in mid-2007 to USD 4.6 billion by January 2009; UBS from USD 116 billion to USD 35 billion; HSBC from USD 215 billion to USD 97 billion; and Citigroup from USD 255 billion to USD 19 billion.

Securitisation channels have shut down in the crisis process from 2008 onward, and banks that rely on the originate-to-distribute model have substantially reduced their volumes of new lending, thus leading to a sharp reduction in revenues. Some banks, in recent times, are attempting to shift back to a more traditional on balance sheet banking model. The growth of derivatives during the boom years decoupled from the growth of the real economy. There will now be a reduction in that decoupling effect. As a response, indeed, derivatives will not disappear, but their volumes may shrink and become more aligned with the size of real economies. However, as a result of the crisis, access to short-term funding channels has been severely compromised, and a number of banks became reliant on government support. This opened criticism in the financial industry of substantial malpractice in highly geared investments and questionable risk management practices. More importantly, it has raised questions on the integrity of the sophisticated conventional modern financial system in which regulators are trying desperately to catch up with market innovations, particularly in the space of derivatives, debt markets and speculation.

That period in the markets provoked thoughts on failures in conventional risk management techniques and the need for a better alternative. Therefore, "this crisis has been a wake-up call for reassessing the effectiveness of international financial architecture and in particular for mechanisms to head off systemic risk", stated Reza Moghadam, director of the IMF's strategy, policy and review department (Wroughton, 2009).

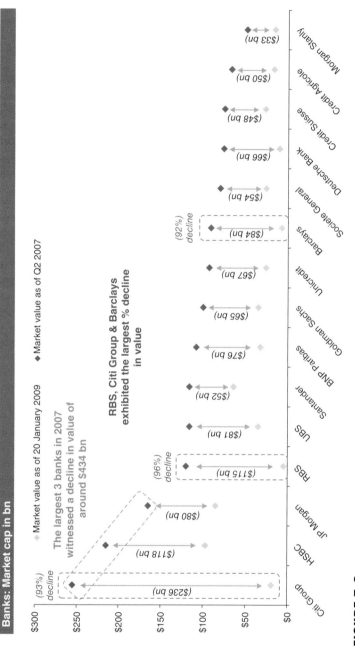

FIGURE 5.2 Decline in market value of leading banks in 2009

Source: Authors' analysis based on figures from Bloomberg, 20 January 2009

It should be noted that the conventional systems have pretty much forgotten about ethics; this is an important cause of the financial crisis. The fragility of the conventional system operating on the basis of speculation, manipulation and interest rates was underlined by the infamous 2001 Nobel Prize-winning economist Joseph Stiglitz (2008) who argued that: "The present financial crisis springs from a catastrophic collapse in confidence. The banks were laying huge bets with each other over loans and assets. Complex transactions were designed to move risk and disguise the sliding value of assets … Financial markets hinge on trust, and that trust has eroded. It was all done in the name of innovation, and any regulatory initiative was fought away with claims that it would suppress that innovation."

In addition, the crisis has highlighted shortcomings in banks' pricing, monitoring and managing of risk. Too much reliance has been placed on quantitative models, based on historical data, to make assessments of current and future risks. The inappropriate use of financially innovative structured products has led to tremendous wealth destruction.

The crisis cannot be explained by the argument that it occurred because of liquidity, which was being there one day and gone the next. When trust and confidence disappeared and investors asked for their money back, it became apparent that real liquidity had not been created in the first place, a situation that should not occur under an aspirational Islamic financial system where there is a partner, rather than a debtor, relationship with depositors.

Derivatives and the Crisis: A Source of the Financial Crisis

Derivatives are financial weapons of mass destruction … I view derivatives as time bombs, both for the parties that deal in them and the economic system.
—Warren Buffet, Berkshire Hathaway Annual Report, 2002

Following the outbreak of the crisis, it became fashionable to malign derivatives for doing much damage to the global economy. Politicians and the media held derivatives responsible for massive corporate losses and the downfall of companies like insurer AIG and Lehman Brothers. Some have gone so far as to suggest that derivatives were the main contributing factor to the credit crisis and to the wider global recession.

Bartram (2009) disagrees with this approach, as he argues that blaming derivatives is like blaming a car for causing a crash, rather than the reckless driver who was behind the wheel. The cause of the global recession in reality is manifold and the reason for many corporate failures is varied too, he adds. However, derivatives are complex securities that transfer one kind of risk but create newer risks which are difficult to assess. They break down the relationships between lender and borrower and encourage risk-taking at the originator level (Ahmed, 2009). One of the interviewees for this research, Engel (2010), argues that derivatives should not be blamed for the mess that happened in the financial sector.

As financial products, derivatives are great risk transfer tools: they help stop systemic collapse in the financial sector. For example, when Enron collapsed, many feared that several top banks would go under because of their huge exposure to Enron. It was derivatives that spread the risk among several banks and saved the system from a total meltdown. While it is true that bankers make derivatives look very complicated, once they are broken down into little boxes and pieces, their structure can be understood with greater ease.

Searching for the Causes of the Crisis

A number of economists have tried to determine the causes of the crisis. Some consider financial liberalisation and deregulation to be the cause in an environment where the financial systems of many countries are not sound as a result of improper regulation and supervision. Others feel that the ultimate cause is the bursting of the speculative bubble in asset prices driven initially by excessive risk-taking and the use of innovative complex structures. It has also been argued that the root cause of the crisis was the maturity mismatch and liquidity mismanagement where long-term assets were far greater than short-term liabilities.

The available literature on the financial crisis thus indicates as many opinions as there are researchers. However, even though all these factors may have had some role to play in the crisis, no consensus seems to have developed so far in pinpointing the ultimate cause or the cause of all causes. In the absence of a proper understanding on the ultimate cause, conflicting remedies have been proposed. Consequently, the proposals for government bailouts, stricter regulations and supervision have been unable to step beyond the basic principles of the conventional banking mechanism.

In pre-crisis times, most conventional banks employed intense financial-leveraging techniques to magnify their gains in expansionary economic times. The use of leverage amplifies returns during a boom cycle, but it can also have a reverse effect during a recessionary phase when managements not only have to write down losses on their declining asset portfolios, but also have to pay interest on their outstanding loans – the exact situation that most conventional banks were faced with.

Banks created complex opaque financial instruments that produced new risks, which were not well understood (Ahmed, 2009). This decomposing of risk through financial engineering and product development made risk management a serious scientific process, as risk management became often dependent on sophisticated mathematical models.

It had become apparent that, during the process of financial crisis, at many banks, multiple lines of defence failed – business managers, risk managers, audit and control. Coupled with these failures was weakness in board risk oversight. The crisis revealed that very few firms have a true 'culture' of risk management that will not be compromised when competition heats up, regulatory pressure abates or management changes.

The weaknesses of the system have to be studied in a comprehensive manner, and as a result of such an approach, the key factors causing the crisis can be identified at three levels: instrumental (the use of innovative complex products), organisational (financial institutions engaged in excessive risk-taking) and regulatory (a deregulated environment and lax regulations) (Ahmed, 2009). However, the industry debate has focused on pure risk management failures, particularly the shortcomings of risk models in measuring risks accurately, without addressing the broader issue of how risk is managed at the highest macroeconomic levels and how the whole financial system is based on greed and lack of morality.

When the financial crisis erupted, most people referred to 'greed' as the source behind the crisis – the ultimate cause; the worship of markets in general and financial markets in particular is considered the source of 'greed'. However, the main causes stem from the creation of (excessive) debt, de-linkage of wealth creation from debt creation, and the making of money (debt) by banks, which may be linked to the 'greed' of those involved in such processes. These factors have led to debts growing faster than wealth, which must eventually be equalised by a crash resulting in business failures, unemployment and ultimately gross inequalities of income and wealth. An economy with a heavy reliance on debt can lead to nothing but high risk and volatility.

After the crisis, the global economy was not expected to rebound quickly, but rather to return to trend growth rates, with persistent unemployment and budget deficits. Figure 5.3 offers a stylised illustration of global macroeconomic and credit conditions over recent years. The financial crisis may be behind us but the sovereign risk challenges, with huge public debts, definitely represent a rocky road ahead. World economies went from low risk aversion during the boom in 2006 to high risk aversion during the peak of the panic in 2009. A decade later, the worldwide economic recovery remains fragile. Trade and currency wars between the US and China, the global recession, the budget deficit in the US and sovereign debt issues in the Eurozone are still sources of high concern to investors. 'Slowbalisation' seems to be the name of the game for years to come across the globe.

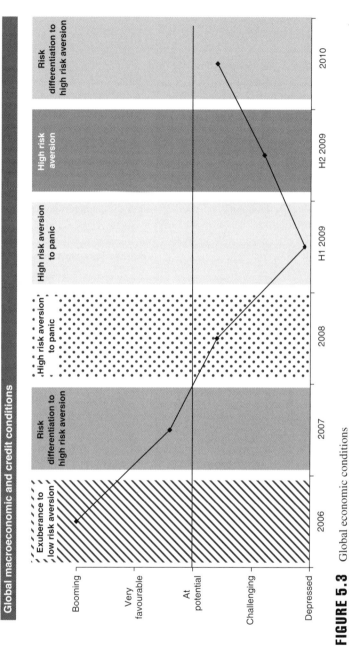

FIGURE 5.3 Global economic conditions

Source: Authors' analysis based on figures from Moody's (2010a)

THE FINANCIAL CRISIS AND THE NEED FOR AN ALTERNATIVE SYSTEM

The crisis highlighted shortcomings in the existing conventional banking system. Unlike in the wake of earlier crises, the world economy and its financial markets will not resume their former pattern. The consequences of the crisis indicate that there will be a fundamental systemic change to the banking industry. In supporting this, a 2009 report by PricewaterhouseCoopers (PWC, 2009) claimed that the nature of the banking system will change. Unsustainable, overleveraged structures will be replaced by simpler and more transparent forms of banking, and some activities may be subject to limitations in a new model that represents a renaissance of classical banking. Thus, it is expected that there should be a new financial culture with a greater focus on 'what you have' in terms of resources, rather than 'what you can' create through financial innovation (PWC, 2009). The developments thus show that regulators and financial institutions must look beyond mere survival mode, accept that the facts have changed, and focus on achieving a sustainable banking model – a model that enjoys trust, is reliable, stable, ethical and transparent. In other words, the rules of the game have to and will change under the new circumstances. This is echoed by Keynes: "When the facts change, I change my mind" (PWC, 2009).

In an attempt to overcome the failures of the conventional financial system, the world has started to look for an alternative method of banking and finance. Calls have been promoting traditional old style banking without the destructive power of derivatives and toxic assets, regulators have been reducing interest rates across the world, hoping to stimulate the stagnant economy, and experts are starting to look for a more ethical mode of finance. Amid all these searches, it so happens that Islamic banking is one of the very few alternatives that are available today, and within the gloom of the global crisis, investors are turning to Islamic finance as the less risky and more ethical option. Islamic finance is gaining credibility as an alternative; the fact that the Wall Street banking model based on open-ended innovation and leverage failed has made people search for ethical alternatives.

THE FINANCIAL CRISIS AND ISLAMIC FINANCE AND BANKING AS AN ALTERNATIVE OPTION

Islamic Finance: No Subprime Exposures But Not Fully Immune

The foundational principles and operational mechanisms of IBF were discussed in Chapter 2, which made reference to the ethical sources of IBF. Despite such foundational ethical claims, on the surface the story of Islamic banking as more resilient than conventional banking, which has been repeated in a world torn by a financial tsunami, is attractive. Unfortunately, at least in the form in which it is currently practised, such expectations of IBF are not entirely true.

Since the main liquidity for Islamic banks comes from the GCC region, it should be mentioned that many Islamic banks, especially in the GCC, have not been immune to the financial crisis. The liquidity squeeze in the region has put pressure on these banks just as much as on their conventional peers.

In examining the propensity of IBF for crisis, it can be seen that Islamic banks mainly carry four main asset classes within their investment portfolios: property, equity, *sukuk* and managed funds (which include underlying assets mainly comprising infrastructure, private equity, real estate and stocks). In the financial crisis process, it is observed that such assets have all lost value (Moody's, 2009a). In addition, the volume of *sukuk* issuance dramatically declined between September 2008 and summer 2009, although it started to take off later in 2009 (Standard & Poor's, 2010a). However, Islamic banks, due to the immaturity of the industry coupled with constraints imposed by the *Shari'ah*, have been relatively protected because they had no exposure to subprime assets and their derivatives, such as dubiously rated collateralised debt obligations (CDOs) and special investment vehicles (SIVs) securitised debt-based assets.

Table 5.1 describes the impact of the financial crisis on Islamic banking.

It can be argued that IFIs around the world have generally displayed strong resilience amid the global financial debacle. One obvious reason for their proven ability to weather the storm is embedded within the core principles of Islamic banking: both speculation and interest are prohibited. In addition, the subprime crisis was driven by a number of factors that in combination led to the accumulation of risks, which were again magnified through the use of complex, often highly structured financial products – all of which were explicitly *riba*-based. However, it may be that the Islamic finance industry was not as badly affected as its conventional counterpart because of its comparative lack of sophistication and *Shari'ah* restrictions rather than anything different in its current activities. It is a fact that re-packaging of debt obligations into several layers without a substantial trace to the underlying asset is difficult to achieve through *Shari'ah* engineering. Islamic securities should be asset-based. Furthermore, a direct link to the asset is the substantial basis of asset-generating returns. Moreover, *Shari'ah* disallows the trading of future obligations until the asset is actually delivered.

Based on the observed progress, it can be argued that IFIs are not risk-immune, but their capacity to resist the crisis was bolstered by the natural conservatism inherent in the principles of Islamic finance, which is based on ethical norms of Islamic moral economy.

TABLE 5.1 The impact of the crisis on Islamic banking

The 2008–2009 economic crisis impacted banks globally, with large markets for Islamic finance no exception
– Global banks suffered USD 700 billion losses in 2008
– GCC economies have also felt the crunch, with little or no growth in 2009
– Equity markets have also seen steep declines in spite of a partial recovery in 2009
– Banks in the GCC have faced challenging times, with scarce liquidity, a rising perception of risk, and the ever-present reality of credit defaults
Since 2008, Islamic banks have not been immune from the crisis
– Islamic banking penetration is up in key markets with Islamic banks outperforming in asset growth
– However, both market values and profitability of Islamic banks have come under pressure, narrowing the gap with conventional peers
■ Revenues have declined significantly from 2008, particularly driven by a drop in income from investing activity
■ A number of Islamic banks have been harder hit by non-performing loans (NPLs) than their conventional peers and continue to face the risk from real estate concentrations even as their operational efficiency continues to lag that of their conventional peers
– Liquidity continues to be a significant constraint for Islamic banks. While Islamic banks maintain their market share of deposits, it will be subject to increased competition in the 'war for deposits'

Source: Based on data from McKinsey & Company (2009)

Islamic Banks Affected by the Financial Crisis: No Man is an Island

Similar to other institutions, Islamic banks do not operate in isolation. They are part of local, regional and increasingly global interdependent financial markets. In this respect, although they are less sensitive to the monetary fluctuations of the West, they remain dependent on the real economic cycle. The Islamic financial market will always need to interact and engage with the conventional one – it does not exist in some isolated bubble; therefore some level of 'contamination' may be difficult to avoid.

The credit crisis highlighted the globalised nature of the world we live in: imagining that a subprime crisis could never happen in Islamic finance would be to encourage complacency. As the financial crisis gradually turned into a real economic downturn, asset quality ultimately deteriorated and Islamic banks' high exposures to the real estate sector turned out to be a curse rather than a blessing. For example, the Gulf countries now contemplate the effects of property and stock market declines coupled with lower economic growth prospects in the short term, and Islamic and conventional institutions alike are feeling the pain of reduced liquidity and credit losses. This is due to the fact that the global financial and economic crisis did not spare the once-booming economies of the Middle East, and the Gulf Arab states in particular. However, in general, the macroeconomic repercussions were milder in the region, where recovering oil prices and large amounts of liquidity in numerous Sovereign Wealth Funds allowed governments to take interventionist counter-cyclical measures to stimulate their domestic economies and support flagship government-owned banks and companies.

As such, Islamic banks have been facing three series of cyclical challenges, which again reflect their current structural strengths and weaknesses (Moody's, 2009c):

(i) Managing short-term liquidity has been made more difficult.
(ii) Investment portfolios, concentrated on illiquid and cyclical asset classes, have been impaired.
(iii) Access to long-term funding has been postponed, forcing banks to reduce the maturity profile of their assets.

With the financial crisis, market disruptions made it difficult for Islamic banks to continue fuelling their aggressive pre-crisis growth as key funding sources dried up. Customer deposits shrank as money that had entered in 2008 left the market leaving governments to prop up deposits single-handedly, and IFIs, particularly in the GCC, started to raise deposit rates to ensure retention. Governments stepped in to ease short-term liquidity positions; however, this did not alleviate the overall long-term position gap. To help manage their liquidity, Islamic banks will have to develop creative funding strategies and improve their internal capabilities to understand and forecast their liquidity needs.

However, despite such constraints, which are expected to be temporary, Islamic banks have had the capacity to resist due to a number of buffers in the following format:

(i) Their credit portfolios have been essentially domestic, with limited pressure on asset quality so far.
(ii) Their entrenchment in the retail banking arena, with high customer loyalty and deposit stability, limits the probability of massive bank runs.
(iii) High capitalisation and ample core liquidity often provide a relatively higher amount of confidence to counterparts.

In the economic downturn, falling asset prices, credit seizures and liquidity crunches created a difficult situation where retail-funded commercial Islamic banks are better placed than their rivals. They enjoy low leverage and abundant liquidity. Islamic investment banks, meanwhile, are wholesale-funded with a concentrated deposit base and are also highly exposed to cyclical and illiquid asset classes such as real estate, private equity and venture capital. Consequently, they have suffered far more, with two of them defaulting: Global Investment House and The Investment Dar, both within the GCC. Another Islamic finance company whose survival has come under pressure for the same reasons is Tamweel, which is merging with its rival Amlak in the United Arab Emirates.

In general, Islamic banking had shown stronger performance than conventional banking. In 2009, amid the peak of the global crisis, more *Shari'ah* banks were launched and more markets opened up to Islamic products. While most conventional banks suffered substantial losses and severe asset reductions, assets in Islamic finance grew to USD 822 billion in 2009, an increase of 29% compared with 2008, with the opening of 20 Islamic banks, according to Maris Strategies and the Banker (Oakley, 2009).

Traditionally, IFIs have not been heavily leveraged. The primary reasons for conservative financial leverage maintenance are:

(i) IFIs have limited incentives to grow debt-like liabilities because their assets tend to be highly profitable;

(ii) They needed to set aside extra capital buffers to prepare for expansion;

(iii) Funding is usually cheap, thanks to easy access to non-remunerated *qardh hasan* current account deposits; and

(iv) The necessity to set aside capital charges for specific risks like displaced commercial risk (DCR), reputational risk and concentration risks as per Basel II's Pillar 2 (Moody's, 2009d).

These capital and liquidity buffers, previously criticised by opponents of Islamic finance as a burden on profitability, have perhaps been one of the most important strengths of the IFIs amid the crisis because they provided a financial institution with surplus cash to use as a shock absorber. As a result, under the difficult economic conditions of the crisis, most IFIs were able to seek out opportunities by using their surplus liquidity to aggressively boost deposit volumes and thus to increase their market shares by growing lending volumes, while maintaining their focus on the retail and corporate sectors. For example, this is a strategy employed by GCC banks to de-couple their retail lending business from global markets by focusing on extending credit locally. According to Thun (2010), one of the interviewees for this research, with few exceptions (especially in Dubai), funding has been less of a constraint for IFIs because of the market's perception that these players will be more resilient than their conventional peers to global credit turmoil. Thus, the market has acknowledged that Islamic banks cannot carry assets such as highly leveraged structured instruments or global investment banks' shares on their balance sheets because these are considered *haram* and therefore are not eligible for investment according to the *Shari'ah* boards' *fatawa*.

In practice, customers are switching their savings from conventional banks (perceived as riskier) to Islamic banks (perceived as less directly exposed to subprime). This activity has been recorded in a number of countries, especially the UAE, Kuwait and Bahrain. The latest figures on these banks show an increase of 34.4% in their Q3 2008 deposit base over the previous year (Moody's, 2009a). This retail entrenchment is a good strategic shift – one suitable for the current environment with wholesale funding restricted and liquidity ratios lower (albeit not severely so).

Moreover, wholesale-funded IFIs were affected by their inability to access the retail deposit segment for funding, as retail deposits are more granular, more stable and cheaper, while wholesale depositors are savvy and constantly arbitrage institutions in need of funding. It is no coincidence that Islamic intermediaries like Global Investment House (GIH) in the field of merchant banking and Amlak and Tamweel in specialised mortgage finance found it extremely difficult to fund their businesses (Alvi, 2009a).

Islamic investment banks that operate largely as private equity firms have been feeling the impact of global market conditions because they have invested in real estate markets and companies outside the Gulf region, through private equity transactions. Falling real estate prices, the credit crunch, and the economic recession in Europe and the US lessened the value of these investments and pushed these Islamic investment banks to either enlist their generally sophisticated clients' support to share any losses or to write down losses to preserve their reputations. Effectively illustrating this is Arcapita Bank, which reported significantly deteriorated liquidity; its 2008 financial performance declined versus historical levels, and between January and June 2009 its credit rating was downgraded by Standard & Poor's from BBB to BB-; this is a four-notch downgrade in less than six months. In June 2009, Arcapita requested to withdraw its rating.

Although GCC countries, home to most IFIs, announced that they stand ready to support their financial systems if needed, providing support to IFIs is more complicated than for conventional banks, because governments are limited to using the same mechanisms as those for conventional institutions. For instance, interest-based repo facilities or traditional deposits are not *Shari'ah*-compliant, which by definition implies limitations on the instruments that governments have to intervene with the liquidity of Islamic banks. The UAE has based its support for IFIs on *wakala*, which has required some time to implement (Standard & Poor's, 2010a).

Failures in Islamic Finance: *Sukuk* Defaults

Defaults in the sukuk *market are a sign of market maturity; however, it comes at severe costs, the most expensive of which is reputational risk.*
—Badlisyah Abdul-Ghani, CEO of CMB Islamic Bank (2009)

Sukuk issuers such as the Kuwait-based Investment Dar Company defaulted on their *sukuk* as part of a general debt restructuring program. Another noticeable example is the Saudi Arabia-based Saad Group, which defaulted on its debt in the recent past, including the Golden Belt *sukuk* that it issued in 2007. This was followed by the Dubai debt bombshell, which put *sukuk* in the spotlight for all the wrong reasons. Nakheel, the property arm of Dubai World, responsible for key developments in the region such as the Jumeira Palm and The World, issued three *sukuk* to finance its investments. Three years after issuing the world's biggest *sukuk*, Dubai's Nakheel grabbed the headlines once again, this time through default. On 25 November 2009, the Government of Dubai announced that it intended to restructure part of the debt (approximately USD 26 billion) of Dubai World, the Emirate's largest state-owned conglomerate. Nakheel asked for trading to be suspended on all three of its listed *sukuk* until it was in a position to provide clarification to investors and the market. On 14 December 2009, Abu Dhabi provided USD 10 billion to help Dubai to meet its obligations, including USD 4.1 billion needed to repay Nakheel, with the rest of the money to be used to pay trade creditors and contractors as well as meeting interest expenses and company's working capital (Oakley, 2009). Indeed, Dubai's woe did hit the reputation of IBF. As a response, Dubai first had announced that it would restructure the debt, then two weeks later it announced that it would repay, possibly on the back of market reaction. Dubai realised that it could not afford the damage of not repaying. But the damage may have already been done.

The market conditions during the 2008/2009 crisis had resulted in other defaults in the Islamic finance sector, such as the Saad Group, Investment Dar and the East Cameron Gas Company. These failures have brought several key risk management issues like enforcement of judgments in the GCC, transparency, corporate governance and asset-based *sukuk* into the limelight.

These episodes reminded investors that default can and does happen in the *sukuk* market, as in any other part of the financial sector. However, *sukuk* default is a new phenomenon, as the market is still in its infancy. This represents an interesting development, and it should help investors to understand what could happen in the case of default and what the legal and financial repercussions could be. According to Professor Habib Ahmed of Durham University (cited in Newby, 2009), "Islamic economists have been saying that Islamic finance was not affected directly by the subprime problems. The Nakheel problem shows that

Islamic finance can have similar problems if wrong investments are made … This case is a wake-up call for Islamic finance to focus more on ethical and moral issues that it has been ignoring for so long."

Recent *sukuk* defaults highlight the issues Sheikh Taqi Usmani battled with, as he rejected the 'opaque' *musharakah/mudarabah* type whereby investors did not really know what 'assets' as *sukuk* holders they were getting but did not care as they relied on the creditworthiness of obligor. *Ijara*, although not perfect, at least gives *sukuk* holders the ability to assess the value of what they are getting for their money (inflated or otherwise). In addition, the rating agencies were concerned only with the credit rating of the obligor (because of the purchase undertaking), whereas a proper *musharakah/mudarabah sukuk* would have forced them to look at the merits of the underlying business – and perhaps to reject them on that basis.

During the financial crisis, the default of a couple of *sukuk* was thus possibly partly responsible for the recent slowdown in issuance. The silver lining was that these defaults should provide the market with useful information on how *sukuk* will behave following default.

According to Standard & Poor's (2010a), despite its relative recovery in 2009, major hurdles remain on the path to *sukuk* market development, including:

(i) Difficult market conditions, which are slowing the planned issuance of numerous *sukuk*;

(ii) Uncertainty about the legal recourse to the underlying asset as demonstrated by the recent defaults;

(iii) The lack of standardisation, notably when it comes to *Shari'ah* interpretation; and

(iv) The low liquidity of the *sukuk* market, which constrains investors trying to exit the market in times of turbulence or access the market looking for distressed sellers.

The need to address those issues in a well-regulated Islamic finance market is even more crucial due to its nascent stage of development. Any failure in the Islamic financial sector now will hurt its reputation and could threaten its survival. "If there is a failure of the bond market in California, nobody will question whether there is a systemic risk to the global bond market. But if a *sukuk* fails, it will raise questions on the entire Islamic finance" said the economist Mirakhor, a former IMF executive director (Oana, 2009).

Islamic Banking Emerging Stronger from the Crisis

It should be considered that lower volumes, shrinking margins and deteriorating asset quality will all weigh on IFIs' profitability and ultimately their capitalisation. However, once again, the impact will be more manageable than for their conventional peers. Fortunately, Islamic banks have been very profitable in the past and have therefore accumulated large amounts of capital, making them capable of absorbing these sorts of shocks. Conventional banks have had greater appetite for exotic asset classes, like bank bonds, hedge funds and direct exposures to global financial institutions and insurers, than have Islamic banks. In that sense, asset-quality deterioration at conventional banks may be more pronounced. In addition, conventional peer banks used to be less well capitalised and less liquid, and hence will find it more difficult to book new business in the current market conditions. To grow today, a bank must have accumulated excess liquidity and capital in the past: most commercial Islamic banks have, some conventional banks have not.

Wilson (2009) points out that Islamic banks have been less adversely affected by the crisis than major international banks. He argues that, as the latter have been weakened by the recent financial crisis, this undoubtedly presents an opportunity for Islamic banks, especially in the GCC, which have been less adversely affected. GCC-based investors in conventional banks, such as Prince Waleed's Kingdom Holdings, which holds 5% of Citibank, and the Abu Dhabi and Qatar Investment Authorities, which hold significant stakes in Barclays, have seen the value of their investments plummet. In contrast, the value of Al Rajhi Bank and KFH investments in retail Islamic banking affiliates in Asia has been much more resilient.

The Islamic financial industry is therefore expected to emerge stronger from the crisis, provided some conditions are met: more innovation bound with the ethical norms of the Islamic moral economy, enhanced transparency, more robust risk management architecture and culture, and, most importantly, less deviation from the core *Shari'ah* principles. These are the lessons to be learnt from the financial crisis, as it has forced Islamic banks to do a complete reassessment of their policies and attitudes not only to whether they are merely Islamising conventional products but also to whether the financing is beneficial to the real economy. In an interview with *Arab News* (2009), Sheikh Esam M. Ishaq stated, "I think in a way the financial crisis is a blessing in disguise for Islamic banking because Islamic banks unfortunately were far down the road in trying to mimic and replicate anything and everything that was there in the conventional banking sector." Hence, the call exists for a return to the foundational basics of Islamic finance to overcome or at least moderate the consequences of potential financial crises.

Paradoxically, the reputation of Islamic banks has benefited from the recent crisis (albeit with some exceptions), reflecting their conservative approach to business, a close proximity to their domestic and regional deposit franchises, their balanced and ordered appetite for growth, and their focus on the basics of banking as opposed to over-innovation, with an emphasis on their domestic market first. All these factors, which used to be perceived as weaknesses before the credit crisis began, are now being used as shields against the potential damage of imported stress. Investors may therefore view IFIs as safer havens less prone to excessive financial shocks. Several Islamic banks therefore are in a position to gain market share at the expense of conventional peers, which have been weakened by toxic subprime assets. Furthermore, a global economic recovery is likely to benefit the GCC as oil and gas prices rebound, resulting in fresh liquidity being pumped into Islamic banks to fuel further expansion (Wilson, 2009).

It is quite clear that the policies implemented and practised by Islamic banks have luckily worked to their advantage so far. From a risk management perspective, however, (and in light of the financial crisis) IFIs are using unstable policies without growing their liquid asset supply and monitoring their risk levels. As the market matures and the crisis deepens, the negative impact of these policies could lead to bankruptcies due to inaccurate liquidity management and defective asset qualities. That said, the chances of an IFI becoming insolvent are low due to the availability of government support – especially in the GCC – and support from other financial institutions.

From a conceptual perspective, Islamic banks will probably be the big winners when the crisis ends, provided that the abovementioned conditions are fulfilled. As a sub-set of ethical finance, Islamic banking is now considered not so much a niche business standing at the margins, but rather as representative of a credible, viable and sustainable alternative business model for sound, ethical and socially responsible banking (Oakley, 2009). Many now believe that mainstream finance has moved too far into excess leverage, meaningless innovation and value-destroying investments. As a rule, Islamic bankers tend to view a monetary, banking and financial system as existing to serve the real economy and not being served by it. In a sense, the Islamic banking model inherently calls for social and economic responsibility from those who create money with credit, encouraging balance, care, honesty and transparency in doing business. What Islamic banking also promotes is that debt is a responsibility and should not be overly traded; that money is a measure of value, not a commodity; and finally that human factors, rather than simply profits, are the cornerstone of any economic and financial system. In that sense, by endogenising such features into its operations, IFIs will undoubtedly find their reputations strengthened, and Islamic finance as a whole will come out stronger from this crisis. At this stage, supervisory authorities and IFIs have a golden opportunity to achieve the true goals of the Islamic moral economy and to create a stable Islamic financial system that can resist economic shocks and that truly operate on the basis of profit and loss sharing (PLS) (Awan, 2008). The credit crunch has shaken confidence in the existing Western regulations and created the need for a better, more transparent system; this has opened the door for Islamic bankers to take up the opportunity. Indeed at the 5th World Islamic Economic Forum (WIFE) in Jakarta on 2 March 2009, Muslim leaders, including Indonesian President Susilo

Bambang Yudhoyono and Malaysian Prime Minister Abdullah Badawi, called on the Muslim world to leverage the global financial crisis by turning "adversity into opportunity" (Parker, 2009).

In short, Islamic banking has suffered from the liquidity drought, to the point where a few of the sector's investment banks have defaulted; but as an industry it now has a track record of resilience, which had not been tested before. It is true that Islamic finance has been more conservative because of *Shari'ah* rules, which has resulted in Islamic financiers steering clear of toxic repackaged credit instruments. By partially following the core principles of *Shari'ah* IFIs were more financially stable than their conventional peers. Therefore, a true *Shari'ah*-compliant financial model can be a panacea if it is followed purely, without deviation.

DEVIATIONS FROM THE FOUNDATIONAL *SHARI'AH* PRINCIPLES: EVALUATING THE OPERATIONS OF ISLAMIC FINANCE

The social failure and the deviation of Islamic finance from its foundational aims have been articulated by a number of studies (Asutay, 2007; Asutay and Zaman, 2009). An important part of this criticism is related to the notion of *Shari'ah* compliance, as the real issue in Islamic banking is the excessive reliance on form in the sense of technical norms at the expense of substance or the foundational norms. A critical examination of the developments and trends in Islamic finance indicates that the convergence has been from Islamic finance to conventional finance in terms of operations and functioning; and that Islamic banking, in its current state, does not necessarily uphold the full spirit of an Islamic moral economy (Asutay, 2007). The financial crisis, being an extremely difficult lesson, should encourage IBF institutions to overcome this apparent divergence and the growing dichotomy between the ideals of an Islamic moral economy and the realities of today's Islamic banking (Asutay, 2009b). Indeed, a number of scholars are of the view that some IFIs have deviated to a great extent from the fundamental basis of Islamic finance. Currently, most Islamic finance is work in progress. Some Islamic banks have succumbed to the influence of conventional banking. Notably controversial examples include the contemporary mechanisms of *tawarruq* or fixed-income instruments, IFIs' reluctance to hold PLS assets, and the issuance of 'asset-based' *sukuk* with no real recourse to the underlying assets.

Tawarruq: A Contentious Islamic Finance Instrument

One major example of the apparent divergence between theory and practice is the excessive use of *murabahah*, which gives a fixed return. This has been dubbed '*murabahah* syndrome', with an ironic feeling about operations of IFIs. This practice, referred to as *tawarruq* in Arabic (meaning 'cash generation'), has been under criticism from many *Shari'ah* scholars, such as Sheikh Muhammad Taqi Usmani, Dr Abdul Latif Al Mahmood and others. It was initially approved as an interim solution until IFIs move to genuine commodity *murabahah*, but it seems that several banks took advantage of this interim approval and prefer to stick to *tawarruq* as it bears minimal commodity risks for the bank and replicates a conventional loan. Figure 5.4 shows that IFIs have a long-standing bias toward simple products that use mostly *murabahah* and *ijarah* structures, both of which offer more predictable returns, and have similar profiles to conventional products. Furthermore, they do not bear the challenges in terms of governance, profit calculation and allocation of more complex structures, like *musharakah* and *mudarabah*, which allow for more advanced financing offerings such as private equity.

Sheikh Muhammad Taqi Usmani, as cited by Ayub (2007:446), states about *tawarruq* and fixed-income instruments: "*Shari'ah* scholars have allowed their use for financing purposes only in those spheres where *musharakah* cannot work and that, too, with certain conditions. This allowance should not be taken as a permanent rule for all sorts of transactions and the entire operations of Islamic banks should not revolve around it."

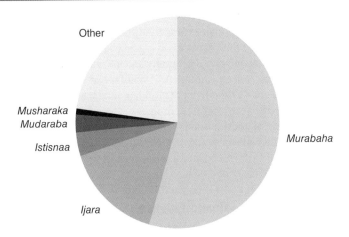

Islamic products distribution

Murabaha and Ijara have the highest share between the Islamic products

FIGURE 5.4 Asset breakdown for a sample of leading Islamic banks (excluding fixed assets and cash
Source: Based on data from Oliver Wyman (2009)

The problem is that for many banks *tawarruq* has become an essential tool for conducting day-to-day business (Davies, 2009).

Practically, however, fixed-income *murabahah* is being used to a very large extent and the use of the PLS mode is negligible, even in institutions in which the honourable Sheikh Usmani used to serve as *Shari'ah* supervisor or member of the *Shari'ah* board.

Lack of Appetite for Risk-Sharing Assets

One of the major criticisms of Islamic banks is their reluctance to hold risk-sharing assets. By design, because of the prohibition of interest and pure debt, and the sharing of risks, Islamic banks should engage in partnerships and equity-sharing financial assets, but in practice the portion of such assets on the balance sheets of Islamic banks is minimal. For example, Table 5.2 shows the asset composition of selected banks from 1999 to 2002. It is evident that Islamic banks' first preference is for financial instruments that are generated through debt creation, sale contracts and leasing instruments. Informal observation of more recent balance sheets shows a similar picture.

Islamic banks' reluctance with regard to risk-sharing instruments such as *musharakah* and *mudarabah* is problematic for achieving the true potential and promise of the system. The reason for shying away from such instruments is a lack of appetite for risky assets, which in turn is due to Islamic banks' attempts to emulate conventional commercial banks where preservation of depositors' principal is their foremost objective. By investing in financing and trade-related instruments, Islamic banks are able to provide low-risk and good fee investment opportunities; they want the best of both worlds. There are also pressures on Islamic banks to make their investment accounts behave like conventional deposits in terms of return profile. These pressures are twofold – namely, from the marketplace and from the banking supervisor in some countries (IFSB, 2007).

TABLE 5.2 Asset composition of selected Islamic banks

	1999	2000	2001	2002
Murabahah and deferred sales	80.1%	83.0%	86.7%	84.3%
Istisna'a	10.8%	8.7%	7.5%	7.0%
Ijara	2.5%	2.4%	1.9%	2.9%
Mudarabah	1.6%	1.6%	1.2%	3.1%
Musharakah	0.9%	0.8%	1.3%	1.2%
Qard ul-hassan	0.2%	0.3%	0.4%	0.5%
Other	0.2%	0.2%	0.5%	3.0%

Source: Askari et al. (2009:95). © John Wiley & Sons, Inc. Reproduced with permission

The real issue in Islamic banking, as mentioned above, is the excessive reliance on form at the expense of substance. By promoting risk-sharing through asset-based equity-type facilities on the assets side and profit-sharing investment accounts on the funding side, Islamic finance could in principle contribute to a better balance between debt and equity, thereby fostering stability. However, in practice, the use of equity-type financing facilities is limited due to risks linked to considerations of asymmetric information and adverse selection (IFSB, 2007).

IFIs should change this business model and expand their portfolio to include risk-sharing instruments. Islamic banks often claim that their reluctance is a direct reflection of depositors' low appetite for risk-sharing products. However, it is possible that depositors' low appetite for such instruments is due to a lack of transparency and confidence in the ability of the financial intermediary. Therefore, Islamic banks should consider doing a better job of selecting and monitoring risk-sharing assets, and enhance the transparency of the investment process by informing depositors through good estimates of exposures to risks taken by the bank on investing in risk-sharing instruments (Askari et al., 2009). The long-term sustainable growth of Islamic banking will depend largely on the development of risk-sharing products.

Sukuk

While there are many *sukuk* structures (14 described by Accounting and Auditing Organization for Islamic Financial Institutions (AAOIFI)), the majority of those applied (be they *ijarah*, *musharakah* or *mudarabah*) effectively 'reduce' to a form that is an Islamic equivalent of a conventional unsecured bond. Much complexity is generated by asset-based aspects of the structure, but the ultimate objective is to replicate the risk-and-return characteristics of a fixed-income bond. Moreover, most originators in these structures do not intend to sell the contributed assets, and the transfer of assets is often not legally perfected or registered (Dey and Holder, 2008). Most *sukuk* transactions are therefore 'asset-based' rather than 'asset-backed'.

This disparity between the 'ideal' and the 'reality' of *sukuk* was highlighted by AAOIFI in February 2008 following a well-publicised criticism of the *mudarabah sukuk* structure by the prominent *Shari'ah* scholar and Chairman of the AAOIFI *Shari'ah* Board, Sheikh Taqi Usmani. AAOIFI then published a statement containing six principles regarding *sukuk* structures. Subsequently, many sources attributed the market decline to this statement. In reality, the decline in *sukuk* market volume in 2008 was probably due more to prevailing global credit market conditions (it was a very difficult time to raise funds, whether conventional or Islamic) rather than to any direct reaction to the AAOIFI statement. In the midst of this global turmoil and the market pause, the AAOIFI comment has provided for some self-reflection in the industry.

While there was some debate regarding the method of its release, the AAOIFI's comments constituted a positive effort toward improving transparency and bringing the 'substance' of *sukuk* products closer to the basic tangible and risk-sharing principles on which there is an almost universal consensus; it is in the implementation of these principles that matters become complex for investors.

To date, many of the current *sukuk* types adhere to AAOIFI in form, but not in substance. The highly successful Indonesian sovereign *sukuk* (USD 650 million) issued in April 2009 shows there is still heavy demand for these unsecured, asset-'based' structures (Moody's, 2009d).

The term 'based' is often used to reference a 'looser' asset security structure that has little or no legal relevance in the event of a corporate default or distress. There is no scope in the courts for such vagaries – either the investors have a legally enforceable claim on assets or they do not. So when crunch time comes, those investors in asset-based structures are left with nothing: no assets, no security, just an unsecured claim in substance like a debt of the company. The majority of investors happily accept these structures. Many investors – Islamic and non-Islamic alike – simply want a fixed-income bond: rough estimates put the market size at USD 45–50 trillion and it is this powerful investor demand that primarily drives the shape of the market (Moody's, 2010b).

HOW TO ACHIEVE THE FULL POTENTIAL OF ISLAMIC FINANCE

Although Islamic banking offers a combination of both equity- and non-equity-based instruments, the system's preference for equity contracts often makes it more efficient and stable than debt-based conventional systems. Sadr and Iqbal (2002) presented empirical evidence based on data gathered over 15 years from the Agricultural Bank of Iran demonstrating that equity-based financing increases transparency, monitoring and supervision, and thus improves efficiency and stability of the financial system.

The operations of IFIs demonstrate that they tend to shy away from equity- and partnership-based instruments for several reasons, such as the inherit riskiness and additional costs of monitoring such investments, low appetite for risk, and lack of transparency in the markets. Consequently, bank portfolios are often not diversified either geographically or by product. This unwillingness to take on risk reflects lack of transparency in the Islamic banking system, which dampens confidence and trust among investors and market participants. The result is that depositors and investors become more risk averse, and so banks become even more risk averse, thus creating a vicious circle which results in a severe financial and economic crisis. In theory, Islamic financial principles contribute to the stability of the financial system. Islamic modes of finance, particularly the profit-sharing principle, provide a loss-absorption feature to financial institutions. The original concept of Islamic financing is undoubtedly in favour of equity participation rather than creation of debt, because it is only equity that brings an equitable and balanced distribution of wealth in society. A debt-ridden economy, on the other hand, tends to concentrate wealth in the hands of the rich and creates a bubble economy which fuels inflation and brings many other social and economic evils (Usmani, 2008). However, the practice is very different from the theory. All of these deviations between theory and practice of Islamic finance mean that the system is not functioning at its full potential and has adapted itself to a limited functionality. In fact, due to these deviations, the Islamic banking system is exposed to risks that it is not supposed to be exposed to. These deviations and other greedy banking practices, hence, have created additional risks both at the institutional and systematic levels. In a 'pure' *Shari'ah* system, finance would be based around equity rather than debt and, although cycles would occur, they would not be on the same scale and crashes could be avoided. Therefore, Islamic banking needs to develop more ideal equity-based Islamic products and shift away from those based on debt. The Holy Prophet (Peace be upon him) declared that "Allah Almighty remains with trade-partners (to help and support them) unless one of them becomes dishonest to the other."[1] Also, in the *Hadith*, debt presents a troubling face once the possibility of deferment arises, as it might with a debtor in difficulty. Such Islamic sentiments, under the conditions of the financial crisis, have also been raised by contemporary researchers and financiers; for example, Davis (2009a) states that "Debt is the weapon used to conquer and enslave societies, and interest is its ammunition."

In addition, IFIs – in theory – should be less exposed to asset–liability mismatch than their conventional counterparts. This comparative advantage is rooted in the 'pass through' nature of Islamic banks, which act as agents for investors/depositors and pass all profits and losses through to them. Following the theoretical model, any negative shock to an Islamic bank is absorbed by both shareholders and investors/depositors. Thus, the chronic problem of asset–liability mismatch in Islamic banks should not exist; this type of financial intermediation contributes to the stability of the financial system. This is theory; the practice is, however, different, as discussed thoroughly in Chapter 3. IFIs tend to sacrifice a share of their profits for the year to subsidise Profit-Sharing Investment Accounts (PSIAs)' appetite for returns. In order to mitigate the displaced commercial risk, these IFIs resort to the practice of smoothing distributions to PSIAs, utilising Internal Rate of Return (IRRs) and Profit Equalisation Eeserves (PERs). This implies that an Islamic bank that practises distribution smoothing may be subject to higher earnings volatility when it does not have a significant build-up of reserves. This renders the Islamic bank riskier than a conventional bank, given that a conventional bank has hedging mechanisms. If IFIs truly provide real economic distributions to their PSIAs, as the *Shari'ah* requires, these banks will be able to avoid systemic risks and be more resistant to economic shocks.

Regrettably, both Islamic banks and their supervisory authorities in some countries consider unrestricted investment accounts to be a product designed to compete with, and to be an acceptable substitute for, conventional deposits; in such an environment profit smoothing may be considered to be an inherent attribute of the product rather than a means of deliberately avoiding transparency and market discipline, especially if it is combined with in-substance capital certainty (Archer and Karim, 2007). In some such countries unrestricted IAHs may benefit from deposit guarantee schemes; the compliance of such practices with *Shari'ah* principles seems open to doubt. Therefore, if unrestricted IAHs are considered to be virtual depositors, the implications of this in terms of capital adequacy need to be enforced by the regulator by treating these IAHs in the same way as liabilities for the purpose of calculating capital adequacy ratio.

Dar and Presley (2000) argue that Islamic banking is all about taking risk. Depositors keep their money in profit-sharing accounts and so, in theory at least, they participate in both the profits and losses of the banks. In practice, however, banks have consistently given depositors returns that are on par with the interest rates that conventional banks deliver. As their profits declined during the crisis, IFIs started dipping into PERs to keep depositors satisfied, which added significant pressure on IFIs during the years of economic downturn. "Devout Muslims have increasingly migrated to Islamic banks in recent years, but will the trend survive if some of them start losing their money?", wonders Dar (Khalaf, 2009). It is arguable that illiquidity cases like Northern Rock in the UK would have never happened under a pure Islamic system because instead of borrowers funding investments, they would be sharing the risks with other investors and they would not be able to 'withdraw' funding as they did with Northern Rock.

However, many argue that PSIAs would not agree to receive volatile distributions, since they mistakenly believe that IFIs should provide distributions similar to conventional banks. Archer and Karim (2007) suggest that this might be because of the inherent nature of bank depositors (whether Islamic or conventional) whose relatively low net worth means that they are naturally risk averse and prefer to earn stable low returns compared with high-net-worth individuals who invest in shares, funds and all sorts of diversified risky investments. But perhaps it may also have to do with market education about Islamic banking as an alternative system. Many people, particularly after the crisis, started to believe in the Islamic finance system and the benefits it offers. AAOIFI and IFSB are working toward educating the market about the best practices of Islamic finance, but it might be difficult to change the mindset of bank depositors, which has been set in stone over decades.

It should also be noted that some IFIs might mistakenly see no incentives in moving in this direction of fully applying *Shari'ah* principles. It is therefore essential that supervisory authorities, at least in Islamic countries, provide regulatory incentives for IFIs that comply with *Shari'ah* rules and punishments for those that do not comply. Making AAOIFI and IFSB standards mandatory for Islamic banks should be a step in the right direction.

As has been discussed in the previous chapter, the IFSB supervisory discretion formula for calculating CAR gives a natural incentive to IFIs to engage in providing true economic returns to PSIAs and to stop the smoothing practice. However, this formula is not obligatory in most countries and is applied on a jurisdictional basis, i.e. if an individual IFI has little or no displaced commercial risk, it still has to abide by the regulatory imposed α factor. One way for regulators and supervisors to resolve this 'one-size-fits-all' issue and indirectly incentivise IFIs to engage in the 'passing through' to PSIAs mechanism is imposing a variable α factor on banks (Farook, 2008). The IFSB already provides this flexibility to each regulator. This would, however, require accounting technology that would calculate an individual bank's exposure to displaced commercial risk, as this is quite achievable. Central banks, for instance, can design a formula to calculate individual displaced commercial risk exposure for each Islamic bank. Based on this exposure, the central bank can impose a variable α factor that will determine the capital that each bank must hold against its RWAs funded by PSIAs. In addition, banks can be given further α factor relief based on the extent of disclosure provided, with more disclosures allowing more haircuts on the extent of RWAs funded by PSIAs included in the denominator of the CAR equation (Farook, 2008). If the measure is variable and banks have the opportunity to reduce their CAR by reducing the PSIAs' displaced commercial risk charge, they will do whatever is in their capacity to diminish it. This may include ensuring a more efficient asset allocation strategy, reducing dependence on fixed rate instruments, and improving disclosure directed toward IAHs, educating them about the nature of their relationship with the bank and the rationale behind the profit share distributed to them, even if it happens to be lower than conventional-based market deposit rates.

This will of course have a positive effect on the broader Islamic financial system, as IFIs will be more resistant to systemic risks because they will actually share the effects of shocks with PSIAs, who will also get to bear the fruit of expansionary cycles.

Even liquidity, which both academics and practitioners identify as one of the highest risks facing Islamic banks, acted in some way as a financial crutch for Islamic banks in recent years. IFIs have traditionally held high levels of cash/liquid assets, ideally to buffer against their high liquidity risk. This excessive liquidity syndrome of IFIs in fact reduced their liquidity risk during the economic downturn when the money market dried up and several banks went under because of liquidity issues.

CONCLUSION

The Chinese use two brush strokes to write the word crisis. One brush stroke stands for danger; the other for opportunity. In a crisis, be aware of the danger, but recognise the opportunity.

—John F. Kennedy

The current bleak economic environment represents a golden opportunity for IBF, as the fundamental weaknesses in the Wall Street banking model have been exposed, requiring substantive change to the whole banking system. If it was not for this crisis, the inherent stability and risk management techniques within Islamic finance would not have gained so much attention.

Although IFIs have been more resilient to the financial turbulence than their conventional peers, the shift in the environment did negatively affect some of them. IFIs are not risk-immune; they face their own liquidity and asset decline challenges but to a limited degree. So far, Islamic banks have been closely mimicking Western products and hence they are being exposed to similar risks. No major collapse has occurred in Islamic finance as a result of the crisis, but Islamic banking has been hit by defaults, for example, the slump in Dubai real estate and debt restructuring. Even if Islamic finance had been prevailing, at its current state, the crisis could have happened but at a less severe level. Islamic finance has not yet provided a more principled mode of finance than the debunked Wall Street model because the embedded ethical foundations have not been explored yet (Asutay, 2009b).

NOTE

1. Abu Dawood, Chapter 27, *Hadith* no. 3383.

CHAPTER 6

Research Framework and Methodology

The literature review and the examination of other studies about risk management in Islamic banking have shaped the research methodologies used in this study. The previous chapters thoroughly reviewed and synthesised the literature relating to, first, the theoretical overview of Islamic banking with specific reference to risk management; second, the difference between conventional and Islamic banking from a risk management perspective; third, the empirical studies regarding risk management in Islamic banking; and, finally, the impact of the recent financial crisis on the future of Islamic banking. This chapter discusses the research methods employed in this research, and also presents the appropriate analytical tools utilised.

The chapter defines the research objectives and questions introduced earlier in Chapter 1; this is followed by the research hypotheses presented in the Research Hypotheses section. The chapter later discusses research design and methodologies, and explores the advantages and disadvantages of each by identifying the research methodology and design for this research. The subsequent sections explain the research design, strategy, methods for primary data collection, and chosen data analysis methods or tools. An explanation of the questionnaire and interview design and the pilot study are also included.

RESEARCH QUESTIONS AND OBJECTIVES

As stated in Chapter 1, the aim of this study is to explore and evaluate the risk profile of Islamic banks. At the heart of this research is the question of whether Islamic banks are more or less risky than their conventional peers as perceived by the participants. A review of the existing literature does not provide a clear-cut answer to this question, which is expected to be explored by primary data. In other words, this is clearly an empirical question, the answer to which requires feedback from the market place. This study, however, is not merely another addition to the available literature. It distinguishes itself by extracting empirical evidence from the perceptions of banking professionals and from the recent crisis.

Given the complexity of the topic, there are several questions that this research sets out to answer:

(i) What is the difference between risk management for conventional and Islamic financial institutions (IFIs)?

(ii) What are the additional risks faced by Islamic banks?

(iii) How do the Islamic banks perceive their own risks?

(iv) How advanced are the current risk management practices used by IFIs?

(v) How do regulators expect to respond to the new risks inherent in Islamic banks?

(vi) Was Basel II drafted with conventional banking model in mind?

(vii) What does Basel III carry for Islamic banking?

(viii) What are the appropriate capital requirement levels for Islamic banks?

(ix) What possible *Shari'ah*-compatible risk management instruments are available at the present and for the future?

(x) Can conventional risk mitigation techniques be adopted by Islamic banks or does Islamic banking need to engineer its own?

(xi) Is Islamic banking actually more resilient than conventional banking?

(xii) What effects did the recent crisis have on Islamic banking?

(xiii) Are Islamic banks recession proof?

(xiv) Will the Islamic banking principles offer a role model for the future?

(xv) Could the crisis have occurred under an Islamic banking system?

(xvi) Can Islamic banking survive without proper hedging tools?

(xvii) Is hedging *Shari'ah*-compliant?

(xviii) What are the main divergences between the current practice and the moral principles of Islamic banking?

(xix) What is the next chapter for risk management in Islamic banking?

Following a structured approach, answers for each of these questions are explored through collecting primary data.

After the research questions were identified, an attempt was made to operationalise them within the context of the broader objectives. Thus, the operationalised objectives are:

(i) To ascertain the fundamental principles underlying risk management in Islamic banking and the unique risks facing IFIs;

(ii) To investigate the effect of different control variables like region, country, respondent's position, nature of FI, nature of operations and accounting standards on the participants' perception on nature of risks, risk measurement and risk management and mitigation approaches of IFIs in comparison to those of conventional banks and with reference to the market conditions in which IFIs operate;

(iii) To evaluate the applicability of IFSB Standards and Guidelines with respect to risk management and capital adequacy, and how could they operate in a Basel II (and potentially Basel III) era;

(iv) To investigate the real roots of the recent crisis with a view to drawing some lessons for IFIs;

(v) To examine the dichotomy between the theory and practice of Islamic banking; and

(vi) To explore the next chapter for risk management in Islamic banking.

In answering the research questions, the impact of various categories of respondents and their profile indicators on risk perception are also investigated.

RESEARCH HYPOTHESES

Having reviewed the related literature, identified research issues and formulated research objectives and questions, what follows is the formulation of the research hypotheses.

A research hypothesis is the statement created by a researcher when they speculate upon the outcome of a piece of research or experiment. It is a tentative generalisation, the validity of which remains to be tested. It is often a statement of the expected relationship between two or more variables. The hypothesis requires more work by the researcher in order to either confirm or disprove it (Creswell and Clark, 2007). Research hypotheses determine the parameters of the research questions; therefore the methods used in testing the hypotheses should be relevant to the research questions and objectives (Robson, 2011).

For this study, research hypotheses were developed based on the main findings of prior research literature as well as by referring to the researcher's wide practical experience in Islamic banking and also the unique characteristics of IFIs as compared to conventional banks. The hypotheses are related to the opinions of several groups of respondents about risk management in Islamic banking.

As discussed in the section 'Research Design', in order to follow a structured approach that facilitated data collection and analysis, the questionnaire and interview format was utilised; this is divided into 10 main parts. Research questions and hypotheses are categorised in relation to the topical aspect of each part in the questionnaire and interviews. The findings from questionnaire and interview data analysis are tested against those hypotheses and, as a result, conclusions will be drawn accordingly. In addition, the researcher further formulated sub-hypotheses in order to further investigate the impact of various categories of respondents on risk perception.

The research hypotheses and sub-hypotheses are listed and categorised as follows:

Section A – Risk perception and risks in Islamic banking

Hypothesis 1: The main risks facing Islamic banks are reputational risk, *Shari'ah*-non-compliance risk, asset–liability management risk, liquidity risk and concentration risk.

H_{1-1}: *There is no statistically significant difference among the respondents in relation to their perception of the various risks facing IFIs according to region.*

H_{1-2}: *There is no statistically significant difference among the respondents in relation to their perception of the various risks facing IFIs according to the country in which they operate.*

H_{1-3}: *There is no statistically significant difference among the respondents in relation to their perception of the various risks facing IFIs according to the respondent's position.*

H_{1-4}: *There is no statistically significant difference among the respondents in relation to their perception of the various risks facing IFIs according to accounting standards.*

H_{1-5}: *There is no statistically significant difference among the respondents in relation to their perception of the various risks facing IFIs according to the nature of the financial institution.*

Section B – Islamic finance contracts

Hypothesis 2: Islamic bankers prefer mark-up based contracts (*murabahah*, *wakalah*, *salam*, *istisna'a* and *ijarah*) and shy away from profit-sharing contracts (*musharakah* and *mudarabah*).

H_{2-1}: *There are no statistically significant differences among the respondents' use of Islamic finance contracts according to region.*

H_{2-2}: *There are no statistically significant differences among the respondents' use of Islamic finance contracts according to the respondent's position.*

H_{2-3}: *There are no statistically significant differences among the respondents' use of Islamic finance contracts according to the nature of the financial institution.*

H_{2-4}: *There are no statistically significant differences among the respondents' use of Islamic finance contracts according to the nature of activities.*

Hypothesis 3: Profit-sharing contracts are perceived as more risky than mark-up based contracts in the Islamic finance industry.

H_{3-1}: *There are no statistically significant differences among the respondents' risk perceptions about Islamic finance contracts according to region.*

H_{3-2}: *There are no statistically significant differences among the respondents' risk perceptions about Islamic finance contracts according to the respondent's position.*

H_{3-3}: *There are no statistically significant differences among the respondents' risk perceptions about Islamic finance contracts according to the nature of the financial institution.*

H_{3-4}: *There are no statistically significant differences among the respondents' risk perceptions about Islamic finance contracts according to accounting standards.*

H_{3-5}: *There are no statistically significant differences among the respondents' risk perceptions about Islamic finance contracts according to the nature of activities.*

Section C – Additional risk issues facing IFIs

Hypothesis 4: There is no substantial difference between risk management in Islamic banking and conventional banking.

H_{4-1}: *There are no statistically significant differences among respondents' perceptions about additional risk management issues in Islamic banking according to the nature of the financial institution.*

H_{4-2}: *There are no statistically significant differences among respondents' perceptions about additional risk management issues in Islamic banking according to region.*

H_{4-3}: *There are no statistically significant differences among respondents' perceptions about additional risk management issues in Islamic banking according to the respondent's position.*

H_{4-4}: *There are no statistically significant differences among respondents' perceptions about additional risk management issues in Islamic banking according to the nature of activities.*

H_{4-5}: *There are no statistically significant differences among respondents' perceptions about additional risk management issues in Islamic banking according to accounting standards.*

Section D – Capital adequacy for Islamic banks

Hypothesis 5: It is generally known that capital requirement levels should be lower in IFIs than in conventional banks.

Hypothesis 6: Basel II was drafted with conventional banking very much in mind. IFIs should follow their own standards, e.g. IFSB Principles on capital adequacy.

H_{6-1}: There are no statistically significant differences among the respondents' views about capital adequacy for Islamic banks according to region.

H_{6-2}: There are no statistically significant differences among the respondents' views about capital adequacy for Islamic banks according to the nature of the financial institution.

H_{6-3}: There are no statistically significant differences among the respondents' views about capital adequacy for Islamic banks according to the nature of activities.

Section E – Islamic banking and the global credit crisis

Hypothesis 7: Islamic banking is more resilient to economic shocks than conventional banking but not recession proof.

H_{7-1}: There are no statistically significant differences among the respondents' perceptions about the credit crisis and Islamic banking according to region.

H_{7-2}: There are no statistically significant differences among the respondents' perceptions about the credit crisis and Islamic banking according to the nature of the financial institution.

H_{7-3}: There are no statistically significant differences among the respondents' perceptions about the credit crisis and Islamic banking according to the nature of activities.

H_{7-4}: There are no statistically significant differences among the respondents' perceptions about the credit crisis and Islamic banking according to accounting standards.

H_{7-5}: There are no statistically significant differences among the respondents' perceptions about the credit crisis and Islamic banking according to the respondent's position.

Section F – Risk management and reporting

Hypothesis 8: Not many Islamic banks use the more technically advanced risk measurement and reporting techniques.

H_{8-1}: *There are no statistically significant differences among respondents in the frequency of producing risk management reports according to region.*

Section G – Risk measurement

Hypothesis 9: The use of risk measurement techniques is less advanced among Islamic banks than their conventional peers.

H_{9-1}: *There are no statistically significant differences among respondents in the use of risk measurement techniques according to region.*

H_{9-2}: *There are no statistically significant differences among respondents in the use of risk measurement techniques according to the respondent's position.*

H_{9-3}: *There are no statistically significant differences among respondents in the use of risk measurement techniques according to the nature of the FI.*

H_{9-4}: *There are no statistically significant differences among respondents in the use of risk measurement techniques according to the nature of activities.*

H_{9-5}: *There are no statistically significant differences among respondents in the use of risk measurement techniques according to accounting standards.*

Section H – Risk mitigation

Hypothesis 10: Islamic banks use a number of risk mitigation tools that are intended to be *Shari'ah*-compliant and that are less advanced than those utilised by conventional banks.

H_{10-1}: *There are no statistically significant differences among respondents in the use of risk mitigation techniques according to region.*

H_{10-2}: *There are no statistically significant differences among respondents in the use of risk mitigation techniques according to the respondent's position.*

H_{10-3}: *There are no statistically significant differences among respondents in the use of risk mitigation techniques according to the nature of the financial institution.*

H_{10-4}: *There are no statistically significant differences among respondents in the use of risk mitigation techniques according to the nature of activities.*

H_{10-5}: *There are no statistically significant differences among respondents in the use of risk mitigation techniques according to accounting standards.*

Section I – Islamic banking in practice

Hypothesis 11: Most IFIs abandoned conservative risk management *Shari'ah* principles in favour of copying conventional structures.

H_{11-1}: *There are no statistically significant differences among respondents' perceptions about the current practices in Islamic banking according to the nature of the financial institution.*

H_{11-2}: *There are no statistically significant differences among respondents' perceptions about the current practices in Islamic banking according to region.*

H_{11-3}: *There are no statistically significant differences among respondents' perceptions about the current practices in Islamic banking according to the respondent's position.*

Section J – The next chapter in Islamic banking

Hypothesis 12: Islamic banking has a great potential to become a strong alternative financing system provided that it goes back to its roots.

H_{12-1}: *There are no statistically significant differences among respondents' recommended growth strategies for Islamic banks according to region.*

H_{12-2}: *There are no statistically significant differences among respondents' recommended growth strategies for Islamic banks according to the respondent's position.*

H_{12-3}: *There are no statistically significant differences among respondents' recommended growth strategies for Islamic banks according to the nature of the financial institution.*

H_{12-4}: *There are no statistically significant differences among respondents' recommended growth strategies for Islamic banks according to the nature of activities.*

H_{12-5}: *There are no statistically significant differences among respondents' recommended growth strategies for Islamic banks according to accounting standards.*

General Hypothesis: Hypothesis 13 is a general hypothesis that is not linked to a specific part of the questionnaire, which aims to develop a conclusion from the main narrative and analysis of the entire research. This hypothesis expects significant differences between the perceptions of Islamic and conventional bankers, with the former being biased in favour of the Islamic banking model and the latter being biased toward their banking model.

Hypothesis 13: Perceptions of Islamic and conventional bankers differ significantly in relation to risk and risk management issues in Islamic banking and finance (IBF), as Islamic bankers are more biased toward their business model, and vice versa.

RESEARCH METHODOLOGY

Research methodology is the approach a researcher follows in carrying out a research project. Bryman (2008) defines methodology as "the practices and techniques used to gather, processes, manipulate and interpret information that can then be used to test ideas and theories about social life". Thus, research methodology provides a framework for the methods used in collecting, analysing and reporting data.

According to the literature, there are two types of research methodologies: qualitative and quantitative. Quantitative methodology is designed to reach conclusions based on numerical data, for example, by means of testing the strengths of the relationship between dependent and independent variables (Creswell, 1994). It involves the collection of data so the information can be quantified and subjected to statistical treatment in order to support or refute alternative knowledge claims. The main motive in quantitative methodology is to explain and examine a subject matter by correlating various variables.

Qualitative research methodology, on the other hand, places an emphasis on words instead of quantification when a researcher collects and analyses data (Bryman, 2008). Therefore, qualitative methodology is a set of research techniques used to interpret a phenomenon. It should be noted that when the motivation for a research is exploratory and evaluatory, it is constructed as a qualitative research methodology (Cresswell and Clark, 2007).

This research is designed as a qualitative research study, as it aims to explore the opinions and also to evaluate the risk perceptions of respondents to develop a better understanding of risk practices in Islamic finance industry.

RESEARCH DESIGN

Research design is a framework for a certain set of criteria that would generate suitable evidence for the researcher in the desired area of investigation. It therefore provides structure for the collection and analysis of data (Bryman, 2008).

The objective of research design is to guide the research process from beginning to end by providing the framework within which all the necessary work will be completed. Social research should be constructed with a particular design in mind before a researcher starts collecting and analysing data.

Creswell and Clark (2007) and Bryman (2008) regard a successful research design to comprise of the following tasks:

(i) Define the research problem;
(ii) Determine the problem-solving information that is needed and when it is needed;
(iii) Design the exploratory, descriptive or casual phases of the research;
(iv) Specify the measurement and scaling procedures;
(v) Construct and pre-test a questionnaire or an appropriate form for data collection;
(vi) Specify the sampling process and sample size;
(vii) Develop a plan of data analysis and tabulation;
(viii) Specify the time and financial constraints; and
(ix) Follow up on the completed research study.

Research design, by considering the abovementioned tasks, can be classified in numerous ways depending on the objective of the categorisation criteria. The most common classification is according to the particular approach taken – exploratory research, descriptive research and explanatory research, which are explored as follows:

Exploratory research is conducted to provide insights into and comprehension of the problem situation confronting the researcher. It helps the researcher solve an issue that has not been studied extensively previously. As the general nature of a research problem and the relevant variables are investigated, exploratory research is typically inevitable when the data that are sought are loosely defined, resulting in an unstructured working format. This does not mean that the research is non-systemic but rather of a qualitative nature providing room for interpretative explanations (Creswell and Clark, 2007).

Descriptive research's main intention is to describe something pertaining to characteristics, functions or any phenomena. It is conducted to describe what exists. Thus, it is a type of research where the researchers use past events to explain existing observable facts. Descriptive research is characterised by the prior formulation of explicit hypotheses, thereby stressing the importance of clearly defined research problems. This leads to a research design that is more structured, consisting of numerous planning and statistical methodologies (Bryman, 2008).

Explanatory research, on the other hand, recognises cause-and-effect relationships between variables in the problem model, which is characterised by a structured design and a considerable amount of planning. This design sees how various independent variables are manipulated in order to check how a dependent variable is affected within a relatively controlled environment. There are, however, disadvantages of explanatory research. Some of the most common issues include it being expensive, and having administrative problems (Creswell and Clark, 2007).

When one considers the relationship between the three previously discussed types of research design, choosing a research approach is not an easy decision. The best way is to rationalise the chosen design(s) by examining the situation at hand. The selected design should be relevant to the problem being studied and the procedure of conducting the research should be economically feasible and realistically attainable. Thus, the nature of the study and the resources available to the researcher will greatly influence the research design.

The framework of the present study contains characteristics of both exploratory and descriptive research designs. This study benefits from the use of both the survey technique and semi-structured interviews to search the particularities of risk management in Islamic banking. This enables the researcher to explore the subject matter through the perceptions of banking professionals (explorative). The descriptive nature of the research stems from the fact that it benefits from the available body of knowledge and literature as discussed in the literature review section. Therefore, the chosen research design in this research is mixed research design. This study does not warrant the use of explanatory research, as it does not examine any direct cause–effect relationships.

RESEARCH STRATEGY

Another important aspect of a piece of research is the research strategy. Research strategy is the approach to the study, and is related to how the connection between theory and empirical data can be made. It is a fact that "social research attempts to connect theory with empirical data – the evidence we observe from the social world. In other words, the relationship between research and theory", and how it is done is explained by the research strategy (Asutay, 2011). In social research, there are two main research strategies: deductive and inductive reasoning methods.

Deductive theory represents the most common view of the nature of the relationship between theory and social research. The researcher, on the basis of what is known in a particular domain and of theoretical considerations in relation to that domain, deduces a hypothesis that must then be subject to empirical scrutiny (Bryman, 2008). The researcher begins with a theory about the topic to be researched, which is then narrowed down to a more specific hypothesis that needs to be tested. This ultimately leads to the researcher being able to test the hypothesis with specific data to reach a conclusion confirming or rejecting the hypothesis (Creswell, 1994).

The inductive approach on the other hand moves from specific observations or findings to a broader generalisation and theory. In other words, the researcher begins with specific observations or arguments, formulates tentative hypotheses to be explored, and finally develops a general theory (Blaikie, 2007).

Since this research is oriented toward an explorative approach, it commences with exploring the field, and with the data collected from the field; it generates particular hypotheses to be tested with the data collected from the field. In other words, since this study begins with the specific and then moves to the general, it therefore follows a deductive strategy.

RESEARCH METHOD

Research method includes the techniques, tools and procedures, by which the data is collected, analysed and interpreted for the research project (Bryman, 2008). Creswell (1994:64) defines research method as "the practices and techniques used to gather, processes, manipulate and interpret information that can then be used to test ideas and theories about social life".

According to the literature there are two types of research methods: qualitative and quantitative. The quantitative method is designed to reach conclusions based on numerical data, while qualitative research method places an emphasis on words instead of quantification. Therefore, the qualitative method is a set of research techniques used to interpret a phenomenon. Quantitative analysis depends heavily on statistical significance, while qualitative analysis mainly uses simple human judgement in interpreting and organising the collected data (Oppenheim, 2001).

Quantitative measurement is perceived as more accurate, valid, reliable and objective than qualitative measurement, due to the former's scientific nature. However, this does not mean that qualitative research is less valuable. Instead of focusing on numbers, qualitative research focuses on observations and words, stories, visual depictions, interpretations and other expressive descriptions. Qualitative approaches have the advantage of allowing for more diversity in responses as well as the capacity to adapt to new developments or issues during the research process itself. While qualitative research can be expensive and time-consuming to conduct, many fields of research employ qualitative techniques that have been specifically developed to provide more succinct, cost-efficient and timely results.

Generally speaking, a research method that combines two or more research methods provides better interpretation as the information missed by one method might be captured by the other and thus an enhanced and integrated result may emerge from the analysis. According to Creswell and Clark (2007:13), mix methods research "provides more comprehensive evidence for studying a research problem than either qualitative or quantitative research alone. Researchers are given permission to use all of the tools of data collection available rather than being restricted to the types of data collection typically associated with qualitative research or quantitative research. Mixed methods research helps answer questions that cannot be answered by qualitative or quantitative approaches alone."

This research hence triangulation- or mixed method-based, as it benefits from quantitative and qualitative research methods. While the quantitative research method is in the form of a self-administered questionnaire, the qualitative research method in this study is based on semi-structured interviews. Both the survey questionnaire and the semi-structured interviews are developed from the same perspective and are expected to achieve the same objective of finding relevant responses to the research questions. It should be noted that research related to the literature review being descriptive research further contributes to the triangulation nature of the research.

Research Method: Data Collection

As mentioned above, two main data collection methods are utilised in this study, namely questionnaire and interviews. The following sections explore the details of both methods of data collection.

The survey questionnaire A questionnaire is a research instrument which consists of a series of questions and other prompts for the purpose of gathering information from respondents. It is very popular, since many different types of primary data can be collected including attitudinal, motivational, behavioural and perceptive aspects of the subject being studied (De Vaus, 2002).

In designing the questionnaire, it is important that the questions address the aims of the study. The questionnaire is considered to be effective if it suits the research objectives and questions. A good questionnaire has to be clear and unambiguous, and encourage respondent participation (Creswell, 1994).

If properly designed and implemented, surveys can be an efficient and accurate means of determining information about a given population. Results can be provided relatively quickly and, depending on the sample size and methodology chosen, they are relatively inexpensive. Survey questionnaires have many advantages over other methods of data collection (De Vaus, 2002).

Some advantages of questionnaires can be listed as follows:

 (i) The responses are gathered in a standardised way, so questionnaires are more objective, certainly more so than interviews;
 (ii) It can be completed at the convenience of the respondents;
(iii) Generally it is relatively quick to collect information using a questionnaire;
(iv) Low cost of data collection and processing;
 (v) As the questionnaire can be anonymous, it gives the respondents freedom and encouragement to answer questions honestly, especially sensitive questions; and
(vi) It can cover a large sample of respondents at the same time.

On the other hand, the questionnaire method has some disadvantages which have to be taken into consideration. Oppenheim (2001) highlights the following problems:

 (i) Some respondents may not be willing to answer the questions;
 (ii) Respondents may answer superficially especially if the questionnaire takes a long time to complete. The common mistake of asking too many questions should be avoided;
(iii) The validity of the responses may be compromised by a biased view of the respondent;
(iv) No opportunity to correct misunderstandings or to probe, or to offer explanations or help;
 (v) Questionnaires are standardised so it is not possible to explain any points in the questions that participants might misinterpret; and
(vi) Respondents' inability to answer a question might affect the response rate and reliability.

Despite the disadvantages of the questionnaires, they are rather useful and efficient in aiming to collect data related to the perceptions and opinions of individuals on a particular subject. This study utilised a questionnaire survey in collecting primary data from bankers and financiers in the form of their opinions and perceptions in mapping out the risks and aspects of risk management in IBF. Thus, a questionnaire survey is considered one of the main methods of primary data collection for this study.

Open-ended versus closed questions   In terms of questionnaire design, the questions included may be divided into those which are 'open-ended' and those which are 'closed'. In open-ended or free-response questions, respondents are free to reply to the questions in any way they wish and the answers have to be recorded in full. In 'closed' questions, respondents are offered a choice of alterative replies and they must reply in one of a predetermined number of ways, such as 'yes', 'no' or 'don't know' (De Vaus, 2002). The advantages of using closed-ended questionnaires are that this technique is easier and quicker for the respondents to answer; they require no writing. In addition, closed-ended questionnaires are easier to code and statistically analyse as quantification is straightforward. Disadvantages of closed questions are loss of spontaneity and expressiveness, and perhaps the introduction of bias by 'forcing' respondents to choose between given alternatives or by making them focus on alternatives that might have not occurred to them (Oppenheim, 2001). On the other hand, open-ended questions have many advantages, stemming from the fact that respondents are encouraged to structure the answer as they wish. This provides a means for obtaining information which cannot be obtained adequately by the use of a closed question (Creswell, 1994). Another advantage of the open-ended question is the information which the respondents indicate with respect to their level of knowledge or degree of expertise. The disadvantage of open-ended questions is that they produce a mass of different words meaning the same thing, or a number of similar words meaning different things. It can therefore be stated that open-ended questions are easy to ask, difficult to answer, and more difficult to analyse. Oppenheim (2001) explains that these free-response questions require drawing up some system of categories known as coding. The design of such coding framework and the actual coding operation require trained staff and are extremely time-consuming; for this reason researchers have to curb their desire to have too many open-ended questions (Oppenheim, 2001).

Level and characteristics of measurements   The level of scales measurement of a variable in statistics is a classification that is used to describe the nature of data contained within numbers assigned to objects and therefore within the variable. According to De Vaus (2002), there are three main levels of measurement scales. These are:

(i) Nominal scale, in which a distinction between categories of a variable can be made, but one cannot rank the categories in any order. The nominal scale is used to measure qualitative variables and yields frequency data that may be subjected to non-parametric statistical tests, such as gender.

(ii) Ordinal scale, in which it is meaningful to rank the answers by categories, but it is not possible to quantify precisely how much difference there is between categories (such as more than, less than, equal to).

(iii) Interval/ratio scale, in which ranking of categories can be made and it is also possible to quantify the differences between the categories precisely. Likert scales are very commonly used with interval procedures.

Sampling in the questionnaire   A sample is a small selected portion of the whole population. According to Bryman (2008:85), "a sample is the segment of population that is selected to be investigated". The size of the sample must be sufficient in order to represent the population which the study is intended to investigate. The sample size depends on the homogeneity of the population. If the pilot study indicates that there is a considerable heterogeneity of the population, then it is important to choose a larger sample. As Robson (2011:164) contends, if the population is heterogeneous and the main interest of the study is to generalise the findings to the population from which the sample was drawn, then a larger sample is needed. In addition, a larger sample size will decrease the probability of sampling error.

According to Bryman (2008), sample sizes smaller than 500 cases and larger than 30 cases tend to be suitable for most studies. As far as the survey sample in this study is concerned, there were obviously some real cost and time constraints which limited the sample size. The target population is the wider group of banking professionals worldwide, both Islamic and conventional banking practitioners, whose perceptions about risk management in Islamic banking could shape the outcome of this study. The significant diversity and dispersion of the population meant the time and cost constraints would be unusually high due to the inherent extra complications associated with such a target population. Caught between these challenges and the strong desire to make the sample size as large as possible, the researcher completed 77 questionnaires out of which five were not fit for purpose. The sample size for this study, upon which both descriptive and inferential statistical analysis will be performed, is therefore 72 questionnaires.

There are different sampling strategies such as simple random sampling, systematic sampling, stratified sampling, cluster sampling, panel sampling and others, each with their own advantages and disadvantages.

According to Robson (2011), a variety of sampling methods can be employed, individually or in combination. Factors commonly influencing the choice between these designs include:

  (i) Nature and quality of the research;
  (ii) Availability of auxiliary information about units on the research;
  (iii) Accuracy requirements, and the need to measure accuracy;
  (iv) Whether detailed analysis of the sample is expected; and
  (v) Cost/operational concerns.

It should be noted that the snowball sampling method is used for this research, which is a sampling method used to obtain research and knowledge from extended associations through previous acquaintances; it uses recommendations to find people with the specific range of skills that has been determined as being useful. It is referred to metaphorically as snowball sampling because as more relationships are built through mutual association, more connections can be made through those new relationships and a plethora of information can be shared and collected, much like a snowball that rolls and increases in size as it collects more snow. Snowball sampling is a useful tool for building networks and increasing the number of participants. However, the success of this technique depends greatly on the initial contacts and connections made (Babbie, 2010).

Snowball sampling has a number of advantages over other sampling methods. It is possible for the surveyors to include people in the survey that they would not have known. It is also useful for locating respondents of a specific population if they are difficult to locate. The advantage of this is that the researcher can quickly find respondents who are experts in their fields. This leads to having the most well-known experts for the sampling group, and also can help the researcher find lead users more simply (Babbie, 2010). The method is, however, heavily reliant on the skill of the researcher in conducting the actual sampling, and that individual's ability to vertically network and find an appropriate sample. To be successful requires previous contacts within the target areas, and the ability to keep the information flow going throughout the target group. Identifying the appropriate person to conduct the sampling, as well as locating the correct targets is a time-consuming process which renders benefits that only slightly outweighing the costs. Another disadvantage of snowball sampling is the lack of definite knowledge as to whether or not the sample is an accurate reading of the target population. By targeting only a few select people, it is not always indicative of the actual trends within the result group (Babbie, 2010).

The experience in conducting this research indicates that due to the nature of the research as well as the subject matter, the snowball sampling strategy proved to be a very successful strategy.

Operationalising the questionnaire

(i) Questionnaire design and structure The questionnaire was primarily developed by the researcher drawing on conclusions from the literature review, which included articles, books, PhD theses and exploratory surveys on the topic of risk management in Islamic banking. In particular, the survey by Khan and Ahmed (2001) was useful in developing the questions. In addition, the researcher's extensive practical experience in Islamic banking played a role in designing the questionnaire.

The nine-page questionnaire (reproduced in Appendix 1) was drawn up with 22 main questions, most having a number of sub-statements.

The survey was mainly dominated by closed questions in a manner that ensured that respondents could answer all the questions as easily as possible, with a box-ticking response. However, at the end of the questionnaire, an open-ended question option was provided for the respondents to raise any issue which they might have in mind in relation to the subject of the questionnaire. The type of questions used in the questionnaire varies according to the type of information required to test the research hypotheses. The questions are mostly multiple choice in order to cover all the relevant data.

The questionnaire was split into five main parts:

Part One, General and Background Information, covers the control variables of the survey by acquiring background data of the respondents and their organisations. The aim of obtaining data for this section is to use it as control variables to investigate whether these variables had any effect on the respondents' answers in the other sections.

The second part, Risk Perception, is used to elicit opinions of respondents on different risk management issues in Islamic banking. This part is subdivided into three main sections: Section 1 covers the inherent risks, risk measurement and severity of risks facing Islamic banks, in addition to seeking the respondents' perception of different Islamic banking contracts; Section 2 deals with capital adequacy for Islamic banks; while Section 3 is intended to gather the respondents' views on the impact of the recent credit crisis on Islamic banking. Part Two consists of 10 questions. The five-point Likert scale is used, providing options for each question, so the respondents are able to express their preference in terms of how strongly they agree or disagree with statements. In Question 7 the five-point Likert scale is used to express the degree of importance (ranking from Very Unimportant = 1 to Very Important = 5). However, the respondents are given space at the end of the question to provide additional comments.

In the third part, Risk Management and Mitigation, respondents are requested to provide feedback on the use of risk management and mitigation techniques at their organisations, if applicable. This part consists of four closed-ended questions through which respondents have to express their views on risk management and mitigation techniques employed by the banks. Replies from the respondents were obtained by asking each one to answer questions using a five-point Likert scale for Question 17, while respondents had to choose from listed options for Questions 18, 19 and 20.

Part Four, Islamic Banking in Practice, investigates whether there is a dichotomy between the practice and ideals of Islamic banking. It consists of one closed-ended question, Question 21, which is subdivided into four statements. Replies from the respondents were obtained by asking each one to answer questions using a five-point Likert scale (ranking from Strongly Disagree = 1 to Strongly Agree = 5).

Finally, *Part Five, The Next Chapter in Islamic Banking*, explores different growth strategies for IFIs. Respondents were asked to rank the importance of each strategy according to their perception. While Q22 is a closed-ended question, respondents are given space at the end of the question to provide additional comments.

(ii) Administration and sampling The list of institutions and respondents to approach was taken from the contact list at the European Islamic Investment Bank Plc (EIIB). Between February 2010 and November 2010, questionnaires were sent to 110 Islamic banker professionals in 19 countries.

In the process of conducting the questionnaire, a cover letter for each questionnaire was provided to explain the purpose of the research, as well as to highlight the importance of the individual's response. The letter aimed at assuring respondents that the information provided is confidential, anonymous and would be used only for the purpose of the research.

The sample included Islamic and conventional bankers, auditors, lawyers, rating analysts, *Shari'ah* scholars, consultants and brokers from various countries and regions.

The final return date for the questionnaire was 30 November 2010. Questionnaires were distributed via email, fax, post and in person. Fifty-eight questionnaires were initially returned – an initial response rate of 52.7%. Follow-up reminders increased the total to 77 returned questionnaires from 18 countries. However, out of the 77 surveys returned, five were not useable because the researcher felt that the answers were inconsistent or that that the respondents were biased in their replies, which could influence the validity and reliability of the findings.

The final sample comprised 72 surveys from 18 countries – a final response rate of 65.5%. The sample represented a diverse geographic spread of institutions, and respondents were spread across different departments and held different positions within their organisations. The sample size and distribution is within acceptable limits.

Table 6.1 provides a breakdown of the response rate; however, detailed analysis of the sample according to respondents' roles, countries and regions, and nature of institution is provided in Chapter 7.

Pilot study A pilot study is a small-scale preliminary study conducted before the main research in order to check the feasibility or to improve the design of the

TABLE 6.1 Questionnaire response rate

Distributed	Received	Not Valid	Valid	Response Rate
110	77	5	72	65.5%

research. The questionnaire must be evaluated rigorously before final administration (De Vaus, 2002). A pilot test is important as it highlights any shortcomings before the document is fully launched. The objective is to check the overall presentation, clarity and reasonableness in terms of the length of the questions and the depth of the information sought (Bryman, 2008). Also, piloting is important to check the uniformity of interpretation of each respondent, and whether respondents are answering the questions correctly (Dillman, 2000).

The drafted questionnaires for this study were first pilot tested on a group of 10 bankers working in London. The respondents were asked the following questions:

(i) Is the questionnaire too long?
(ii) Were the instructions clear?
(iii) Were any of the statements ambiguous?
(iv) Did they find any of the questions sensitive?
(v) Whether they had any comments and suggestions.

The feedback of this piloting provided the following observations:

(i) Q7: Some respondents did not understand what is meant by Displaced Commercial Risk.
(ii) Q7: There was some ambiguity concerning which risks fall under market risk.
(iii) Q11: Some sub-statements are unclear.

This feedback was then incorporated into the questionnaire and a further random sample of seven bankers was selected for second piloting. This time the results from the pilot test resulted in no noticeable difference to the original questionnaire. This produced the final version used for this research.

Interviews An interview is a qualitative research technique that allows face-to-face interaction. It involves asking questions and receiving answers from respondents in an identified research area. As compared to questionnaires, it can lead to increased insight into respondents' thoughts, feelings and behaviour rather than simple answers.

Robson (2011) classifies interviews into structured, semi-structured and unstructured interviews. The different types can, to some extent, be linked to the depth of response sought. Oppenheim (2001) classifies interviews into essentially two kinds:

(i) Exploratory interviews, depth interviews or free-style interviews; and
(ii) Standardised interviews such as used, for example, in public opinion polls, market research and government surveys.

Oppenheim (2001) provides some advantages of interviews compared to questionnaires:

  (i) Improved response rate;
 (ii) Interviews can give a prepared explanation of the purpose of the study more convincingly than a cover letter;
(iii) Flexibility, as questions that are inappropriate to a particular interviewee can be omitted or additional ones included;
 (iv) Gives the interviewer the opportunity to probe further into a subject to extract more details from the interviewee;
  (v) In interviews it is easier to keep the attention of the respondent; and
 (vi) Enhancing data validity: due to human interaction, interview results have less chance of being biased and unreliable.

However, interviews have some common disadvantages. Creswell and Clark (2007) argue that the disadvantages of using interviews are to some extent a reflection of their advantages. Obviously, interviews are much more expensive than questionnaires. The larger or the more dispersed the sample, the greater the cost. Travel costs and call-backs add to this. The cost factor also enters the data processing stage: since interviews are used particularly where many open-ended questions have to be asked, there will be a major and costly coding operation allied to the use of interviews. Analysis of interview data may be challenging as the data collected usually contains non-standard responses. Moreover, interviews tend to be time-consuming, as they require lots of preparation and coordination with the interviewees.

Operationalising interviews This study collected qualitative data by conducting exploratory semi-structured interviews because exploratory interview is essentially heuristic, which helps to develop ideas and research hypotheses rather than to gather facts and statistics (Oppenheim, 2001). In addition, Bryman (2008) describes the in-depth interview as an engaged conversation between two people. In the interview, the researcher puts themselves in the participant's situation to try to understand that person's point of view (De Vaus, 2002). The researcher needs to listen and pay constant attention to the participants as they are responding, repeatedly attempting to understand the meaning of what is being said and how the person has shaped their perspective. In this way, interviewing is more than 'collecting data'. Furthermore, interviewing allows the researcher and the participant to connect in a profound way, reducing the distance between them (Creswell and Clark, 2007). This type of interview is often unstructured and therefore permits the interviewer to encourage a respondent to talk at length about the topic of interest in a flexible approach (Robson, 2011).

(i) Interview structure The interview script was developed within the context of the original research questions and hypotheses. The script helps to guide the interview sessions. The interview is divided into six main parts corresponding to the six research parts introduced under the structured approach in the Interview Analysis section. This facilitated data collection and analysis. The interview script covers the same topics as the questionnaire, as the main purpose of the semi-structured interview is to prove or disprove the conclusions derived from the questionnaire data analysis.

(ii) Administration of the interview and sampling The snowball sampling method, as discussed before, was used for the interview sampling to obtain perceptions and knowledge from an extended network of respondents, through previous acquaintances. The researcher utilised his network of initial contacts and connections to find participants with valuable experience and knowledge in Islamic banking and risk management. From June 2010 to January 2011, in-depth semi-structured interviews were completed with 37 Islamic banking professionals. The interviewees included a mix of senior banking executives and heads of business units who work at either Islamic banks or conventional banks with Islamic activities/windows, researchers, academics, *Shari'ah* scholars, consultants and specialised analysts at rating agencies. Five of the respondents in the interview were also included in the sample for questionnaires.

Out of the 37 interviews conducted, four interviews were discarded because the researcher felt that the interviewees were biased in their replies or were not well informed about the issues discussed. Therefore, the final sample included only 33 respondents (five of whom were included in the questionnaire sample) who were knowledgeable about the topic and contemporary developments, and whose replies could be taken, with a high level of confidence, as bias-free.

Out of the 33 interviews that comprise the final sample, 21 interviews were conducted face-to-face, either in London or in the participants' cities. The researcher utilised his numerous business trips to arrange for these face-to-face interviews. Seven interviews were conducted via teleconference, and five interviews were conducted via video conference facilities. Both the teleconferences and the video conferences were dialled from the researcher's primary location in London. The final sample was diverse both geographically and by participants' roles.

Interviews were conducted to gather primary data for this research to support the primary data generated through quantitative method, namely the questionnaire. It should be noted that the preparation for the interview was carefully planned and professionally conducted. When possible, these interviews were audio recorded with the permission of the interviewee. When recording was not possible because of the spontaneous arrangement of the interview, notes were taken in shorthand by the interviewer. Even when an interview was being recorded, shorthand notes were also kept.

However, the interview sample was not as big as the questionnaire sample for a number of reasons:

  (i) In-depth interviews take much more time than structured questionnaires;
 (ii) Interviews require one-on-one interaction;
(iii) Travelling to meet interviewees was difficult due to time and cost constraints;
 (iv) Despite exploiting video conference and teleconference facilities to conduct some interviews, several potential interviewees did not have the time or the wish to participate; and
  (v) Some potential interviewees were located in remote time zones (like America and Southeast Asia), which added to the difficultly of arranging suitable interview times.

Despite these difficulties, the sample size and distribution are within acceptable limits and therefore allow for reliable data.

Table 6.2 combines the geographic distribution with the position of interviewees. It is obvious that interviewees represent a wide range of expertise and roles.

Validity and reliability of the data Validity refers to whether the questionnaire or interviews measure what they intend to measure, which is crucial,

TABLE 6.2 Breakdown of interview sample

Position	Country									
	Bahrain	Egypt	France	Kuwait	Malaysia	Qatar	Syria	UAE	UK	Total
Consultant		3%		3%				3%	6%	15%
Conventional Banker		3%				3%			6%	12%
Islamic Banker	6%	6%			3%				9%	24%
Lawyer		3%						3%	3%	9%
Rating Agency Analyst			3%					3%	15%	21%
Researcher	3%	3%							3%	9%
Shari'ah Scholar	3%						3%	3%		9%
Total	12%	18%	3%	3%	3%	3%	3%	12%	42%	100%

regardless of the method used to collect such data, as invalidity makes the results worthless. Validity depends largely on how honest and accurate the responses given by the respondents are, which is a difficult factor to measure.

Reliability refers to the consistency of the questions. This means that if the research were to be carried out by other independent researchers employing the same methodology and strategy, they would arrive at a similar conclusion, all other things being equal (Creswell, 1994). If a method of collecting evidence is reliable it means that anybody using this method, or the same person using it at another time, would come up with the same results. According to Oppenheim (2001), the key components of data reliability include consistency, precision and explicability of results, which suggests that the researcher should be consistent when collecting the data and should aim for a high degree of precision and accuracy, which of course will be subject to many factors outside the control of the researcher. However, the researcher should try to minimise bias in the data collection process.

In this study, the validity and reliability of the data were proved acceptable for a number of reasons:

(i) The use of multiple methods of data collection;

(ii) The use of a cover letter explaining the purpose of the research and assuring the confidentiality of responses;

(iii) The questionnaire was subjected to a sequence of pilot tests which involved every question being scrutinised and edited when necessary;

(iv) Collected raw data was screened and filtered for errors;

(v) Personal close follow-up with the questionnaire respondents via telephone calls and emails to ensure elimination of any confusion or lack of clarity that might arise;

(vi) Checking consistency of answers in questionnaires through multiple questions asking about the same point;

(vii) Five questionnaires were excluded from inclusion in the final sample as the researcher felt the inconsistency in the answers might spoil the data;

(viii) Four interviews were discarded for the same reasons;

(ix) Personally assuring the interviewees involved in the semi-structured interviews of the anonymity of both their identity and personal responses; and

(x) Sending the draft questionnaire and interview script to a number of PhD students and academics to seek their opinions on the proposed drafts and their potential effect of the data validity and reliability.

Cronbach's alpha test Cronbach's alpha is the most common form of internal consistency reliability coefficients; it ranges in value from 0 (when the true score is not measured at all and there is only an error component) to 1 (when all items measure only the true score and there is no error component). The higher the value

TABLE 6.3 Reliability statistics
(Cronbach's alpha coefficient)

Cronbach's Alpha	No. of Items
0.912	105

of alpha, the more reliable the scale is. As a rule of thumb, alpha should be at least 0.7 (De Vaus, 2002).

Table 6.3 reveals that the Cronbach's alpha coefficient for respondent groups for the 105 items that used the scale was 0.912 (>0.70), which should be taken as confirming the reliability of the contents of the questionnaire used in this study.

Research Method: Data Analysis

Data analysis is one of the most difficult parts of the research process. Having chosen the appropriate method of analysis, the choice of statistics is affected by the method of analysis itself, the level of measurement of variables and the complexity of research questions (De Vaus, 2002). This section provides a detailed description of the methods used to analyse the assembled qualitative and quantitative data.

Quantitative data analysis An initial screening of the questionnaire was carried out regarding the completeness and eligibility of the responses. As a result of this initial screening, only 72 out of the 77 returned questionnaires were included in the final sample.

The questionnaires were numbered and data was checked for errors. Cross-tabulations were carried out to check the inconsistency of the data (skip errors, missed answers, values outside the range). In addition, the frequency distribution for all question items was checked and corrected if required. Once all the errors had been corrected, raw data was coded and saved as a new master file for statistical analysis. The final complete sample was then entered directly into the Statistical Package for Social Science (SPSS) programme. Initially, all the variables were created, and then the actual questionnaires were entered. This enables the data to be created in statistical tables in order to facilitate inferential statistical analysis.

Most questions in the questionnaire are designed along a five-point Likert scale in order to measure the respondents' opinions about sets of statements, which make codification and analysis of the data easier and more efficient.

The following statistical techniques are utilised:

(i) Descriptive analysis methods Descriptive statistics are summaries of data, which can be tabular, numerical or graphical. Different types of descriptive statistics such as the mean, the mode, the median, the frequency distribution, the minimum, the maximum and percentages are calculated, and these are presented in Chapters 7, 8, 9 and 10.

(ii) Non-parametric tests The main objective of statistical analysis applied in this research is to test whether there are significant differences in perceptions of respondents through various control variables at the overall sample level and among various groups of respondents. Significance testing is usually concerned with accepting or rejecting hypotheses or propositions, and can be conducted by parametric and non-parametric tests. Non-parametric tests were considered to be appropriate for this study because the data collected was mainly nominal and ordinal; the responses were not normally distributed; and the sample size was relatively small. Parametric tests usually suit samples which are drawn from a normally distributed population and data collected on an interval or ratio scale (Hebel, 2002).

The following non-parametric techniques were used:

(a) Chi-Square test The Chi-Square test is used to measure the association between dependent variables and independent variables (Saunders et al., 2007). The test is appropriate for testing the goodness-of-fit variables because the test can be applied to determine whether or not an observed set of frequencies matches some expected set of frequencies. The Chi-Square test was used to verify the existence of any significant differences in the responses regarding the degree of response for each statement. A significance level of 5% is used for this study as justification for rejecting the null hypothesis.

(b) Kruskal-Wallis and Mann-Whitney U test The Kruskal-Wallis (K-W) test is a non-parametric method for testing equality of population medians among groups. It is identical to a one-way analysis of variance with the data replaced by their ranks. It is an extension of the Mann-Whitney U test to three or more groups.

The K-W test allows researchers to measure the possible differences between two or more groups in relation to particular control variables. In this study, the K-W test of significance was intensively used for the inferential statistical analysis to test the impact of control variables like region, country, respondent's position, nature of financial institution, nature of activities and accounting standards on the perception of survey participants. The significance level used for this Kruskal-Wallis test is 5%.

(c) Spearman's Rank Correlation Coefficient Spearman's Rank Correlation Coefficient is a measure of correlation, which shows how closely two sets of data are linked. It can be done only on data that can be put in order, highest to lowest (Bryman, 2008). In this study, the Spearman's Rank Correlation Coefficient is used to test whether there is correlation between different groups of respondents.

(iii) Factor analysis Factor analysis as an inferential statistical analysis tool is used as a data-reduction method to reduce a large number of variables to a small number of factors to facilitate the process of summarising the data which has been collected. Pallant (2007) states that in order to conduct factor analysis the Kaiser-Meyer-Olkin (KMO) test and Bartlett's test need to be conducted. For factor analysis to be considered appropriate, the Bartlett's test of sphericity value should be significant ($p < 0.05$), while for the KMO test, the suggested minimum outcome must be at least 0.6 (KMO score ranging from 0 to 1). The KMO test's benchmarks are as follows: if the KMO measure is in the 0.90s, the sampling is considered marvellous. If the outcome is in the 0.80s, then the sampling is considered meritorious; if it is in the 0.70s, then the sample is middling; if it is in the 0.60s, then the sample is mediocre; if it is in 0.50s, then the sample is deemed miserable; and lastly, if it is below 0.50, then the sample is unacceptable (Pallant, 2007).

In this study, factor analysis was used for Questions 11 and 16 to test whether the observed variables can be explained largely or entirely in terms of a much smaller number of components. This also helps to organise large numbers of factors into components generated by the study.

(iv) MANOVA Multivariate analysis of variance (MANOVA) is a generalised form of univariate analysis of variance (ANOVA). It is used when there are two or more dependent variables (Tabachnick and Fidell, 2006). MANOVA tests aim to establish whether mean difference among groups on a combination of dependent variables is likely to occur by chance (Pallant, 2007). In this study, after conducting factor analysis, the MANOVA test was computed for Questions 11 and 16 in order to investigate if there is any significant difference between the component groups identified by factor analysis in relation to some control variables. This helps to locate the impact or significance of each control variable on the generated distribution and components.

(v) Friedman test The Friedman test is used to find a tendency for some variables to receive higher ranks than others, for example, assigning the ranks of 1 to 10 to the most preferred and least preferred variables respectively (Creswell, 1994). The Friedman test ranks the scores for each of the cases and then calculates the mean score for each sample. If there is no significant difference between the samples, their mean score ranks should be similar (Bryman, 2008). The Friedman test determines whether the rank totals for each condition or variable differ significantly from the values which would be expected by chance (Bryman, 2008).

In this study, the Friedman test was used in Questions 9 and 10 to examine whether there is a significant difference between the respondents' perceptions in ranking the given options. The significance level used for this Friedman test is 1%.

(vi) Interpretative analysis In addition to these quantitative methods, an interpretative approach was employed to provide further meaning to the results of the questionnaires and in-depth understanding of the issues in an integrated manner. This interpretative approach introduces interaction between the primary data findings and the literature review in order to provide better understanding of the findings of the questionnaire analysis.

Qualitative data analysis Analysis of qualitative data collected through semi-structured interviews is more complex and demanding than analysis of quantitative data. This means that unless great care is taken in analysis, it may cause real harm to the research itself (Robson, 2011).

Since the interviews were based on open-ended questions, the researcher transcribed all recorded interviews and read the interview notes and then transferred them into segments representing complete thoughts on a single question or topic, in line with the original research questions. All transcribed interviews were broken into coded segments representing complete thought statements. Answers were codified according to the most common responses provided by interviewees. After coding, the interview segments were transferred from word-processing format to a spreadsheet for further analysis.

As Charmaz (1983:114) states "Codes serve to summarise, synthesise, and sort many observations made of the data...coding becomes the fundamental means of developing the analysis...Researchers use codes to pull together and categorise a series of otherwise discrete events, statements, and observations which they identify in the data...At first the data may appear to be a mass of confusing, unrelated, accounts. But by studying and coding, the researcher begins to create order." Thus, the qualitative data collected through interview was analysed by the use of coding analysis, which was conducted manually rather than with the help of software such as n-vivo.

The findings generated through coding analysis were also subjected to interpretative analysis with the objective of developing a better understanding of the data and findings. This social constructivist-oriented method helps to develop an integrative approach to the data to render a rich qualitative analysis.

DIFFICULTIES AND LIMITATIONS

This study, as any research, has experienced a number of challenges and constraints, which may have limited the range of the study both for the questionnaire and the interviews. These issues are as follows:

Limitation of the time available to the researcher was no doubt a restricting factor as he was unable to increase the sample size, since to do so would have called for more resources than were at his disposal. The coverage of the sample used in this research, for both the questionnaire and the interviews, could be extended to a larger number of banks across a wider range of countries to enrich the findings. However, due to limitations of time and costs this was unfortunately not possible. Also, more comprehensive data collection may help address some of the other data-related issues recognised in this research.

The fact that the researcher is an Islamic banker known to most of the respondents added some sensitivity. Some respondents were worried about the conflict of interest and potential use of the information provided by the researcher's employer, despite assurances that the researcher is acting in his personal rather than professional capacity.

It should also be noted that some respondents expressed a degree of suspicion concerning the objectives of the study despite assurances regarding anonymity and strict confidentiality.

Other difficulties include:

(i) Incomplete questionnaires and ineligible text;
(ii) Void or biased responses; and finally
(iii) Due to the sampling technique limitations which have been highlighted, this study is unable to use more robust statistical tools in analysing the data, such as parametric statistical tools, which arguably are more powerful.

CONCLUSION

This chapter aimed to render a discussion of the research process by identifying the details of the research and its conduct. Initially, the research objectives and questions were developed and then the research propositions were formulated. The chapter began by explaining the importance of research design and its significant role in planning the overall research project. It also explained the chosen research methodology for this research and the justification thereof. Research methods in the form of survey questionnaires and semi-structured interviews were discussed in some detail, emphasising their relevance to this research as confirmed by both the research questions and hypotheses. Data reliability and validity were also discussed with relevance to this study. In addition, the stages of conducting the fieldwork were briefly explained with emphasis on the practical phases of collecting the primary data.

The final part of this chapter discussed the statistical techniques which were used to analyse the collected data. In this research, non-parametric statistical tests were used due to violations of the distribution assumptions of parametric tests, namely due to not having normally distributed data. Having discussed the research instrument, the survey and interview samples, the pilot study, the administration of the research instruments and the form of data analysis, the book continues with the following chapters presenting the findings of the empirical work conducted.

CHAPTER 7

Profiling Perspectives of Risk Dimensions in Islamic Finance

Descriptive Questionnaire Data Analysis

This chapter, the first of the empirical chapters, summarises the descriptive findings from the collected primary data in terms of providing a quantitative analysis of respondents' answers to the self-administered questionnaire. The questionnaire follows the structure explained in Chapter 6, Research Framework and Methodology, with the aim of empirically answering the research questions.

The chapter begins by providing a descriptive analysis of the general characteristics of the respondents. Then the research questions and hypotheses, explained in the previous chapter, are tested and general observations are made of the findings. Cross-tabulation and descriptive statistics are used to provide indications of respondents' perceptions. The findings are examined with respect to the extant literature review, while the second part of quantitative analysis – inferential statistics – is presented in the Chapter 8. A more complete discussion of the research findings will be provided in Chapter 10 in the context of existing knowledge and information, and also in association with the findings of the qualitative interview analysis, which will be separately presented in Chapter 9.

DATA ANALYSIS AND RESULTS

As mentioned in Chapter 6, the questionnaire survey was conducted between February and November 2010. The questionnaires were distributed to 110 respondents in 18 selected countries among six global regions. The final sample comprised of 72 surveys – a final response rate of 65.5%. The sample represented a diverse geographic spread of institutions, and respondents were spread across different departments and held different positions within their organisations.

Characteristics of the Respondents

The first part of the questionnaire aimed at identifying different characteristics of the respondents. Among the many variables used in the study, the main control

TABLE 7.1 Geographic distribution of the study sample

Country	Number of Questionaires	Percent of Final Sample
UK	21	29%
Egypt	9	13%
Bahrain	6	8%
France	4	6%
Germany	4	6%
Qatar	4	6%
Kuwait	3	4%
Malaysia	3	4%
Saudi Arabia	3	4%
Syria	3	4%
UAE	3	4%
Switzerland	2	3%
US	2	3%
Jordan	1	1%
Pakistan	1	1%
Palestine	1	1%
Singapore	1	1%
Turkey	1	1%
Total	**72**	**100%**

variables used to assess the respondents' profiles are the primary location of the financial institution, nature of operations and activities, and the accounting standards used. These control variables aim to test the effect of these characteristics on the respondents' answers.

Table 7.1 depicts the findings in relation to the primary country of operation of the financial institution, which indicates that the majority of participating banks are located in the UK followed by Egypt, Bahrain and France. GCC countries and Malaysia follow, while Jordan, Pakistan, Palestine, Singapore and Turkey are each represented by one financial institution in the sample.

In addition, Table 7.2 combines the financial institution's main region of operation with the respondents' positions. As can be seen in Table 7.2, Heads of Risk Management and Risk Managers represent more than 32% of the sample, followed by General Managers and Managing Directors. Respondents included only one

TABLE 7.2   Breakdown of the positions of the participants

Participant's Role	Americas	Europe	GCC	Other	Other Middle East	Southeast Asia	Total (Count)	Total (%)
Analyst	1	2			2		5	7%
Auditor		2					2	3%
CEO		2	1		1	1	5	7%
Chief Financial Officer			1	1			2	3%
Consultant		2					2	3%
Director		5			1		6	8%
General Manager			4		6		10	14%
Head of Investment Banking			1				1	1%
Head of Risk Management		8	3				11	15%
Managing Director		1	4		3		8	11%
Risk Manager	1	4	3	1		3	12	17%
Senior Analyst		3	1				4	6%
Senior Trader		1	1				2	3%
Shari'ah Scholar					1		1	1%
Solicitor		1					1	1%
Total (Count)	**2**	**31**	**19**	**2**	**14**	**4**	**72**	
Total (%)	3%	43%	26%	3%	19%	6%		100%

Head of Investment Banking and one *Shari'ah* scholar. The participants' length of service at their organisations does not form part of this questionnaire.

The nature of the participating financial institutions is also investigated. As can be seen in Table 7.3, out of the 72 institutions that participated in this study, 34.7% were fully fledged Islamic banks, with the remainder being conventional banks with Islamic activities (19.4%), conventional banks (27.8%) and others (18.1%).

Since the operational nature of the participating institutions has implications for some of the questions in the questionnaire, the nature of activities of the financial institutions is also examined. As depicted in Table 7.4, respondents are almost equally distributed among retail banking (14%), commercial banking (15%) and investment banking (15%). Twenty-four percent of respondents stated that their

TABLE 7.3 Nature of financial institution

Nature of Institution	Region						
	Americas	Europe	GCC	Other	Other Middle East	Southeast Asia	Total
Audit Firm		3%					3%
Brokerage					1%		1%
Consulting Firm		3%					3%
Conventional Bank	3%	11%	4%		10%		28%
Conventional Bank with Islamic activities		10%	10%				19%
Fully Fledged Islamic Bank		7%	13%	3%	7%	6%	35%
Law Firm		3%					3%
Rating Agency		7%					7%
Sharia'a Scholar					1%		1%
Total	**3%**	**43%**	**26%**	**3%**	**19%**	**6%**	**100%**

TABLE 7.4 Activities of financial institution

	Conventional Bank	Conventional Bank with Islamic activities	Fully Fledged Islamic Bank	Others	Total
Commercial banking	4%	7%	4%		15%
Integrated banking	8%	4%			13%
Investment banking	6%	3%	7%		15%
Private Equity House			1%		1%
Retail & commercial banking	10%	3%	11%		24%
Retail banking		3%	11%		14%
Other				18%	18%
Total	**28%**	**19%**	**35%**	**18%**	**100%**

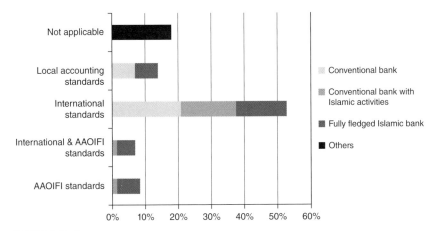

FIGURE 7.1   Accounting standards used by financial institution

institutions offer both retail and commercial banking, while 14% considered their institution an integrated bank or private equity house. The 'Other' category (18%) comprises of audit, consulting and law firms, together with rating agencies and *Shari'ah* scholars.

Finally, the accounting standards utilised by the sampled financial institutions were also asked about in the questionnaire. As illustrated in Figure 7.1, the majority of the participating banks use international accounting standards (53%), 8.3% use AAOIFI standards, 13.9% use local accounting standards, while 6.9% of respondents said their institutions adapt both AAOIFI and international standards concurrently. Eighteen percent of respondents fall under the 'Not Applicable' category as these respondents are not working for financial institutions.

Locating Risk Perception

Perceptions of risk issues in Islamic banks

Overall risks faced by Islamic banks   Respondents were asked in Question 7 to express their perceptions of the severity of risks facing Islamic financial institutions (IFIs) by indicating the degree of importance of each risk on a five-point Likert scale (ranking from Very Unimportant = 1 to Very Important = 5). In addition, Question 8, being an open-ended question, requested respondents to list any additional risk(s) – in order of seriousness – that could affect IFIs.

The descriptive statistics in Table 7.5 demonstrate the importance attached to each of the risk areas by the participants as faced by their financial institution. As can be seen from Table 7.5, the mean values for the risk categories are between

TABLE 7.5 Descriptive statistics for each type of risk (aggregate results)

Risk	n	Mean	Median	Mode	Chi-Square
Liquidity Risk	72	4.01	4	5	0.000
Asset-Liability Management Risk	72	3.94	4	5	0.000
Reputation Risk	72	3.92	4	5	0.000
Concentration Risk	72	3.81	4	5	0.000
Credit Risk	72	3.75	4	4	0.000
Shari'ah- Non-Compliance Risk	72	3.71	4	3	0.000
Legal Risk	72	3.49	3	3	0.000
Corporate Governance Risk	72	3.21	3	2	0.108 N/S
Displaced Commercial Risk	69	2.94	3	4	0.160 N/S
Operational Risk	72	2.93	3	3	0.000
Equity Investment Risk	72	2.86	3	3	0.046
Fiduciary Risk	70	2.74	3	2	0.004
Market Risk	71	2.72	2	2	0.002

Notes: n = Number of responses; N/S indicates that the differences between the responses are not significant at 5% using the Chi-Square test of significance

4.01 and 2.72, the median is between 4 and 2, and the mode is between 5 and 2. However, due to the nature of the data collected using a Likert scale, the median and the mode seem to be more appropriate measurements for this study. According to Howell (1997), the major advantage of the median and the mode is that unlike the mean, they are unaffected by extreme scores. Another advantage of these measures, when contrasted with the mean, is that they do not require any assumptions about the interval properties of the scale.

Furthermore, the Chi-Square test, a non-parametric test, is used to explore frequency data in order to test whether the data represents good fit or not. This study uses a significance level of 5%. Since, for this question, for most risks (except displaced commercial risk and corporate governance risk) the p-value is less than 0.05, it is concluded that for most risks there is goodness of fit between the data.

On an aggregate level, as can be seen from Table 7.5, liquidity risk is perceived as the most severe risk facing IFIs with the highest mean value of 4.01 followed by asset–liability management (ALM) risk (3.94) and reputation risk (3.92). Concentration, credit and *Shari'ah*-non-compliance risks followed the initial risk categories but were not recognised as being as critical as the top risks by the participants. Among the risks listed, market risk was considered as the least risky (2.72).

It is no surprise that liquidity and ALM risks are ranked as the highest risks facing the industry. The limited range of possible funding sources for IFIs and the consistent focus on longer-term assets lead to concentrated liabilities, imbalanced funding mixes and stretched capital management strategies. The two risks are closely correlated and the impact of liquidity risk is magnified by the lack of money-market instruments to manage liquidity. These two risks, together with reputation and concentration risks, support Research Hypothesis 1 about the top risks facing IFIs.

Shari'ah-non-compliance risk has been ranked sixth as it is likely to be a significant and unique risk for IFIs, since *Shari'ah*-compliance should be the core focus of every IFI. Any divergence from *Shari'ah* principles exposes the IFI to a wide range of risks at different levels as discussed in previous chapters.

Operational risk has been ranked tenth by respondents; this is not in line with the researcher's expectations as operational risk could be critical to IFIs due to their specific contractual features. In addition, because of the relatively new nature of Islamic banking, a lot of the issues related to operations need to be instituted. These include people risk, creating computer programmes and legal documents, etc. It should be noted that Research Hypothesis 1 does not consider operational risk to be among the top five risks; however, a higher ranking was expected.

Market risk (incorporating rate-of-return risk, currency risk, commodity risk, benchmark risk and mark-up risk) is incurred on instruments like commodities and currencies traded in well-traded markets; this appears to be less risky for Islamic banks. This risk arises from movements in the prices of goods/securities which are usually a part of the trading book of a bank. On the banking book, conventional banks trade in currencies, indices and bonds to boost their profitability and to keep a part of their assets in liquid money-market instruments. Market risk tends to be more speculative in nature. However, the majority of *Shari'ah* scholars forbid the sale of debt, and trading in *sukuk* is almost non-existent among IFIs as most of them hold the *sukuk* until maturity. Islamic banks, however, can trade in commodities and asset-backed securities; however, not too many IFIs are involved in this, and this may be a reason for the low ranking of market risk.

Equity investment risk was intentionally separated from market risk in the questionnaire as profit and loss sharing (PLS) through *musharakah* and *mudarabah* contracts should be the essence of Islamic banking. Unfortunately, IFIs in practice tend to allocate limited funds to equities and therefore equity investment risk was ranked among the lowest risks recognised by bankers. As more IFIs shift their strategic attention to equities after the drying up of international money markets and the attractive equity investment opportunities emerging following the recent crisis, equity investment risk is expected to attract more attention in the Islamic banking world.

Of note is the low rank given to displaced commercial risk, as the practice of smoothing investment returns through Profit Equalisation Reserves (PERs), Investment Risk Reserves (IRRs) and active management of *mudarib* fees is a very common feature of IFIs to avoid random, business and confidence-driven liquidity crises. In addition, it was observed that some respondents did not understand what is meant by displaced commercial risk, despite its being defined in the question-naire. This was reflected in the relatively lower number of responses for this risk category (69) compared to the others.

In order to examine the risk perceptions further, Table 7.6 breaks down the risk perceptions according to the nature of the financial institutions: Islamic banks, conventional banks (including those offering Islamic activities) and Others. For each category of financial institution, the mean ranking of risk categories are presented.

The results depicted in Table 7.6 can be summarised as follows:

(i) The top four risks identified by Islamic bankers are the same top four risks ranked by the total sample in aggregate (see Table 7.5).

(ii) Three out of the top four risks identified by Islamic bankers are also listed by conventional bankers among the top four risks.

(iii) Only two out of the top four risks identified by Islamic bankers are among the top four risks ranked by Others; these are reputation and ALM risks.

(iv) Different patterns exist for the last four risk categories; however, no trends could be identified.

(v) Islamic bankers' risk perception of corporate governance risk (2.96) is notice-ably lower than the risk perception of conventional bankers (3.29) and Others (3.46). This is contrary to the literature review, which indicates that weak cor-porate governance structure is a general feature of Islamic banking. Also, the inferential statistics analysis in Chapter 8 proves that corporate governance is the most statistically significant risk facing IFIs across a number of control variables. In fact, corporate governance is a significant risk facing IFIs. How-ever, the Islamic bankers included in this sample are mainly from the Middle East and the GCC, and their risk perceptions are influenced by cultural and social aspects.

It should also be noted that the results in Table 7.6 indicate that bankers, whether Islamic or non-Islamic, have a better understanding of the Islamic bank-ing model and its risk architecture than non-bankers (Others), who tend to be more theoretical in their approach.

In supporting the findings in Table 7.6, Table 7.7 spreads the responses of each group across the five scaling criteria through frequency distribution. This provides a better understanding of the risk perception of each group and helps to reach significant findings.

TABLE 7.6 Risk perception among different groups

Islamic Banks		Conventional Banks		Others	
Risk	**Mean**	**Risk**	**Mean**	**Risk**	**Mean**
Liquidity Risk	4.48	Liquidity Risk	3.79	Reputation Risk	4.23
ALM Risk	4.44	Credit Risk	3.62	Shari'ah-Non-Compliance Risk	4.00
Reputation Risk	4.44	ALM Risk	3.62	ALM Risk	3.85
Concentration Risk	4.36	Concentration Risk	3.47	Credit Risk	3.69
Shari'ah-Non-Compliance Risk	4.24	Legal Risk	3.47	Liquidity Risk	3.69
Credit Risk	3.96	Reputation Risk	3.41	Concentration Risk	3.62
Legal Risk	3.56	Corporate Governance Risk	3.29	Market Risk	3.54
Equity Investment Risk	3.16	Shari'ah-Non-Compliance Risk	3.21	Corporate Governance Risk	3.46
Operational Risk	3.00	Displaced Commercial Risk	3.18	Legal Risk	3.38
Corporate Governance Risk	2.96	Operational Risk	2.85	Operational Risk	3.00
Fiduciary Risk	2.79	Fiduciary Risk	2.71	Equity Investment Risk	2.92
Displaced Commercial Risk	2.76	Equity Investment Risk	2.62	Fiduciary Risk	2.75
Market Risk	2.48	Market Risk	2.58	Displaced Commercial Risk	2.64

Note: Conventional banks include Islamic subsidiaries

As depicted by the frequency distribution in Table 7.7, there is similarity in risk perceptions between Islamic and conventional bankers. This will be further emphasised by the results of the Kruskall-Wallis test of significance in Chapter 8, which proves that there is a general trend in terms of risk perception that can be attributed to prevailing market conditions.

Finally, under open-ended Question 8, two respondents added political and country risks as additional risks facing IFIs. Most Muslim countries have a high degree of corruption, political instability and weak currencies, which add political and country risks for IFIs. However, the lesson from the recent political unrest and revolutions in the Middle East is that political risk indeed matters and remains an important risk category area considering the volatility of the political circumstances. However, as an Islamic finance risk category, this was largely ignored. It should be also acknowledged that political risks are hard to predict and are not recurring. However, considering the recent and current political developments in the Middle East, if the questionnaire is to be administered now, namely after the eruption of the Middle Eastern revolutions, political risk would most likely attract much higher scores given that most Islamic banks are located in, or directly affected by, Middle Eastern events, with the Middle East being the main liquidity source for IFIs. Lastly, in locating the risk categories for the IFI, one respondent mentioned regulatory risk, and another added technical risks.

Perceived risk levels of Islamic finance contracts The questionnaire also aims at locating the perceptions and opinions of the respondents on various Islamic modes of financing. While Question 9 covers the intensity of use of different Islamic finance contracts, Question 10 searches for feedback on the risks inherent or perceived to be attached in those contracts. Question 9 is applicable only to IFIs and conventional banks with Islamic activities, while such restriction does not hold for Question 10.

(i) Intensity of use of different Islamic financial contracts Table 7.8 summarises the mean values of Islamic finance contracts. As expected, *murabahah* contracts are by far the most-used contracts. This '*murabahah* syndrome' has been under criticism from many Islamic economists and some *Shari'ah* scholars, but unfortunately still remains the backbone of Islamic banking and finance (IBF). In addition to the findings in this study, other studies in the literature also demonstrate that *murabahah* has been intensively used by IFIs for money-market transactions, investment and retail activities. Recently, more banks began using *walaka* for money-market transactions to replace the commodity *murabahah*, which brings about more complications and raises *Shari'ah* concerns.

The low mean values for *musharakah* and *mudarabah* in Table 7.8 reflect Islamic banks' reluctance to hold risk-sharing assets. In addition, the analysis

TABLE 7.7 Frequency distribution of risk perceptions

Risk	Islamic Banks					Conventional Banks					Others				
	VI	I	N	U	VU	VI	I	N	U	VU	VI	I	N	U	VU
Credit Risk	20%	60%	16%	4%	0%	18%	38%	35%	6%	3%	23%	31%	38%	8%	0%
Market Risk	8%	24%	8%	28%	32%	6%	12%	21%	55%	6%	23%	38%	15%	15%	8%
Operational Risk	8%	20%	44%	20%	8%	3%	29%	26%	32%	9%	8%	31%	23%	31%	8%
Equity Investment Risk	16%	24%	36%	8%	16%	9%	18%	26%	21%	26%	8%	15%	46%	23%	8%
Liquidity Risk	64%	24%	8%	4%	0%	35%	26%	24%	12%	3%	38%	23%	15%	15%	8%
ALM Risk	60%	28%	8%	4%	0%	29%	26%	24%	18%	3%	38%	31%	15%	8%	8%
Displaced Commercial Risk	8%	20%	36%	12%	24%	15%	39%	12%	15%	18%	9%	18%	27%	18%	27%
Shari'ah-Non-Compliance Risk	44%	36%	20%	0%	0%	15%	18%	41%	26%	0%	38%	23%	38%	0%	0%
Concentration Risk	52%	36%	8%	4%	0%	26%	24%	26%	18%	6%	23%	23%	46%	8%	0%
Reputation Risk	52%	40%	8%	0%	0%	26%	26%	18%	21%	9%	46%	38%	8%	8%	0%
Fiduciary Risk	8%	17%	33%	29%	13%	18%	6%	24%	35%	18%	8%	8%	42%	33%	8%
Corporate Governance Risk	12%	20%	32%	24%	12%	24%	26%	12%	32%	6%	31%	23%	15%	23%	8%
Legal Risk	16%	44%	24%	12%	4%	26%	12%	44%	18%	0%	15%	23%	46%	15%	0%

Note 1: Scale: 1 = Very Unimportant (VU), 2 = Unimportant (U), 3 = Neutral (N), 4 = Important (I), 5 = Very Important (VI)
Note 2: Conventional banks include Islamic subsidiaries

TABLE 7.8 Intensity of use of Islamic finance contracts

Risk	n	Mean	Median	Mode	Chi-Square
Murabaha	39	6.95	1	1	0.00
Wakala	39	5.56	2	2	0.00
Ijarah	39	4.28	4	4	0.00
Mudaraba	39	4.00	4	4	0.01
Istisna'a	39	2.46	6	6	0.00
Musharaka	39	2.41	6	5	0.00
Salaam	39	2.33	6	7	0.00

Notes: n = Number of responses; Question 9 is applicable only to IFIs
and conventional banks with Islamic activities

revealed that *salam* has a long way to go before becoming commonly used by
Islamic banks. It is evident from the responses that the banks' first preference is
for financial instruments that are generated through debt-creating, sale contracts
and leasing instruments. This is enhanced by the responses about risk perception
in different modes of financing.

These findings are supported by the results of the Chi-Square test as reported
in Table 7.8, which indicated that the Chi-Square values related to the goodness
of fit of the risk categories are highly significant ($p < 1\%$).

In addition, as depicted in Table 7.9, Spearman's Rank Correlation Coefficient
between the medians of Islamic banks and conventional banks offering Islamic
products shows that at 5% significance level the rankings of the two groups are
correlated ($\rho = 0.9420 > 0.714$).

TABLE 7.9 Correlation between Islamic and conventional banks in using Islamic
finance contracts

	Islamic Banks Median	Conventional Banks Median	Difference	(Difference) 2
Murabaha	1	1	0	0
Wakala	2	2.5	0.5	0.25
Mudaraba	4	3	−1	1
Ijarah	4	4	0	0
Musharaka	5	6	1	1
Istisna'a	6	6	0	0
Salam	6	5	−1	1
Spearman's Rank Correlation Coefficient				**0.94196**

TABLE 7.10   Risk perception in Islamic finance contracts

Risk	n	Mean	Median	Mode	Chi-Square
Mudaraba	72	6.21	1	1	0.00
Musharaka	72	5.89	2	1	0.00
Istisna'a	70	4.20	3.5	3	0.00
Salaam	71	3.75	4	5	0.00
Ijarah	71	3.73	4	2	0.01
Wakala	72	2.26	6	6	0.00
Murabaha	72	1.90	7	7	0.00

Notes: n = Number of responses

(ii) Perceptions of risks attached to various Islamic finance contracts   Table 7.10 emphasises the perception that the profit-sharing modes of financing have higher risks, while fixed-income contracts (such as *ijara* and *murabahah*) are perceived as least risky. The main reason for higher concern regarding partnership contracts may be that 'principals' invested are not guaranteed under partnership modes of finance. In addition, these instruments are usually of a long-term nature. This is particularly true for real estate projects, while fixed-income contracts are perceived to have shorter maturities and to be less risky, with some 'implied' guarantees. Even though *ijarah* contracts may be long term, they can be adjusted to reflect changing market conditions. It is important to note that the manipulation of the contracts by Islamic finance practitioners resulted in the equity and risk-sharing contracts, for instance *wakala*, sharing the same risk characteristics as fixed-income contracts. This created a gap in risk perceptions among different groups of respondents. These findings are supported by the results of the Chi-Square test, which indicate the presence of goodness of fit for the financial contracts with high significance level (p < 1%).

In addition, as shown in Table 7.11, Spearman's Rank Correlation Coefficient between the medians of Islamic banks and conventional banks offering Islamic products shows that at 5% significance level the rankings of the two groups are correlated ($\rho = 0.8929 > 0.714$).

In furthering the analysis, intensity of use of Islamic finance contracts were correlated with the attached risk perceptions regarding the respective financial contracts. This is depicted in Figure 7.2, which demonstrates that Islamic finance contracts that are perceived as higher risk (like *mudarabah* and *musharakah*) are much less used by banks than less risky contracts. In fact, *murabahah* scored the lowest mean on the risk matrix (1.90) compared to the highest mean on the intensity of use (6.95). This reflects the extent to which banks are shying away from

TABLE 7.11 Correlation between Islamic and conventional banks in risk perception about Islamic finance contracts

	Islamic Banks Median	Conventional Banks Median	Difference	(Difference)2
Murabaha	7	7	0	0
Mudaraba	1	1	0	1
Wakala	6	6	0	1
Ijarah	4	4	0	1
Musharaka	2	2	0	1
Istisna'a	3	4	1	1
Salam	4	4	0	1
Spearman's Rank Correlation Coefficient				**0.89286**

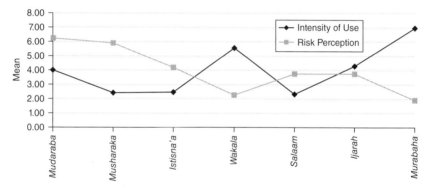

FIGURE 7.2 Islamic finance contracts: Intensity of use versus risk perception

risk-taking or equity participation. Manipulation of the contracts changed the risk characteristics of these contracts from principles defined by Islamic finance. This manipulation caused the Islamic finance contracts to behave differently and thus they are perceived differently by practitioners on the risk scale. Thus, the FIs are heavily using less risky products regardless of the aspirational expectations related to asset-based Islamic finance.

Additional risk issues facing IFIs Question 11 asked respondents for their views on some risk and risk management issues related to IFIs that were identified in the literature review. This is a closed question that provided 11 statements and respondents were requested to express their preference in terms of how strongly

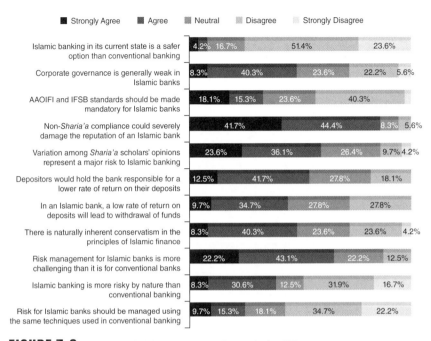

FIGURE 7.3 Additional risk management issues facing IFIs

they agreed or disagreed with each statement. The five-point Likert scale was used with answers labelled 'strongly agree', 'agree', neutral', 'disagree' and 'strongly disagree'. The findings based on frequency results are summarised in Figure 7.3 and Table 7.12, which ranks the importance of statements according to their mean values.

As can be seen in Table 7.12, the Chi-Square values indicate that the responses for all these statements but one are significant at the 5% level. Furthermore, the findings indicate that the majority of respondents (56.9%) believe that risk for Islamic banks should be managed using different techniques than those used in conventional banking. Although more than 48% of respondents consider that the Islamic finance principles contain naturally built-in conservatism, around 75% of respondents think that the malpractices in Islamic banking in its current state made it a riskier mode of finance than conventional banking.

The following salient points are identified in Table 7.12 and Figure 7.3:

(i) The findings demonstrate that, although respondents do not perceive Islamic banking to be by nature a more risky model than conventional banking, Islamic banks as they stand today could be more risky than conventional banks.

TABLE 7.12 Frequency results of responses to statements under Question 11

Statement	SA	A	N	D	SD	n	Mean	Median	Mode	Chi-Square
Non-*Sharia'a* compliance could severely damage the reputation of an Islamic bank	41.7%	44.4%	8.3%	5.6%	0.0%	72	**4.22**	4	4	**0.00**
Risk management for Islamic banks is more challenging than it is for conventional banks	22.2%	43.1%	22.2%	12.5%	0.0%	72	3.75	4	4	0.00
Variation among *Sharia'a* scholars' opinions represent a major risk to Islamic banking	23.6%	36.1%	26.4%	9.7%	4.2%	72	**3.65**	4	4	**0.00**
AAOIFI and IFSB standards should be made mandatory on Islamic banks	18.1%	15.3%	23.6%	40.3%	2.8%	72	3.51	4	4	0.44
Depositors would hold the bank responsible for a lower rate of return on their deposits	12.5%	41.7%	27.8%	18.1%	0.0%	72	**3.49**	4	4	**0.00**
In an Islamic bank, a low rate of return on deposits will lead to withdrawal of funds	9.7%	34.7%	27.8%	27.8%	0.0%	72	3.26	3	4	0.00
There is naturally inherent conservatism in the principles of Islamic finance	8.3%	40.3%	23.6%	23.6%	4.2%	72	**3.25**	3	4	**0.00**
Corporate governance is generally weak in Islamic banks	8.3%	40.3%	23.6%	22.2%	5.6%	72	3.24	3	4	0.00
Islamic banking is more risky by nature than conventional banking	8.3%	30.6%	12.5%	31.9%	16.7%	72	**2.82**	3	2	**0.00**
Risks for Islamic banks should be managed using same techniques used in conventional banking	9.7%	15.3%	18.1%	34.7%	22.2%	72	2.56	2	2	0.01
Islamic banking in its current state is a safer option than conventional banking	4.2%	4.2%	16.7%	51.4%	23.6%	72	**2.14**	2	2	**0.00**

Notes: n = Number of responses; Scale: 1 = Strongly Disagree (SD), 2 = Disagree (D), 3 = Neutral (N), 4 = Agree (A), 5 = Strongly Agree (SA)

(ii) As the findings show, risk management for IFIs is more challenging than it is for conventional banks.

(iii) The findings indicate that risks for IFIs cannot be managed using conventional risk management tools and techniques.

(iv) The findings in Table 7.12 and Figure 7.3. show that not only do IFIs face some risks that are different from those faced by their conventional peers, but these risks are also more serious and not well understood.

(v) It can be generalised from the findings that *Shari'ah* principles carry natural inherent conservatism.

(vi) It is important to state that despite the principles of Islamic finance, depositors seek competitive rates of return from IFIs.

(vii) In addition to the risk categories identified in the previous section, displaced commercial risk and *Shari'ah* standardisation are obvious examples of additional challenges facing IFIs.

(viii) As a particular risk area for Islamic banking, the *Shari'ah*-non-compliance risk could be a severe risk for IFIs. This is emphasised by the responses under Question 7.

(ix) As the findings demonstrate, the majority of respondents do not believe that AAOIFI and IFSB standards should be made mandatory for Islamic banks.

(x) Importantly, the results also demonstrate that weak corporate governance is noticeable among IFIs.

Gauging perceptions of capital adequacy for Islamic banks This section addresses capital adequacy issues facing IFIs as perceived by the participants. It tackles the research questions concerning whether the Basel II and Basel III Accords were drafted with the conventional banking model in mind, and also aims to identify the appropriate capital requirement levels for Islamic banks as perceived by the participants.

As shown by Figure 7.4, the majority of respondents (59.7%) expressed their adherence to the Basel II guidelines. Interestingly, 12.9% of the participants stated that their institution used IFSB standards on capital adequacy, and 6.9% stated that they used local standards imposed by the regulator (mainly Egyptian banks), which are highly likely to be derived mainly from Basel II guidelines.

Among those implementing Basel II (43 respondents), the majority of the participants stated that their institution used the less sophisticated approaches to calculate credit, market and operational risks due to their relatively limited size of operations and the absence of advanced IT systems, as summarised in Table 7.13. Conventional multinational banks use a combination of different approaches for different portfolios; however, the 'Advanced' techniques dominate. As the findings demonstrate, among IFIs, it is mainly the Islamic windows of big international

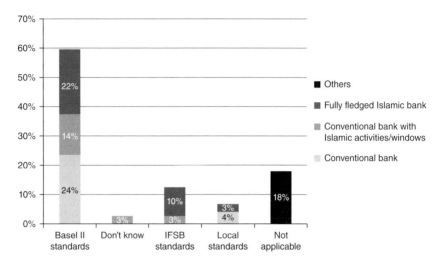

FIGURE 7.4 Frequency distribution of capital adequacy standards used by respondents

TABLE 7.13 Descriptive statistics for Question 13: Capital requirement methodologies used

	n	Percentage of Total
Credit Risk		
Standardised Approach	25	59.5%
Foundation IRB	5	11.9%
Advanced IRB	12	28.6%
Total	**42**	**100.0%**
Market Risk		
Standardised Approach	29	69.0%
Internal Models Approach	13	31.0%
Total	**42**	**100.0%**
Operational Risk		
Basic Indicator Approach	24	57.1%
Advanced Measurement Approach	18	42.9%
Total	**42**	**100.0%**

Notes: n = Number of responses; for multinational banks that use more than one methodology, the most advanced methodology is the one counted

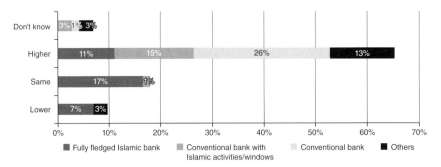

FIGURE 7.5 Evaluating capital requirements for Islamic banks versus conventional banks

banks that selected the 'Advanced' capital adequacy approaches as they make use of the infrastructure and systems available at their parent companies.

The participants were asked to evaluate the capital requirements for Islamic and conventional banks. The responses to Question 14 in Figure 7.5 and Table 7.14 produced unexpected findings, as more than 65% of participants believe that capital requirements for IFIs should be higher than those for their conventional peers. This could be understood as meaning, as things stand today, that Islamic banking carries more risks and hence should have higher capital buffers in order to enable IFIs absorb unexpected losses.

The participants' opinions on Basel II and IFSB Capital Adequacy Standards were also requested, as Question 15 of the questionnaire asked respondents for their views on additional capital adequacy issues. This closed question provided five statements, and respondents were requested to express their preference in terms of how strongly they agree or disagree with each statement. The results, using the five-point Likert scale, are summarised below. The frequency results for the whole sample are summarised by Figure 7.6, while Table 7.15, which breaks down the findings for Islamic bankers and non-Islamic bankers (including Islamic subsidiaries, conventional banks and others), ranks the importance of statements according to their mean values.

From Table 7.15 and Figure 7.6, the following generalisation can be made:

(i) On aggregate level, the majority of respondents had 'No' views about the new Basel III standards and their effects on Islamic banking and financial stability in general. This shows that there is still lack of clarity about Basel III and its potential impacts. Around one-third of respondents do not believe that the new standards, with their stricter capital, leverage and liquidity rules, are likely to prevent another financial crisis. Almost the same percentage of

TABLE 7.14 Evaluating capital requirements for Islamic banks versus conventional banks

	Region	Fully Fledged Islamic Bank	Conventional Bank	Conventional Bank with Islamic Activities	Others	Total
Don't know	Europe			1.4%	2.8%	4.2%
	GCC		1.4%	1.4%	0.0%	2.8%
Higher	Americas		2.8%		0.0%	2.8%
	Europe	5.6%	11.1%	6.9%	11.1%	34.7%
	GCC	2.8%	2.8%	8.3%	0.0%	13.9%
	Other Middle East	1.4%	9.7%		1.4%	12.5%
	Southeast Asia	1.4%			0.0%	1.4%
Lower	Europe				1.4%	1.4%
	GCC	2.8%			0.0%	2.8%
	Other	1.4%			0.0%	1.4%
	Other Middle East	1.4%			1.4%	2.8%
	Southeast Asia	1.4%			0.0%	1.4%
Same	Europe	1.4%		1.4%	0.0%	2.8%
	GCC	6.9%			0.0%	6.9%
	Other	1.4%			0.0%	1.4%
	Other Middle East	4.2%			0.0%	4.2%
	Southeast Asia	2.8%			0.0%	2.8%
Total		**34.7%**	**27.8%**	**19.4%**	**18.1%**	**100%**

respondents do not think that the Basel III standards will be easily applicable to IFIs. The breakdown between Islamic and non-Islamic bankers reveals the same pattern.

(ii) A similar pattern exists between the two groups regarding their views about the failings of Basel II to prevent the recent crisis. The majority of respondents support this view, with zero responding 'D' or 'SD' on the need to review Basel II standards.

(iii) While most non-Islamic bankers (46.8%) believe that Basel II standards should be equally applied to IFIs without modification, most Islamic bankers support the opposite (44%). On aggregate level no consensus pattern is obvious, with the 'SA' and 'A' side scoring slightly higher than the 'D' and 'SD' side.

(iv) A similar pattern exists between the views of the two groups regarding the use of the IFSB standards by IFIs with the majority favouring the 'SA' and 'A' side over the 'D' and 'SD' side.

TABLE 7.15 Breakdown of perceptions of capital adequacy standards

Fully Fledged Islamic Banks

Statement	SA	A	N	D	SD	n	Mean	Median	Mode	Chi-Square
Basel II standards should be reviewed after failing to prevent the current crisis	40.0%	48.0%	12.0%	0.0%	0.0%	25	4.28	4	4	0.00
IFSB standard on Capital Adequacy should be used by Islamic banks rather than Basel II	24.0%	12.0%	44.0%	16.0%	4.0%	25	3.36	3	3	0.02
Stricter capital, leverage, and liquidity rules, as proposed under Basel III, are likely to prevent another financial crisis.	4.0%	20.0%	48.0%	24.0%	4.0%	25	2.96	3	3	0.00
Basel II standards should be equally applied to Islamic banks without modification	4.0%	32.0%	20.0%	32.0%	12.0%	25	2.84	3	2	0.11
The proposed Basel III rules would be easily applicable to Islamic banks	0.0%	8.0%	48.0%	36.0%	8.0%	25	2.56	3	3	0.00

Non-Islamic Bankers (including Islamic subsidiaries and conventional banks)

Statement	SA	A	N	D	SD	n	Mean	Median	Mode	Chi-square
Basel II standards should be reviewed after failing to prevent the current crisis	36.2%	51.1%	12.8%	0.0%	0.0%	47	4.23	4	4	0.00
Basel II standards should be equally applied to Islamic banks without modification	21.3%	25.5%	25.5%	23.4%	4.3%	47	3.36	3	3	0.11
IFSB standard on Capital Adequacy should be used by Islamic banks rather than Basel II	21.3%	14.9%	36.2%	21.3%	6.4%	47	3.23	3	3	0.02
The proposed Basel III rules would be easily applicable to Islamic banks	0.0%	6.4%	74.5%	10.6%	8.5%	47	2.79	3	3	0.00
Stricter capital, leverage and liquidity rules, as proposed under Basel III, are likely to prevent another financial crisis.	2.1%	6.4%	57.4%	31.9%	2.1%	47	2.74	3	3	0.00

Notes: n = Number of responses; Scale: 1 = Strongly Disagree (SD), 2 = Disagree (D), 3 = Neutral (N), 4 = Agree (A), 5 = Strongly Agree (SA)

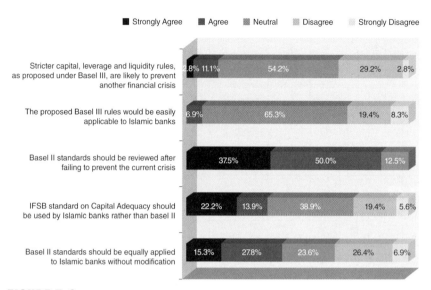

FIGURE 7.6 Perceptions about capital adequacy standards

(v) As shown in Table 7.15, Islamic and non-Islamic bankers rank the statements differently. This divergence in the mean rankings reflects differences in risk perceptions.

It should be noted that these findings are supported by the Chi-Square values as depicted in Table 7.15, which indicate that the data for all statements but one represent a good fit at the 5% level.

The credit crisis and Islamic banks This last section of Part Two of the questionnaire aimed to reveal the respondents' views on different issues relating to the global crisis. This closed question provided nine statements and respondents were requested to express their opinion in terms of how strongly they agree or disagree with each statement. The frequency results for the entire sample are summarised by Figure 7.7, while Table 7.16 breaks down the findings for Islamic bankers and non-Islamic bankers (including Islamic subsidiaries, conventional banks and others), and ranks the importance of statements according to their mean values.

The findings in Figure 7.7 and Table 7.16 can be generalised as follows:

As can be seen from the responses, both groups support the view that IFIs are more resilient to economic shock than their conventional peers. Seventy-two percent of Islamic bankers ranked this statement either 'SA' or 'A', while 40% of non-Islamic bankers chose either 'SA' or 'A'.

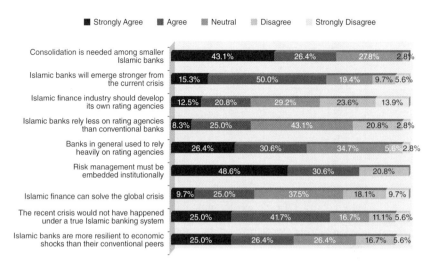

FIGURE 7.7 Perceptions of Islamic banking and the global financial crisis

In addition, on aggregate level more than 66% of respondents support the view that the crisis would not have happened under a true Islamic banking system. This was further emphasised by the 34.7% who believe that Islamic finance can solve the global crisis. A breakdown of the two groups shows varying patterns: 76% of Islamic bankers, the total of 'Strongly Agree' or 'Agree', stated that the crisis would not have happened under a true Islamic banking system, a view shared by circa 61% of non-Islamic bankers. However, while the majority of the former support the view that Islamic finance can solve the global crisis, the majority of non-bankers are not of this view.

Furthermore, most respondents (56.9%) agree that banks in general heavily relied on rating agencies. The same view is shared among the Islamic and non-Islamic bankers. In aggregate, there was no consensus as to whether Islamic banks rely less or more on rating agencies than do conventional banks; however, surprisingly enough, more non-Islamic bankers believe that IFIs rely less on rating agencies than do Islamic bankers, with the majority of these declining such a view.

Moreover, some respondents believe that conventional rating agencies do not fully understand and appreciate certain aspects of IFIs, principally the fiduciary aspect, and that conventional rating methodologies do not recognise the need for a different approach to capital adequacy calculation and accounting standards. However, there is no consensus either on the aggregate level or by non-Islamic bankers as to whether the Islamic finance industry needs to develop its own rating agencies. The majority of Islamic bankers did not support such a view (44%). Although there are some important differences between Islamic and conventional banks that

TABLE 7.16 Perceptions of Islamic banking and the financial crisis

Total Sample

Statement	SA	A	N	D	SD	n	Mean	Median	Mode	Chi-Square
Risk management must be embedded institutionally	48.6%	30.6%	20.8%	0.0%	0.0%	72	4.28	4	5	0.00
Consolidation is needed among smaller Islamic banks	43.1%	26.4%	27.8%	2.8%	0.0%	72	4.10	4	5	0.00
Banks in general used to rely heavily on rating agencies	26.4%	30.6%	34.7%	5.6%	2.8%	72	3.72	4	3	0.00
The recent crisis would not have happened under a true Islamic banking system	25.0%	41.7%	16.7%	11.1%	5.6%	72	3.69	4	4	0.00
Islamic banks will emerge stronger from the current crisis	15.3%	50.0%	19.4%	9.7%	5.6%	72	3.60	4	4	0.00
Islamic banks are more resilient to economic shocks than their conventional peers	25.0%	26.4%	26.4%	16.7%	5.6%	72	3.49	4	4	0.00
Islamic banks rely less on rating agencies than conventional banks	8.3%	25.0%	43.1%	20.8%	2.8%	72	3.15	3	3	0.00
Islamic finance could have solved the global crisis	9.7%	25.0%	37.5%	18.1%	9.7%	72	3.07	3	3	0.00
Islamic finance industry should develop its own rating agencies	12.5%	20.8%	29.2%	23.6%	13.9%	72	2.94	3	3	0.00

Fully Fledged Islamic Banks											
Statement	SA	A	N	D	SD	n	Mean	Median	Mode	Chi-Square
Risk management must be embedded institutionally	32.0%	40.0%	28.0%	0.0%	0.0%	25	4.04	4	4	0.00
Banks in general used to rely heavily on rating agencies	28.0%	48.0%	20.0%	4.0%	0.0%	25	4.00	4	4	0.00
Islamic banks are more resilient to economic shocks than their conventional peers	40.0%	32.0%	8.0%	20.0%	0.0%	25	3.92	4	5	0.01
The recent crisis would not have happened under a true Islamic banking system	20.0%	56.0%	16.0%	8.0%	0.0%	25	3.88	4	4	0.00
Consolidation is needed among smaller Islamic banks	28.0%	36.0%	32.0%	4.0%	0.0%	25	3.88	4	4	0.01
Islamic banks will emerge stronger from the current crisis	24.0%	32.0	36.0%	8.0%	0.0%	25	3.72	4	3	0.02
Islamic finance can solve the global crisis	16.0%	40.0%	32.0%	12.0%	0.0%	25	3.60	4	4	0.01
Islamic banks rely less on rating agencies than conventional banks	12.0%	20.0%	24.0%	36.0%	8.0%	25	2.92	3	2	0.20
Islamic finance industry should develop its own rating agencies	20.0%	12.0%	24.0%	28.0%	16.0%	25	2.92	3	2	0.74

(continued)

TABLE 7.16 (Continued)

Non-Islamic Bankers (including Islamic subsidiaries, conventional banks and others)

Statement	SA	A	N	D	SD	n	Mean	Median	Mode	Chi-Square
Risk management must be embedded institutionally	57.4%	25.5%	17.0%	0.0%	0.0%	47	4.40	5	5	0.00
Consolidation is needed among smaller Islamic banks	51.1%	21.3%	25.5%	2.1%	0.0%	47	4.21	5	5	0.00
The recent crisis would not have happened under a true Islamic banking system	27.7%	34.0%	17.0%	12.8%	8.5%	47	3.60	4	4	0.03
Banks in general used to rely heavily on rating agencies	25.5%	21.3%	42.6%	6.4%	4.3%	47	3.57	3	3	0.00
Islamic banks will emerge stronger from the current crisis	10.6%	59.6%	10.6%	10.6%	8.5%	47	3.53	4	4	0.00
Islamic banks rely less on rating agencies than conventional banks	6.4%	27.7%	53.2%	12.8%	0.0%	47	3.28	3	3	0.00
Islamic banks are more resilient to economic shocks than their conventional peers	17.0%	23.4%	36.2%	14.9%	8.5%	47	3.26	4	4	0.04
Islamic finance industry should develop its own rating agencies	8.5%	25.5%	31.9%	21.3%	12.8%	47	2.96	3	3	0.08
Islamic finance can solve the global crisis	6.4%	17.0%	40.4%	21.3%	14.9%	47	2.79	3	3	0.00

Notes: n = Number of responses; Scale: 1 = Strongly Disagree (SD), 2 = Disagree (D), 3 = Neutral (N), 4 = Agree (A), 5 = Strongly Agree (SA)

must be properly understood and considered, these can be incorporated within the existing rating frameworks.

The results also demonstrate that more than 69% of respondents support consolidation among smaller Islamic banks; the prevailing opinion is that there are far too many Islamic banks to serve this growing market, but only a handful have the size necessary to compete on a global stage. The same pattern could be traced on breaking down the findings among the two groups.

Lastly, the findings in Table 7.16 and Figure 7.7 show that, on aggregate level, most respondents agreed that Islamic banks will emerge stronger from the crisis as they provide an ethical banking alternative (65.3%). A similar pattern exists between the two groups, as 56% of Islamic bankers and 70.2% of non-Islamic bankers support the view that Islamic banks will emerge stronger from the crisis.

Perceptions of Risk Management and Mitigation

The third part of the questionnaire aims to examine the risk management and hedging techniques used within individual Islamic banks. Risk mitigation has recently come under the spotlight within Islamic banking in particular with the emergence of a number of defaults in the Gulf region. Traditionally, the unique nature of risks faced by Islamic banks, combined with the restrictions added by *Shari'ah*, makes risk mitigation for Islamic banks a difficult and complex process. There are risks that Islamic banks, similar to their conventional counterparts, can manage and control through appropriate risk policies, controls and traditional risk management tools. However, there are other risks that banks cannot eliminate and that can only be reduced or moderated by transferring or selling those risks in well-defined markets. The challenge is, however, that most of the conventional hedging tools do not so far comply with the *Shari'ah* requirements, which limits the available tools of risk management for Islamic banks.

Risk management and reporting   The first part of this section aims to depict the findings related to risk management reporting used by the institutions of the participants. Table 7.17 shows the different risk management reports that participating banks produce and the frequency of publishing those reports, while Table 7.18 shows the frequency distribution of the findings among Islamic and conventional banks (including Islamic subsidiaries).

As depicted by Table 7.17, the most widely used reports in general are capital requirement, liquidity risk and credit exposure reports, followed by industry concentration risk and profit rate risk reports. The commodity risk report is the least used with 29% of respondents indicating it is not used. Some institutions produce other specific reports not listed in the questionnaire like market risk reports (10%), stress-testing reports (5%), counterparty concentration reports (7%) and collateral management reports (3%).

TABLE 7.17   Risk management reports – market practice

Report	Daily	Weekly	Monthly	Yearly	Never	Don't Know	Total Responses
Capital requirement report	44%	24%	31%	—	—	2%	**100%**
Operational risk report	37%	17%	37%	2%	—	3%	**97%**
Profit rate risk report	56%	10%	29%	—	—	3%	**98%**
Foreign exchange risk report	42%	20%	29%	—	—	3%	**95%**
Liquidity risk report	61%	25%	14%	—	—	—	**100%**
Commodity risk report	39%	5%	24%	0%	29%	3%	**100%**
Country risk report	54%	17%	29%	—	—	—	**100%**
Equity mark-to-market report	51%	12%	22%	5%	5%	5%	**100%**
Classified accounts report	27%	3%	47%	17%	—	2%	**97%**
Industry concentration risk report	42%	—	53%	2%	—	2%	**98%**
Credit exposure report	68%	3%	29%	—	—	—	**100%**
Large exposure report	58%	—	34%	—	3%	3%	**98%**
Other risk reports							
Market risk	5%	—	5%	—	—	—	**10%**
Stress testing	0%	—	5%	—	—	—	**5%**
Counterparty concentration	3%	—	3%	—	—	—	**7%**
Collateral management	3%	—	—	—	—	—	**3%**

In terms of frequency of producing these reports, the credit exposure report is the most produced daily report, followed by the liquidity risk report and profit rate risk report. The classified accounts report is the least produced daily report (27%) as banks tend to produce it on a monthly basis. As the findings show, 31 institutions indicate that they produce industry concentration risk report on a monthly basis, followed by classified accounts report (47%) and operational risk report (37% respondents). A small number of respondents indicated that they produce some reports annually. Finally, few respondents indicated that they do not know the frequency of reports' production; this is because these respondents work in non-risk management rules like traders and financial officers.

The analysis in Table 7.18 in a comparative manner shows that IFIs use the same risk management techniques as conventional banks for managing the risks, in particular liquidity, credit and market risks. Nevertheless, the spread and frequency of utilising these techniques is lower among Islamic banks compared to their conventional peers. Generally, IFIs still use less technically advanced risk

TABLE 7.18 Risk management reports – Islamic versus conventional banks

Fully Fledged Islamic Banks

Report	Daily	Weekly	Monthly	Yearly	Never	Don't Know	Total Responses
Capital requirement report	36%	24%	36%	—	—	4%	**100%**
Operational risk report	32%	8%	44%	4%	—	4%	**92%**
Profit rate risk report	48%	8%	36%	—	—	4%	**96%**
Foreign exchange risk report	28%	24%	32%	—	—	8%	**92%**
Liquidity risk report	52%	36%	12%	—	—	—	**100%**
Commodity risk report	8%	—	20%	—	68%	4%	**100%**
Country risk report	28%	32%	40%	—	—	—	**100%**
Equity mark-to-market report	16%	12%	36%	12%	12%	12%	**100%**
Classified accounts report	—	4%	48%	40%	—	—	**96%**
Industry concentration risk report	16%	—	76%	4%	—	—	**96%**
Credit exposure report	48%	8%	44%	—	—	—	**100%**
Large exposure report	28%	—	56%	—	8%	8%	**100%**
Other risk reports							**0%**
Market risk	4%	—	4%	—	—	—	**8%**
Stress testing	—	—	8%	—	—	—	**8%**
Counterparty concentration	4%	—	4%	—	—	—	**8%**
Collateral management	4%	—	—	—	—	—	**4%**

Conventional Banks (including Islamic subsidiaries)

Report	Daily	Weekly	Monthly	Yearly	Never	Don't Know	Total Responses
Capital requirement report	50%	24%	26%	—	—	—	**100%**
Operational risk report	41%	24%	32%	—	—	3%	**100%**
Profit rate risk report	62%	12%	24%	—	—	3%	**100%**
Foreign exchange risk report	53%	18%	26%	—	—	—	**97%**
Liquidity risk report	68%	18%	15%	—	—	—	**100%**
Commodity risk report	62%	9%	26%	—	—	3%	**100%**
Country risk report	74%	6%	21%	—	—	—	**100%**
Equity mark-to-market report	76%	12%	12%	—	—	—	**100%**

(continued)

TABLE 7.18 (*Continued*)

Report	Daily	Weekly	Monthly	Yearly	Never	Don't Know	Total Responses
Classified accounts report	47%	3%	47%	—	—	—	**97%**
Industry concentration risk report	62%	0%	35%	—	—	3%	**100%**
Credit exposure report	82%	0%	18%	—	—	—	**100%**
Large exposure report	79%	0%	18%	—	—	—	**97%**
Other risk reports							
Market risk	6%	—	6%	—	—	—	**12%**
Stress testing		—	3%	—	—	—	**3%**
Counterparty concentration	3%	—	3%	—	—	—	**6%**
Collateral management	3%	—	—	—	—	—	**3%**

measurement approaches as they are still in the emerging phase and do not have sufficient resources and systems to use more technically advanced techniques. The most widely used report among IFIs on a daily basis is liquidity risk report, followed by credit exposure report and profit rate risk report. Commodity risk and equity mark-to-market reports are the least used by IFIs in this survey.

Risk measurement In addition to risk management reports, financial institutions use various techniques to measure and analyse risks. Table 7.19 exhibits different techniques used to measure and assess risks. There may be a variety of formats in which these techniques can be used, ranging from simple analysis to sophisticated models. The most common technique used by IFIs as indicated by respondents is maturity matching analysis (88%), followed by reliance on external ratings provided by rating agencies (84%), internal based rating and gap analysis (76% each). Only 56% indicated they use Value at Risk (VaR) models, while simulation techniques are used by just six IFIs in the sample to assess different risks.

Comparing these figures to the responses by conventional bankers emphasises the fact that risk management techniques in Islamic banking are not as sophisticated as in the conventional banking world. The most common technique used by conventional banks is external ratings provided by rating agencies (94.1%), followed by maturity matching analysis (91.2%), internal based rating (88.2%) and duration analysis (85.3%).

Moreover, the results for this question confirm those obtained by Question 11 as reported in the preceding section. As discussed in the section 'Additional risk issues facing IFIs' in Chapter 8, more than 65% of respondents either 'Agree' or 'Strongly Agree' that risk management for IFIs is more challenging as compared to the conventional banks. In addition, around 57% of respondents believe that risk management for IFIs should not use the same tools as conventional banks.

TABLE 7.19 Risk measurement techniques

(a)

Risk Management Technique	Fully Fledged Islamic Banks		Conventional Banks	
	Total Responses	Percentage	Total Responses	Percentage
Internal based ratings	19	76.0%	30	88.2%
Credit ratings by rating agencies	21	84.0%	32	94.1%
Gap analysis	19	76.0%	28	82.4%
Duration analysis	17	68.0%	29	85.3%
Maturity matching analysis	22	88.0%	31	91.2%
Earnings at risk	11	44.0%	27	79.4%
Value at risk	14	56.0%	23	67.6%
Stress testing	15	60.0%	22	64.7%
Simulation techniques	6	24.0%	16	47.1%
Risk Adjusted Rate of Return on Capital (RAROC)	8	32.0%	26	76.5%
Others				

(b)

Ranking	Fully Fledged Islamic Banks	Conventional Banks
1	Maturity matching analysis	Credit ratings by rating agencies
2	Credit ratings by rating agencies	Maturity matching analysis
3	Internal based ratings	Internal based ratings
4	Gap analysis	Duration analysis
5	Duration analysis	Gap analysis
6	Stress testing	Earnings at risk
7	Value at risk	RAROC
8	Earnings at risk	Value at risk
9	RAROC	Stress testing
10	Simulation techniques	Simulation techniques

Notes: a) Question 18 is applicable only to respondents in the banking field, whether Islamic or conventional; b) Conventional banks include Islamic subsidiaries

Risk mitigation A comparative analysis was conducted on risk mitigation between Islamic and conventional banks. As can be seen in Figure 7.8, 72.2% of respondents believe that risk mitigation techniques in Islamic banking are less advanced than conventional banking. Table 7.20 provides detailed analysis of the findings.

The results depicted in Table 7.20 can be summarised as follows:

(i) The majority of respondents (72.2%) believe that risk mitigation in Islamic banking is less advanced than conventional banking. The main responses came from fully fledged Islamic banks in the GCC (12.5%), followed by conventional banks in Other Middle East (9.7%) and Islamic subsidiaries in the GCC (6.9%).

(ii) 15.3% of the respondents indicated that they 'Don't know' whether risk mitigation techniques in Islamic banking are more or less advanced than those used is conventional banking. Within this category, conventional banks in Europe, conventional banks in the GCC, and Islamic subsidiaries in Europe had the main responses with 2.8% of total responses each.

(iii) 12.5% of respondents believe that risk mitigation techniques are similar in Islamic and conventional banking. The main responses in this category came from Europe (4.2%), followed by Americas, GCC and Southeast Asia with 1.4% each;

(iv) No respondents believe that risk mitigation techniques are more advanced in Islamic banking than in conventional banking.

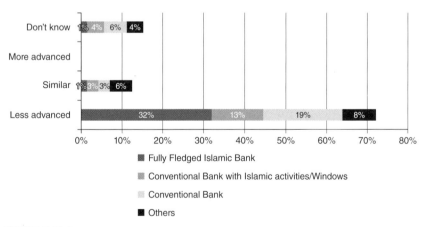

FIGURE 7.8 Risk mitigation in Islamic banking versus conventional banking

TABLE 7.20   Risk mitigation in Islamic banking

	Region	Fully Fledged Islamic Bank	Conven- tional Bank	Conventional Bank with Islamic Activities	Others	Total
Don't know	Europe	0.0%	2.8%	2.8%	1.4%	**6.9%**
	GCC	0.0%	2.8%	1.4%	1.4%	**5.6%**
	Other Middle East	1.4%	0.0%	0.0%	1.4%	**2.8%**
Less advanced	Americas	0.0%	1.4%	0.0%	1.4%	**2.8%**
	Europe	6.9%	6.9%	5.6%	1.4%	**20.8%**
	GCC	12.5%	1.4%	6.9%	1.4%	**22.2%**
	Other	2.8%	0.0%	0.0%	1.4%	**4.2%**
	Other Middle East	5.6%	9.7%	0.0%	1.4%	**16.7%**
	Southeast Asia	4.2%	0.0%	0.0%	1.4%	**5.6%**
Similar	Americas	0.0%	1.4%	0.0%	1.4%	**2.8%**
	Europe	0.0%	1.4%	1.4%	1.4%	**4.2%**
	GCC	0.0%	0.0%	1.4%	1.4%	**2.8%**
	Southeast Asia	1.4%	0.0%	0.0%	1.4%	**2.8%**
Total		**34.7%**	**27.8%**	**19.4%**	**18.1%**	**100%**

In searching for risk and risk management attitudes in Islamic banks, the participants were also asked to express their opinions on risk mitigation techniques. These results obtained from Question 19 were confirmed by the poor responses for Question 20 about the techniques IFIs use to mitigate their risks as summarised in Table 7.21.

This question is only applicable to fully fledged Islamic banks and Islamic subsidiaries of conventional banks as the listed risk mitigation techniques are all *Shari'ah*-compliant. As summarised in Table 7.21, collateral arrangements is the most commonly used technique (92.3%), followed by Islamic currency forwards (82.1%) and guarantees (76.9%). Dual currency *murabahah* represented under 'Others' is the least used risk mitigation techniques at 2.6% of responses.

The reasons for the lack of usage of *Shari'ah*-compliant risk mitigation techniques may be because those techniques are subject to different interpretation by *Shari'ah* scholars. Other reasons may include that, as previously indicated in Table 7.8, *salam* and *istisna'a* contracts are not widely used in IFIs. As explained in Chapter 3, there have been substantial efforts in developing *Shari'ah*-compliant

TABLE 7.21   Risk mitigation techniques

Risk Mitigation Technique	Total Responses	Percentage of Total Sample
On-balance sheet netting	25	64.1%
Collateral arrangements	36	92.3%
Islamic options	10	25.6%
Islamic swaps	14	35.9%
Guarantees	30	76.9%
Islamic currency forwards	32	82.1%
Parallel contracts	12	30.8%
Other (please specify)	1	2.6%

Notes: Question 20 is applicable only to Islamic banks and conventional banks with Islamic activities. Total sample for this question = 39 respondents

hedging instruments; however, much of this progress remains localised with limited scope for cross-border application and further work is still needed.

Evaluating the Practice of Islamic Banking

This last section aims to analyse the opinions and the evaluation of the participants on the practice of Islamic banking. One of the main statements considered in this section is the proposition that Islamic banking has been diverting from its roots by mimicking conventional banks. In doing so, Question 21, a closed question, provided four statements, and respondents were requested to express their preference in terms of how strongly they agree or disagree with each statement. The frequency results for the entire sample are summarised by Figure 7.9, while Table 7.22 breaks down the findings between Islamic bankers and non-Islamic bankers (including Islamic subsidiaries, conventional banks and others) and ranks the importance of statements according to their mean values.

As can be seen from the findings depicted in Table 7.22 and Figure 7.9, on both aggregate and individual levels, the majority of respondents either 'Strongly Agree' or 'Agree' with the four statements. Although Islamic finance provides an ethical banking alternative, IFIs need to reform before they can exploit the ethical foundation in the Islamic banking model. The responses of Islamic bankers and non-Islamic bankers were close, with the former's responses being closer to 'SA' than the latter. These findings are supported by the significant results of the Chi-Square test ($p < 1\%$). However, the mean rankings for the responses of Islamic bankers are higher than those of non-Islamic bankers across all statements, reflecting higher risk perceptions.

TABLE 7.22 Breakdown of perceptions about current practices in Islamic banking

Total Sample

Statement	SA	A	N	D	SD	n	Mean	Median	Mode	Chi-Square
There is difference between the current practice and principles of Islamic banking	33.3%	33.3%	31.9%	1.4%	0.0%	72	3.99	4	4	0.00
Islamic banks need to reform to be successful	31.9%	29.2%	34.7%	4.2%	0.0%	72	3.89	4	3	0.00
Islamic banks have been mimicking conventional models	25.0%	40.3%	27.8%	6.9%	0.0%	72	3.83	4	5	0.00
Islamic finance provides an ethical banking alternative	27.8%	27.8%	41.7%	2.8%	0.0%	72	3.81	4	3	0.00

Fully Fledged Islamic Banks

Statement	SA	A	N	D	SD	n	Mean	Median	Mode	Chi-Square
There is difference between the current practice and principles of Islamic banking	44.0%	32.0%	20.0%	4.0%	0.0%	25	4.16	4	4	0.01
Islamic finance provides an ethical banking alternative	44.0%	20.0%	36.0%	0.0%	0.0%	25	4.08	4	5	0.00
Islamic banks need to reform to be successful	28.0%	40.0%	28.0%	4.0%	0.0%	25	3.92	4	4	0.01
Islamic banks have been mimicking conventional models	28.0%	44.0%	16.0%	12.0%	0.0%	25	3.88	4	5	0.00

Non-Islamic Bankers (including Islamic subsidiaries, conventional banks and others)

Statement	SA	A	N	D	SD	n	Mean	Median	Mode	Chi-Square
There is difference between the current practice and principles of Islamic banking	27.7%	34.0%	38.3%	0.0%	0.0%	47	3.89	4	4	0.00
Islamic banks need to reform to be successful	34.0%	23.4%	38.3%	4.3%	0.0%	47	3.87	4	3	0.00
Islamic banks have been mimicking conventional models	23.4%	38.3%	34.0%	4.3%	0.0%	47	3.81	4	3	0.00
Islamic finance provides an ethical banking alternative	19.1%	31.9%	44.7%	4.3%	0.0%	47	3.66	4	3	0.00

Notes: n = Number of responses; Scale: 1 = Strongly Disagree (SD), 2 = Disagree (D), 3 = Neutral (N), 4 = Agree (A), 5 = Strongly Agree (SA)

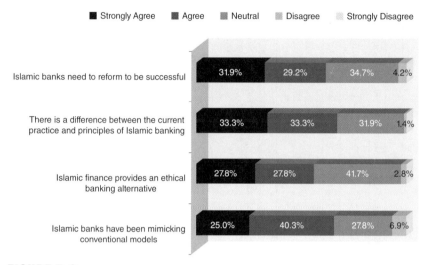

FIGURE 7.9 Frequency distribution for Question 21: current practices in Islamic banking

The Future of Islamic Banking

The last section of the questionnaire includes a forward-looking question that explores different strategies IFIs should follow in order to prepare for the future. The participants were provided a number of statements and asked to express their opinions. The results related to the growth strategies for IFIs are presented in Table 7.23.

Table 7.23 reveals that both Islamic and non-Islamic bankers (including Islamic subsidiaries, conventional banks and others) consider improved risk management and mitigation practices among the top priorities IFIs should focus on in their development plans. While Islamic bankers ranked 'Enhanced morality – back to roots' second (mean = 5.96), non-Islamic bankers ranked it in fourth place (mean = 5.60). 'Diversification' was highly ranked by both groups, while mergers and acquisitions, and organic growth in home market received lower ranking. Non-Islamic bankers ranked 'Standardisation' higher than Islamic bankers.

These findings are supported by the significant results of the Chi-Square test for most strategies. In addition, Spearman's Rank Correlation Coefficient shows that at the 5% significance level the rankings of the two groups are correlated (ρ= 0.9405>0.643) as depicted in Table 7.24.

TABLE 7.23   Growth strategies for IFIs

Total Sample				
Strategy	**n**	**Mean**	**Median**	**Mode**	**Chi-Square**
Improved risk management	72	6.75	2	1	0.0
Better risk mitigation	72	6.33	2	2	0.0
Enhanced morality – back to roots	72	5.72	3	5	0.0
Diversification – reduce concentration	72	5.24	3	3	0.0
Innovation	72	3.26	6	8	0.0
Standardisation	72	3.14	7	7	0.0
Mergers and acquisitions	72	3.08	6	6	0.0
Organic growth in home market	72	2.49	7	8	0.0

Fully Fledged Islamic Banks				
Strategy	**n**	**Mean**	**Median**	**Mode**	**Chi-Square**
Improved risk management	25	6.64	2	1	0.0
Enhanced morality – back to roots	25	5.96	3	1	0.1
Better risk mitigation	25	5.88	3	4	0.0
Diversification – reduce concentration	25	4.44	4	8	1.0
Innovation	25	3.72	5	6	0.3
Mergers and acquisitions	25	3.32	6	6	0.1
Organic growth in home market	25	3.16	7	8	0.1
Standardisation	25	2.88	7	7	0.0

Non-Islamic Bankers (including Islamic subsidiaries, conventional banks and others)				
Strategy	**n**	**Mean**	**Median**	**Mode**	**Chi-Square**
Improved risk management	47	6.81	2	1	0.0
Better risk mitigation	47	6.57	2	2	0.0
Diversification – reduce concentration	47	5.66	3	3	0.0
Enhanced morality – Back to roots	47	5.60	4	5	0.0
Standardisation	47	3.28	6	8	0.0
Innovation	47	3.02	6	8	0.0
Mergers and acquisitions	47	2.96	6	6	0.0
Organic growth in home market	47	2.13	7	8	0.0

TABLE 7.24   Correlation between perceptions of Islamic and conventional banks about growth strategies for IFIs

	Islamic Banks Median	Conventional Banks Median	Difference	(Difference)2
Improved risk management	2	2	0	0
Enhanced morality – back to roots	3	4	1	1
Mergers and acquisitions	6	6	0	0
Organic growth in home market	7	7	0	0
Better risk mitigation	3	2	−1	1
Innovation	5	6	1	1
Diversification – reduce concentration	4	3	−1	1
Standardisation	7	6	−1	1
Spearman's Rank Correlation Coefficient				**0.94048**

CONCLUSION

This chapter is the first empirical analysis chapter of the quantitative data assembled through survey questionnaire where mainly descriptive statistics were applied to the primary data. Frequency distribution is among the descriptive statistics used, in addition to Spearman's Rank Correlation Coefficient test and Chi-Square test. The analyses produced results on different aspects of risk management in Islamic banking, which are summarised and explained in the context of the research objectives.

The findings in this chapter show that, although IFIs face additional risks to those faced by conventional financial institutions, both Islamic and conventional bankers have similar perceptions about risk management in Islamic banking. Liquidity, ALM and concentration risk were among the top risks identified by both groups. Moreover, profit-sharing modes of financing and product-deferred sales are perceived to be more risky than *murabahah, wakalah* and *ijarah*. This explains why IFIs shy away from such instruments due to their lack of appetite for risky assets, which in turn is due to IFIs trying to emulate the conventional model. The manipulation of the contracts by Islamic finance practitioners, in order to mimic conventional products, made the risk perception of equity and risk-sharing contracts, for instance *wakalah*, similar to risk perception of fixed-income contracts like *murabahah*. This manipulation caused the contracts to behave differently and created a gap in risk perceptions.

The findings also indicate that, although IFIs are doing comparatively well in terms of their general risk management and reporting, they are still perceived as using less advanced risk management approaches. *Shari'ah*-compatible risk mitigation techniques are also not widely used by IFIs. Developing *Shari'ah*-compliant risk mitigation and hedging tools, in addition to improving risk management and reporting practices, represents a serious challenge to Islamic banking in order to lift itself to the next level. Most IFIs use Basel II capital adequacy standards, with greater use of basic and standardised approaches rather than advanced models. This is due to the relative simplicity of their capital requirements. The majority of respondents perceived that Basel II could be applied to IFIs, but with a few amendments.

It is interesting to note that both Islamic and non-Islamic bankers share the view that, although IFIs have shown resilience, they are not immune from economic shocks. Broadly speaking, Islamic banking had a relatively 'mild crisis' in that it suffered less damage as a result of the global economic and financial turmoil of the past few years than conventional banking.

Empirical evidence shows that Islamic banking is expected to emerge stronger from the crisis, provided some conditions are met, such as: 'further innovation', 'enhanced transparency', 'more robust risk management architecture and culture' and above all 'enhanced *Shari'ah*-compliance'.

After providing some descriptive analysis of the general characteristics of the sample, and examining the research questions and hypotheses, the findings of this chapter will be further analysed by the inferential statistical analysis in Chapter 8, which studies the attitudes of the respondents by providing a comparative analysis between several identified groups or respondents' categories.

Analysing Perceptions of Risk and Risk Management Dimensions and Issues

Inferential Statistical Analysis

This chapter is a continuation of Chapter 7 in analysing the quantitative data represented by the survey questionnaire. In this chapter inferential statistics are employed for exploring and analysing the opinions and attitudes of the respondents by providing a comparative analysis between several identified groups or respondent categories. In addition, the chapter considers some determinants and factors which contribute to the perception and knowledge of the respondents concerning risk management in Islamic banking.

As mentioned earlier in the research methodology chapter, the analysis in the present chapter employs several inferential statistics tools for non-parametric data analysis, ranging from cross-tabulation, the Friedman test, the Kruskall-Wallis test, and the Chi-Square test to factor analysis and MANOVA multivariate analysis of variance. Each of these statistical analyses will be used in the relevant section of the chapter; a brief description of it will be presented prior to its application, and the result will subsequently be interpreted. The chapter is divided into six broad sections in line with the main parts of the questionnaire and in accordance to the thematic division used in the interview analysis in Chapter 9. Each section is developed to find satisfactory answers to one or more of the main research questions and their sub-questions as previously explained in the book. This chapter concludes with a brief summary of the overall analysis and findings.

It should be noted that in order to avoid unnecessary detail, various analyses were brought together under one table to consolidate the analysis in a concise manner.

RISK PERCEPTION

It is highly expected that the respondents have different risk perceptions and understanding of risk management in Islamic banking according to their background, region, position within the organisation, nature of financial institution and other control variables. Therefore, this section analyses the respondents' opinions according to the selected category of their profile.

Risk Issues in Islamic Banks

Overall risks faced by Islamic banks The first factor to be examined is the respondents' perceptions about the severity of risk facing IFIs. Descriptive statistics for Question 7, in Chapter 7, showed that Islamic and conventional bankers share similar views about the top risks facing IFIs, unlike non-bankers who adopted a more theoretical approach in their views. This section will investigate further to examine the difference in perceptions among different subgroups of respondents. For this purpose, the researcher has employed the Kruskall-Wallis (K-W) test for region, country, respondent's position, nature of Financial Institution, nature of activities and accounting standards

The first control variable is 'Region'. The results from the K-W test for the entire research sample in Table 8.1 indicate that there is no statistically significant difference among various regions in risk perception (p-value > 0.05) except for corporate governance risk (p-value = 0.002), which is also evident from the mean ranking. With a 'relaxation' of the confidence level to 0.06, we can accept displaced commercial risk as significant as well.

Repeating the K-W test with 'Region' as the control variable for different samples of data, in terms of the institutional setting of respondents, gives consistent results, as illustrated by Table 8.2, which confirms that there is a difference in risk perception of corporate governance risk among regions for fundamental market reasons. In other words, there is a significant difference between regions when institutional settings were also considered.

In addition, examining the mean rankings across different regions for corporate governance risk confirms the existence of a structural pattern. As apparent from Table 8.3, the rankings do not change much when conducting K-W with different samples identifying different institutional settings. The inclusion of conventional banks and non-bankers in the test sample gives similar results. 'Americas' disappear when conventional banks are excluded from the test sample as there were no respondents from IFIs in the 'Americas' in this research sample. Also, the difference in values between the highest and the lowest mean rankings is noticeable, which confirms that the distribution of corporate governance risk is significantly different across regions.

TABLE 8.1 K-W test results by region for Question 7 for entire research sample

Risk	Region	N	K-W Test Mean Rank	Chi-Square	Asymp. Sig.
Credit Risk	Americas	2	54	6.05	0.301
	Europe	31	32.19		
	GCC	19	40.13		
	Other	2	22.25		
	Other Middle East	14	37.54		
	Southeast Asia	4	47.38		
	Total	72			
Market Risk	Americas	2	63	10.568	0.061
	Europe	30	41		
	GCC	19	29		
	Other	2	31.75		
	Other Middle East	14	36.04		
	Southeast Asia	4	20.25		
	Total	71			
Operational Risk	Americas	2	38	4.496	0.48
	Europe	31	35.58		
	GCC	19	41.68		
	Other	2	37.75		
	Other Middle East	14	28.39		
	Southeast Asia	4	46		
	Total	72			
Equity Investment Risk	Americas	2	63	10.34	0.066
	Europe	31	40.37		
	GCC	19	36.29		
	Other	2	48		
	Other Middle East	14	27		
	Southeast Asia	4	21.75		
	Total	72			
Liquidity Risk	Americas	2	23	5.89	0.317
	Europe	31	39.42		
	GCC	19	38.18		

(*continued*)

TABLE 8.1 (*Continued*)

Risk	Region	N	K-W Test Mean Rank	Chi-Square	Asymp. Sig.
	Other	2	43.25		
	Other Middle East	14	26.79		
	Southeast Asia	4	43.25		
	Total	72			
ALM Risk	Americas	2	24.5	3.482	0.626
	Europe	31	39.53		
	GCC	19	37.39		
	Other	2	32.5		
	Other Middle East	14	29.57		
	Southeast Asia	4	41		
	Total	72			
Displaced Commercial Risk	Americas	2	36	11.002	**0.051**
	Europe	29	28.64		
	GCC	19	45.79		
	Other	2	49.5		
	Other Middle East	13	34.04		
	Southeast Asia	4	25.25		
	Total	69			
Shari'ah-**Non-Compliance Risk**	Americas	2	42.5	4.49	0.481
	Europe	31	39.11		
	GCC	19	36.18		
	Other	2	52.25		
	Other Middle East	14	27.93		
	Southeast Asia	4	36.88		
	Total	72			
Concentration Risk	Americas	2	41	5.869	0.319
	Europe	31	37.9		
	GCC	19	35.21		
	Other	2	51		
	Other Middle East	14	28.21		
	Southeast Asia	4	51.25		
	Total	72			

TABLE 8.1 *(Continued)*

Risk	Region	N	K-W Test Mean Rank	Chi-Square	Asymp. Sig.
Reputation Risk	Americas	2	33	3.644	0.602
	Europe	31	34.68		
	GCC	19	35.53		
	Other	2	58.5		
	Other Middle East	14	36.64		
	Southeast Asia	4	45.5		
	Total	72			
Fiduciary Risk	Americas	2	33	4.978	0.419
	Europe	30	34.12		
	GCC	19	33.89		
	Other	2	13.75		
	Other Middle East	13	42.77		
	Southeast Asia	4	42		
	Total	70			
Corporate Governance Risk	Americas	2	57	19.086	**0.002**
	Europe	31	45.98		
	GCC	19	29.21		
	Other	2	49.25		
	Other Middle East	14	26.07		
	Southeast Asia	4	17.5		
	Total	72			
Legal Risk	Americas	2	26	2.067	0.84
	Europe	31	38.19		
	GCC	19	34.58		
	Other	2	48.5		
	Other Middle East	14	33.93		
	Southeast Asia	4	40.75		
	Total	72			

TABLE 8.2 K-W test results by region for Question 7 for selected sample data

Risk	Fully Fledged Islamic Banks, Conventional Banks with Islamic Activities and Conventional Banks		Fully Fledged Islamic Banks and Conventional Banks with Islamic Activities		Fully Fledged Islamic Banks	
	Chi-Square	Asymp. Sig.	Chi-Square	Asymp. Sig.	Chi-Square	Asymp. Sig.
Credit Risk	6.037	0.303	2.65	0.618	2.384	0.666
Market Risk	8.4	0.136	2.962	0.564	1.331	0.856
Operational Risk	4.181	0.524	4.241	0.374	1.222	0.874
Equity Investment Risk	9.399	0.094	3.188	0.527	6.795	0.147
Liquidity Risk	5.266	0.384	0.096	0.999	0.938	0.919
ALM Risk	2.404	0.791	0.894	0.925	3.006	0.557
Displaced Commercial Risk	9.785	0.082	7.992	0.092	7.219	0.125
Shari'ah-Non-Compliance Risk	4.609	0.465	1.387	0.846	6.283	0.179
Concentration Risk	7.318	0.198	2.751	0.6	4.077	0.396
Reputation Risk	4.388	0.495	2.795	0.593	2.223	0.695
Fiduciary Risk	5.846	0.322	3.128	0.537	9.058	0.06
Corporate Governance Risk	17.733	**0.003**	14.866	**0.005**	9.745	**0.045**
Legal Risk	2.656	0.753	2.904	0.574	3.398	0.494

There is a pattern regardless of the nature of the respondents included in the sample, which implies that there are structural issues determined by the nature of the market, which can be explained by fundamental market reasons. Although corporate governance practices have material impacts on a bank's risk profile, IFIs do not generally have robust corporate governance frameworks in place particularly in the Gulf Cooperation Council (GCC), Middle East and Southeast Asia.

The same pattern could be identified, although to a lesser extent, when examining concentration risk, one of the main risks identified by respondents, as explained in the previous chapter. Table 8.4 confirms that there are fundamental market reasons for the difference in mean ranking among different regions. The mean ranking for the K-W test for the full sample ranks 'Southeast Asia' first (51.25), followed by 'Other' (51), then 'Americas' (41), while 'Other Middle East' comes last with mean rank of 28.21. This ranking changes little when conducting the K-W test for different samples using different institutional settings, which confirms that for concentration risk there is a significant difference between regions when institutional settings are also applied.

TABLE 8.3 K-W test mean rankings for corporate governance risk for different sample data

Corporate Governance Risk	Full Sample		Fully Fledged Islamic Banks, Conventional Banks with Islamic Activities and Conventional Banks		Fully Fledged Islamic Banks and Conventional Banks with Islamic Activities		Fully Fledged Islamic Banks	
Region	Mean Rank	Rank	Mean Rank	Rank	Mean Rank	Rank	Mean Rank	Rank
Americas	57	1st	47.75	1st	N/A	N/A	N/A	N/A
Europe	45.98	3rd	39.78	3rd	28.75	1st	19	1st
GCC	29.21	4th	24.74	4th	17.34	3rd	13.61	3rd
Other	49.25	2nd	41.25	2nd	27.75	2nd	18.75	2nd
Other Middle East	26.07	5th	22.25	5th	12.1	4th	8.3	4th
Southeast Asia	17.5	6th	14.88	6th	10.38	5th	7.13	5th

TABLE 8.4 K-W test mean rankings for concentration risk for different sample data

Concentration Risk	Full Sample		Fully Fledged Islamic Banks, Conventional Banks with Islamic Activities and Conventional Banks		Fully Fledged Islamic Banks and Conventional Banks with Islamic Activities		Fully Fledged Islamic Banks	
Region	Mean Rank	Rank	Mean Rank	Rank	Mean Rank	Rank	Mean Rank	Rank
Americas	41	3rd	31.75	4th	N/A	N/A	N/A	N/A
Europe	37.9	4th	34.83	3rd	21.38	3rd	16.8	2nd
GCC	35.21	5th	26.58	5th	17.59	5th	12.28	3rd
Other	51	2nd	38.75	2nd	24.75	2nd	13.5	5th
Other Middle East	28.21	6th	22.25	6th	17.8	4th	8.8	4th
Southeast Asia	51.25	1st	40.13	1st	25.88	1st	14.88	1st

Furthermore, examining the mean rankings across different raw data for other significant risks like credit and liquidity risks (as identified by the respondents in Chapter 7) shows that rankings remain very similar between fully fledged Islamic banks and fully fledged Islamic banks combined with Islamic subsidiaries of conventional banks. However, adding conventional banks with no Islamic activities to the sample changes the rankings slightly as summarised in Tables 8.5 and 8.6. Under credit risk, for instance, when only fully fledged Islamic banks are included in the sample, 'Southeast Asia' ranks first (15.63), followed by 'Other Middle East' (13.2), 'Europe' (13.1), 'GCC' (13) and 'Other' (7). Also, the difference in values between the mean rankings is minimal, reflecting the close perception among different regions. When the institutional sample settings change to include Islamic subsidiaries as well, this pattern of mean rankings remains very similar. However, changing the institutional sample settings to include conventional banks changes the rankings and the gap between mean values becomes wider. Of note is the existence of the same pattern when non-bankers are also included in the sample. This shows that for credit risk there is a difference between regions when conventional banks and other non-banking respondents are also considered. Islamic and conventional bankers have different risk perceptions about credit risk across various regions.

Table 8.6 shows that the same trend exists for liquidity risk. K-W test results for different institutional samples indicate a similar pattern between samples of fully fledged Islamic banks and fully fledged Islamic banks combined with Islamic

TABLE 8.5 K-W test mean rankings for credit risk for different sample data

Credit Risk	Full Sample		Fully Fledged Islamic Banks, Conventional Banks with Islamic Activities and Conventional Banks		Fully Fledged Islamic Banks and Conventional Banks with Islamic Activities		Fully Fledged Islamic Banks	
Region	Mean Rank	Rank	Mean Rank	Rank	Mean Rank	Rank	Mean Rank	Rank
Americas	54	1st	44.25	1st	N/A	N/A	N/A	N/A
Europe	32.19	5th	25.45	5th	18.58	4th	13.1	3rd
GCC	40.13	3rd	32.61	3rd	20.72	3rd	13	4th
Other	22.25	6th	18	6th	11	5th	7	5th
Other Middle East	37.54	4th	30.17	4th	21	2nd	13.2	2nd
Southeast Asia	47.38	2nd	38.75	2nd	24.63	1st	15.63	1st

TABLE 8.6   K-W test mean rankings for liquidity risk for different sample data

Liquidity Risk	Full Sample		Fully Fledged Islamic Banks, Conventional Banks with Islamic Activities and Conventional Banks		Fully Fledged Islamic Banks and Conventional Banks with Islamic Activities		Fully Fledged Islamic Banks	
Region	Mean Rank	Rank	Mean Rank	Rank	Mean Rank	Rank	Mean Rank	Rank
Americas	23	6th	17.75	6th	N/A	N/A	N/A	N/A
Europe	39.42	3rd	33.65	3rd	19.29	5th	12	5th
GCC	38.18	4th	30.58	4th	20.47	2nd	14.61	2nd
Other	43.25	2nd	34.75	2nd	20	3rd	12	3rd
Other Middle East	26.79	5th	22.67	5th	20.2	1st	12.3	1st
Southeast Asia	43.25	1st	34.75	1st	20	3rd	12	3rd

subsidiaries. Also, there is another similar pattern between the full sample and a sample comprising fully fledged Islamic banks, Islamic subsidiaries and conventional banks. This emphasises that Islamic and conventional bankers have different risk perceptions about liquidity risk across various regions, while the perceptions of Islamic subsidiaries is the same as that of fully fledged Islamic banks.

The findings indicate that there is an observed pattern which can be generalised to most of the risk categories. This can be explained only by market realities.

The K-W test was conducted in a similar manner according to 'country' as control variable; the results confirm those produced by the test conducted according to 'Region'.

In addition, an attempt was made to test the impacts of 'respondent's position' and 'accounting standards' on risk perception; however, the results show that there are no significant differences, as summarised in Table 8.7.

Finally, conducting the K-W test to examine the significance of perceived differences among various risk groups for the entire research sample according to the 'Nature of Financial Institution' provided dispersed results. Table 8.8 shows that liquidity, ALM, *Shari'ah*-non-compliance, concentration, reputation and displaced commercial risks have significant p-values, while the remaining risks do not.

Further examination of the mean rankings for risks with significant p-value, as summarised in Table 8.9, confirms the dispersion of data as no trend could be established. In general, fully fledged Islamic banks and conventional banks

TABLE 8.7 K-W test results by respondent's position and accounting standards for Question 7 for entire research sample

	K-W According to Respondent's Position			K-W According to Accounting Standards		
Risk	Chi-Square	df	Asymp. Sig.	Chi-Square	df	Asymp. Sig.
Credit Risk	11.817	14	0.621	1.098	4	0.778
Market Risk	20.115	14	0.127	1.616	4	0.656
Operational Risk	15.095	14	0.372	3.472	4	0.324
Equity Investment Risk	7.749	14	0.902	6.584	4	0.086
Liquidity Risk	13.051	14	0.522	7.051	4	0.07
ALM Risk	7.108	14	0.93	5.677	4	0.128
Displaced Commercial Risk	15.899	13	0.255	5.266	4	0.153
Shari'ah-Non-Compliance Risk	22.246	14	0.074	6.074	4	0.108
Concentration Risk	16.891	14	0.262	5.79	4	0.122
Reputation Risk	13.971	14	0.452	4.421	4	0.219
Fiduciary Risk	17.288	14	0.241	0.525	4	0.913
Corporate Governance Risk	18.487	14	0.186	5.596	4	0.133
Legal Risk	11.305	14	0.662	0.668	4	0.881

TABLE 8.8 K-W test results by nature of financial institution for Question 7 for entire research sample

Risk	Chi-Square	df	Asymp. Sig.
Credit Risk	2.943	3	0.4
Market Risk	6.238	3	0.101
Operational Risk	3.237	3	0.357
Equity Investment Risk	3.599	3	0.308
Liquidity Risk	8.818	3	**0.032**
ALM Risk	9.381	3	**0.025**
Displaced Commercial Risk	13.528	3	**0.004**
Sharia'a Non-Compliance Risk	15.674	3	**0.001**
Concentration Risk	16.629	3	**0.001**
Reputation Risk	11.257	3	**0.01**
Fiduciary Risk	0.796	3	0.851
Corporate Governance Risk	1.511	3	0.68
Legal Risk	4.146	3	0.246

TABLE 8.9 K-W test results by risk categories in relation to nature of financial institution for Question 7 for entire research sample

Risk		Liquidity Risk		ALM Risk		Displaced Commercial Risk		*Shari'ah-*Non-Compliance Risk		Conc. Risk		Rep. Risk	
Nature of FI	N	Mean Rank	Rank	Mean Rank	Rank	Mean Rank	Rank	Mean Rank	Rank	Mean Rank	Rank	Mean Rank	Rank
Fully Fledged Islamic Bank	25	44.64	1st	45.18	1st	31.98	2nd	46.88	1st	48.48	1st	44.7	1st
Islamic Subsidiary	14	38.29	2nd	35.64	2nd	52	1st	25.46	4th	27.93	3rd	32.5	3rd
Conventional Bank	20	28	4th	27.05	4th	29.13	4th	27.73	3rd	35.85	2nd	25.93	4th
Others	13	32	3rd	35.27	3rd	30.36	3rd	41.92	2nd	23.69	4th	41.31	2nd
Total	72												

with Islamic activities have higher mean values than conventional banks alone and 'Others', particularly for liquidity, Asset-Liability Management (ALM) and displaced commercial risks. This trend, nonetheless, slightly changes for concentration and reputation risks. Also of note is the proximity of mean value among fully fledged Islamic banks and Islamic subsidiaries, which reflects the similar perception of risks in Islamic banking. One possible reason for this is the similar knowledge and awareness of Islamic banking products and structures among those professionals with hands-on experience in Islamic banking. This confirms the findings of the section 'Locating Risk Perception' in Chapter 7.

Based on the above results, it can be concluded that three control variables (region, country and nature of FI) contribute to some significant differences about risk perception among respondents, but not for all risks. In addition, this can also be supported by the fact that there is no significant difference in perception levels between respondents from stand-alone Islamic banks and Islamic subsidiaries. Initially it was expected that respondents from stand-alone Islamic banks would have stronger perceptions compared to those from Islamic subsidiaries for two reasons: firstly, stand-alone Islamic banks have been in existence for much longer than Islamic subsidiaries, and, secondly, respondents from stand-alone Islamic banks have the advantage of dealing with only Islamic banking products and services, whereas Islamic subsidiaries still need to operate side-by-side with their respective conventional counterpart in sharing the same operating platforms and buildings. Nevertheless, the results have indicated otherwise. Differences could be spotted between perceptions of conventional banks and stand-alone Islamic banks, and more noticeably between the perceptions of bankers and non-bankers, represented by 'Others'. This could be because bankers, whether Islamic or non-Islamic, have hands-on experience and better understanding of the Islamic banking model and its risk architecture than non-bankers, who tend to be more theoretical in their approach.

Islamic finance contracts Questions 9 and 10 seek respondents' views on various Islamic modes of financing. Question 9 targets institutions that use Islamic finance contracts only. Therefore, when conducting the K-W test for Question 9, only stand-alone Islamic banks and Islamic subsidiaries were included in the data analysis.

Intensity of use of different Islamic finance contracts Table 8.10 shows that regardless of the respondent's position or the nature of activities, banks use Islamic finance contracts in similar patterns; all products had p-value > 0.05. However, K-W test results according to 'Region' indicate that there is significant difference in the use of *mudarabah* across different regions. Moreover, there is significant difference in the use of *wakala* and *salaam* according to the nature of financial institution.

The Friedman test is used to find a tendency for some variables to receive higher ranks than others, i.e. to test whether the ranking is significant or not. The results of the test reflect that ranking for this question is significant.

As can be seen in Table 8.11, 'Other Middle East' and 'Southeast Asia' use *mudarabah* the most, with mean values of 32.5 and 27.13 respectively, while 'Europe' (17.71) and the 'GCC' (16.74) rank lower on the use of *mudarabah* as financial institutions in these regions tend to rely more on *murabahah*, *wakala* and *ijarah*. This should be explained by the economies of the regions in question, as the lack of financial depth may necessitate greater use of equity financing.

TABLE 8.10 K-W test results for Question 9 for selected sample data

Contract	K-W According to Region		K-W According to Respondent's Position		K-W According to Nature of FI		K-W According to Nature of Activities	
	Chi-Square	Asymp. Sig.	Chi-Square	Asymp. Sig.	Chi-Square	Asymp. Sig.	Chi-Square	Asymp. Sig.
Murabahah	0.867	0.929	6.847	0.445	0.178	0.674	2.81	0.729
Wakala	1.273	0.866	6.472	0.486	6.875	**0.009**	6.946	0.225
Mudarabah	10.283	**0.036**	3.999	0.78	3.692	0.055	1.334	0.931
Ijarah	7.573	0.109	10.752	0.15	0.111	0.739	4.572	0.47
Musharakah	2.085	0.72	5.511	0.598	0.727	0.394	2.85	0.723
Istisna'a	2.07	0.723	3.622	0.822	2.064	0.151	8.831	0.116
Salaam	4.794	0.309	10.661	0.154	4.729	**0.03**	3.073	0.689
Friedman test	0.00							

TABLE 8.11 K-W test mean rankings for *mudarabah* according to region

	Region	N	Mean Rank
Mudarabah	Europe	12	17.71
	GCC	16	16.47
	Other	2	16.50
	Other Middle East	5	32.50
	Southeast Asia	4	27.13
	Total	39	

TABLE 8.12 K-W test mean rankings for *wakala* and *salaam* according to nature of financial institution

	Nature of Financial Institution	N	Mean Rank
Wakala	Fully Fledged Islamic Bank	25	17.08
	Conventional Bank with Islamic Activities/ Windows	14	25.21
	Total	39	
Salaam	Fully Fledged Islamic Bank	25	22.86
	Conventional Bank with Islamic Activities/ Windows	14	14.89
	Total	39	

As depicted by Table 8.12, Islamic subsidiaries (25.21) tend to use *wakala* to a greater extent than do fully fledged Islamic banks (17.08), while the picture is reversed for the use of *salaam*, where the disparity between mean values of the two groups is wide

In addition, Question 9 was re-tested, excluding Islamic subsidiaries from the sample. However, there were no significant differences between the use of different contracts across the different control variables: region, respondent's position, nature of activities and accounting standards.

Risk perception for different Islamic finance contracts Unlike Question 9, which targeted financial institutions using Islamic finance contracts, Question 10 seeks risk perceptions for these contracts. The feedback of all respondents is valuable; therefore the K-W test is conducted on the entire research sample.

As can be seen in Table 8.13, the results of the Friedman test reflect that ranking for this question is significant, indicating that there is a significant difference between risk perceptions of Islamic contracts.

TABLE 8.13 K-W test results for Question 10 (risk seriousness) by region for entire sample

Contract	Region	N	K-W Test Mean Rank	Chi-Square	Asymp. Sig.
Murabahah	Americas	2	28.75	11.554	**0.041**
	Europe	31	38.63		
	GCC	19	43.13		
	Other	2	54		
	Other Middle East	14	25.93		
	Southeast Asia	4	20.63		
	Total	72			
Wakala	Americas	2	33	4.682	0.456
	Europe	31	32.26		
	GCC	19	37.29		
	Other	2	33		
	Other Middle East	14	42.14		
	Southeast Asia	4	49.38		
	Total	72			
Mudarabah	Americas	2	28.25	1.983	0.851
	Europe	31	36.77		
	GCC	19	37		
	Other	2	28.25		
	Other Middle East	14	34.64		
	Southeast Asia	4	46.75		
	Total	72			
Ijarah	Americas	2	33.25	4.637	0.462
	Europe	31	35.85		
	GCC	19	34.08		
	Other	2	39.5		
	Other Middle East	13	43.88		
	Southeast Asia	4	20.25		
	Total	71			
Musharakah	Americas	2	36.75	3.503	0.623
	Europe	31	39.85		
	GCC	19	33.05		

TABLE 8.13 *(Continued)*

Contract	Region	N	K-W Test Mean Rank	Chi-Square	Asymp. Sig.
	Other	2	36.75		
	Other Middle East	14	37.64		
	Southeast Asia	4	22.63		
	Total	72			
Istisna'a	Americas	2	46.5	6.413	0.268
	Europe	29	37.4		
	GCC	19	33.21		
	Other	2	46.5		
	Other Middle East	14	27.5		
	Southeast Asia	4	49.63		
	Total	70			
Salaam	Americas	2	59.75	4.569	0.471
	Europe	31	35.13		
	GCC	19	35.53		
	Other	2	28.75		
	Other Middle East	13	33		
	Southeast Asia	4	46.5		
	Total	71			
Friedman test	0.00				

K-W test results according to 'region', as illustrated in Table 8.13, indicate that *murabahah* is the only contract that reflects significant results across regions. This is expected because *murabahah* is extensively used globally. Moreover, mean rankings for *murabahah*, shown in Table 8.14, show that 'Other' regions, like Turkey and Pakistan, have a higher ranking (54.0) than the 'GCC' (43.13) and Europe (38.63), while the remaining regions follow. This can be attributed to two main reasons. First, the European and GCC markets are more sophisticated in their financial awareness of risk management, product structures and the use of risk-hedging techniques than are Turkey and Pakistan, a fact which has a direct impact on risk perception among those markets. Second, at the time of conducting this questionnaire, European and GCC markets enjoyed stable political environments and 'relatively' less volatile business cycles compared to 'Others'.

Repeating the K-W test with 'Region' as the control variable for different institutional samples of data gives consistent results, as depicted by Table 8.15,

TABLE 8.14 K-W test mean rankings for *murabahah* according to region for entire research sample

Contract	Region	N	K-W Test Mean Rank	Chi-Square	Asymp. Sig.
Murabahah	Americas	2	28.75	11.554	**0.041**
	Europe	31	38.63		
	GCC	19	43.13		
	Other	2	54.0		
	Other Middle East	14	25.93		
	Southeast Asia	4	20.63		
	Total	72			

TABLE 8.15 K-W test results by region for Question 10 for selected institutional data

	Fully Fledged Islamic Banks, Conventional Banks with Islamic Activities and Conventional Banks		Fully Fledged Islamic Banks and Conventional Banks with Islamic Activities		Fully Fledged Islamic Banks	
	Chi-Square	Asymp. Sig.	Chi-Square	Asymp. Sig.	Chi-Square	Asymp. Sig.
Murabahah	14.146	**0.015**	13.497	**0.009**	9.788	**0.044**
Wakala	4.339	0.502	3.369	0.498	3.927	0.416
Mudarabah	2.043	0.843	1.896	0.755	2.255	0.689
Ijarah	6.546	0.257	2.152	0.708	4.189	0.381
Musharakah	2.647	0.754	3.601	0.463	4.015	0.404
Istisna'a	7.964	0.158	3.241	0.518	5.859	0.21
Salaam	5.065	0.408	1.954	0.744	1.937	0.747

which confirms that there is a difference in the risk perception of *murabahah* among regions in comparing according to institutional nature for fundamental market reasons.

In addition, examining the mean rankings across different regions for *murabahah* confirms the existence of a structural pattern. As apparent from Table 8.16, the rankings are similar when conducting the K-W with different raw data. The inclusion of conventional banks and non-bankers in the test sample gave similar results.

TABLE 8.16 K-W test mean rankings for *murabahah* according to region for selected institutional data

Murabahah	Full Sample		Fully Fledged Islamic Banks, Conventional Banks with Islamic Activities and Conventional Banks		Fully Fledged Islamic Banks and Conventional Banks with Islamic Activities		Fully Fledged Islamic Banks	
Region	K-W Test Mean Rank	Rank	K-W Test Mean Rank	Rank	K-W Test Mean Rank	Rank	K-W Test Mean Rank	Rank
Americas	28.75	4th	23	4th	N/A		N/A	
Europe	38.63	3rd	34.48	2nd	23.83	2nd	17.1	2nd
GCC	43.13	2nd	34.42	3rd	22	3rd	14.78	3rd
Other	54	1st	43.5	1st	27	1st	19	1st
Other Middle East	25.93	5th	19.13	5th	10	4th	7.9	4th
Southeast Asia	20.63	6th	16	6th	9.5	5th	7.25	5th

The region 'Americas' disappears when conventional banks are excluded from the test sample as there were no respondents from Islamic banks in the Americas in this research sample.

As depicted by Table 8.16, there is a general pattern in terms of perception of *murabahah*-related issues. Such regional and institutional differences can be attributed to market conditions prevailing in each region.

Furthermore, using the entire research sample, attempts were made to test the impact of the respondents' positions, nature of financial institution, nature of activities and accounting standards on risk perception. However, the results, as depicted in Table 8.17, show that there are no significant differences except for *murabahah* contracts, which had significant risk perception according to accounting standards ($p = 0.028$), and nature of financial institution (0.03).

Additional risk issues facing IFIs Question 11 aimed at exploring the perceptions of the participants in relation to a number of risks-related statements. For this, the K-W test was employed to determine if there were any statistically significant differences across the categories of respondent profiles.

Table 8.18 shows the K-W test results for the 'Nature of financial institution' variable. Statements 1, 2, 3, 4, 8, 10 and 11 are statistically significant, which reflects that there are significant differences in risk perception among respondents according to the nature of their financial institution. It should be noted that insignificant categories are eliminated and hence are not depicted in the table. Table 8.18 also breaks down the mean rankings for these statements.

TABLE 8.17   K-W test results for Question 10 (perceived risk seriousness) for entire sample data

Contract	K-W According to Respondent's Position		K-W According to Nature of Financial Institution		K-W According to Accounting Standards		K-W According to Nature of Activities	
	Chi-Square	Asymp. Sig	Chi-Square	Asymp. Sig	Chi-Square	Asymp. Sig	Chi-Square	Asymp. Sig
Murabahah	19.85	0.14	8.75	**0.03**	10.90	**0.028**	4.08	0.67
Wakala	17.98	0.21	2.23	0.53	3.87	0.42	2.68	0.85
Mudarabah	14.02	0.45	0.27	0.97	2.82	0.59	4.36	0.63
Ijarah	13.99	0.45	7.07	0.07	6.13	0.19	9.06	0.17
Musharakah	19.02	0.16	1.50	0.68	3.18	0.53	2.34	0.89
Istisna'a	19.46	0.15	0.49	0.92	4.87	0.30	1.69	0.95
Salaam	18.39	0.19	0.97	0.81	3.52	0.48	1.69	0.95

TABLE 8.18   K-W test results for Question 11 for the full research sample according to nature of financial institution

		Statement						
		1	2	3	4	8	10	11
Chi-Square		9.73	28.631	7.969	36.833	12.224	23.692	15.743
Asymp. Sig.		**0.021**	**0.00**	**0.047**	**0.00**	**0.007**	**0.00**	**0.001**
Nature of Financial Institution	N	Mean Rank						
Fully Fledged Islamic bank	25	28.68	21.92	37.06	55.5	38.9	23.86	42.92
Conventional Bank with Islamic Activities	14	41.36	33	25	26.21	23.79	30.46	39.14
Conventional Bank	20	46.05	44.55	37.48	22.45	34.35	47.4	38.85
Others	13	31.62	55.92	46.31	32.65	48.88	50.54	17.69
Total	72							

Note: Only statements with significant p-value are displayed in the table

Statements:

1. Risks for Islamic banks should be managed using the same techniques used in conventional banking.

2. Islamic banking is more risky by nature than conventional banking.

3. Risk management for Islamic banks is more challenging than it is for conventional banks.

4. There is naturally inherent conservatism in the principles of Islamic finance.

5. In an Islamic bank, a low rate of return on deposits will lead to withdrawal of funds.

6. Depositors would hold the bank responsible for a lower rate of return on their deposits.

7. Variation among *Shari'ah* scholars' opinions represents a major risk to Islamic banking.

8. *Shari'ah*-non-compliance could severely damage the reputation of an Islamic bank.

9. AAOIFI and IFSB standards should be made mandatory for Islamic banks.

10. Corporate governance is generally weak in Islamic banks.

11. Islamic banking in its current state is a safer option than conventional banking.

Studying the mean ranking for each statement does not reveal a certain pattern governing the data; the data is widely dispersed with no clear trend of ranking according to nature of financial institution.

Repeating the K-W test for the entire research sample using other control variables (such as region, position of respondent, nature of activities and accounting standards) gives similar results; as seen in Table 8.19, which confirms that there is a significant difference in risk perception among various groups. With a 'relaxation' of the significance level to 0.06, more statements can be considered significant. An attempt was made to study the mean ranking for each statement within each test; however, the results did not reveal a certain pattern, and the data is widely dispersed with no clear ranking trend.

Factor analysis for Question 11   In order to provide further statistical robustness to the analysis, factor analysis was conducted. Factor analysis seeks to discover if the observed variables can be explained largely or entirely in terms of a much smaller number of variables called 'factors'.

As there are 11 statements for Question 11, all analysing the respondents' perceptions of different risk issues in Islamic banking, the researcher felt that reducing these statements into a more manageable number would enhance the analysis and would tell more about how respondents perceived these issues. Hence, factor analysis is deemed to be relevant in this respect as the main task of factor analysis is to cluster the related group of variables through their common variance (Pallant, 2007).

In order to test the factorability of the data in terms of sampling adequacy, there are two statistical measures available in the SPSS software that can be used: Bartlett's test of sphericity and the Kaiser-Meyer-Olkin (KMO) test. As laid down in Pallant (2007), for the factor analysis to be considered appropriate, the Bartlett's

TABLE 8.19 K-W test results for Question 11 for the full research sample according to various control variables

Statement	Region		Position of Respondent		Nature of Activities		Accounting Standards	
	Chi-Square	Asymp. Sig.	Chi-Square	Asymp. Sig.	Chi-Square	Asymp. Sig.	Chi-Square	Asymp. Sig.
1	9.695	**0.084**	18.272	0.195	7.736	0.258	9.534	**0.049**
2	29.87	**0.00**	32.308	**0.004**	31.623	**0.00**	22.755	**0.00**
3	11.308	**0.046**	23.068	**0.059**	9.59	0.143	5.236	0.264
4	24.749	**0.00**	24.06	**0.045**	18.209	**0.006**	15.894	**0.003**
5	9.5	0.091	18.734	0.175	5.504	0.481	6.408	0.171
6	10	0.075	18.471	0.186	1.598	0.953	0.937	0.919
7	19.217	**0.002**	24.05	**0.045**	14.798	**0.022**	7.077	0.132
8	4.523	0.477	18.66	0.178	12.829	**0.046**	8.222	0.084
9	16.245	**0.006**	16.724	0.271	11.293	0.08	8.495	0.075
10	33.479	**0.00**	25.222	**0.032**	25.108	**0.00**	17.862	**0.001**
11	14.644	**0.012**	22.839	0.063	23.755	**0.001**	21.018	**0.00**

test of sphericity value should be significant ($p < 0.05$), while for the KMO test, the suggested minimum outcome must be at least 0.6 (KMO score ranging from 0 to 1). The KMO test's benchmarks are as follows: for a KMO measure in the 0.90s the sampling is considered marvellous. If the outcome is in the 0.80s, then the sampling is considered meritorious, if it is in 0.70s then the sample is middling, if it is in the 0.60s then the sample is mediocre, if it is in the 0.50s then the sample is deemed miserable and lastly if it is below 0.50 then the sample is unacceptable (Pallant, 2007).

Table 8.20 presents the results of KMO and also Bartlett's test for this factor analysis.

The outcome of the KMO measure for all 11 items combined, related to risk perception, produced the value of 0.760, which is higher than 0.60, therefore the

TABLE 8.20 KMO and Bartlett's test results for the 11 items combined

Kaiser-Meyer-Olkin Measure of Sampling Adequacy		0.760
Bartlett's Test of Sphericity	Approx. Chi-Square	268.223
	df	55
	Sig.	0.000

factor analysis is appropriate for this study. In addition, the significant p-value as presented in the table of 0.000 is significantly lower than critical p-value of 0.05. Therefore, the identity matrix can be rejected. Based on the very encouraging results from both tests, factor analysis may be performed.

The second step is to choose the most suitable method of data extraction. As discussed in Chapter 6, the researcher selected principal component analysis (PCA) as it is deemed the most suitable method for the data at hand. PCA involves determining the patterns with the objective of studying the similarities and the differences among the components of the data set.

After determining the factors, the next step in order to facilitate the interpretation selection of rotation method is very important. In this regard, orthogonal (uncorrelated) and oblique (correlated) approaches are the two main techniques to rotation (Pallant, 2007). The results of the orthogonal rotation are easier to interpret, describe and report (Field, 2009). There are various rotational approaches in SPSS within both the orthogonal and oblique categories. Varimax, Quartimax and Equamax are the typical orthogonal approaches of rotation, whereas Direct Oblimin, Quartimin and Promax are the oblique methods. Varimax is the most commonly used orthogonal technique in order to reduce the number of variables whereas the Direct Oblimin technique is generally used for the oblique method. The researcher opted for Varimax rotation with Kaiser Normalization, as Table 8.21 suggests.

Table 8.21 presents the output of the number of factors that are retained according to Kaiser's criterion, in which all the eigenvalues are more than 1.0. In this situation, there are three factors that will be retained, since the eigenvalues are 3.732, 1.887 and 1.439 respectively. The screen plot, which is basically a graph of the eigenvalues, shows that the 11 variables could be reduced to only three as the graph slopes down steeply before becoming parallel to the horizontal line. It is therefore clear from the plot that there is only a three-factor solution to this question. Hence it was decided to retain the three factors.

According to Pallant (2007), the eigenvalue has to be greater than 1.0 to be regarded as significant and to be used in determining the factors. The assumption here is that the eigenvalues stand for the amount of total variation represented by the factors and this means that an eigenvalue of 1.0 or above indicates a high level of variation. Table 8.21 shows that there are three factors with an eigenvalue greater than 1.0. This means that the original 11 items can be simply reduced to three factors. The three-component solution explained 64.2% of the variance with component 1 contributing 33.9%, component 2 contributing 17.1% and component 3 contributing 13.1%. The explanatory power of the first factor is very high.

Table 8.22 further provides Rotated Component Matrix by distributing all variables to the identified three components. The factors in each component have some common characteristics and measure the same phenomenon, and therefore

TABLE 8.21 Total variance explained for Question 11

Compo-nent	Initial Eigenvalues			Extraction Sums of Squared Loadings			Rotation Sums of Squared Loadings		
	Total	% of Vari-ance	Cumu-lative %	Total	% of Vari-ance	Cumu-lative %	Total	% of Vari-ance	Cumu-lative %
1	3.732	33.926	33.926	3.732	33.926	33.926	3.103	28.214	28.214
2	1.887	17.151	51.076	1.887	17.151	51.076	2.013	18.296	46.509
3	1.439	13.078	64.155	1.439	13.078	64.155	1.941	17.646	64.155
4	0.982	8.929	73.084						
5	0.675	6.136	79.219						
6	0.571	5.190	84.410						
7	0.443	4.023	88.433						
8	0.370	3.366	91.799						
9	0.349	3.171	94.970						
10	0.299	2.722	97.692						
11	0.254	2.308	100.000						

Note: Extraction method: PCA

each component is named with a general description of the factors or variables it includes. For instance, factors in component 1 deal with the respondents' risk perception. The factors in component 2 deal with *Shari'ah* principles and their impact on the risk profile of an IFI, while the factors in component 3 deal with the rate of return paid by an IFI and the effect of this on depositors' behaviour and perception of how safe the IFI is. Thus the results indicate that all these statements can be explained with three main components. Figure 8.1 provides a screen plot of the factor analysis results for Question 11.

After conducting factor analysis between groups, a MANOVA test was computed in order to investigate if there is any significant difference between the three component groups in relation to the same control variables. This will help to locate the impact or significance of each control variable on the established distribution.

The outputs of the relevant tests are presented in Tables 8.23 to 8.25 in terms of data conforming to the assumptions before the main MANOVA analysis. In this sense, the sig. value of Box's Test of Equality of Covariance Matrices should not be lower than 0.001 in terms of not violating the assumption (Tabachnick and Fidell, 2006). In this example, the output of Box's Test shows that there is no violation of assumption of homogeneity of variances of variance-covariance matrices since the sig. value of 0.248 is higher than the critical value of 0.001.

TABLE 8.22   Rotated component matrix[a] for Question 11

	Component		
	1 Risk Perception	**2 *Shari'ah* Compliance**	**3 Rate of Return**
1 – Risks for Islamic banks should be managed using same techniques used in conventional banking	**0.134**	−0.770	−0.168
2 – Islamic banking is more risky by nature than conventional banking	**0.806**	−0.237	0.061
3 – Risk management for Islamic banks is more challenging than it is for conventional banks	**0.521**	0.301	0.400
4 – There is naturally inherent conservatism in the principles of Islamic finance	−0.484	**0.627**	−0.289
5 – In an Islamic bank, a low rate of return on deposits will lead to withdrawal of funds	0.062	−0.012	**0.882**
6 – Depositors would hold the bank responsible for a lower rate of return on their deposits	−0.010	−0.059	**0.886**
7 – Variation among *Shari'ah* scholars' opinions represents a major risk to Islamic banking	**0.584**	−0.448	−0.006
8 – *Shari'ah*-non-compliance could severely damage the reputation of an Islamic bank	0.038	**0.647**	−0.098
9 – AAOIFI and IFSB standards should be made mandatory on Islamic banks	−0.693	**0.419**	0.112
10 – Corporate governance is generally weak in Islamic banks	**0.790**	−0.145	0.253
11 – Islamic banking in its current state is a safer option than conventional banking	−0.693	−0.241	**0.121**

Notes: Extraction method: PCA.
Rotation method: Varimax with Kaiser Normalization.
[a] Rotation converged in five iterations

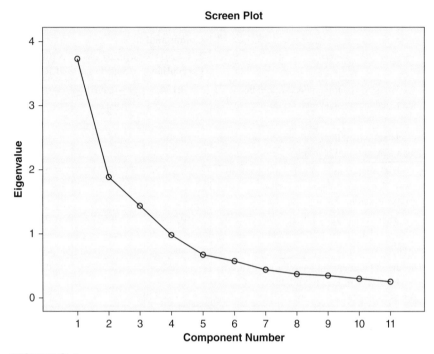

FIGURE 8.1 Screen plot for Question 11

Additionally, the output of the Levene's Test of Equality of Error Variances is explored. The results in the Sig. column show that sig. values of 'Risk Perception' (0.806), '*Shari'ah* Compliance' (0.121) and 'Rate of Return' (0.112) are higher than 0.05. Thus, there is no violation of the assumption of equality of variances for these three factors.

After performing Box's Test of Equality of Covariance Matrices and Levene's test, the set of multivariate tests was employed. Pallant (2007) states that multivariate tests of significance demonstrate if there are any significant differences among groups; the sig. value should be lower than 0.05 in order to find a statistically significant result. There are several statistics which are also used in the SPSS such as Pillai's Trace, Wilks' Lambda, Hotelling's Trace and Roy's Largest Root. In this research Wilks' Lambda result is taken into account since it is one of the most commonly used statistics (Tabachnick and Fidell, 2006). The results of the Wilks' Lambda show that there is a statistically significant difference between regions in relation to the perceptions of the three components since the sig. value of 0.00 is quite a bit lower than the critical level of 0.05.

TABLE 8.23   Box's Test of Equality of Covariance Matrices[a]

Box's M	27.466
F	1.209
df1	18
df2	544.584
Sig.	0.248

Notes: Tests the null hypothesis that the observed covariance matrices of the dependent variables are equal across groups.
[a] Design: Intercept + Region

TABLE 8.24   Levene's Test of Equality of Error Variances[a]

	F	df1	df2	Sig.
Risk Perception	0.458	5	66	0.806
Shari'ah Compliance	1.818	5	66	0.121
Rate of Return	1.867	5	66	0.112

Notes: Tests the null hypothesis that the error variance of the dependent variable is equal across groups.
[a] Design: Intercept + Region

TABLE 8.25   Multivariate Tests

Effect		Value	F	Hypothesis df	Error df	Sig.	Partial Eta Squared
Intercept	Pillai's Trace	0.995	4017.889[a]	3.000	64.000	0.000	0.995
	Wilks' Lambda	0.005	4017.889[a]	3.000	64.000	0.000	0.995
	Hotelling's Trace	188.339	4017.889[a]	3.000	64.000	0.000	0.995
	Roy's Largest Root	188.339	4017.889[a]	3.000	64.000	0.000	0.995
Region	Pillai's Trace	0.568	3.083	15.000	198.000	0.000	0.189
	Wilks' Lambda	**0.472**	**3.693**	**15.000**	**177.077**	**0.000**	**0.222**
	Hotelling's Trace	1.036	4.330	15.000	188.000	0.000	0.257
	Roy's Largest Root	0.951	12.550[b]	5.000	66.000	0.000	0.487

Notes
[a] Exact statistic
[b] Computed using alpha = 0.05

Since multivariate tests suggest that there is a statistically significant difference, a further investigation is conducted. This is in order to reveal if there is a difference in terms of region on 'Risk Perception', '*Shari'ah* Compliance' and 'Rate of Return', or only to some extent. Tests of Between-Subjects Effects provide this information. Bonferroni adjustment, which is one of the most commonly employed methods, gives this information when the alpha level of 0.05 is divided by the number of dependent variables (Pallant, 2007). In this example, there are three dependent variables, therefore 0.05 is divided by three and the new alpha level is 0.0167. As can be seen in the Tests of Between-Subjects Effects in Table 8.26, the results indicate that the dependent variables 'Risk Perception' and '*Shari'ah* Compliance' have significant values of 0.000, while 'Rate of Return' has a sig. value of 0.671, which is higher than the critical value of 0.0167 for this example.

TABLE 8.26   Tests of Between-Subjects Effects

Source	Dependent Variable	Type I Sum of Squares	df	Mean Square	F	Sig.	Partial Eta Squared
Corrected Model	Risk Perception	18.683[a]	5	3.737	11.212	0.000	0.459
	Shari'ah Compliance	14.314	5	2.863	6.937	0.000	0.344
	Rate of Return	1.537	5	0.307	0.638	0.671	0.046
Intercept	Risk Perception	738.561	1	738.561	2216.046	0.000	0.971
	Shari'ah Compliance	886.673	1	886.673	2148.655	0.000	0.970
	Rate of Return	629.139	1	629.139	1305.938	0.000	0.952
Region	**Risk Perception**	**18.683**	**5**	**3.737**	**11.212**	**0.000**	**0.459**
	***Shari'ah* Compliance**	**14.314**	**5**	**2.863**	**6.937**	**0.000**	**0.344**
	Rate of Return	1.537	5	0.307	0.638	0.671	0.046
Error	Risk Perception	21.996	66	0.333			
	Shari'ah Compliance	27.236	66	0.413			
	Rate of Return	31.796	66	0.482			
Total	Risk Perception	779.240	72				
	Shari'ah Compliance	928.222	72				
	Rate of Return	662.472	72				
Corrected Total	Risk Perception	40.679	71				
	Shari'ah Compliance	41.549	71				
	Rate of Return	33.333	71				

Notes
[a] R Squared = 0.459 (Adjusted R Squared = 0.418)

Furthermore, Tests of Between-Subjects Effects provide the effect size. Partial Eta Squared is used to determine the impact of independent variables on dependent variables, and it signifies the percentage of the variance in the dependent variable which is explained by the independent variable (Pallant, 2007). In this question, the effect of 'Region' (independent variable) on 'Risk Perception' and *'Shari'ah* Compliance' (dependent variables) can be evaluated by the Partial Eta Squared, which is depicted in the Tests of Between-Subjects Effects in Table 8.26. The importance of this impact is explored using the effect size values. Cohen (2005) categorises an effect size of 0.01 as a small effect and 0.06 as a medium effect whereas 0.14 is a large effect.

The effect size values for this case are 0.459 and 0.344, which are deemed large effect sizes using Cohen's. These results signify that 45.9% and 34.4% of the variances in 'Risk Perception' and *'Shari'ah* Compliance' scores are explained respectively by the region.

MANOVA test according to nature of financial institution for Question 11
After conducting a MANOVA test with 'Region' as the independent variable, another MANOVA test was computed with 'nature of financial institution' as the independent variable in order to investigate if there is any significant difference between the three dependent factors identified by the factor analysis.

In this case, the output of Box's Test, as shown in Table 8.27, shows that there is no violation of the assumption of homogeneity of variances of variance-covariance matrices since the sig. value of 0.080 is higher than the critical value of 0.001.

Additionally, the output of the Levene's Test of Equality of Error Variances is explored in Table 8.28. The results in the Sig. column show that sig. values of 'Risk Perception' (0.753), *'Shari'ah* Compliance' (0.427) and 'Rate of Return' (0.077) are higher than 0.05. Thus, there is no violation of the assumption of equality of variances for these three factors.

TABLE 8.27 Box's Test of
Equality of Covariance Matrices[a]

Box's M	29.551
F	1.497
df1	18
df2	9866.884
Sig.	0.080

Notes: Tests the null hypothesis that the observed covariance matrices of the dependent variables are equal across groups.
[a] Design: Intercept + Nature Financial Institution

TABLE 8.28 Levene's Test of Equality of Error Variances[a]

	F	df1	df2	Sig.
Risk Perception	0.400	3	68	0.753
Shari'ah Compliance	0.938	3	68	0.427
Rate of Return	2.386	3	68	0.077

Notes: Tests the null hypothesis that the error variance of the dependent variable is equal across groups.
[a] Design: Intercept + Nature Financial Institution

TABLE 8.29 Multivariate tests[c]

Effect		Value	F	Hypothesis df	Error df	Sig.	Partial Eta Squared
Intercept	Pillai's Trace	0.995	4340.694[a]	3.000	66.000	0.000	0.995
	Wilks' Lambda	0.005	4340.694[a]	3.000	66.000	0.000	0.995
	Hotelling's Trace	197.304	4340.694[a]	3.000	66.000	0.000	0.995
	Roy's Largest Root	197.304	4340.694[a]	3.000	66.000	0.000	0.995
Nature of FI	Pillai's Trace	0.621	5.921	9.000	204.000	0.000	0.207
	Wilks' Lambda	**0.478**	**6.335**	**9.000**	**160.777**	**0.000**	**0.218**
	Hotelling's Trace	0.890	6.396	9.000	194.000	0.000	0.229
	Roy's Largest Root	0.534	12.100[b]	3.000	68.000	0.000	0.348

Notes
[a] Exact statistic.
[b] The statistic is an upper bound on F that yields a lower bound on the significance level.
[c] Design: Intercept + Nature Financial Institution

The results of the Wilks' Lambda in Table 8.29 show that there is a statistically significant difference according to nature of financial institution since the sig. value of 0.00 is quite a bit lower than the critical level of 0.05.

Since the multivariate test suggests that there is a statistically significant difference, a further investigation is conducted. Tests of Between-Subjects Effects provide this information. In this case, there are three dependent variables, therefore 0.05 is divided by three and the new alpha level is 0.0167. As can be seen in the Tests of Between-Subjects Effects in Table 8.30, the results indicate that the dependent variables 'Risk Perception' and '*Shari'ah* Compliance' have significant values of 0.000, while 'Rate of Return' has a sig. value of 0.234, which is higher than the critical value of 0.0167 for this example. Furthermore, the effect size values as evaluated by the Partial Eta Squared for this case are 0.301 and 0.336, which are deemed large-effect sizes using Cohen's. These results signify that 30.1% and

TABLE 8.30   Tests of Between-Subjects Effects

Source	Dependent Variable	Type III Sum of Squares	df	Mean Square	F	Sig.	Partial Eta Squared
Corrected Model	Risk Perception	12.240[a]	3	4.080	9.755	0.000	0.301
	Shari'ah Compliance	13.952[b]	3	4.651	11.459	0.000	0.336
	Rate of Return	2.014[c]	3	0.671	1.457	0.234	0.060
Intercept	Risk Perception	715.613	1	715.613	1711.036	0.000	0.962
	Shari'ah Compliance	799.581	1	799.581	1970.166	0.000	0.967
	Rate of Return	570.736	1	570.736	1239.172	0.000	0.948
Nature of FI	**Risk Perception**	**12.240**	**3**	**4.080**	**9.755**	**0.000**	**0.301**
	***Shari'ah* Compliance**	**13.952**	**3**	**4.651**	**11.459**	**0.000**	**0.336**
	Rate of Return	2.014	3	0.671	1.457	0.234	0.060
Error	Risk Perception	28.440	68	0.418			
	Shari'ah Compliance	27.597	68	0.406			
	Rate of Return	31.319	68	0.461			
Total	Risk Perception	779.240	72				
	Shari'ah Compliance	928.222	72				
	Rate of Return	662.472	72				
Corrected Total	Risk Perception	40.679	71				
	Shari'ah Compliance	41.549	71				
	Rate of Return	33.333	71				

[a] R Squared = 0.301 (Adjusted R Squared = 0.270).
[b] R Squared = 0.336 (Adjusted R Squared = 0.306).
[c] R Squared = 0.060 (Adjusted R Squared = 0.019)

33.6% of the variances in 'Risk Perception' and '*Shari'ah* Compliance' scores are explained respectively by the nature of financial institution.

Conducting the MANOVA test according to 'Region' and 'Nature of Financial Institution' as independent variables provided consistent results. It can be concluded that 'Risk Perception' and '*Shari'ah* Compliance' are significant dependent variables and have strong explanatory power, while 'Rate of Return' does not follow the pattern.

Capital Adequacy for Islamic Banks

This section addresses capital adequacy challenges facing IFIs. It tackles the controversial issues regarding the applicability of the Basel II and Basel III Accords to IFIs, and the appropriate capital requirement levels for Islamic banks.

TABLE 8.31 K-W test results by region for Question 15 (capital adequacy) for entire research sample

	Statement									
	1		**2**		**3**		**4**		**5**	
Chi-Square	18.081		24.185		20.089		20.24		5.502	
Asymp. Sig.	**0.003**		**0.000**		**0.001**		**0.001**		0.358	
Region	**N**	**Mean Rank**	**N**	**Mean Rank**	**N**	**Mean Rank**	**N**	**Mean Rank**	**N**	**Mean Rank**
Americas	2	59.25	2	22	2	27.5	2	57	2	28
Europe	31	45.13	31	24.66	31	30.26	31	45.06	31	32.06
GCC	19	23.16	19	51.24	19	50.71	19	24.24	19	40.39
Other	2	18	2	48.5	2	59	2	28.75	2	28
Other Middle East	14	34.54	14	42.86	14	33.29	14	32.39	14	39.93
Southeast Asia	4	37.75	4	37.25	4	21.88	4	36.38	4	48.88
Total	72		72		72		72		72	

The results of the K-W test in Table 8.31 show that all statements are statistically significant (p-value < 0.05) except for Statement 5 (p-value $= 0.358$) implying that regional differences in relation to capital adequacy are significant. Statements as depicted in the following tables and their coding are:

1. Basel II standards should be equally applied to Islamic banks without modification.
2. IFSB standards on Capital Adequacy should be used by Islamic banks rather than Basel II.
3. Basel II standards should be reviewed after failing to prevent the financial crisis.
4. The proposed Basel III rules would be easily applicable to Islamic banks.
5. Stricter capital, leverage and liquidity rules, as proposed under Basel III, are likely to prevent another financial crisis.

Conducting the K-W test with 'Nature of Financial Institution' as the control variable for the entire research sample gives different results, as illustrated by Table 8.32. All statements are statistically insignificant except Statement 5, which shows different views between bankers (whether Islamic or conventional) and non-bankers, which is also evident from the mean ranking. This implies that the nature of financial institution is not a statistically determining factor; and that the opinions of the respondents are rather similar.

TABLE 8.32 K-W test results by nature of financial institution for Question 15 (capital adequacy) for entire research sample

	Statement									
	1		**2**		**3**		**4**		**5**	
Chi-Square	5.611		5.127		5.781		4.07		9.79	
Asymp. Sig.	0.132		0.163		0.123		0.254		**0.02**	
Nature of Financial Institution	**N**	**Mean Rank**	**N**	**Mean Rank**	**N**	**Mean Rank**	**N**	**Mean Rank**	**N**	**Mean Rank**
Fully Fledged Islamic bank	25	30.92	25	37.9	25	37.4	25	31.86	25	39.98
Conventional Bank with Islamic Activities	14	33.93	14	45.71	14	46.14	14	34.57	14	40.75
Conventional Bank	20	45	20	32.05	20	32	20	39.73	20	38.78
Others	13	36.92	13	30.73	13	31.31	13	42.54	13	21.73
Total	72		72		72		72		72	

Furthermore, repeating the K-W test with 'Nature of Activities' and 'Respondent's Position' as control variables for the entire research sample gives results consistent with those of K-W according to 'Nature of Financial Institution', as illustrated by Tables 8.33 and 8.34 respectively. For 'Nature of Activities', statements are statistically insignificant except for Statements 1 and 3, while as depicted by Table 8.34 for 'Respondent's Position', all statements are statistically insignificant except Statement 5. This reflects the difference in opinions among different groups regarding the newly developed Basel III capital and liquidity standards and their applicability to Islamic banking.

The Credit Crisis and Islamic Banks

This section of the questionnaire seeks respondents' views on different issues relating to the recent global crisis. For this purpose, Question 16 of the survey presented nine statements to respondents. This part applied to all the respondents, which means replies from all institutional samples of data were obtained by asking respondents to answer using a five-point Likert scale (ranking from Strongly Agree = 5 to Strongly Disagree = 1). Table 8.35 employs the K-W test to examine the significant difference among respondents' perceptions according to 'Region'.

TABLE 8.33 K-W test results by nature of activities for Question 15 for entire research sample

| | \multicolumn{10}{c}{**Statement**} | | | | | | | | | |
	\multicolumn{2}{c}{**1**}	\multicolumn{2}{c}{**2**}	\multicolumn{2}{c}{**3**}	\multicolumn{2}{c}{**4**}	\multicolumn{2}{c}{**5**}
Chi-Square	8.467		12.532		11.053		13.98		14.255	
Asymp. Sig.	0.206		**0.051**		0.087		**0.03**		**0.027**	
Nature of Activities	**N**	**Mean Rank**	**N**	**Mean Rank**	**N**	**Mean Rank**	**N**	**Mean Rank**	**N**	**Mean Rank**
Commercial Banking	11	34.91	11	39.68	11	38.95	11	29.23	11	42.86
Integrated Banking	9	38.67	9	37.5	9	39	9	40.61	9	36.33
Investment Banking	11	44.09	11	23.86	11	24.23	11	48.32	11	37.91
Private Equity House	1	67	1	11.5	1	27.5	1	44	1	43
Retail & Commercial Banking	17	37.35	17	39.79	17	38.35	17	33.26	17	45.71
Retail Banking	10	22.9	10	50.4	10	49.55	10	24.7	10	31
Other	13	36.92	13	30.73	13	31.31	13	42.54	13	21.73
Total	72		72		72		72		72	

Statements tested in this section and their coding are as follows:

1. Islamic banks are more resilient to economic shocks than their conventional peers.
2. The recent crisis would not have happened under a true Islamic banking system.
3. Islamic finance could have solved the global crisis.
4. Risk management must be embedded institutionally.
5. Banks in general used to rely heavily on rating agencies.
6. Islamic banks rely less on rating agencies than conventional banks.
7. The Islamic finance industry should develop its own rating agencies.
8. Islamic banks will emerge stronger from the crisis.
9. Consolidation is needed among smaller Islamic banks.

The results in Table 8.35 show that most statements are statistically significant (p-value < 0.05). With a 'relaxation' of the confidence level to 0.06, we can accept all statements except Statements 6 and 9. Mean rankings reveal that,

TABLE 8.34   K-W test results by position of respondent for Question 15 for entire research sample

	Statement									
	1		**2**		**3**		**4**		**5**	
Chi-Square	12.056		12.503		16.546		19.49		29.835	
Asymp. Sig.	0.602		0.566		0.281		0.147		**0.008**	
Position of Respondent	**N**	**Mean Rank**	**N**	**Mean Rank**	**N**	**Mean Rank**	**N**	**Mean Rank**	**N**	**Mean Rank**
Analyst	5	43	5	32.5	5	29.3	5	44	5	43
Senior Analyst	4	37.75	4	27.75	4	21.88	4	44	4	13
Auditor	2	42.25	2	42	2	16.25	2	57	2	13
CEO	5	36.9	5	34.3	5	29.3	5	37	5	34.7
CFO	2	9	2	64.5	2	59	2	13.5	2	13
Consultant	2	27.25	2	42	2	43.25	2	23.75	2	13
Director	6	39.17	6	22	6	29	6	48.33	6	31.92
General Manager	10	37.8	10	36.6	10	37.85	10	33.85	10	47.7
Head of Investment Banking	1	3	1	64.5	1	59	1	3.5	1	13
Head of Risk Management	11	33.27	11	37.95	11	36.91	11	39.91	11	33.64
Managing Director	8	37.81	8	38.88	8	40.44	8	28.75	8	48.06
Risk Manager	12	41.63	12	35.17	12	38.75	12	34.33	12	41.92
Senior Trader	2	41	2	38	2	59	2	44	2	57.25
Shari'ah Scholar	1	3	1	64.5	1	59	1	13.5	1	13
Solicitor	1	51.5	1	32.5	1	27.5	1	44	1	43
Total	72		72		72		72		72	

although there is no clear pattern that could be traced, the 'GCC' and 'Other' categories are usually ranked at the top for most statements. This emphasises the fact that respondents from these two regions are more aggressive than those from other regions in their views about the credit crunch and Islamic finance. Thus the findings indicate that there are statistically different and significant opinions among the respondents coming from different regions.

TABLE 8.35 K-W test results by region for Question 16 for entire research sample

Statement	1	2	3	4	5	6	7	8	9
Chi-Square	11.052	19.879	27.446	14.571	10.877	4.863	18.587	11.171	3.695
Asymp. Sig.	**0.05**	**0.001**	**0.00**	**0.012**	**0.054**	0.433	**0.002**	**0.048**	0.594
Region	Mean Rank								
Americas	30.25	29	9	55	30.75	33	38	31	44.5
Europe	28.39	27.08	26.1	42.5	33.89	34.16	25.11	30.05	39.06
GCC	44.76	50.87	51.37	38.05	47.42	43.16	49.32	48.29	29.5
Other	52.5	41	56.5	17.25	52.75	51.25	43.5	31	32
Other Middle East	38.86	41.93	35.43	26.71	29.29	33.57	41.89	38.04	38.93
Southeast Asia	47	23.75	54	17.25	24.88	27.63	40.75	30.63	39.63

Note: N for all statements = 72

In addition, attempts were made to test the impacts of 'Nature of Financial Institution', 'Nature of Activities', 'Accounting Standards' and 'Respondent's Position' on the responses; the results are summarised in Tables 8.36 to 8.39.

With the exception of Statement 3 (p = 0.005), there is no statistically significant difference among all other statements. Mean ranking for Statement 3, as seen in Table 8.36, shows that fully fledged Islamic banks are far more aggressive in their belief that Islamic finance could have solved the global crisis than other categories (46.2), followed by Islamic subsidiaries (40.25), then by Others

TABLE 8.36 K-W test results by nature of financial institution for Question 16 for entire research sample

Statement	1	2	3	4	5	6	7	8	9
Chi-Square	4.614	1.698	12.818	4.531	5.573	5.631	2.965	4.369	4.238
Asymp. Sig.	0.202	0.637	**0.005**	0.21	0.134	0.131	0.397	0.224	0.237
Region	Mean Rank								
Fully Fledged Islamic bank	41.6	38.46	46.2	30.44	42.02	31.48	35.64	37.3	31.54
Conventional Bank with Islamic Activities	38.21	35.29	40.25	36.07	36.82	42.93	43.32	43.07	33.96
Conventional Bank	34.95	38.75	27.38	40.83	28.1	33.23	37.05	29.53	43.1
Others	27.23	30.58	27.85	41.96	38.46	44.27	29.96	38.62	38.62

Note: N for all statements = 72

TABLE 8.37 K-W test results by nature of activities for Question 16 for entire research sample

Statement	1	2	3	4	5	6	7	8	9
Chi-Square	12.156	8.402	11.446	12.029	4.862	15.608	10.263	6.527	2.581
Asymp. Sig.	**0.059**	0.21	0.076	0.061	0.562	**0.016**	0.114	0.367	0.859
Region	Mean Rank								
Commercial Banking	41.36	41.59	46.73	36.86	37.41	31.32	39.86	34.27	35.77
Integrated Banking	38.94	32.61	27.61	45.5	24.22	35.89	34.61	29.11	39.39
Investment Banking	27.55	25.95	29.45	42.95	33.68	22.68	28.32	29.82	36.27
Private Equity House	7	39.5	34	55	42.5	1.5	19	18.5	12.5
Retail & Commercial Banking	39.29	40.85	39.88	30.03	39.38	37.59	37.35	40.38	38.21
Retail Banking	49.05	46	46.75	22.95	41.6	49.5	52.3	45.4	31.7
Other	27.23	30.58	27.85	41.96	38.46	44.27	29.96	38.62	38.62

Note: N for all statements = 72

TABLE 8.38 K-W test results by accounting standards for Question 16 for entire research sample

Statement	1	2	3	4	5	6	7	8	9
Chi-Square	6.86	7.494	11.839	8.564	11.496	6.621	10.72	5.72	4.252
Asymp. Sig.	0.143	0.112	**0.019**	0.073	**0.022**	0.157	**0.03**	0.221	0.373
Region	Mean Rank								
AAOIFI standards	52.5	51.5	54.83	28.17	45.42	49.5	57	43.25	22.25
International & AAOIFI standards	40.9	49.1	54.5	45.6	58.9	29.7	49.8	52.6	33.1
International standards	36.79	33.74	34.33	38.32	34.61	34.32	33.12	32.76	39.08
Local accounting standards	35.65	39.4	36	22.95	24.6	30.3	38.9	35.85	34.2
N/A	27.23	30.58	27.85	41.96	38.46	44.27	29.96	38.62	38.62

Note: N for all statements = 72

and Conventional Banks. This is consistent with the K-W test result according to 'Region' as the control variable (Table 8.35) because respondents from the 'GCC' and 'Other' regions in this research sample are mainly fully fledged Islamic banks and Islamic subsidiaries.

TABLE 8.39 K-W test results by respondent's position for Question 16 for entire research sample

Statement	1	2	3	4	5	6	7	8	9
Chi-Square	17.068	19.453	19.773	13.82	23.564	14.194	23.054	15.677	17.272
Asymp. Sig.	0.253	0.148	0.137	0.463	**0.052**	0.435	**0.059**	0.333	0.242
Region	**Mean Rank**								
Analyst	36.9	40.1	24	39.9	19	33	40.2	24.3	52
Senior Analyst	26.13	35	39.63	40.75	21.25	45.25	21.5	34.63	45.88
Auditor	30.25	51.5	14	55	63	33	47	25.75	57
CEO	32.1	33.3	39	39.9	46	24.1	18.5	26.4	38.1
CFO	63.5	63.5	56.5	40.75	52.75	39.75	68	55.25	32
Consultant	41.25	51.5	41.5	31.5	63	51.25	43.5	55.25	29.25
Director	21	20.83	15.67	42.42	30.33	41.17	18.42	35.17	33.83
General Manager	30	41.2	34.5	27.65	30.75	31.75	40.8	33.5	28.1
Head of Investment Banking	63.5	39.5	69	55	63	57.5	68	67	32
Head of Risk Management	38.23	36.59	41.27	37.77	43.55	32.55	39.14	40.82	30.45
Managing Director	46.94	45.5	41.5	25.44	28.94	49.81	40	43.31	34.06
Risk Manager	40	26.25	38.79	36.13	33.92	30.42	32.88	32.88	47.04
Senior Trader	30.25	29	34	55	42.5	33.75	47	37.5	22.25
Shari'ah Scholar	63.5	63.5	69	8	63	69.5	68	67	12.5
Solicitor	19	8.5	34	55	42.5	33	38	18.5	12.5

Note: N for all statements = 72

The same statements are further investigated in relation to the nature of activities. As depicted by Table 8.37, only Statement 6 is statistically significant. With a relaxation of the confidence level to 0.06, one can also accept Statement 1. For both Statements 1 and 6, 'Retail Banking' is the most aggressive category according to mean rankings, and 'Private Equity Houses' is by far the least aggressive. Other categories fall in between, although no particular trend can be established. These results confirm the K-W test results according to 'Region' (Table 8.35), as out of the 10 retail banks included in the research sample, five are located in the 'GCC' and one is located in 'Other'. It should be noted that the sole Private Equity

House in this research sample is also located in the 'GCC'. Furthermore, results from Table 8.37 are also consistent with the K-W test results according to 'Nature of Financial Institution' (Table 8.36) because 8 out of the 10 retail banks included in the research sample are fully fledged Islamic banks, and the other two are Islamic subsidiaries. The one Private Equity House is also a fully fledged Islamic bank.

Table 8.38 shows that only Statements 3, 5 and 7 are statistically significant according to accounting standards. Mean rankings reflect that for these three statements, 'AAOIFI' and 'International & AAOIFI standards' are always top ranked, followed by other criteria. These results confirm the K-W results for the previous control variables in Tables 8.35 to 8.37; therefore the results indicate that the perceived views in relation to accounting standards are statistically significant for these three statements.

The potential impact of the respondents' positions on the same statements is also investigated. The p-values in Table 8.39 show that there are no significant differences according to respondent's position. By relaxing the confidence level to 0.06, one can also accept Statements 5 and 7. No pattern could be concluded by studying the mean ranking. The only obvious conclusion is that *Shari'ah* scholars ranked the highest mean and solicitors had the lowest mean values for most, but not all, statements. This is expected because *Shari'ah* scholars tend to be more conservative in their views about Islamic banking and *Shari'ah* compliance, while solicitors usually focus more on legal structures rather than the *Shari'ah* side of transactions.

Factor analysis for Question 16 (credit crisis and Islamic finance) To locate the perception of the participants regarding the credit crisis in relation to a number of issues related to Islamic finance, they were provided with a number of statements. The opinions are analysed through factor analysis.

As previously explained, factor analysis seeks to discover if the observed variables can be explained largely or entirely in terms of a much smaller number of variables called the factors.

As there are nine statements for Question 16, analysing the respondents' perceptions toward Islamic banking and the global credit crisis, the researcher felt that reducing these statements to a more manageable number would enhance the analysis and tell more about how respondents perceived these issues. Hence, factor analysis is deemed to be relevant in this respect as the main task of factor analysis is to cluster the related group of variables through their common variance.

In order to test the factorability of the data in terms of sampling adequacy, Table 8.40 presents the results of KMO and also Bartlett's Test for this factor analysis.

The outcome of the KMO measure for all nine items combined, related to the respondents' perceptions, showed the value of 0.844, which is higher than 0.60,

TABLE 8.40 KMO and Bartlett's Test results for the nine items combined

Kaiser-Meyer-Olkin Measure of Sampling Adequacy		0.844
Bartlett's Test of Sphericity	Approx. Chi-Square	173.046
	df	36
	Sig.	0.000

implying that factor analysis is appropriate for this study. In addition, the significant p-value of 0.000 is significantly lower than critical p-value of 0.05. Therefore, the identity matrix can be rejected. Based on the very encouraging results from both tests, factor analysis may be performed.

In the second step, PCA is used for data extraction, and then Varimax rotation is used in order to reduce the number of variables as in Table 8.41, which presents the output of the number of factors that are retained according to Kaiser's criterion, in which all the eigenvalues are more than 1.0. In this situation, there are three factors that will be retained, since the eigenvalues are 3.170, 1.356 and 1.332 respectively.

The results indicate that these three components can explain 64.9% of the total variation, which satisfies the use of factor analysis.

Figure 8.2, which is basically a graph of the eigenvalues, shows that the nine variables could be reduced to only three as the graph slopes down steeply before

TABLE 8.41 Total variance explained for Question 16

	Initial Eigenvalues			Rotation Sums of Squared Loadings		
Component	Total	% of Variance	Cumulative %	Total	% of Variance	Cumulative %
1	3.682	40.906	40.906	3.170	35.225	35.225
2	1.136	12.617	53.523	1.356	15.064	50.289
3	1.031	11.456	64.980	1.322	14.691	64.980
4	0.746	8.287	73.267			
5	0.637	7.081	80.348			
6	0.523	5.813	86.161			
7	0.459	5.098	91.260			
8	0.402	4.472	95.732			
9	0.384	4.268	100.000			

Note: Extraction method: PCA

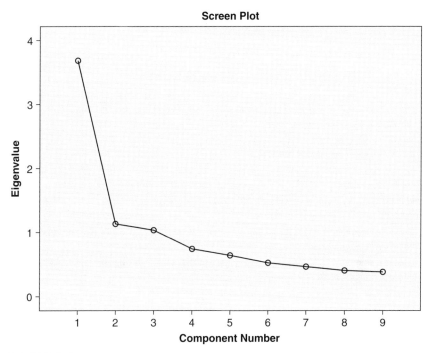

FIGURE 8.2   Screen plot for Question 16

becoming parallel to the horizontal line after the third component. It is clear from the plot that there is only a three-factor solution to this question. Therefore, it was decided to retain the three factors.

Table 8.41 shows that there are three factors with an eigenvalue greater than 1.0; this means that the original nine items can be simply reduced to three factors. The three-component solution explains 64.9% of the variance with component 1 contributing 40.9%, component 2 contributing 12.6% and component 3 contributing 11.5%. The explanatory power of the first factor is very high.

Table 8.42 further provides a rotated component matrix by distributing all variables to the identified three components. The test results showed no component for factor 2; therefore the researcher accepted factors 1 and 3 only. The factors in each component have some common characteristics and measure the same phenomenon and therefore each component is named with a general description of the factors or variables it includes. For instance, factors in component 1 deal with 'resilience of IFIs'. The factors in component three deal with 'risk management must be embedded institutionally'. The former includes seven statements,

TABLE 8.42 Rotated component matrix[a] for Question 16

	Component		
	1. Resilience of IFIs	**2.**	**3. Risk management must be institutional**
Islamic banks are more resilient to economic shocks than their conventional peers	**0.776**	−0.050	−0.238
The recent crisis would not have happened under a true Islamic banking system	**0.764**	0.081	−0.082
Islamic finance could have solved the global crisis	**0.643**	0.468	−0.146
Risk management must be embedded institutionally	−0.100	−0.189	**0.834**
Banks in general used to rely heavily on rating agencies	**0.552**	0.447	0.358
Islamic banks rely less on rating agencies than conventional banks	**0.454**	−0.029	−0.583
Islamic finance industry should develop its own rating agencies	**0.743**	0.265	−0.075
Islamic banks will emerge stronger from the crisis	**0.706**	−0.007	−0.211
Consolidation is needed among smaller Islamic banks	−0.012	−0.906	**0.156**

Notes: Extraction method: PCA.
Rotation method: Varimax with Kaiser Normalization.
[a] Rotation converged in nine iterations

while the latter includes only two components. Thus, the heavy weight is with the 'resilience of IFIs' component.

MANOVA test according to region for Question 16 After conducting factor analysis between groups a MANOVA test was computed in order to investigate if there is any significant difference between the two factors in relation to same control variables. This will help to locate the impact or significance of each control variable on the established distribution.

The MANOVA test was conducted according to 'Region' as the independent variable with the objective of testing the significance of 'Region' on the identified two components. In this case, the output of the Box's Test in Table 8.43 shows that there is no violation of assumption of homogeneity of variances of variance-covariance matrices since the sig. value of 0.013 is higher than the critical value of 0.001.

TABLE 8.43 Box's Test of
Equality of Covariance Matrices[a]

Box's M	24.157
F	2.342
df1	9
df2	824.888
Sig.	**0.013**

Note: Tests the null hypothesis that the
observed covariance matrices of the dependent variables are equal across groups.
[a] Design: Intercept + Region

TABLE 8.44 Levene's Test of Equality of Error Variances[a]

	F	df1	df2	Sig.
Resilience of IFIs	0.625	5	66	**0.681**
Risk management is institutional	1.398	5	66	**0.236**

Notes: Tests the null hypothesis that the error variance of the dependent variable is equal
across groups.
[a] Design: Intercept + Region

Additionally, the output of the Levene's Test of Equality of Error Variances
(Table 8.44) is explored. The results in the Sig. column show that sig. values of
'Resilience of IFIs' (0.681) and 'Risk management must be institutional' (0.236)
are higher than 0.05. Thus, there is no violation of the assumption of equality of
variances for these two factors.

The results of the Wilks' Lambda in Table 8.45 show that there is a statistically
significant difference according to the region since the sig. value of 0.01 is quite
a bit lower than the critical level of 0.05.

Since the multivariate test suggests that there is a statistically significant difference, a further investigation is conducted. Tests of Between-Subjects Effects
provide this information. In this case, there are two dependent variables, therefore 0.05 is divided by two and the new alpha level is 0.025. As can be seen
in the Tests of Between-Subjects Effects in Table 8.46, the results indicate that
'Resilience of IFIs' has significant values of 0.000, while 'Risk management must
be institutional' has a sig. value of 0.242, which is higher than the critical value
of 0.025 for this example. Furthermore, the effect size values as evaluated by the
Partial Eta Squared for 'Resilience of IFIs' is 0.320, which are deemed large-effect
sizes using Cohen's criteria. It can be concluded that these results, which signify

TABLE 8.45 Multivariate tests[c]

Effect		Value	F	Hypothesis df	Error df	Sig.	Partial Eta Squared
Intercept	Pillai's Trace	0.975	1255.030[a]	2.000	65.000	0.000	0.975
	Wilks' Lambda	0.025	1255.030[a]	2.000	65.000	0.000	0.975
	Hotelling's Trace	38.616	1255.030[a]	2.000	65.000	0.000	0.975
	Roy's Largest Root	38.616	1255.030[a]	2.000	65.000	0.000	0.975
Region	Pillai's Trace	0.370	2.992	10.000	132.000	0.002	0.185
	Wilks' Lambda	**0.646**	**3.175[a]**	**10.000**	**130.000**	**0.001**	**0.196**
	Hotelling's Trace	0.524	3.354	10.000	128.000	0.001	0.208
	Roy's Largest Root	0.473	6.249[b]	5.000	66.000	0.000	0.321

Notes
[a] Exact statistic.
[b] The statistic is an upper bound on F that yields a lower bound on the significance level.
[c] Design: Intercept + Region

TABLE 8.46 Tests of Between-Subjects Effects

Source	Dependent Variable	Type III Sum of Squares	df	Mean Square	F	Sig.	Partial Eta Squared
Corrected Model	Resilience of IFIs	13.209[a]	5	2.642	6.221	0.000	0.320
	Risk management is institutional	2.821[b]	5	0.564	1.384	0.242	0.095
Intercept	Resilience of IFIs	313.934	1	313.934	739.239	0.000	0.918
	Risk management is institutional	438.911	1	438.911	1076.963	0.000	0.942
Region	**Resilience of IFIs**	**13.209**	**5**	**2.642**	**6.221**	**0.000**	**0.320**
	Risk management is institutional	2.821	5	0.564	1.384	0.242	0.095
Error	Resilience of IFIs	28.028	66	0.425			
	Risk management is institutional	26.898	66	0.408			
Total	Resilience of IFIs	877.837	72				
	Risk management is institutional	1292.250	72				
Corrected Total	Resilience of IFIs	41.237	71				
	Risk management is institutional	29.719	71				

Notes
[a] R Squared = 0.320 (Adjusted R Squared = 0.269).
[b] R Squared = 0.095 (Adjusted R Squared = 0.026)

32% of the variances in 'Resilience of IFIs' scores, are explained respectively by region.

An attempt was also made to see the effect of 'Nature of FI' on the identified components in factor analysis through MANOVA. However, no significant results could be established.

RISK MANAGEMENT AND REPORTING

This part of the questionnaire examines the risk management and hedging techniques used within IFIs. Question 17 covers the frequency of producing risk management reports as perceived by the participants, and is applicable only to financial institutions.

As depicted by Table 8.47, the K-W test for fully fledged Islamic banks, conventional banks with Islamic activities, and conventional banks shows that, statistically, there is a significant difference among various regions in the frequency of producing risk reports (p-value < 0.05) except for Commodity Risk Report (0.094), Industry Concentration Risk Report (0.129), Credit Exposure Report (0.091) and Large Exposure Report (0.071). Hence, for the rest of the reports there are significant differences in the perceptions of the participants. Thus, for most of the reports region is a significant factor.

Repeating the K-W test with 'Region' as the control variable for various institutional samples of data gives different results as the removal of conventional banks from the sample shows that the distribution of frequency of producing reports becomes the same across more reports, i.e. fewer risk reports show statistical significance in the frequency of production across regions. By removing Islamic subsidiaries from the sample and conducting the K-W test on fully fledged Islamic banks exclusively, only two reports (FX Risk Report and Credit Exposure Report) become statistically significant across various regions.

The results reflect the risk management culture difference between Islamic and conventional banks. By conducting the K-W test on fully fledged IFIs only, there was little significance between the responses across different regions. However, expanding the sample to include Islamic subsidiaries of conventional banks increased the significant difference in risk reporting across regions. When the sample was expanded further to incorporate conventional banks, the significance in difference becomes more noticeable.

Tables 8.48 to 8.55 examine the mean rankings for reports with statistically significant differences in frequency of production.

In this particular case mean ranking requires clarification. Since during coding 'daily reporting' was assigned value 1, and 'never' was assigned value 5, this has

TABLE 8.47 K-W test results for Question 17 (risk reporting) by region for selected sample data

Frequency of Producing:	Fully Fledged Islamic Banks, Conventional Banks with Islamic Activities and Conventional Banks			Fully Fledged Islamic Banks and Conventional Banks with Islamic Activities			Fully Fledged Islamic Banks		
	Chi-Square	df	Asymp. Sig.	Chi-Square	df	Asymp. Sig.	Chi-Square	df	Asymp. Sig.
Capital Requirement Report	28.727	5	**0.00**	11.746	4	**0.019**	7.89	4	0.096
Operational Risk Report	18.01	5	**0.003**	3.534	4	0.473	2.208	4	0.698
Profit Rate Risk Report	20.859	5	**0.001**	8.04	4	0.09	4.539	4	0.338
FX Risk Report	19.469	5	**0.002**	10.321	4	**0.035**	9.646	4	**0.047**
Liquidity Risk Report	19.312	5	**0.002**	8.026	4	0.091	5.357	4	0.253
Commodity Risk Report	9.405	5	0.094	6.636	4	0.156	7.297	4	0.121
Country Report	11.58	5	**0.041**	6.554	4	0.161	5.218	4	0.266
Equity Mark-to-Market Report	12.611	5	**0.027**	11.406	4	0.022	6.464	4	0.167
Classified Accounts Report	16.91	5	**0.005**	9.651	4	**0.047**	5.386	4	0.25
Industry Concentration Risk Report	8.537	5	0.129	3.168	4	0.53	3.153	4	0.533
Credit Exposure Report	9.479	5	0.091	10.937	4	**0.027**	12.452	4	**0.014**
Large Exposure Report	10.155	5	0.071	9.408	4	0.052	7.111	4	0.13

impact on the mean ranking. In other words, the better mean value here would be the lower value indicating better disclosure.

The results presented in this section so far indicate a particular pattern. The trend is obvious: conventional banks, concentrated in Europe and the Americas, produce risk reports more frequently than Islamic banks. Risk management and reporting is more advanced in conventional banking than in Islamic banking.

TABLE 8.48 Frequency of producing Capital Requirement Report

Region	Fully Fledged Islamic Banks, Conventional Banks with Islamic Activities and Conventional Banks			Fully Fledged Islamic Banks and Conventional Banks with Islamic Activities			Fully Fledged Islamic Banks		
	N	Mean Rank	Rank	N	Mean Rank	Rank	N	Mean Rank	Rank
Americas	2	13.5	1st	N/A	N/A	N/A	N/A	N/A	N/A
Europe	20	18.3	2nd	12	13.46	1st	5	8	1st
GCC	19	32.03	4th	16	20.75	3rd	9	12.5	3rd
Other	2	23.5	3rd	2	14.75	2nd	2	8.75	2nd
Other Middle East	12	47.63	6th	5	31.9	5th	5	19.5	5th
Southeast Asia	4	37.5	5th	4	24.38	4th	4	14.38	4th
Total	59			39			25		

TABLE 8.49 Frequency of producing Operational Risk Report

Region	Fully Fledged Islamic Banks, Conventional Banks with Islamic Activities and Conventional Banks			Fully Fledged Islamic Banks and Conventional Banks with Islamic Activities			Fully Fledged Islamic Banks		
	N	Mean Rank	Rank	N	Mean Rank	Rank	N	Mean Rank	Rank
Americas	2	11.5	1st	N/A	N/A	N/A	N/A	N/A	N/A
Europe	20	19.5	2nd	12	15.17	1st	5	9.1	1st
GCC	19	33.08	4th	16	19.94	3rd	9	12.22	3rd
Other	2	27.5	3rd	2	17	2nd	2	10.25	2nd
Other Middle East	11	40.18	6th	4	24.13	5th	4	14.63	5th
Southeast Asia	3	38.17	5th	3	23.83	4th	3	13.83	4th
Total	57			37			23		

TABLE 8.50 Frequency of Producing Profit Rate Risk Report

Region	Fully Fledged Islamic Banks, Conventional Banks with Islamic Activities and Conventional Banks			Fully Fledged Islamic Banks and Conventional Banks with Islamic Activities			Fully Fledged Islamic Banks		
	N	Mean Rank	Rank	N	Mean Rank	Rank	N	Mean Rank	Rank
Americas	2	17	1st	N/A	N/A	N/A	N/A	N/A	N/A
Europe	20	18.95	2nd	12	13.67	1st	5	7.9	1st
GCC	19	33.11	4th	16	20.56	2nd	9	12.61	2nd
Other	2	32.5	3rd	2	21.5	3rd	2	12.75	3rd
Other Middle East	12	41.88	6th	5	27.5	5th	5	16.5	5th
Southeast Asia	3	33.83	5th	3	22.5	4th	3	13	4th
Total	58			38			24		

TABLE 8.51 Frequency of producing FX Risk Report

Region	Fully Fledged Islamic Banks, Conventional Banks with Islamic Activities and Conventional Banks			Fully Fledged Islamic Banks and Conventional Banks with Islamic Activities			Fully Fledged Islamic Banks		
	N	Mean Rank	Rank	N	Mean Rank	Rank	N	Mean Rank	Rank
Americas	2	13	1st	N/A	N/A	N/A	N/A	N/A	N/A
Europe	19	19.18	2nd	11	13.5	1st	5	8	1st
GCC	19	29.97	4th	16	17.66	3rd	9	9.67	2nd
Other	2	29.5	3rd	2	17.25	2nd	2	10.75	3rd
Other Middle East	11	39.91	5th	4	29.5	5th	4	18.75	5th
Southeast Asia	3	46	6th	3	27.5	4th	3	17.5	4th
Total	56			36			23		

TABLE 8.52   Frequency of producing Liquidity Risk Report

Region	Fully Fledged Islamic Banks, Conventional Banks with Islamic Activities and Conventional Banks			Fully Fledged Islamic Banks and Conventional Banks with Islamic Activities			Fully Fledged Islamic Banks		
	N	Mean Rank	Rank	N	Mean Rank	Rank	N	Mean Rank	Rank
Americas	2	18.5	1st	N/A	N/A	N/A	N/A	N/A	N/A
Europe	20	19.78	2nd	12	13.5	1st	5	7	1st
GCC	19	33.13	4th	16	22	3rd	9	14.44	3rd
Other	2	31.25	3rd	2	21	2nd	2	12.5	2nd
Other Middle East	12	41.25	6th	5	24.4	4th	5	14.8	4th
Southeast Asia	4	37.63	5th	4	25.5	5th	4	15.25	5th
Total	59			39			25		

TABLE 8.53   Frequency of producing Country Report

Region	Fully Fledged Islamic Banks, Conventional Banks with Islamic Activities and Conventional Banks			Fully Fledged Islamic Banks and Conventional Banks with Islamic Activities			Fully Fledged Islamic Banks		
	N	Mean Rank	Rank	N	Mean Rank	Rank	N	Mean Rank	Rank
Americas	2	16.5	1st	N/A	N/A	N/A	N/A	N/A	N/A
Europe	20	25.13	2nd	12	18.79	1st	5	13.9	3rd
GCC	19	27.47	3rd	16	16.53	2nd	9	9.17	1st
Other	2	33.75	4th	2	20.75	3rd	2	12.25	2nd
Other Middle East	12	39	5th	5	28.1	5th	5	16.9	5th
Southeast Asia	4	44.25	6th	4	27	4th	4	16	4th
Total	59			39			25		

TABLE 8.54   Frequency of producing Equity Mark-to-Market Report

Region	Fully Fledged Islamic Banks, Conventional Banks with Islamic Activities and Conventional Banks			Fully Fledged Islamic Banks and Conventional Banks with Islamic Activities			Fully Fledged Islamic Banks		
	N	Mean Rank	Rank	N	Mean Rank	Rank	N	Mean Rank	Rank
Americas	2	15.5	1st	N/A	N/A	N/A	N/A	N/A	N/A
Europe	20	22.55	2nd	12	15.13	1st	5	8.9	1st
GCC	19	30.34	3rd	16	18.03	2nd	9	11.94	3rd
Other	2	36.75	4th	2	23	3rd	2	13.25	4th
Other Middle East	12	39.96	6th	5	33.8	5th	5	19.8	5th
Southeast Asia	4	39.63	5th	4	23.75	4th	4	11.88	2nd
Total	59			39			25		

TABLE 8.55   Frequency of producing Classified Accounts Report

Region	Fully Fledged Islamic Banks, Conventional Banks with Islamic Activities and Conventional Banks			Fully Fledged Islamic Banks and Conventional Banks with Islamic Activities			Fully Fledged Islamic Banks		
	N	Mean Rank	Rank	N	Mean Rank	Rank	N	Mean Rank	Rank
Americas	2	8.5	1st	N/A	N/A	N/A	N/A	N/A	N/A
Europe	20	20	2nd	12	14.75	1st	5	11.9	3rd
GCC	19	33.95	4th	16	19.78	3rd	9	12.28	4th
Other	2	32.5	3rd	2	17	2nd	2	7.5	1st
Other Middle East	10	37.7	6th	4	32.5	5th	4	18.5	5th
Southeast Asia	4	37.25	5th	4	20.88	4th	4	10.25	2nd
Total	57			38			24		

RISK MEASUREMENT

This section expands the descriptive analytical analysis conducted in Chapter 7 by examining the impact of various control variables on respondents' views regarding the use of numerous techniques to measure and analyse risk. For this purpose, the researcher used K-W to determine if there were any statistically significant differences across the categories of respondent profiles, specifically region, respondent's position, nature of financial institution, nature of activities and accounting standards. Since this question targets financial institutions only, the sample used for this question is restricted to bankers.

'Region' and 'Nature of Financial Institution' are the control variables selected for analysis by mean ranking, being the control variables with the most significant results, and because these two variables are most essential to the difference in risk management techniques among banks. As can be seen in Table 8.56, 'Region' has five significant risk management techniques, and 'Nature of Financial Institution' has three significant techniques. Thus, they have more significant variables compared to others, which justifies their further analysis.

Table 8.57 shows that conventional banks in relation to their regional location, concentrated outside of the GCC and Middle East, use more advanced risk management techniques than Islamic banks. The 'Americas' are the most advanced across all techniques, followed often by 'Other' or 'Europe'. The rest

TABLE 8.56   K-W test results for Question 18 (risk measurement) for selected sample data according to various control variables

Risk Management Technique	Region		Respondent's Position		Nature of Financial Institution		Nature of Activities		Accounting Standards	
	Chi-Square	Asymp. Sig.	Chi-Square	Asymp. Sig.	Chi-Square	Asymp. Sig.	Chi-Square	Asymp. Sig.	Chi-Square	Asymp. Sig.
Internal based ratings	6.223	0.285	9.79	0.459	1.612	0.447	3.067	0.69	3.699	0.296
Credit ratings by rating agencies	1.58	0.904	6.81	0.743	3.396	0.183	8.01	0.156	11.78	**0.008**
Gap analysis	17.56	**0.004**	10.8	0.372	0.516	0.773	6.884	0.229	7.119	0.068
Duration analysis	15.69	**0.008**	14.2	0.163	2.468	0.291	6.559	0.256	7.151	0.067
Maturity matching analysis	8.155	0.148	5.78	0.833	0.344	0.842	10.79	0.056	6.028	0.11
Earnings at risk	8.58	0.127	10.0	0.438	7.754	**0.021**	10.14	0.071	4.029	0.258
Value at risk	10.98	0.052	13.0	0.222	1.926	0.382	5.731	0.333	5.134	0.162
Stress testing	17.48	**0.004**	9.70	0.466	4.91	0.086	7.604	0.179	5.687	0.128
Simulation techniques	14.60	**0.012**	19.2	**0.038**	6.64	**0.036**	13.05	**0.023**	7.708	0.052
RAROC	19.65	**0.001**	16.0	0.097	12.29	**0.002**	10.79	0.056	7.373	0.061

TABLE 8.57 K-W test mean rankings for risk measurement by region for selected sample data

Risk Management Technique		Gap analysis		Duration analysis		Stress testing		Simulation techniques		RAROC	
Nature of Financial Institution	N	Mean Rank	Rank	Mean Rank	Rank	Mean Rank	Rank	Mean Rank	Rank	Mean Rank	Rank
Americas	2	36	1st	36.5	1st	41	1st	48.5	1st	42.5	1st
Europe	20	33.05	4th	35.03	3rd	36.58	3rd	36.7	2nd	33.65	3rd
GCC	19	34.45	3rd	31.84	4th	30.13	4th	28.32	4th	36.29	2nd
Other	2	36	1st	36.5	1st	41	1st	33.75	3rd	27.75	4th
Other Middle East	12	18.79	6th	19.29	6th	21.33	5th	21.46	5th	15.46	6th
Southeast Asia	4	21.25	5th	21.75	5th	11.5	6th	19	6th	20.38	5th
Total	59										

Note: Only techniques with significant p-value are further analysed by mean ranking

TABLE 8.58 K-W test mean rankings for risk measurement by nature of financial institution for selected sample data

Risk Management Technique		Earnings at Risk		Simulation Techniques		RAROC	
Nature of Financial Institution	N	Mean Rank	Rank	Mean Rank	Rank	Mean Rank	Rank
Fully Fledged Islamic Bank	25	23.98	3rd	26.08	3rd	22.44	3rd
Conventional Bank with Islamic Activities	14	34.18	2nd	27.43	2nd	38.29	1st
Conventional Bank	20	34.6	1st	36.7	1st	33.65	2nd
Total	59						

Note: Only techniques with significant p-value are further analysed by mean ranking

of the regional samples include mostly Islamic banks; their use of sophisticated risk measurements, however, is not as significant as in conventional banks in the Americas and Europe, as evidenced from mean ranking.

These results in Table 8.58 confirm that there is a particular trend determined by the market realities. The use of risk management techniques in IFIs is not as sophisticated or as widely spread as in the conventional banking world. Fully fledged Islamic banks rank third across all techniques as not many IFIs use the more technically advanced risk measurement approaches, which is evidenced from the mean ranking in Table 8.58.

RISK MITIGATION

As previously discussed, risk mitigation and hedging are controversial issues in Islamic banking. Different mitigation techniques are subject to different interpretations by *Shari'ah* scholars. There have been substantial efforts in developing *Shari'ah*-compliant hedging instruments, which are the subject of this section. These include: on balance sheet netting, collateral arrangements, Islamic options, Islamic swaps, guarantees, Islamic currency forwards and parallel contracts. However, much of this progress remains localised with limited scope for cross-border application and further work is still needed as evident from the results of the K-W test in Table 8.59. Question 20 targets institutions that use Islamic finance contracts only; therefore, when conducting the K-W test, only stand-alone Islamic banks and Islamic subsidiaries were included in the raw data in relation to five control variables: region, respondent's position, nature of financial institution, nature of activities and accounting standards.

'Nature of Financial Institution' is the control variable selected for analysis by mean ranking as it has the highest number of significant results and because this variable is most essential to the difference in risk mitigation techniques among financial institutions, as illustrated in Table 8.60.

These results confirm that there is a general trend determined by the market realities. With the exception of Islamic swaps and Islamic currency forwards, fully fledged Islamic banks fell behind Islamic subsidiaries in using all other risk mitigation techniques. The latter group tends to benefit from the already

TABLE 8.59 K-W test results for Question 20 (risk mitigation) for selected sample data according to various control variables

Risk Mitigation Technique	Region Chi-Square	Asymp. Sig.	Respondent's Position Chi-Square	Asymp. Sig.	Nature of Financial Institution Chi-Square	Asymp. Sig.	Nature of Activities Chi-Square	Asymp. Sig.	Accounting Standards Chi-Square	Asymp. Sig.
On balance sheet netting	9.65	0.086	22.841	**0.011**	44.91	**0.00**	8.483	0.132	5.371	0.147
Collateral arrangements	11.25	**0.047**	22.177	**0.014**	53.14	**0.00**	8.599	0.126	5.248	0.155
Islamic options	16.94	**0.005**	20.417	**0.026**	46.59	**0.00**	15.034	**0.01**	9.811	**0.02**
Islamic swaps	14.65	**0.012**	21.024	**0.021**	44.73	**0.00**	12.76	**0.026**	12.991	**0.005**
Guarantees	8.64	0.124	24.37	**0.007**	52.24	**0.00**	11.293	**0.046**	6.088	0.107
Islamic currency forwards	9.98	0.076	23.579	**0.009**	54.59	**0.00**	8.787	0.118	5.287	0.152
Parallel contracts	10.30	0.067	18.794	**0.043**	45.59	**0.00**	12	**0.035**	6.838	0.077

TABLE 8.60 K-W test mean rankings by nature of financial institution for selected sample data

Risk Mitigation Technique	N	On Balance Sheet Netting	Collateral Arrange-ments	Islamic Options	Islamic Swaps	Guarantees	Islamic Currency Forwards	Parallel Contracts
Nature of Financial Institution	N				Mean Rank			
Fully Fledged Islamic Bank	25	19.2	19.94	19.68	20.02	18.88	20.22	19.46
		(2nd)	(2nd)	(2nd)	(1st)	(2nd)	(1st)	(2nd)
Conventional Bank with Islamic Activities	14	21.43	20.11	20.57	19.96	22	19.61	20.96
		(1st)	(1st)	(1st)	(2nd)	(1st)	(2nd)	(1st)
Total	39							

Note: Ordering in parentheses refers to mean ranking

developed risk mitigation platforms at their conventional parents. However, of notice is that the difference in the value of mean ranking between the two groups is small, which reflects that IFIs are progressing in the use of risk mitigation but that still the use of risk mitigation techniques in IFIs is not as developed as in conventional banking.

ISLAMIC BANKING IN PRACTICE

This section examines the proposition that Islamic banking has been diverting from its roots by mimicking conventional banks. In doing so, a K-W test was conducted using the entire sample according to nature of financial institution.

This section aims to test the participants' perceptions in relation to the following statements. The coding of the statements as they appear in the tables is as follows:

1. Islamic banks have been mimicking conventional models.
2. Islamic finance provides an ethical banking alternative.
3. There is a difference between current practice and the principles of Islamic banking.
4. Islamic banks need to reform to be successful.

As depicted by Table 8.61, only Statement 3 is statistically significant, reflecting the similarities in views among respondents about the diversion

TABLE 8.61   K-W test results by nature of financial institution for Question 21 for entire research sample

Nature of Financial Institution		Statement							
		1		2		3		4	
Chi-Square		7.566		4.589		12.812		7.171	
Asymp. Sig.		**0.056**		0.205		**0.005**		0.067	
Nature of Financial Institution	N	Mean Rank	Rank	Mean Rank	Rank	Mean Rank	Rank	Mean Rank	Rank
Fully Fledged Islamic Bank	25	38.22	2nd	42.3	1st	40.94	2nd	37.24	2nd
Conventional Bank with Islamic Activities	14	26.79	4th	37.86	2nd	29.89	4th	27	4th
Conventional Bank	20	34.23	3rd	30.15	4th	27.18	3rd	35.2	3rd
Others	13	47.15	1st	33.65	3rd	49.42	1st	47.31	1st
Total	72								

between principles and current practices in Islamic banking. However, with a 'relaxation' of the confidence level to 0.06, Statement 1 can also be accepted as statistically significant. Furthermore, mean rankings reflect a pattern across all statements, with the exception of Statement 2. Non-bankers (Others) scored the highest mean, followed by fully fledged Islamic banks, conventional banks and Islamic subsidiaries respectively. This reflects the risk appetite of each group. Interestingly, Islamic bankers are more critical of the current practices in the industry than their conventional peers. This could be explained by the fact that Islamic bankers are more educated about the underlying principles of Islamic finance and have a better understanding of current structures than conventional bankers. The 'Others' category comprises *Shari'ah* scholars, consultants, researchers, etc., whose better understanding of the ideologies of Islamic banking is reflected in their lack of satisfaction with Islamic banking in its current state (highest mean ranking for three statements).

Repeating the K-W test with 'Region' as the control variable for the entire research sample gives different results, as illustrated by Table 8.62. All statements are statistically insignificant, except Statement 2, which shows the common dissatisfaction with the current status of Islamic banking across all regions.

Despites the similarities between views of respondents across various regions (only Statement 2 has a significant p-value), the mean ranking results show dispersed results; no trend can be established across various regions.

TABLE 8.62 K-W test results by region for Question 21 for entire research sample

Region		Statement							
		1		2		3		4	
Chi-Square		8.202		19.551		4.25		3.227	
Asymp. Sig.		0.145		**0.002**		0.514		0.665	
Region	N	Mean Rank	Rank	Mean Rank	Rank	Mean Rank	Rank	Mean Rank	Rank
Americas	2	51.75	1st	9.5	6th	24.75	6th	27.5	6th
Europe	31	40.45	2nd	29.24	4th	35.92	4th	38.42	2nd
GCC	19	26.92	5th	46.71	2nd	36.66	3rd	38	3rd
Other	2	51.75	1st	62.5	1st	60.5	1st	50	1st
Other Middle East	14	35.39	4th	42.5	3rd	34.11	5th	32.14	4th
Southeast Asia	4	40	3rd	23.75	5th	42.5	2nd	27.5	5th
Total	72								

In addition, an attempt was made to test the impact of the 'Respondent's Position' on the views; however, the results show that there are no significant differences as all p-value > 0.05.

THE NEXT CHAPTER IN ISLAMIC BANKING

The last section of the questionnaire is a forward-looking question that explores different strategies IFIs should follow in order to prepare for the day after tomorrow. For this, eight statements were provided to the respondents to disclose their opinion. The data was analysed through K-W test.

As shown in Table 8.63, 'Nature of Financial Institution' is the only control variable whose results had some statistically significant outcomes across different groups. 'Organic growth in home market' and 'Standardisation' had p-values of 0.036 and 0.015 respectively. The mean rankings of these two strategies according to 'Nature of Financial Institution' are examined in Table 8.64. As regards other control variables, the opinions do not show differences but rather convergence.

As can be seen from Table 8.63, no particular pattern could be identified. For 'Organic growth in home market', conventional banks were more aggressive with a high mean value (46.6), followed by others (38.46), fully fledged Islamic bank (31.68) and finally Islamic subsidiaries (28.86). However, this trend was almost reversed for 'Standardisation' with Islamic subsidiaries having the highest mean value (49.68), which is much higher than the rest of the categories. Conventional banks rank last with a mean of 28.65.

TABLE 8.63 K-W test results for Question 22 for the entire sample according to various control variables

Strategy	Region Chi-Square	Asymp. Sig.	Respondent's Position Chi-Square	Asymp. Sig.	Nature of Financial Institution Chi-Square	Asymp. Sig.	Nature of Activities Chi-Square	Asymp. Sig.	Accounting Standards Chi-Square	Asymp. Sig.
Improved risk management	5.22	0.389	15.3	0.358	2.59	0.458	1.991	0.921	3.607	0.462
Enhanced morality – back to roots	9.10	0.105	11.82	0.621	5.49	0.139	9.002	0.173	3.799	0.434
Mergers and acquisitions	3.80	0.578	17.49	0.231	1.28	0.732	5.956	0.428	6.094	0.192
Organic growth in home market	10.83	0.055	13.98	0.451	8.57	**0.036**	2.965	0.813	2.216	0.696
Better risk mitigation	9.07	0.106	16.07	0.309	7.28	0.063	9.697	0.138	3.556	0.469
Innovation	1.42	0.921	12.13	0.596	3.04	0.385	12.17	0.058	1.435	0.838
Diversification – reduce concentration	5.09	0.404	17.36	0.238	5.06	0.167	6.979	0.323	6.118	0.191
Standardisation	7.14	0.21	21.59	0.087	10.5	**0.015**	5.246	0.513	5.301	0.258

TABLE 8.64 K-W test mean rankings by nature of financial institution for entire sample

Strategy Nature of Financial Institution	N	Organic Growth in Home Market Mean Rank	Rank	Standardisation Mean Rank	Rank
Fully Fledged Islamic Bank	25	31.68	3rd	38.88	2nd
Conventional Bank with Islamic Activities	14	28.86	4th	49.68	1st
Conventional Bank	20	46.6	1st	28.65	4th
Others	13	38.46	2nd	29.81	3rd
Total	72				

CONCLUSION

This chapter represents the second part of the quantitative analysis for the questionnaire. The objective of this chapter was to gauge the perception of the respondents regarding different risk management and capital adequacy issues in

Islamic banking, the effect of the recent global crisis on Islamic banking, and what the future holds for the industry. Various inferential statistical tools were employed to examine the relationship between the characteristics of the sample respondents and their risk perceptions. K-W analysis was the most-performed test to find out if there were any significant differences caused by the category to which the respondents belonged, and the results of testing were subsequently interpreted.

'Region' was the control variable that displayed the most statistically significant differences among respondents' perceptions for different parts of the questionnaire. Analysis according to 'Nature of Financial Institution', 'Nature of Activities' and 'Respondent's Position' also revealed some general trends that can be attributed to prevailing market conditions. 'Accounting Standards' was used as control variable as well; however, the results did not often provide much statistical significance for this category.

The differences among respondents' answers were scrutinised to test if there were significant differences related to characteristics. Chapter 9 takes the analysis one step further by qualitatively analysing the field interviews conducted with Islamic banking professionals, while further analysis was then carried out to make more sense of the available facts. Detailed analysis of the findings of this chapter, within the context of the findings of descriptive statistical analysis of the questionnaire and the interview analysis, is provided in an integrated manner in Chapter 10.

CHAPTER 9

Exploring Perceptions of Risk and Risk Management Practices in Islamic Banking

Interview Data Analysis

This chapter focuses on the qualitative analysis of data assembled through individual in-depth interviews with Islamic banking professionals. In analysing the data, focused coding technique is used. The objective is to explore the responses of the interviewees in relation to risk practices as conducted in their financial institutions and banks. It is also considered that the findings from this chapter can help to substantiate the findings established in the earlier analyses, but also to develop further meaning in relation to the risk management practices.

In this chapter, the primary data collected through in-depth interviews is summarised and analysed. The outcomes and results are matched with the research objectives. Although the outcomes from the interviews are mainly discussed in this chapter, views and quotes from interviewees are used as supporting arguments throughout this book.

It should be noted that the focused coding method based on thematic understanding is utilised as the main method of analysis.

INTERVIEW ANALYSIS

A detailed explanation in relation to the process and analysis of interviews was given in Chapter 6 on the research methodology. It should be reiterated that the interviews conducted with bankers, financiers and *Shari'ah* scholars were audio recorded with the permission of the interviewees. When recording was not possible because of the spontaneity with which the interview was arranged, notes were taken in shorthand by the interviewer, and even when an interview was being recorded, shorthand notes were also kept.

Interviews were transcribed and the interview notes were read several times, which helped to create the thematic areas but also the focused coding. In other words, notes were transferred into segments representing complete thoughts on a single question or topic, in line with the original research questions. All transcribed interviews, thus, were broken into coded segments representing complete thought statements. After coding, the interview segments were transferred from word-processing format to a spreadsheet for further analysis.

FORMING THE MAIN INTERVIEW THEMES

The interview themes and questions were designed within the context of the main research questions and hypotheses explained in Chapter 6. The interviews covered the same topics as the questionnaire, as the main purpose of the semi-structured interviews was to prove or disprove the conclusions driven from the questionnaire data analysis. The main themes were:

1. Risk perception in Islamic banking;
2. Capital adequacy for Islamic banks;
3. Islamic banking and the global credit crisis;
4. Risk mitigation in Islamic banking;
5. The dichotomy between the theory and practice of Islamic banking; and
6. The next chapter in Islamic banking.

It should be noted that a theme may have occurred several times within an interview, but, for purposes of analysis, a theme was counted only once per interview.

INTERVIEW QUESTIONS

Prior to the interviews, an interview guide was prepared by listing the important topics to be covered and drafting a list of questions to be explored with the respondents, including sub-topics. Nevertheless, in-depth interviews are never rigidly defined. They are, by nature, structured to allow respondents the freedom to express their thoughts, feelings and insights. Therefore, during the interviews, the phrasing of questions and their order or sequence were redefined to fit the characteristics of each interview.

The following were the main interview questions:

Theme A – Risk perception in Islamic banking

 (i) What are the main risks facing Islamic banks?
(ii) Does the risk perception in Islamic banks differ from conventional banking, and in what sense? Are Islamic banks riskier than their conventional counterparts?

(iii) Do you believe that Islamic banking products are structured differently as compared to conventional banking products?

(iv) Do you think IFIs actually favour mark-up based contracts over profit-sharing contracts? Why?

Theme B – Capital adequacy for Islamic banks

(i) How suitable are the Basel II standards to Islamic banking?

(ii) Do Islamic banks need to reserve more or less capital compared to their conventional peers?

(iii) What impact will Basel III have on Islamic banks? Will the Basel III standards consider Islamic banking?

(iv) Are the Basel III new regulatory standards more likely to prevent a major crisis similar to the recent one? Has Basel II failed in preventing the crisis?

Theme C – Islamic banking and the global credit crisis

(i) There is much debate about the resilience of Islamic banking against the financial crisis. Do you think that Islamic banking has really been resilient to the crisis, or does it suffer from the same flaws as conventional banking?

(ii) Could the recent crisis have occurred under an Islamic banking system? Will the Islamic finance industry gain confidence after the current financial crisis?

Theme D – Risk mitigation in Islamic banking

(i) What do you think about risk mitigation in Islamic banking? Do you consider it *Shari'ah*-compliant? How important is hedging to the industry?

Theme E – The dichotomy between the theory and practice of Islamic banking

(i) How *Shari'ah*-compliant is Islamic banking within current practice? Do you believe that Islamic banks need to reform in order to be successful?

Theme F – The next chapter in Islamic banking

(i) What strategies should Islamic banks focus on over the coming decade? What do you believe are the catalysts for the growth of Islamic banking?

RESULTS AND DATA ANALYSIS

Risk Perception in Islamic Banking

This first part of the interview analysis aims at the participants' opinions regarding risk management issues in Islamic banking. Questions 1, 2, 3 and 4 explore how the risk perception in Islamic banking differs from conventional banking, the unique risk characteristics of Islamic financial institutions (IFIs), the risks inherent in Islamic banking contracts, and the risk management techniques used by IFIs. Tables 9.1 to 9.6 present the findings from the focused coding analysis for Question 1 about the main risks facing Islamic banks. The results of the analysis for Question 2 are presented in Tables 9.7 to 9.9, while Tables 9.10 to 9.12 summarise the findings for Question 3, which asks the participants whether they believe that Islamic banking products are structured differently to conventional products.

As can be seen from Table 9.1, several weaknesses and vulnerabilities among IFIs have been identified by the respondents in the areas of risk management and governance, particularly in terms of the handling of asset–liability maturity mismatches, *Shari'ah*-non-compliance, reputational risk and real estate exposure and concentration risk. Respondents identified *Shari'ah*-non-compliance, liquidity, concentration, asset-liability management (ALM) and reputational risks as the main risk facing IFIs. Tables 9.2 to 9.6 examine the respondents' answers regarding each of these identified risks.

Some interviewees, particularly *Shari'ah* scholars and researchers, regarded *Shari'ah*-non-compliance as a major risk, as it can have a material impact on the IFIs' risk profile, and its ripple effect can create other risks, particularly reputational and legal risks. Islamic finance disputes in courts, especially in international deals, are decided by judges trained under common law and not particularly under

TABLE 9.1 Results for Question 1

Question 1	What are the main risks facing Islamic banks?
Focused Coding	
1	*Shari'ah*-non-compliance risk
2	Liquidity risk
3	ALM risk
4	Concentration risk
5	Reputational risk
Theme: Main risks facing IFIs are liquidity risk, ALM risk, concentration risk, *Shari'ah*-non-compliance risk and concentration risk.	

TABLE 9.2 Focused coding number 1 for Question 1

Shari'ah non-compliance risk	
Interview 1	The risk of being perceived as non-*Shari'ah*-compliant could severely damage the creditworthiness of an IFI
Interview 3	AAOIFI has taken some steps in this regard with its institutional certifications of *Shari'ah* compliance
Interview 4	Interface between *Shari'ah* and civil systems create range of risks

Islamic jurisprudence. This requires an interface between *Shari'ah* and civil law, thus adding additional legal risks. Moreover, respondents widely felt that the application of *Shari'ah* compliance as a commercial and defensive legal tool, like the case where the distressed Investment Dar Company's own *Shari'ah* board retracted its approval, undermines the credibility and ethical ethos that underpins Islamic finance. Given the consequences of such reversals, it is key for the industry that the approval process be extensively documented, formalised and open to inspection. One *Shari'ah* scholar in interview 3 expressed the view that Accounting and Auditing Organization for Islamic Financial Institutions (AAOIFI) has taken some steps in this regard with its institutional certifications of *Shari'ah* compliance, but for a deeper, stable and more liquid market the concept needs to gain wider acceptance.

As depicted by Tables 9.3 and 9.4, several respondents recognised liquidity and ALM risks as the most severe risks facing IFIs and stated that IFIs need to factor liquidity more fully into risk management. Respondents believe that both liquidity and ALM risks are strongly correlated. In the absence of a wide pool of *Shari'ah*-compliant and sufficiently liquid investment vehicles (especially in fixed income), IFIs find it difficult to manage their balance sheet from an ALM perspective, especially with regard to liquidity and margin-rate risk. IFIs use cash from deposits and short-term liquid assets to finance long-term liabilities. As a result, the liability makeup affects their funding structures differently and reflects an institution's specific ALM policies. Most respondents therefore believe that IFIs' funding mix tends to be imbalanced, with the dominance of deposits, PSIAs and equity making IFIs' funding profile predominantly short-term at a time when the maturity of their asset classes is widening. To mitigate nascent maturity mismatches, some IFIs started issuing medium-term *sukuk* to lengthen the maturity profile of their funding, but *sukuk* still represent a minor share of total

TABLE 9.3 Focused coding number 2 for Question 1

Liquidity risk	
Interview 13	IFIs suffer from managing excessive liquidity, especially with regard to the management of short-term liquidity and overnight liquidity
Interview 27	The liquidity/leverage trade-off for many IFIs is a double-edged sword
Interview 30	Liquidity management is structurally difficult at IFIs
Interview 33	Liquidity is one of the most critical issues for IFIs

TABLE 9.4 Focused coding number 3 for Question 1

ALM risk	
Interview 23	Handling of asset–liability maturity mismatches is a challenge

TABLE 9.5 Focused coding number 4 for Question 1

Concentration risk	
Interview 9	Reliance on limited funding sources
Interview 12	Concentration risk is a time bomb that might bring down many IFIs, particularly in the GCC
Interview 25	Real estate financing is one of IFIs' preferred habitats hence creating scary concentrations
Interview 29	High concentration risk made it necessary for IFIs to maintain strong capitalisation

TABLE 9.6 Focused coding number 5 for Question 1

Reputational risk	
Interview 18	Because Islamic banking is at the infancy stage of development, its reputational risk is critical

liabilities. Subordinated *sukuk* and hybrid instruments have not been used yet; these are more expensive funding sources and incentives to issue them are limited given the relative abundance of capital in the region. IFIs are also increasingly focusing on retail deposits to boost liquidity, due to the deposits' sticky nature. As a result, according to the responses given by the interviewees, the Islamic banking industry is faced with a conundrum: its institutions maintain high concentrations in current/short-term liabilities, but, at the same time, they are exposed to highly profitable, but illiquid, long-term assets (e.g. property and infrastructure, and *sukuk*), and they have limited access to long-term funding solutions.

As Table 9.4 shows, some respondents opined that IFIs tend to have a concentration base of assets and/or deposits; they face high concentration by name and sector, as well as high geographical concentration. This is inflated by the IFIs' limited geographic reach, as most IFIs are domestic players and only very few have material operations outside their home country. The limited scope of eligible assets creates asset concentration risk. Non-deposit liabilities could have concentration risk as well, due to the relatively small number of IFIs available to participate in the inter-bank market. There is also a limited range of *Shari'ah*-compliant instruments available for managing or transferring risks. Participants opined that the focus on tangibles had led to increased property-related financings at IFIs, affected by the relatively undiversified nature of the economies. As real estate markets are highly volatile in the GCC, the concentration risk is magnified. The recent crash in the property market has put several Islamic banks whose assets are heavily concentrated in real estate in dire straits.

Reputational risk is the last among the top risks facing IFIs as identified by interviewees. Some participants, principally conventional bankers, indicated that reputational risk can have a material impact on the risk profile of an Islamic bank because the industry is still at the infancy stage of development.

Finally, it is interesting to note that the analysis of Question 1 revealed that the views of Islamic bankers, conventional bankers and rating agency analysts were quite similar. *Shari'ah* scholars and researchers, on the other hand, had different perceptions, which tend to be more academic in nature. Some respondents also expressed the view that due to the nature of Islamic finance contracts, risks are strongly bundled together.

Question 2 examines the difference in risk management perceptions in Islamic banking versus conventional banking. The results obtained are summarised in Tables 9.7 to 9.9.

TABLE 9.7 Results for Question 2

Question 2	Does the risk perception in Islamic banks differ from conventional banking, and in what sense? Are Islamic banks riskier than their conventional counterparts?
Focused Coding	
1	There are specific challenges in the management of risks in Islamic banks
2	Islamic banking, as it stands today, carries more risks than the conventional model
Theme: Risk management for Islamic banks is more challenging than it is for conventional banks. Theoretically, Islamic banks are safer than conventional banks. Practically, the story is different.	

TABLE 9.8 Focused coding number 1 for Question 2

There are specific challenges in the management of risks in Islamic banks	
Interview 6	Risk management is not the same for conventional and Islamic banking
Interview 12	Risk management in Islamic banking is still evolving
Interview 21	There are distinguishable elements of an IFI's risk profile that need to be evaluated differently to those of a conventional bank
Interview 24	The Islamic financial model works on the basis of risk-sharing
Interview 27	Risks in IFIs must be assessed in an integrated manner
Interview 29	Risk management in Islamic banking is still below the desired level
Interview 31	Risk management for Islamic banks is far more of a complex issue when compared to conventional banking
Interview 33	Since the risk management needs of Islamic banking are not being met yet, the system is not functioning at its full potential

TABLE 9.9 Focused coding number 2 for Question 2

Islamic banking, as it stands today, carries more risks than the conventional model	
Interview 12	Unfortunately, Islamic bankers made the industry more risky than conventional banking
Interview 14	Many IFIs swapped basic PLS concepts for conventional-like products
Interview 18	Islamic banking suffers from weak risk management practices
Interview 26	Islamic banking in its current practice is riskier than conventional banking
Interview 29	IFIs face a whole additional array of risks not faced by conventional banks

As Table 9.8 shows, most interviewees believe that Islamic banking in its current state can be riskier than conventional banking because of the additional risk management and mitigation challenges and constraints the industry faces. As stated by the interviewees, since the risk management needs of Islamic banking are not yet being met, the system is not functioning at its full potential.

As depicted in Table 9.9, interviewees believe that no financial system is perfect. Although Islamic banking by default enjoys better risk management practices built into its principles, these principles tend to be ignored in favour of mimicking conventional risk solutions. Islamic banking products display unique features relating to credit, funding, liquidity and other risks that need to be considered and which have an impact on risk management. Moreover, most interviewees asserted that IFIs paradoxically suffer from weak risk management practices. In fact, IFIs face a number of challenges in terms of risk management. Many *sukuk*

TABLE 9.10 Results for Question 3

Question 3	Do you believe that Islamic banking products are structured differently as compared to conventional banking products?
Focused Coding	
1	Islamic banking transactions have inherent features that induce financial stability
2	Many Islamic banking products aim to essentially replicate the products and processes of the conventional system
Theme: Islamic finance products have special relationships between the contracting parties; however, Islamic banking has so far been unable to escape the trappings of conventional finance.	

TABLE 9.11   Focused coding number 1 for Question 3

Islamic banking transactions have inherent features that induce financial stability	
Interview 8	The overarching principle of Islamic banking and finance (IBF) products is that all forms of interest are forbidden
Interview 12	The PLS principle is a unique feature of Islamic finance

TABLE 9.12   Focused coding number 2 for Question 3

Many Islamic banking products aim to essentially replicate the products and processes of the conventional system	
Interview 14	If IFIs continue to mimic conventional products, they will weaken their value proposition
Interview 17	Many Islamic banking products aim to essentially replicate the products and processes of the conventional system
Interview 20	Theoretically yes, very different. In practice, they are very similar
Interview 30	IFIs are excessively replicating conventional financial instruments

are structured to resemble conventional bonds, meaning the risks of ownership are transferred to the issuer rather than shared by the investors. Whereas risk management is practiced widely in conventional financial markets, it is underdeveloped in Islamic finance. This gives rise to an array of risks which are not well-comprehended yet.

Most respondents agreed that Islamic banking products display unique features, and that developing risk management tools and practices is one of the biggest challenges for Islamic banks. This challenge also offers some opportunities to develop unique solutions that do not suffer from the weaknesses in the conventional banking model. In addition, respondents criticised adopting risk models from the conventional banking practice or making minor adjustments to best practices as this poses major challenges. Participants indicated that, unfortunately, most IFIs closely mimic Western products, and hence IFIs are being exposed to similar risks to their conventional counterparts. Practitioners of Islamic finance to date have been mimicking conventional products. This mimicking has resulted in a close correlation between the two systems. With the absence of advanced risk management and mitigation tools, and with the bundling of risks in Islamic finance contracts, Islamic banking ends up being more risky than the conventional model.

In addition, participants indicated that through *Shari'ah*-compliant engineering most conventional contracts can be copied, at least conceptually. Some interviewees opined that if IFIs continue to mimic conventional products, they will

TABLE 9.13 Results for Question 4

Question 4	Do you think IFIs actually favour mark-up based contracts over profit-sharing contracts? Why?
Focused Coding	
1	IFIs want to share rewards without sharing risks
2	There is lack of appetite for risk-sharing assets
Theme: Fixed income contracts are widely used and the use of the PLS mode is negligible.	

weaken the uniqueness of their value proposition and the powerful nature of their natural factors of differentiation. Participants recognise that Islamic banking might find it difficult to innovate because it exists in a deeply-rooted conventional system. However, they strongly recommended that Islamic banks should start innovating *Shari'ah*-based solutions because if the industry is not innovating authentic products according to genuine *Shari'ah* principles, it might end up with the same failures as conventional banking. Results for Question 4 are depicted in Table 9.13.

As depicted in Tables 9.14 and 9.15, interviewees, particularly *Shari'ah* scholars and consultants, agree that while Islamic banking is asset-based and centres on risk-sharing, in practice IFIs vary in terms of the level of risk-sharing.

TABLE 9.14 Focused coding number 1 for Question 4

IFIs want to share rewards without sharing risks	
Interview 1	Risk-sharing is the exception rather than the rule
Interview 3	This '*murabahah* syndrome' is a disgrace to the industry
Interview 24	Financial engineering in Islamic finance needs to focus on the development of products that foster *Shari'ah* principles instead of focusing only on the risk–return characteristics of the product

TABLE 9.15 Focused coding number 2 for Question 4

There is lack of appetite for risk-sharing assets	
Interview 4	IFIs should engage on partnerships and equity-sharing financial assets, but in practice the portion of such assets on the balance sheets of Islamic banks is minimal
Interview 21	There is limited innovation, most of which is in the form of reverse engineering where the objective is to replicate the behaviour and risk/return profile of conventional products

For example, on the funding side Profit-Sharing Investment Accounts (PSIAs) are being replaced in several IFIs by time deposits based on reverse *murabahah* transactions. These deposits do not have the risk-sharing features of PSIAs, since the return is almost guaranteed. On the asset side, risk-sharing is the exception rather than the rule. Most financing is in the form of *murabahah* or *wakala*, making the IFIs' activities similar to those of conventional banks. Interviewees recommend that practitioners should not create instruments and investments that are identical in substance to conventional ones by combining a redundant succession of trades and labelling them with 'new' Arabic names. The emphasis should be placed on innovation that encourages and favours particular types of investment (such as more tangible risk-sharing ones) and funding that is closer to *Shari'ah* principles. The tendency by some IFIs to blindly replicate and repackage some exotic products of conventional finance through cosmetic changes to make them *Shari'ah*-compliant should be curbed. Respondents expressed their worry that some initiatives to design some forms of '*Shari'ah*-compliant' subprime instrument had been undertaken before the crisis happened – fortunately there was enough wisdom among *Shari'ah* boards that these instruments did not really see the light.

Capital Adequacy for Islamic Banks

This section, through Questions 5, 6, 7 and 8, examines the suitability of the Basel II and III standards for IFIs, compares capital requirement levels between Islamic and conventional banks, and assesses the credibility of Basel II after it failed to prevent one of the most damaging of financial crises. The results obtained are given in Tables 9.16 to 9.28.

Interviewees had varying views about the suitability of Basel II and potentially Basel III to Islamic banking. In general, respondents, particularly bankers and rating agency analysts, agree that with a few amendments Basel II becomes applicable to IFIs. The results of the focused coding analysis are summarised in Tables 9.17 and 9.18.

TABLE 9.16   Results for Question 5

Question 5	How suitable are Basel II (and potentially Basel III) standards to Islamic banking?
Focused Coding	
1	Basel II can be applied to Islamic banks
2	IFIs need their own standards
Theme: With a few amendments Basel II becomes applicable to IFIs.	

TABLE 9.17 Focused coding number 1 for Question 5

Basel II (and potentially Basel III) standards can be applied to Islamic banks	
Interview 13	IFSB Principles are difficult to implement, particularly in the West
Interview 17	Application of Basel II is a matter of adjusting the standards to the needs of Islamic banks
Interview 21	Basel II can be applied to Islamic banks
Interview 30	Applying standards other than Basel II to IFIs will mean that it is not a level playing field

TABLE 9.18 Focused coding number 2 for Question 5

IFIs need their own standards	
Interview 2	The risk-sharing feature necessitates the use of different capital rules
Interview 6	Cannot apply conventional definition of capital to Islamic banking
Interview 9	IFSB principles on capital adequacy provide motivation for better risk management
Interview 12	Basel II was drafted with conventional banking very much in mind
Interview 19	IFSB principles incentivise banks to be more transparent

As demonstrated by Table 9.18, *Shari'ah* scholars and consultants interviewed shared the belief that conventional capital adequacy standards do not fully understand and appreciate certain aspects of IFIs, principally the fiduciary aspect, and that Basel II methodologies do not recognise the need for a different approach to capital adequacy calculation. Another problem mentioned by Islamic bankers related to the lack of ratings in IFIs and their corporate customers, and the fact that there is no historical data to implement Basel II. However, as Table 9.17 depicts, the majority of bankers and analysts interviewed believed that Basel II standards could be applied to Islamic banking with a few amendments to accommodate its unique model. They argue that, although there are some important differences between Islamic and conventional banks that must be properly understood and considered, these can be incorporated within the existing Basel framework. With Basel II being widely applied consistently across the globe, some regulators hesitate to apply bespoke capital rules to Islamic banks in order to ensure a level playing field for all banks.

Question 6 examines the participants' perception regarding the level of capital reserves that IFIs should hold in comparison to capital held by conventional banks. Looking at the theme in Table 9.19 and the respondents' answers in

TABLE 9.19   Results for Question 6

Question 6	Do Islamic banks need to reserve more or less capital than their conventional peers?
Focused Coding	
1	Less capital
2	More capital
Theme: IFIs are exposed to higher risks, thus should reserve more capital.	

TABLE 9.20   Focused coding number 1 for Question 6

Less capital	
Interview 1	If IFIs genuinely apply *Shari'ah* principles, they will require much lower capital reserves than they currently do
Interview 2	The risk-sharing feature necessitates the use of different capital rules. The better the disclosure and risk-sharing the Islamic bank applies, the lower capital it needs to reserve
Interview 23	If PSIAs absorb losses, IFIs should keep less capital aside

TABLE 9.21   Focused coding number 2 for Question 6

More capital	
Interview 8	IFIs have historically been keeping higher capital buffers anyway
Interview 11	IFIs have recently accumulated more capital buffers than their conventional peers due to rising non-performing loans
Interview 21	IFIs are more risky than conventional banks, thus should reserve more capital
Interview 25	Due to their nature of operations, IFIS should reserve more capital

Tables 9.20 and 9.21, it is evident that most interviewees believe that IFIs should hold higher capital levels than their conventional counterparts because the Islamic banking business model in its current state carries more risks.

In theory, the risk-sharing principles inherent in Islamic banking should make IFIs less vulnerable to economic shocks and thus IFIs should need to reserve less capital than their conventional peers as they could 'pass through' economic losses to PSIAs. This is the view expressed by some participants, such as *Shari'ah* scholars and Middle Eastern consultants, as Table 9.20 shows. Unfortunately, the theory is a long way from fact in the current practice, as argued by the participants' views shown in Table 9.21. This submerges the inherent stability within IFIs, rendering them riskier than conventional banks, and hence requiring higher capital buffers. In addition, several bankers and consultants interviewed revealed that many IFIs do not have an internal performance management approach to measure the cost of liquidity and capital in their business decisions. This can lead to suboptimal choices being made by management teams. IFIs thus need to change how they measure performance by taking into consideration actual cost of liquidity and capital. By adjusting for true cost of liquidity and capital, the profitability picture can change considerably. As indicated by the respondent from interview 11, capital levels among IFIs have increased compared to prior years and are at levels much higher than their global peers. However, that extra capital buffer should not be taken for granted and IFIs need to be mindful of rising non-performing loans. Moreover, some interviewees warned that, with the tightening of new Basel III capital standards, IFIs have to pay greater attention to capital management as profitability will be impacted.

It is interesting to note that despite a general lack of absolute clarity about Basel III and its potential impact on IFIs, as indicated by Table 9.22, most interviewees agreed that Basel III is a fact that is here to stay. There is also a general belief among respondents that although Basel III is more demanding than Basel II with regard to addressing systemic risk, it may not be the last of the Basel series. This is mainly because risk is inherent in the complex global financial markets of increasing sophistication. Participants were generally divided among three groups, as summarised by Tables 9.23 to 9.25. The general theme agreed upon by most interviewees is that Basel III will affect all banks; however, its impact on conventional banking will be higher than on Islamic banking.

The first group believed that the Basel III new regulatory standards are still fresh and have a prolonged implementation timeline. No clear idea has yet been

TABLE 9.22   Results for Question 7

Question 7	What impact will Basel III have on Islamic banks? Do the Basel III standards consider Islamic banking?
Focused Coding	
1	Too early to judge
2	Basel III will have bigger impact on conventional banks due to their business models
3	Basel III will impact all banks
Theme: Basel III will affect all banks, however, its impact on conventional banking will be higher than on Islamic banking.	

TABLE 9.23 Focused Coding Number 1 for Question 7

Too early to judge	
Interview 28	The ink is barely dry on the Basel III Accord
Interview 32	Basel III has an extended implementation period making its impact relatively irrelevant for the time being

formed of their potential effects on IFIs. This group consists mainly of analysts at rating agencies and consultants.

Table 9.24 summarises the views of the second group of interviewees, which argued that the counter-cyclical capital buffer concept introduced by Basel III (as opposed to Basel II, which has been widely criticised for encouraging pro-cyclicality) has been at the heart of Islamic banking via profit and loss sharing (PLS) financing. IFIs will be less impacted by Basel III because of smaller market and counterparty risk exposures and lower levels of debt. They are expected to meet the more stringent requirements without raising additional capital. This group was dominated by Islamic bankers.

The third group of participants, comprising of consultants and solicitors, opined that the tightening of capital, leverage and liquidity requirements will affect all banks, Islamic and non-Islamic alike, while the definition of capital and

TABLE 9.24 Focused coding number 2 for Question 7

Basel III will have a bigger impact on conventional banks due to their business models	
Interview 12	Islamic banks have been addressing procyclicality issues way before Basel III proposals
Interview 13	Most IFIs are capital rich and have liquidity buffers, therefore the newly proposed capital and liquidity ratios will have minimal effect

TABLE 9.25 Focused coding number 3 for Question 7

Basel III will impact all banks	
Interview 5	The increased risk-weighting for assets across the board will affect IFIs
Interview 21	Common equity will be squeezed much harder
Interview 23	Any new regulation will affect all banks, whether Islamic or conventional

the deductions in capital calculations are less likely to affect IFIs as their capital structures tend to comprise mainly core Tier 1 capital.

Question 8 aims to get the interviewees' perceptions of the failure of Basel II to prevent the recent crisis and of whether the newly proposed Basel III standards will help to prevent similar crises. Despite divergence among the participants' views, the theme as shown in Table 9.26 is that the shortcomings in Basel II are definitely addressed in Basel III. Participants expressed their doubt that Basel III will succeed in preventing another major crisis because crises are part of business cycles.

There was unarguably divergence among respondents regarding the question on the potential capacity of Basel III to prevent a major crisis such as the recent

TABLE 9.26 Results for Question 8

Question 8	Are the Basel III new regulatory standards more likely to prevent a major crisis like the recent one? Did Basel II fail in preventing the crisis?
Focused Coding	
1	Failings of Basel II needed to be addressed, Basel III addresses those issues
2	The soundness of Basel III is mutually linked to powerful regulatory and economic reinforcements
Theme: Shortcomings in Basel II are definitely addressed in Basel III.	

TABLE 9.27 Focused coding number 1 for Question 8

Failings of Basel II needed to be addressed, Basel III addresses those issues	
Interview 12	Basel II totally failed to prevent the crisis
Interview 25	Basel II got it wrong on different fronts: procyclicality, liquidity, stress-testing, to name a few

TABLE 9.28 Focused coding number 2 for Question 8

The soundness of Basel III is mutually linked to powerful regulatory and economic reinforcements	
Interview 4	Basel III is intended to promote a more resilient banking sector and eliminate systemic risk, but so was Basel II
Interview 14	Don't blame Basel II, blame the system based on greed and lack of morals
Interview 16	Basel II is correct in principle but wrong in implementation

one and whether Basel II had failed in preventing the crisis. As the results in Table 9.26 show, those in the West are focusing on the need for increased buffers for both capital and liquidity, while those in the East are focusing on comprehensive coverage of risk management, enhanced stress-testing and the need for risk and capital management to align and be a core part of a bank's strategy. In general both camps agree that supervisory discretion will influence detailed implementation and leave scope for some jurisdictions to apply a more rigid interpretation of Basel III than elsewhere. Political issues and the debate around the implementation and operation of supervisory challenges mean ongoing fear of an uneven playing field. If different jurisdictions implement Basel III in different ways, issues seen under Basel I and Basel II with respect to international regulatory arbitrage may continue to disrupt the overall stability of the financial system. Moreover, compared with the implementation of Basel II, this enhanced level of dynamism, complexity and interdependency within the global regulatory landscape will add significant challenges to the implementation of Basel III.

A number of respondents, particularly researchers and consultants, believe that the Basel III proposals are unlikely to be the last word on reforms of the banking industry following the credit crunch. Interviewees asserted that Basel III is sometimes sold as the solution to the outstanding issues left by Basel I and II. Some stated that while history does not repeat, it sure does show similarities, and it is very unlikely that Basel III will be the answer to all banking problems. Banks must therefore retain flexibility to accommodate years of fine tuning and future reforms.

During the current tumultuous economic times, a higher capital buffer will generally reduce volatility and improve the intrinsic financial strength of banks. Increased capital requirements, increased cost of funding, and the need to reorganise and deal with regulatory reform will put pressure on margins and operating capacity. Investor returns will decrease at a time when banks need to encourage enhanced investment to rebuild and restore buffers. This will drive banks to go up the risk curve to make up for lost profitability.

Islamic Banking and the Global Credit Crisis

A lot has been said about Islamic finance being resilient in the wake of the global financial crisis, but once the dust of the financial crisis settled, it has become clear that everything is not necessarily well in Islamic finance. The assumption at one point early in the crisis was that Islamic banking would be totally unaffected and would sail through the crisis. However, the crisis has flushed out the false premise that Islamic banking is disconnected from conventional banking, and that it is immune to economic crises.

Questions 9 and 10 aim to explore the market feedback regarding the long-debated issue of whether IFIs are recession proof. Is Islamic banking actually more resilient than conventional banking? Could the crisis have occurred under an Islamic banking system? The results of the focused coding analysis are presented as follows. Results for Question 9 are illustrated in Table 9.29, while Tables 9.30 and 9.31 provide the Focused Coding analysis for Question 9. Results for Question 10 are depicted in Table 9.32, while Tables 9.33 to 9.35 provide the Focused Coding analysis for Question 10.

TABLE 9.29   Results for Question 9

	There is much debate about the resilience of Islamic banking against the financial crisis. Do you think that Islamic banking has really been resilient to the crisis, or does it suffer from the same flaws of conventional banking?
Question 9	
Focused Coding	
1	IFIs were not caught by toxic assets as *Shari'ah* prohibits interest
2	Islamic banking had similar problems to conventional banking
Theme: IFIs have shown some resilience but they are not risk immune.	

TABLE 9.30   Focused coding number 1 for Question 9

IFIs were not caught by toxic assets as *Shari'ah* prohibits interest	
Interview 17	Islamic banks have been lucky so far
Interview 23	IFIs have displayed strong resilience

TABLE 9.31   Focused coding number 2 for Question 9

Islamic banking had similar problems to conventional banking	
Interview 4	To some extent Islamic lenders were not applying best practices and that may have led to the large amount of non-performing loans and others
Interview 13	Lack of liquidity is squeezing *sukuk* issuance
Interview 21	IFIs are part of the globalised financial system – they are not immune from the credit crisis
Interview 25	IFIs have all been penalised by their investment portfolios
Interview 26	The industry faced its greatest ever test. Some IFIs came close to collapse
Interview 33	IFIs have always displayed funding imbalances, but this worsened as the crisis reached its peak

TABLE 9.32   Results for Question 10

Question 10	Could the recent crisis have occurred under an Islamic banking system? Will the industry gain confidence after the current financial crisis?
Focused Coding	
1	The crisis served as a wake-up call for Islamic banks
2	The crisis had a less severe impact on Islamic banking
3	The crisis provides opportunity for IFIs
Theme: Even if Islamic finance had been prevailing, in its current state the crisis could have happened, but at a less severe level. Paradoxically, the reputation of Islamic banking has benefited from the crisis.	

TABLE 9.33   Focused coding number 1 for Question 10

The crisis served as a wake-up call for Islamic banks	
Interview 1	Allowed Islamic banking some time for reflection
Interview 3	In a way the crisis is a blessing in disguise for Islamic banking because IFIs so far have been following a close mimicry of Western products
Interview 32	The shake-out resulting from the crisis has been good for the Islamic finance market

As depicted in Table 9.33, respondents agreed that the credit crisis has allowed the Islamic banking industry some time for reflection. They gave examples of a number of renowned players in the management of Islamic funds, such as The Investment Dar (TID) and Global Investment House (GIH), that suffered major losses during the crisis and have become technically insolvent. Some IFIs had to undertake a painful restructuring process, and the legal battles are still to be fought. The global *sukuk* market is seeing smaller issuance and increasing defaults, led by the bankruptcy of the US-based *sukuk* issuer East Cameron Gas, followed by the Al Gosaibi and Saad Groups of Saudi Arabia.

Most interviewees agree that IFIs should therefore ensure that they do not overlook the lessons to be learnt from the financial crisis. As shown in Table 9.35, respondents believe that since the global economy is still recovering and the growth rate is much slower, IFIs should take this opportunity to clean up the house and tighten up the loose ends.

Interviewees argued that when the financial crisis erupted in mid-2007, the Islamic finance industry remained relatively healthy and insulated, and recorded robust performance. Some commentators wrongly labelled Islamic finance as a

TABLE 9.34 Focused coding number 2 for Question 10

The crisis had less severe impact on Islamic banking	
Interview 16	Although IFIs have been more resilient, the shift in the environment did negatively affect some of them
Interview 20	The crisis highlighted additional risks that IFIs need to carefully understand and mitigate
Interview 24	Islamic banking can also face systemic failure
Interview 27	Islamic banks do not operate in isolation

TABLE 9.35 Focused coding number 3 for Question 10

Crisis provides opportunity for IFIs	
Interview 2	Perceived now as more stable as it has an anti-speculation bent to it
Interview 7	The industry has come out stronger from the global crisis and learnt good lessons
Interview 11	Will emerge stronger from the crisis, provided some conditions are met
Interview 14	IFIs' reputation has benefited from the crisis
Interview 17	IFIs have been lucky so far, and they will be winners after the crisis
Interview 23	Despite flaws in the industry, the crisis has strengthened Islamic banking
Interview 29	The ideals of Islamic finance are receiving more attention in the crisis

'risk-free' sector. However, the significant defaults of TID and Gulf Finance House (GFH) since early 2009 and the growing difficulties of the rest of the Islamic investment banking community makes this assessment dubious, as the structural weaknesses of the Islamic financial industry started to become more obvious. Responses depicted in Table 9.35 reflect that the crisis was a unique opportunity for the industry to prove that it had the capacity and ability to react to and absorb shocks, although this did not apply to all its sub-segments. Some interviewees from rating agencies explained that, while the commercial banking sector seems to have emerged from the crisis relatively unscathed, the investment banking sector could not have been more different, as it suffered a very sudden and sharp dip in performance as losses mounted. And yet, until 2007, IFIs were portrayed by market participants as having significant potential, benefiting from cheap funding, high liquidity, exceptional profits and robust capitalisation. At the time, the combination of these four factors led them to pursue investments in riskier markets and asset classes – such as private equity, infrastructure or real estate, mostly in emerging markets ranging from the Maghreb to Southeast Asia. Some business was also booked in the private equity markets in Europe and the US. While GFH focused more on infrastructure, Arcapita invested heavily in private equity, and both were eager to improve their asset-management capabilities. Moreover, some other *Shari'ah*-compliant investment banks were beginning to discover the merits of unfunded business lines. Respondents gave the examples of Liquidity Management House (LMH, the investment banking subsidiary of leading Kuwait Finance House) and Al Rajhi Capital, which further enhanced their advisory and structuring services, until they eventually became significant players in the GCC's debt and capital markets. However, when the region's economy started to fracture under the stresses of the global liquidity drought, the pro-cyclical nature of IFIs became more pronounced. The illiquid nature of their investments contributed to rapid asset-value decreases at a time when their wholesale and short-term funding features were rapidly damaging their liquidity profile. This structural feature of IFIs' ALM – which was once a benefit when ample liquidity was chasing too few assets – started to turn negative when too many impaired assets were available to serve massive liquidity withdrawals.

Some interviewees explained that lower volumes, shrinking margins and deteriorating asset quality will all weigh on IFIs' profitability and ultimately their capitalisation. However, the impact is more manageable than for conventional banks. Fortunately, IFIs have been very profitable in the past and had therefore accumulated large amounts of capital, making them capable of absorbing these sorts of shocks. Strangely enough, IFIs' reputation has generally benefited from the crisis as it has exposed the weakness of a debt-based financial system. It is therefore the most fortunate time for Islamic banking to re-emphasise its equity-based approach. Interviewees think that this will help the industry to expand not only in the Muslim world but also in the West.

Some researchers interviewed stated that this is not the first time IFIs were tested with a systemic crisis, although previous crises were all on a regional scale. However, the recent crisis, with its unprecedented scale and scope, is the first global crisis to hit Islamic finance. The experiences of Kuwait Finance House in surviving the Kuwait Souq al-Manakh crisis in 1982, of Bank Islam in navigating the Asian financial crisis in 1997–1998, and of a Turkish participation (Islamic) bank in coming out of the economic crisis (2000–2001) should all convey a clear message that Islamic finance does have some inherent qualities that contribute to its resilience. Most interviewees, including non-Islamic bankers, actually see the Islamic financial industry emerging stronger from the crisis, provided some conditions are met as shown in Table 9.35.

In general, most interviewees opined that IFIs will probably be the big winners when the crisis ends. As a sub-set of ethical finance, IFIs are now considered not so much niche businesses standing at the margins, but rather as representatives of a credible, viable and sustainable alternative business model for sound, ethical and socially responsible banking. Many interviewees believe that mainstream finance has moved too far into excess leverage, meaningless innovation and value-destroying investments and therefore IFIs will undoubtedly find their reputations strengthened.

Risk Mitigation in Islamic Banking

Risk mitigation is currently one of the most contentious issues in Islamic banking. The unique nature of risks faced by Islamic banks, combined with the restrictions added by *Shari'ah*, makes risk mitigation for Islamic banks a difficult and complex process. There are risks that Islamic banks, like their conventional counterparts, can manage and control through appropriate risk policies and controls that do not conflict with the *Shari'ah* principles. However, there are other risks that banks cannot eliminate and that can be reduced only by transferring to or selling those risks in well-defined markets. These risks can generate unexpected losses that need capital insulation, and hedging can help to restrict the impact of unexpected loss. In this section of the interview analysis, the participants' opinions and perceptions were sought regarding risk mitigation in Islamic banking. Looking at the theme in Table 9.36 and the respondents' answers in Tables 9.37 and 9.38 shows that risk mitigation has become a must in Islamic banking, provided that it is used merely for hedging and not for speculation.

Respondents almost unanimously agreed that the unique nature of risks faced by IFIs, combined with the restrictions added by *Shari'ah*, make risk mitigation for IFIs a difficult and complex process. However, there was clear disparity among respondents regarding the applicability of *Shari'ah*-compliant hedging solutions. Although derivatives were originally designed to manage or mitigate risks, they

TABLE 9.36 Results for Question 11

Question 11	**What do you think about risk mitigation in Islamic banking? Is it *Shari'ah*-compliant? How important is risk mitigation to the industry?**
Focused Coding	
1	Could be used for hedging purposes only and not for speculative trading activities
2	Hedging is urgently needed by IFIs
Theme: Risk mitigation tools highly demanded among IFIs but still there is a long way to go.	

TABLE 9.37   Focused coding number 1 for Question 11

Could be used for hedging purposes only and not for speculative trading activities	
Interview 1	Should be used solely for hedging and not speculation
Interview 2	The necessities permit forbiddance, but also the necessities are determined based on the degree of necessity
Interview 22	Many IFIs already use Islamic derivatives but they call them something else because *Shari'ah* scholars don't like the word 'derivatives'
Interview 33	IFIs have a limited range of *Shari'ah*-compliant instruments for risk transfer

TABLE 9.38   Focused coding number 2 for Question 11

Hedging is urgently needed by IFIs	
Interview 8	Not having hedging tools puts Islamic banks at competitive disadvantage
Interview 14	Without proper hedging approaches at our disposal, it feels like trying to clap with one hand
Interview 20	Islamic banking is still in its infancy in terms of hedging solutions
Interview 25	Islamic banking is not mature enough to apply existing conventional market risk mitigation and hedging techniques
Interview 27	Today lack of risk-transfer techniques is described as Islamic finance's Achilles heel
Interview 29	Islamic banks need to move quickly toward *Shari'ah*-compliant hedging solutions
Interview 30	There is growing demand for *Shari'ah*-compliant hedging products

have been mutated to trade risks. Some respondents did not have a clear demarcation between the two. They stated that before the crisis, Islamic finance had been criticised because it could not freely hedge its risks using derivatives instruments. Today, this feature has been proven to be truly a blessing in disguise. In addition, the bankers interviewed asserted that even with the *Shari'ah*-approved structures, Islamic hedging currently costs much more than normal conventional hedging; it is documentation intensive and banks have to do dual *murabahahs*, rather than a single standardised transaction. *Shari'ah*-compliant tools are available; they need to be signed and accepted quicker and cheaper.

In general, most interviews reveal that there is growing demand for hedging and *Shari'ah*-compliant derivatives, which should be used merely for hedging and not speculation. Risk mitigation within Islamic banking is still to a large extent a grey area and work in progress.

The Dichotomy Between the Theory and Practice of Islamic Banking

This section examines the proposition that Islamic banking has been diverting from its roots by mimicking conventional banks. The theme in Table 9.39 indicates that although, in theory, the Islamic financial system is more resilient to economic shocks than the debunked Wall Street model, unfortunately the theory is a long way from fact in Islamic banking's current financial practice. The findings from the analysis through focused coding are presented in the following tables.

As Tables 9.40 and 9.41 show, most interviewees criticised Islamic banking for trying to 'shoe-horn' *Shari'ah* principles into conventional product structures; where Islamic products replicate conventional products they are being exposed to the same risks. IFIs are also shying away from being sufficiently socially responsible. A number of respondents are of the view that some IFIs deviated to a great extent from the fundamental basis of Islamic finance; they have succumbed to

TABLE 9.39   Results for Question 12

Question 12	How *Shari'ah*-compliant is Islamic banking within its current practice? Do you believe that Islamic banks need to reform in order to be successful?
Focused Coding	
1	Mimicking conventional became the norm
2	IFIs are in a constant struggle to reconcile faith and finance
Theme: Islamic banking has long been deviating from true *Shari'ah* principles.	

TABLE 9.40   Focused coding number 1 for Question 12

Mimicking conventional became the norm	
Interview 2	With sorrow there is a tendency to mimic everything that is offered by traditional banks
Interview 13	They are still heading in the same direction as conventional banks
Interview 21	Customers are fed up with the market imitating conventional banking
Interview 27	There is lots of form-over-substance compliance in Islamic banking
Interview 33	Big difference between practice and principles

TABLE 9.41 Focused coding number 2 for Question 12

IFIs are in a constant struggle to reconcile faith and finance	
Interview 5	It is not fair to claim that current Islamic banking is merely a disguised version of the conventional substance
Interview 10	IFIs must resolve inner tensions
Interview 16	Everything that is not forbidden in the Holy Quran is ok
Interview 31	You can create and invest in very risky assets and still be *Shari'ah*-compliant

the influence of conventional banking. *Shari'ah* scholars interviewed therefore emphasised that there is an internal logic to *Shari'ah* principles, which IFIs will see only if they stop trying to duplicate conventional structures.

The Next Chapter in Islamic Banking

In this last part of the interview analysis, the participants' opinions and perceptions were sought on the future of IBF with a particular focus on risk management-related issues. The theme in Table 9.42 indicates that various strategies have been suggested by interviewees in order to achieve profitable growth and to enhance IFIs' competitiveness. However, participants asserted that while asset growth is important, addressing risk issues needs to be in place to support sustainable growth. Therefore, strategic focus needs to be timed, with risk management being implemented first, followed by growth. The findings from the analysis through focused coding are presented in Tables 9.43 to 9.46.

TABLE 9.42 Results for Question 13

Question 13	What strategies should Islamic banks focus on over the coming decade? What do you believe are the catalysts for the growth of Islamic banking?
Focused Coding	
1	Enhanced risk management and mitigation
2	Diversification
3	Back to roots
4	Consolidation
Theme: Various strategies suggested. One thing most sides agreed on is the need for enhanced risk management and a return to *Shari'ah* principles.	

TABLE 9.43 Focused coding number 1 for Question 13

Enhanced risk management and mitigation	
Interview 9	The industry urgently needs more advanced risk management architecture
Interview 11	Think capital, think risk … the risk culture must change and must be embedded institutionally
Interview 13	Enhance risk management practices and culture
Interview 20	Without proper risk mitigation, I can't see how Islamic banking will be able to compete in a global competitive environment
Interview 28	Clearly there is substantial room for improvement in risk management
Interview 29	IFIs must manage the funding gap carefully

TABLE 9.44 Focused coding number 2 for Question 13

Diversification	
Interview 25	Concentration kills; IFIs must diversify
Interview 27	Diversification: geographically and operationally

TABLE 9.45 Focused coding number 3 for Question 13

Back to roots	
Interview 4	Back to basics and core values
Interview 19	Innovate do not replicate

TABLE 9.46 Focused coding number 4 for Question 13

Consolidation	
Interview 18	Cross-border consolidation
Interview 21	Mergers and acquisitions; there are far too many small Islamic banks

As the findings in Tables 9.42 depict, recommendations given in terms of strategies that Islamic banks should focus on over the coming decade as catalysts for the growth of Islamic banking are numerous and diverse. Many challenges still lie ahead, as is clear from the interviews. However, the ongoing improvements in banks' risk management and mitigation techniques and prudential frameworks for *Shari'ah*-compliant banking give reasonable hope that the Islamic banking industry's growth will contribute positively to broader financial and economic stability, especially after the financial crisis has proved Islamic finance to be a more ethical and sustainable banking alternative than the debunked Wall Street model.

In particular, IFIs need to improve their liquidity management and diversify their activities from what is mostly a real estate and 'vanilla' lending play, to offer a comprehensive service suite including advanced treasury services, innovative asset-management and securitisation services. This will allow them to address the needs of underserved market segments such as sovereign wealth funds and private wealth clients. The bankers interviewed recommended that there is also a lot to be done in trade finance, which used to be the staple of Islamic finance but for many years has been unfashionable. The corporate finance and liability management areas are also open for huge expansion. IFIs should also exploit consolidation in order to benefit from economies of scale as well as enhancement of scope. Both approaches offer diversification benefits.

CONCLUSION

The objective of this chapter is to analyse the semi-structured interviews conducted with Islamic banking professionals. The responses of the interviewees were first individually recorded and later coded and the results of the coded answers presented in a table. The interview was then organised into various topics to simplify the analysis of the responses given by the interviewees.

As regards the findings, interviewees indicated that the IFIs' unsound risk management architecture is reflected by their concentration risks, poor sector allocation, imprudent liquidity management and imbalanced ALM. In addition, the interviews revealed that the *Shari'ah*-non-compliance risk is a significant risk facing IFIs. It is also noticeable that both Islamic and non-Islamic bankers had similar risk perceptions about risk management in Islamic banking.

In addition, the interview findings indicate that Islamic banking in its current state can be riskier than conventional banking because of the additional risk management and mitigation challenges and constraints the industry faces. As the participants stated, there are several risk management areas where improvement can be made to promote and enhance the functioning of IFIs. Empirical evidence also indicates that many Islamic banking products aim to essentially replicate the products and processes of the conventional system. Most IFIs prefer mark-up based contracts and shy away from profit-sharing contracts that they perceive as more risky.

Interviewees had varying views about the suitability of Basel II and potentially Basel III to Islamic banking and whether IFIs should keep higher or lower capital requirements than their conventional peers. In general, respondents, particularly bankers and rating agency analysts, agree that with a few amendments,

Basel II becomes applicable to IFIs, and that IFIs should hold higher capital levels than their conventional counterparts because the Islamic banking business model in its current state carries more risks. It is interesting to note that, despite a general lack of absolute clarity about Basel III and its potential impact on IFIs, most interviewees agreed that Basel III is a fact that is here to stay.

Furthermore, most interviewees believe that although IFIs have been more resilient to the ongoing crisis than their conventional counterparts, the shift in the environment did negatively affect some of them. Since Islamic finance is not an island, it has suffered from the liquidity drought, to the point where a few IFIs have defaulted, but as an industry it now has a track record of resilience, which had not been tested before. While the global crisis gave Islamic banking an opportunity to prove its resilience, it also highlighted the need to address important challenges. The crisis has led to greater recognition of the importance of liquidity risks, and the need for more advanced risk management and mitigation.

Interviewees are also of the view that IFIs will not achieve their objectives by simply mimicking conventional products. While the ideals of Islamic finance offer some compelling ideas, the reality is that much of Islamic finance today is focused on replicating the conventional system.

Finally, the interviewees almost unanimously agree that there is now an opportunity for Islamic banking to thrive as it has the potential to contribute to a more stable economy. However, in its current form, Islamic banking has little to offer in terms of long-lasting solutions and sustainable financing, as the solution ultimately has to be a moral, not a material one. Islamic banking needs to aim for a truly alternative vision based on the ethical and moral safeguards within authentic Islamic concepts, together with improving risk management and mitigation techniques, enhancing liquidity management and reducing concentrations.

The empirical findings in this chapter provide efficient responses to the research questions and objectives. The findings of the interview analysis having been presented, Chapter 10 combines these findings with the quantitative findings from the questionnaire data analysis in an integrated manner within the context of the existing literature in order to provide a basis for an overall conclusion.

Contextualising the Findings

An Interpretative Discussion

The discussion in this chapter is based on the results of the conceptual aspects of the research that were gained from the literature review and from data collected and analysed in order to investigate risk management issues in Islamic banking. The available studies on similar subjects are mostly theoretical in nature, considering primary data research only. The results of the current study will therefore fill a significant gap in current scholarship by providing vital empirical information about risk management in Islamic banking.

In the last three chapters, Chapters 7, 8 and 9, the findings of the quantitative and qualitative data analysis were presented. This chapter discusses the implications of the findings in relation to the existing body of knowledge in the field. It aims to achieve the objective of giving greater meaning to the results through an interpretative method. The aim of this chapter, hence, is to combine the main results of the empirical chapters so as to conduct an integrated discussion of the hypotheses identified earlier, whereby it will be possible to highlight the contribution of this study.

For the purpose of clarity and to provide a more clearly structured approach to discussion, the flow of this chapter corresponds to the research hypotheses and to the thematic structure used in the questionnaire and interviews. Thus, the main discussion of the chapter is divided into 10 main sections: Risk Perception in Islamic Banking; Islamic Finance Contracts; Additional Risk Issues Facing IFIs; Capital Adequacy for Islamic Banks; Islamic Banking and the Global Credit Crisis; Risk Management and Reporting; Risk Measurement; Risk Mitigation; Islamic Banking in Practice; and, finally, The Future of Islamic Banking.

RISK PERCEPTION IN ISLAMIC BANKING

This section aims to provide a discussion through further interpretation of the results on the overall risks faced by Islamic banks by responding to the hypotheses set in advance.

Hypothesis 1: The main risks facing Islamic banks are reputational risk, *Shari'ah*-non-compliance risk, asset–liability management (ALM) risk, liquidity risk and concentration risk.

In order to identify the main risks facing Islamic financial institutions (IFIs), the findings from the questionnaire and interview analyses were examined side by side, in addition to searching the existing literature review.

The null hypothesis is accepted and the alternative hypothesis is rejected by both quantitative and qualitative analyses.

The descriptive statistics for the entire sample, as in Table 7.5, show that the top five risks facing IFIs according to mean ranking are: liquidity, ALM, reputational, concentration and credit risks. *Shari'ah*-non-compliance risk followed with a close mean rank of 3.71, while market risk was considered the least risky (2.72). Of note is the proximity of mean values among the top risks.

These findings are no surprise, as liquidity management is far from an easy task for IFIs; it is structurally more challenging for IFIs because there is still a significant shortage of liquid instruments, despite the efforts of the various central banks to provide a variety in which Islamic banks can place their surplus cash. In fact, Tamweel and Amlak would have gone insolvent if not for government help. As discussed in Chapter 3, there have been some efforts to improve liquidity management and to develop an Islamic capital market and tradable Islamic financial instruments, but to date these have been limited.

ALM and liquidity risks are closely correlated, as the former is basically the practice of managing risks that arise due to mismatches between the assets and liabilities of a bank. For IFIs, the limited range of possible funding sources leads to concentrated liabilities, imbalanced funding mixes and stretched capital management strategies. Therefore, IFIs' funding bands usually remain imbalanced and IFIs tend to fill the gaps with capital. However, capital is a very expensive way of funding. This is why Islamic banks, particularly in the Gulf Cooperation Council (GCC), engage in higher risk/high yield transactions to make up for the expensive funding via capital and consequently keep shareholders satisfied with high returns. Those IFIs forced themselves, unintentionally, up the risk curve instead of diversifying their risks. This makes the balance sheet of Islamic banks quite polarised, with high real estate assets, which led to Islamic banks having a high concentration risk, on both sides of the balance sheet. A typical balance sheet structure of many IFIs displays high exposure to properties on the assets side and limited funding sources with high reliance on short-term liabilities and capital on the other side. This is a very unfavourable funding continuum, which has led IFIs into a vicious circle of risks.

Moreover, IFIs tend to have a concentration base of assets and/or deposits; they face high concentration by name and sector, as well as high geographical concentration. The limited scope of eligible asset classes creates asset concentration risk. Focus on tangibles had led to increased property-related financings at IFIs, affected by the relatively undiversified nature of the economies. As real estate markets are highly volatile in the GCC, the concentration risk is magnified because concentrations are even more problematic when they are biased toward high-risk sectors. High lending concentrations to construction and real estate companies are common for many IFIs. Moreover, the construction and real estate sectors are highly cyclical, require high capital-intensity, and typically have a long production cycle, leaving IFIs with high exposures to this sector and vulnerable to shifts in the market environment. According to Smith (2010), the combined exposure to the real estate and construction sector is in some cases higher than 100% of Tier 1 capital for Islamic banks, particularly in the GCC.

Respondents also identified credit risk as being among the top risks that face IFIs. Traditionally, a large part of a bank's profit came from lending businesses. Also, the majority of bank losses were related to this aspect of risk management; hence the focus was primarily on credit risk. Credit risk management for IFIs is further complicated by a number of factors such as contractual complications with Islamic banking products creating additional credit risks; difficulty of foreclosure; and lack of credit assessment models, track record, robust ratings, mitigation techniques, etc.

Furthermore, reputational risk is critically important for Islamic banking, as a growing industry that is built on trust and transparency. Finally, *Shari'ah* compliance is inherently and systemically significant to Islamic banking. Any divergence from *Shari'ah* principles exposes the IFI to a wide range of risks at different levels as discussed in previous chapters.

Of note is the political risk. Under Question 8 of the questionnaire, only two respondents added political and country risks as extra risks facing IFIs. However, the lesson from the recent political unrest and revolutions in the Middle East is that political risk – which was previously largely ignored – does matter. Political risks are hard to predict and not recurring. The nature of political risk is that it can strike suddenly and have unpredictable consequences, as has already been witnessed in Tunisia, Egypt, Libya, Syria, Bahrain and Yemen. Political risk has been latent for many years in the Middle East, but has now erupted across most countries in the region. Events just the past few months show that the structural landscape of the region's politics is changing fundamentally. Under these circumstances, long-standing assumptions concerning political risk and its potential economic impact are being challenged. There is no doubt that political change in the Middle East could ultimately be positive as governments that enjoy greater legitimacy tend to be more resilient to economic shocks, which require governments to take tough economic measures. In the short term, however, the process of political change has brought negative economic pressures on the economies of these countries, hence affecting IFIs operating directly or indirectly through the region. On 15 May 2011, Zawya reported that close to USD 1.6 trillion worth of projects were cancelled or on hold in the Middle East and North African (MENA) market, where most IFIs reside and/or operate, because of the recent events.

If the questionnaire was to be redistributed now, after the eruption of the Middle Eastern revolutions, political risk would most likely attract much higher scores given that most Islamic banks are located in, or directly affected by, the Middle East.

Interviewees also indicated that IFIs' unsound risk management architecture is reflected by their concentration risks, poor sector allocation, imprudent liquidity management and imbalanced ALM. In addition, interviews revealed that *Shari'ah*-non-compliance risk is a significant risk facing IFIs. It is also noticeable that both Islamic and non-Islamic bankers had similar risk perceptions about risk management in Islamic banking. This supports Research Hypothesis 1.

This further confirms the findings from the research conducted by Al-Omar and Abdel-Haq (1996), who identified credit and liquidity risks for Islamic banks as higher than those for conventional banks. Also, Khan and Ahmed (2001) found that IFIs face some risks that are different from those faced by conventional financial institutions. They revealed that some of these risks are considered more serious than the conventional risks. While Moody's (2009c) highlighted that IFIs suffer from liquidity management and stated that "liquidity tends to be a financial crutch for Islamic banks", the report indicated that the handling of asset–liability mismatches is not a new problem in Islamic banking; it is as old as Islamic banking itself.

Furthermore, breaking down the descriptive statistics among different groups provided significant findings, as summarised in Table 7.6. Three out of the top four risks identified by Islamic bankers are also listed by conventional bankers among the top four risks. In general, risk perceptions among bankers, whether Islamic or non-Islamic, reflected similar patterns. This was emphasised by the frequency distribution and the Kruskall-Wallis (K-W) test of significance in Chapter 8.

Subsequently, further sub-hypotheses were formulated in order to further investigate the impact of various categories of respondents on risk perception. This was done with the objective of exploring if there are trends and correlations among the different control variables.

The sub-hypotheses are as follows:

H_{1-1}: *There is no statistically significant difference among the respondents in relation to their perception of the various risks facing IFIs according to region.*

As can be seen in Table 8.1, at $\alpha = 0.05$, the null hypothesis is rejected and the alternative hypothesis is accepted, since the tested p-value is lower than the critical p-value for corporate governance risk (p = 0.002), implying that there are statistically significant differences in the risk perception of corporate governance risk among different regions.

The mean rankings for credit, liquidity, corporate governance and concentration risks remain very similar between fully fledged Islamic banks and Islamic subsidiaries, and slightly change when conventional banks are added to the sample; however, the pattern is still obvious. The findings indicate that there is an observed pattern, which can be generalised to most of the risk categories. This can be explained only by market realities. In line with this, Noraini et al. (2009) found no evidence that Islamic bankers in different countries perceived risks differently; that research focused solely on Islamic bankers.

Moreover, the K-W test with 'Region' as the control variable for different samples of data in terms of the institutional nature of respondents consistently show that there is a significant difference between regions in risk perception of corporate governance risk. A bank's corporate governance practices can have a material impact on its risk profile, particularly where governance practices are weak.

This was re-emphasised by the K-W test results for Statement 10 in Question 11 of the questionnaire. When asked how strongly they agree or disagree with the statement 'Corporate governance is generally weak in Islamic banks', the majority of respondents agreed, and the K-W test had very significant results across various control variables as summarised in Table 8.19.

According to a study by Safieddine (2009), there is a need to give special attention to corporate governance issues in IFIs due to the importance of corporate governance for economic development, the growth of Islamic finance, the critical role of governance in financial institutions, and the unique agency issues faced by these institutions. Most of the Islamic banks surveyed by Safieddine (2009) recognise the importance of incorporating governance mechanisms. Some governance instruments, including the board of directors, *Shari'ah* Supervisory Boards and internal control departments, appear to have the qualifications and composition that would equip them to mitigate agency issues; however, deficiencies in the actual practices of governance are still observed, leaving agency issues unresolved. The establishment of a governance committee or an audit committee is not common among the banks surveyed, and clear internal audit functions are not properly established. Therefore, the financial reporting process does not appear to be tightly monitored, and this could potentially result in agency problems. Most importantly, investment account holders (IAHs) and other investors still lack access to relevant information, and they continue to lack influence on management decisions, which expands the divergence between their cash flow and monitoring rights.

Khandelwal (2008) also argues that transparency and corporate governance in the Islamic financial services industry should always be developed and adjusted to meet the specific needs of Islamic banks.

As explained in Chapter 3, IFIs do not generally have robust corporate governance frameworks in place. However, in this they are no different from some of their local conventional peers. For instance, family ownership/majority ownership by a core shareholder group is seen in both segments of an Islamic country's banking system. Their prevalence weakens the rights of minority shareholders, could lead to unmerited appointments or promotion of family members, and could give rise to conflicts of interest between shareholders and bondholders. The lack of genuinely independent directors is a shortcoming of emerging markets in general and impairs a board's ability to maintain accountability and provide strategic guidance. As discussed in Chapter 3, the two cases of Ahmad Hamad Algosaibi & Brothers and the Saad Group in Saudi Arabia raised questions about corporate governance in the Middle East as the two conglomerates were, to a certain degree, a family affair.

In fact, weak corporate governance structures are a general feature of Islamic banking. For a number of IFIs, corporate governance systems are opaque, unaccountable and often heavily 'relationship-based', as opposed to the predominantly rule-based corporate governance systems of conventional banks in developed markets. Often, Islamic banks' ownership structures are complex and not transparent; in addition, developed corporate governance structures comprising qualified independent board members, effective committee structures, protection of minority shareholder interests, etc., are absent. In many cases, the owners or shareholders hold key management positions and dominate the board of directors, thus making it difficult for the board to manage conflicts of interest between the controlling shareholders' interests and those of the minority shareholders.

Banks in the Middle East in general have traditionally enjoyed a cosy relationship with prominent family-owned businesses. The practice of so-called name lending – extending credit based on the reputation and standing of the company's owners rather than on rigorous examination of its financial health – is prevalent.

According to Zawya, most family businesses in the Middle East are less than 65 years old. Many of them began as trading houses and have now become diversified conglomerates. However, a host of challenges facing many family businesses in the Gulf are worth considering:

(i) Succession issues and transferring effective control and knowledge from one generation to the next is a challenge and, as shareholders (family members) become numerous, they impact the efficiency of decision-making.

(ii) Attracting outside talent and relinquishing control when necessary are always important. Over the years, family groups have grown into multi-billion-dollar conglomerates, sometimes without commensurate skill resources.

(iii) Family businesses need to shift from being purely operational to thinking in more strategic terms.

(iv) Separation of management and ownership may be difficult.
(v) Diversification into multiple businesses can lead to over-extension beyond the group's core knowledge and competences.

The GCC Board Directors Institute, a Dubai-based non-profit that seeks to improve corporate governance standards, issued a report in 2009 highlighting the need for reform in the six GCC member states – Bahrain, Kuwait, Oman, Qatar, Saudi Arabia and the United Arab Emirates (UAE). The report *Building Better Boards* notes that only 55% of GCC companies disclose the main executive positions of board members, compared with 100% in Europe, and only 32% of companies disclose other positions held by board members, compared with 97% in Europe. It urges a reduction in the number of boards on which directors serve; the appointment of strong audit, nomination and remuneration committees; efforts to attract more international directors to the boards of Gulf companies; and the promotion of greater corporate transparency (Townsend, 2009).

Corporate governance risk in the GCC, where most Islamic banks reside, has become publicly exposed. Poor corporate governance imposes heavy costs. The need for additional efforts toward improved corporate transparency is paramount. As long as Gulf companies and banks restricted their activities to largely within the region, there was little pressure to change those opaque practices. But growing links with international markets and financial institutions are generating greater demands for reform. Changing corporate practices, however, would not be easy. Governance reform needs to be addressed against the cultural backdrop in the Gulf, which places great emphasis on reputation and discretion.

The same trend could be established when different K-W tests were conducted with different institutional settings. As discussed in the following hypotheses, it was concluded that three control variables (region, country and nature of financial institution) demonstrate some significant differences about risk perception among respondents, but not for all risks.

Furthermore, although statistically corporate governance risk is the sole significant risk identified by respondents, examining the mean ranking of other risks like concentration, credit and liquidity risks reveals a structural pattern determined by market realities. Also, as depicted by Tables 8.4 to 8.6, the differences between the mean rankings is noticeable among different regions for these risks and when conducting the K-W test for different samples using different institutional settings, which confirms that there is significant difference between regions.

H_{1-2}: There is no statistically significant difference among the respondents in relation to their perception of the various risks facing IFIs according to the country in which they operate.

At $\alpha = 0.05$, the null hypothesis is rejected and the alternative hypothesis is accepted. The K-W test was conducted in a similar manner according to 'Country' as control variable; the results confirm those produced by the test conducted according to the 'Region'.

H_{1-3}: *There is no statistically significant difference among the respondents in relation to their perception of the various risks facing IFIs according to the respondent's position.*

At $\alpha = 0.05$, the null hypothesis is accepted and the alternative hypothesis is rejected, since the tested p-value is higher than the critical p-value. Therefore, the results suggest that statistically there are no differences in risk perception among respondents according to their position.

H_{1-4}: *There is no statistically significant difference among the respondents in relation to their perception of the various risks facing IFIs according to accounting standards.*

At $\alpha = 0.05$, the null hypothesis is accepted and the alternative hypothesis is rejected, since the tested p-value is higher than the critical p-value. The results of the K-W test in Table 8.7 show that there are no significant differences among different respondent categories.

H_{1-5}: *There is no statistically significant difference among the respondents in relation to their perception of the various risks facing IFIs according to nature of the financial institution.*

For this hypothesis, the results from the K-W test provided dispersed data. At $\alpha = 0.05$, liquidity, ALM, *Shari'ah*-non-compliance, concentration, reputation and displaced commercial risks had significant p-values, while the remaining risks did not. Therefore, the null hypothesis is accepted and the alternative hypothesis is rejected, since the tested p-value is lower than the critical p-value for most risks. Further examination of the mean rankings for risks with significant p-value, as summarised in Table 8.9, confirms the dispersion of data as no trend could be established. In general, fully fledged Islamic banks and conventional banks with Islamic activities have higher mean values than conventional banks alone and 'Others', particularly for liquidity, ALM and displaced commercial risks. This trend, nonetheless, slightly changes for concentration and reputation risks. Of note also is the proximity of mean value among fully fledged Islamic banks and Islamic subsidiaries, which reflects the similar perception of risks in Islamic banking. One possible reason for this is the similar knowledge and awareness about

Islamic banking products and structures among those professionals with hands-on experience in Islamic banking. This confirms the findings of the descriptive statistics in the section 'Locating Risk Perception' in Chapter 7.

Moreover, this coincides with the findings of the qualitative analysis, as on the basis of the interview findings, there is a high degree of correlation between the responses of the two groups. However, differences generally existed between the responses of bankers and non-bankers.

Based on the above hypotheses and the findings from both the quantitative and qualitative analyses, it can be concluded that three control variables (region, country and nature of financial institution) contribute to some significant differences about risk perception among respondents, but not for all risks. In addition, this can also be supported by the fact that there is no significant difference in perception levels between respondents from stand-alone Islamic banks and Islamic subsidiaries. Initially, it was expected that respondents from stand-alone Islamic banks would have stronger perceptions compared to those from Islamic subsidiaries, for two reasons: firstly, stand-alone Islamic banks have been in existence much longer than Islamic subsidiaries, and, secondly, the respondents from stand-alone Islamic banks have the advantage of dealing with only Islamic banking products and services whereas Islamic subsidiaries still need to operate side by side with their respective conventional counterpart in sharing the same operating platforms and buildings. Nevertheless, the results have indicated otherwise. Differences could be spotted between the perceptions of conventional banks and stand-alone Islamic banks, and more noticeably between the perceptions of bankers and non-bankers, the latter being represented by the category 'Others'. This could be because bankers, whether Islamic or non-Islamic, have hands-on experience and better understanding of the Islamic banking model and its risk architecture than non-bankers, who tend to be more theoretical in their approach.

ISLAMIC FINANCE CONTRACTS

This section aims to provide a discussion through further interpretation of the results on the usage and risk perception of Islamic finance contracts by responding to the hypotheses set in advance.

Intensity of Use of Different Islamic Finance Contracts

Hypothesis 2: Islamic bankers prefer mark-up based contracts (*murabahah, salaam, istisna'a* and *ijarah*) and shy away from profit-sharing contracts (*musharakah* and *mudarabah*).

Descriptive statistics as depicted by Table 7.8 demonstrate that *murabahah* contracts are by far the most used contracts. This '*murabahah* syndrome' has been under criticism from many *Shari'ah* scholars but unfortunately still remains the backbone of IBF; *murabahah* has been intensively used by IFIs for money market transactions, investment and retail activities. Recently, more banks have been using *walaka* for money market transactions to replace the commodity *murabahah*, which involves more complications and raises *Shari'ah* concerns. The low mean for *musharakah* and *mudarabah* reflects Islamic banks' reluctance to hold risk-sharing assets. Moreover, the questionnaire revealed that *salaam* has a long way to go before becoming commonly used by IFIs. It is evident from the responses that the banks' first preference is for financial instruments that are generated through debt-creating, sale contracts and leasing instruments. This is enhanced by the responses about risk perception in different modes of financing. These findings are supported by the results of the Chi-Square test, which indicated that the Chi-Square values of the contracts are very significant ($p < 1\%$).

Moreover, evidence from interview analysis indicates that many Islamic banking products aim to essentially replicate the products and processes of the conventional system. Most IFIs prefer mark-up based contracts and shy away from profit-sharing contracts, which they perceive as more risky, as explained under Hypothesis 3.

Therefore, the hypothesis stating that Islamic bankers prefer mark-up based contracts and shy away from profit-sharing contracts is accepted by both quantitative and qualitative analyses.

Subsequently, the following sub-hypotheses were tested to identify whether there is any statistically significant difference in the level of understanding across various groups of respondents based on the selected control variables.

H_{2-1}: *There are no statistically significant differences among the respondents' use of Islamic finance contracts according to region.*

At $\alpha = 0.05$, the null hypothesis is rejected, since the significant p-value for *mudarabah* is lower than the critical 0.05 p-value; hence the alternative hypothesis is accepted. Inferential statistics in Table 8.11 show that 'Other Middle East' and 'Southeast Asia' use *mudarabah* the most, with mean values of 32.5 and 27.13 respectively, while 'Europe' (17.71) and the 'GCC' (16.74) rank less on the use of *mudarabah*, as financial institutions in these regions tend to rely more on *murabahah*, *wakala* and *ijarah*. This should be explained by the economies of the regions in question.

H_{2-2}: *There are no statistically significant differences among the respondents' use of Islamic finance contracts according to the respondent's position.*

As can be seen in Table 8.10, the results suggest that the null hypothesis is accepted as p-value for all contracts is higher than the critical 0.05 p-value, and hence it can be concluded that 'Respondent's Position' does not play a statistically significant determining role.

H_{2-3}: *There are no statistically significant differences among the respondents' use of Islamic finance contracts according to the nature of the financial institution.*

At $\alpha = 0.05$, the null hypothesis is rejected, since the significant p-values for *wakala* and *salaam* are lower than the critical 0.05 p-value; hence the alternative hypothesis is accepted. This is also emphasised by the findings of the qualitative data analysis, which reflect that fully fledged Islamic banks have some appetite for risk-sharing contracts, although not enough, unlike Islamic subsidiaries and conventional banks, which wish to share rewards without sharing risks, and prefer the use of mark-up based contracts.

H_{2-4}: *There are no statistically significant differences among the respondents' use of Islamic finance contracts according to the nature of activities.*

The results shown in Table 8.10 indicate that the null hypothesis is accepted, which suggests that 'Nature of Activities' plays no statistically significant determining role.

Risk Perception in Different Islamic Finance Contracts

Hypothesis 3: Profit-sharing contracts are perceived as more risky than mark-up based contracts in the Islamic finance industry.

The risk perceptions of the respondents in different modes of financing are summarised in Table 7.9, which shows that respondents perceive *mudarabah* and *musharakah* (mean value of 6.21 and 5.89 respectively) to be riskier than *wakala* and *murabahah* (mean value of 2.26 and 1.90 respectively). The manipulation of the contracts by Islamic finance practitioners in order to mimic conventional products made the risk perception of equity and risk-sharing contracts, for instance *wakala*, similar to the risk perception of fixed-income contracts like *murabahah*. This created a gap in risk perception of different contracts among different groups of respondents. These findings are supported by the results of the Chi-Square test, which indicated that the Chi-Square values of the items are very significant (p < 1%). In addition, the Friedman test of significance in Table 8.13 shows that there is a significant difference with regard to the risk in each mode of financing, at 1% significance level. This explains why IFIs shy away from such instruments – due to their lack of appetite for risky assets – which in turn is due to IFIs trying to emulate the conventional model.

Qualitative analysis confirmed those findings as most interviewees indicated that in general IFIs prefer mark-up based contracts and shy away from profit-sharing contracts, which they perceive as more risky. Therefore, Hypothesis 3 is supported.

Although Islamic banking offers a combination of both equity and non-equity-based instruments, the system's preference for equity contracts – in theory – makes it more efficient and stable than debt-based conventional systems. Sadr and Iqbal (2002) presented empirical evidence based on the data gathered over 15 years from the Agricultural Bank of Iran which demonstrated that equity-based financing increases transparency, monitoring and supervision, and thus improves the efficiency and stability of the financial system. Unfortunately, IFIs tend to shy away from equity- and partnership-based instruments for several reasons, such as the inherent riskiness and additional costs of monitoring such investments, low appetite for risk and lack of transparency in the markets.

> It may be seen that greater reliance on equity financing has to be an indispensable part of the strategy of any system which wishes to actualise the humanitarian goals of need fulfilment, full employment, equitable distribution of income and wealth, and economic stability. And hence the ideals of Islamic economics and finance.
>
> *(Asutay, 2009a)*

The result is as per the expectation of the researcher and further confirms the findings from the research conducted by Noraini et al. (2009), who found that Islamic bankers perceive *salaam* and *istisna'a* to be riskier than *murabahah* and *ijarah,* and that profit-sharing assets (*mudarabah* and *musharakah*) are perceived to be more risky than mark-up based assets, particularly *murabahah* and *ijarah,* with the exception of *salaam.* Also, Khan and Ahmed (2001) found that profit-sharing modes of financing are perceived by bankers to have higher risk, while *murabahah* was ranked as having the least risk, followed by *ijarah.* This is because Islamic debt contracts (like *murabahah*) give the banks a relatively certain income and the ownership of the leased asset remains with the bank. Nagaoka (2007) reflected on the dichotomy in Islamic debt securities and concluded that Islamic finance strongly adheres to financial transactions that involve real assets or those that can be retrieved from the assets while the accumulation of wealth by means of money-chained transactions is considered highly unacceptable in Islamic finance.

The following sub-hypotheses were developed to see if there is any significant difference in the level of knowledge across the groups of respondents for each category. The statistical tests for all the relevant questions in relation to the hypotheses are presented in Tables 8.13 to 8.17.

H_{3-1}: There are no statistically significant differences among the respondents' risk perceptions about Islamic finance contracts according to region.

As depicted in Table 8.13, at $\alpha = 0.05$, the null hypothesis is rejected, since the K-W test results for *murabahah* recorded a lower significant value than the critical p-value. Therefore, the null hypothesis suggests that, statistically, there is a significant difference in the level of risk perception of *murabahah* across different regions. This is expected because *murabahah* is extensively used globally. Moreover, mean rankings for *murabahah*, in Table 8.14, show that 'Other' regions, like Turkey and Pakistan, have a higher ranking (54.0) than the GCC (43.13) and 'Europe' (38.63), while the remaining regions follow. This can be attributed to two main reasons. First, the European and 'GCC' markets are more sophisticated in their financial awareness about risk management, product structures, and the use of risk-hedging techniques than Turkey and Pakistan, a fact which has a direct impact on risk perception among those markets. Second, at the time of conducting this questionnaire, European and GCC markets enjoyed stable political environments and 'relatively' less volatile business cycles compared to 'Others'.

This trend was confirmed when the K-W test was repeated for different institutional data. There is a general pattern in terms of perception of *murabahah*-related issues. Such regional and institutional differences can be attributed to market conditions prevailing in each region.

However, interview data analysis did not reveal such regional differences among respondents when it comes to risk perception of different Islamic finance contracts. Most interviewees, regardless of the region, agreed that risk-sharing among Islamic banks is still the exception rather than the rule.

H_{3-2}: There are no statistically significant differences among the respondents' risk perceptions about Islamic finance contracts according to the respondent's position.

For this hypothesis, the results from the K-W test accept the null hypothesis and reject the alternative hypothesis, since all the Islamic finance modes of finance registered an insignificant p-value of more than the critical p-value of 0.05 as can be seen in Table 8.17. Therefore, it can be concluded that, statistically, there is no significant difference in the level of risk perception of Islamic finance contracts according to the respondent's position.

The qualitative analysis in Chapter 9 reveals that *Shari'ah* scholars and consultants in particular encourage the use of *musharakah* and *mudarabah* contracts more than bankers do. Also, the former consider risk-sharing modes of finances to be less risky, while the latter perceive the mark-up based modes of finance to be less risky.

$H_{3.3}$: *There are no statistically significant differences among the respondents' risk perceptions about Islamic finance contracts according to nature of financial institution.*

As depicted in Table 8.17, at $\alpha = 0.05$, the null hypothesis is rejected and the alternative hypothesis is accepted, since the p-value for *murabahah* (0.03) is lower than the critical p-value of 0.05.

This is also emphasised by the findings of the qualitative data analysis, which reflects that fully fledged Islamic banks believe that *mushrakah* and *mudarabah* are not as risky as perceived by Islamic subsidiaries and conventional banks, the latter tending to find comfort in using *murabahah* and *wakala* products.

$H_{3.4}$: *There are no statistically significant differences among the respondents' risk perceptions about Islamic finance contracts according to the accounting standards used.*

Table 8.17 depicts that at $\alpha = 0.05$, the null hypothesis is rejected, since the K-W test results for *murabahah* recorded a lower significant value (0.028) than the critical p-value. Therefore, the alternative hypothesis suggests that accounting standards plays a statistically significant determining role.

Qualitative data analysis did not test responses against accounting standards used by the financial institution.

$H_{3.5}$: *There are no statistically significant differences among the respondents' risk perceptions about Islamic finance contracts according to nature of activities.*

At $\alpha = 0.05$, the null hypothesis is accepted, since the K-W test results for all contracts recorded a higher p-value than the critical p-value as can be seen in Table 8.17.

ADDITIONAL RISK ISSUES FACING ISLAMIC FINANCIAL INSTITUTIONS

This section aims to provide a discussion through further interpretation of the results on additional risk issues facing IFIs by responding to the hypothesis set in advance.

Hypothesis 4: There is no substantial difference between risk management in Islamic banking and conventional banking.

Descriptive statistics in Chapter 7 indicate that risk management for IFIs is more challenging than it is for conventional banks. Not only do IFIs face some risks that are different from those of their conventional peers, but these risks are also more serious and not well understood. Displaced commercial risk and *Shari'ah* standardisation are obvious examples of additional challenges facing IFIs. The findings also highlighted that corporate governance is generally weak in Islamic banks, which re-emphasises the findings of sub-hypothesis H_{1-1}.

In addition, risk management functions in IFIs in many cases lack influence in the bank's decision-making process. They may in some cases appear strong on paper, although the *de facto* governance behind this is not robust. This could include, for example, a lack of sufficiently senior risk management representation at board level, insufficient powers delegated to risk management, or the presence of strong shareholders or political influences that are able to override or influence decision-making on risk management. Engel (2010) argues that risk managers in IFIs generally lack independence. Rarely can risk managers veto or influence strategy in Islamic banks and they are mostly tasked with managing existing exposures and monitoring disbursed loans, along with other back-office functions.

Furthermore, factor analysis was used in responding to Hypothesis 4. The final outcomes and a detailed discussion of the factor analysis are available in the section 'Additional Risk Issues Facing IFIs' in Chapter 7. The factor analysis results suggest that all 11 variables of risk perception are reduced to three components, namely 'Risk Perception', '*Shari'ah* Compliance' and finally 'Rate of Return'.

The findings from the quantitative analysis echo the interview findings which indicate that Islamic banking in its current state can be riskier than conventional banking. There are several risk management areas where improvement can be made to promote and to enhance the functioning of IFIs. Risks in IFIs must be assessed in an integrated manner and risks for IFIs should not be managed using the same techniques as those used in conventional banking.

The following sub-hypotheses were formulated in order to identify whether there are any significant differences across various groups in the respective control variables.

H_{4-1}: *There are no statistically significant differences among respondents' perceptions about additional risk management issues in Islamic banking according to the nature the of financial institution.*

The results in Table 8.18 suggest that the null hypothesis is rejected in favour of the alternative hypothesis, indicating that there are significant differences according to nature of financial institution. In addition, in order to respond to this hypothesis after conducting factor analysis, further analysis was carried out using a one-way between-groups MANOVA test in order to investigate if there is any significant difference between the three component groups identified under factor analysis in relation to same control variables. This helped to locate the impact or significance of each control variable on the established distribution. The results in Table 8.30 signify that 30.1% and 33.6% of the variances in 'Risk Perception' and '*Shari'ah* Compliance' scores are explained respectively by nature of financial institution.

H_{4-2}: *There are no statistically significant differences among respondents' perceptions about additional risk management issues in Islamic banking according to region.*

As can be seen in Table 8.19, similar conclusions can be derived from this category analysis, where the statistical results reject the null hypothesis. Similarly, after conducting factor analysis further analysis was carried out using a one-way between-groups MANOVA test in order to investigate if there is any significant difference between the three component groups in relation to the same control variables. This helped to locate the impact or significance of each control variable on the established distribution. The results in Table 8.26 signify 45.9% and 34.4% of the variances in 'Risk Perception' and '*Shari'ah* Compliance' scores are explained respectively by the region.

Conducting the MANOVA test according to 'Region' and 'Nature of Financial Institution' as independent variables provided consistent results. It can be concluded that 'Risk Perception' and '*Shari'ah* Compliance' are significant dependent variables and have strong explanatory power, while 'Rate of Return' does not follow the pattern.

H_{4-3}: *There are no statistically significant differences among respondents' perceptions about additional risk management issues in Islamic banking according to the respondent's position.*

Similarly for this sub-hypothesis, the results reject the null hypothesis as Table 8.19 depicts. The p-value for Statements 2, 3, 4, 7 and 10 are lower than the critical p-value of 0.05. It can be concluded that the respondent's position plays a statistically significant determining role.

$H_{4.4}$: *There are no statistically significant differences among respondents' perceptions about additional risk management issues in Islamic banking according to the nature of activities.*

The inferential statistical results in Table 8.19 reject the null hypothesis and accept the alternative hypothesis as the p-value for Statements 2, 4, 7, 8, 10 and 11 are significantly lower than the critical p-value of 0.05.

$H_{4.5}$: *There are no statistically significant differences among respondents' perceptions about additional risk management issues in Islamic banking according to the accounting standards used.*

Similarly, for the accounting standards control variable, the null hypothesis is rejected in favour of the alternative hypothesis, since the p-value recorded for some statements in the Table 8.19 is lower than the critical p-value limit.

CAPITAL ADEQUACY FOR ISLAMIC BANKS

This section aims to provide a discussion through further interpretation of the results on capital adequacy issues facing IFIs by responding to the hypothesis set in advance.

Hypothesis 5: Capital requirements levels should be lower in IFIs than in conventional banks.

The frequency distribution in Figure 7.5 shows that 65.3% of respondents believe that IFIs should hold higher capital levels than their conventional peers. Only 8.3% of respondents indicated that IFIs should hold lower capital levels, 18.1% indicated they should hold the same level, while 6.9% indicated they did not know the answer.

In addition, most interviewees believe that IFIs should hold higher capital levels than their conventional counterparts because the Islamic banking business model in its current state carries more risks.

Therefore, the hypothesis stating that capital requirement levels should be lower in IFIs than in conventional banks is rejected by both quantitative and qualitative analyses, which implies that capital requirement levels should be higher in IFIs than in conventional banks.

The responses are against the researcher's expectations, as most literature reviewed suggests that IFIs should have lower capital requirements than their conventional peers. Archer and Abdel Karim (2007), for instance, argue that the risk-sharing characteristic of Profit-Sharing Investment Accounts (PSIAs) in Islamic banking could greatly enhance risk management and mitigation in IFIs provided that proper pricing, reserving and disclosure are maintained. Therefore, IFIs should be subject to lower capital requirements because according to the Islamic Financial Services Board (IFSB) supervisory discretion formula, α represents the extent of total risk assumed by the PSIA, with the remainder absorbed by the shareholders on account of displaced commercial risk. In line with this, Farook (2008) argues that, if IFIs apply the profit and loss sharing (PLS) principle practically, losses will be shared with PSIAs and hence the Islamic bank will be prone to lower risks leading to lower required minimum capital. The IFSB supervisory discretion formula is a step in the right direction, with α representing the extent of total risk assumed by the PSIA, with the remainder absorbed by the shareholders on account of displaced commercial risk. IFIs that implement the risk-sharing technique practically will be keen on proper disclosure in order to enjoy a higher capital relief.

While the researcher agrees with the concepts discussed in the literature review from an academic point of view, the practice remains different (as depicted by the primary research findings). In order to apply the risk-sharing principle practically, the IFSB standards should be made mandatory for Islamic banks to allow for wider implementation, consistency and standardisation of risk management principles across the Islamic financial industry. This requires collaboration between regulators, IFSB, Accounting and Auditing Organization for Islamic Financial Institutions (AAOIFI), Islamic banks and industry practitioners.

Hypothesis 6: Basel II was drafted with conventional banking very much in mind. IFIs should follow their own standards, e.g. IFSB principles on capital adequacy.

The frequency distribution in Figure 7.6 shows that the majority of respondents believe that Basel II could be applied to IFIs but with a few amendments. In fact, most IFIs use Basel II capital adequacy standards, with greater use of the basic and standardised approaches rather than the advanced models. This is due to the relative simplicity of their capital requirements. Moreover, 87.5% of respondents believe that Basel II standards should be reviewed after failing to prevent the crisis. As depicted in Figure 7.6, there is an obvious lack of clarity on the applicability of the proposed Basel III standards to Islamic banking, as 65.3% of respondents were 'neutral' when asked about the issue, 27.8% either 'disagree' or 'strongly disagree' that the proposed Basel III rules would be easily applicable to Islamic banks. Around one-third of respondents do not believe that the new standards, with their stricter capital, leverage and liquidity rules, are likely to prevent another financial crisis. The break down between Islamic and non-Islamic bankers reveals the same pattern, as shown in Table 7.15.

Interviewees had varying views about the suitability of Basel II and potentially Basel III to Islamic banking. In general, respondents, particularly bankers and rating agency analysts agree that with a few amendments, Basel II becomes applicable to IFIs in order to ensure a level playing field for all banks. It is interesting to note that despite a general lack of absolute clarity about Basel III and its potential impact on IFIs, most interviewees agreed that Basel III is a fact that is here to stay. There is also a general belief among respondents that although Basel III is more demanding than Basel II with regard to addressing systemic risk, it may not be the last of the Basel series. This is mainly because risk is inherent in the complex global financial markets of increasing sophistication. Basel III cannot work on its own. As the regulators recognise, financial stability is about far more than capital and liquidity ratio. Banks will still fail even if higher ratios are implemented. Regulators need to work on other steps to reduce systemic risk including enhanced transparency, risk-sharing and value creation. All these concepts are rooted in Islamic finance, but unfortunately tend to be neglected.

Therefore, Hypothesis 6 is rejected by both quantitative and qualitative analyses.

Although the result is not as per the expectations of the researcher, it confirms the findings of the research conducted by Noraini et al. (2009), who concluded that Basel II could be applied to Islamic banks but with some adaptations and the IFSB could play an important role in this context. In addition, consideration of the implications of Basel III is at an early stage for most IFIs. While Akkizidis and Khandelwal (2007) argue that Basel II is primarily for conventional banks and thus does not offer great help to IFIs, they believe that although Pillars 1 and 2 of Basel II have limited applicability to Islamic banking, the third Pillar of Basel II on market disclosure is largely applicable to IFIs because social responsibility and transparency are of utmost importance in Islamic finance.

Fitch Ratings (2011) expects Basel III to have little impact on IFIs' capital adequacy, as capital ratios are generally sound and consist largely of core Tier 1 capital. Hybrid capital is negligible in the region. However, new liquidity requirements may be significant, as IFIs have a substantial maturity mismatch: customer deposits are contractually short term (albeit very stable), while IFIs are financing increasingly longer-term assets. This may require some adjustment to their liquidity management.

Subsequently, the following sub-hypotheses were developed to see if there is any significant difference in the perception across different groups of respondents for each control variable.

H_{6-1}: *There are no statistically significant differences among the respondents' views about capital adequacy for Islamic banks according to region.*

At $\alpha = 0.05$, the null hypothesis is rejected, since the K-W test results for four statements (out of five) recorded a lower significant value than the critical p-value, as depicted in Table 8.31.

H_{6-2}: *There are no statistically significant differences among the respondents' views about capital adequacy for Islamic banks according to nature of financial institution.*

As Table 8.32 shows, at $\alpha = 0.05$ the null hypothesis is accepted and the alternative hypothesis is rejected for all statements except Statement 5. All statements are statistically insignificant except Statement 5, which shows different views between bankers (whether Islamic or conventional) and non-bankers (p-value = 0.02), which is also evident from the mean ranking. This implies that the nature of financial institution is not a statistically determining factor, and that the opinions of the respondents are rather similar. This coincides with the results of descriptive statistics, in Figure 7.4, as more than 59% of respondents use Basel II standards.

H_{6-3}: *There are no statistically significant differences among the respondents' views about capital adequacy for Islamic banks according to the nature of activities.*

Similarly, for the 'Nature of Activities' control variable, the null hypothesis is rejected since the p-value recorded in the testing is lower than the critical p-value limit for three statements, as depicted in Table 8.33.

H_{6-4}: *There are no statistically significant differences among the respondents' views about capital adequacy for Islamic banks according to respondent's position.*

Similar results also can be found for the 'Respondent's Position' control variable in Table 8.34. At $\alpha = 0.05$, the null hypothesis is rejected and this suggests that the alternative hypothesis is accepted since the p-value recorded in the testing is significantly lower than the critical p-value limit for Statement 5 (0.008). Therefore, it can be concluded that, statistically, there is a significant difference in the respondents' perceptions according to their position.

ISLAMIC BANKING AND THE GLOBAL CREDIT CRISIS

This section aims to provide a discussion through further interpretation of the results on the global credit crisis and Islamic banking by responding to the hypothesis set in advance.

Hypothesis 7: Islamic banking is more resilient to economic shocks than conventional banking but not recession proof.

It is interesting to note that both Islamic and non-Islamic bankers in the questionnaire share the view that Islamic banking is less risky than conventional banking, in theory, due to the naturally inherent conservatism in the *Shari'ah* principles; however, the theory is a long way from fact in current financial practice. Participants asserted that reform is needed within Islamic banking in order for it to be successful and capable of providing an ethical alternative to the debunked Wall Street banking model. Most respondents also support the view that the recent crisis could have been avoided under a genuine Islamic banking system. Although IFIs were by no means unscathed by the crisis, it had a less severe impact than elsewhere and allowed prominent issues to be brought to the forefront. This supports Hypothesis 7.

Factor analysis was used in responding to Hypothesis 7. The final outcomes and a detailed discussion of the factor analysis are available in the section 'The Credit Crisis and Islamic Banks' in Chapter 8. The factor analysis results suggest that all nine variables of perception of the credit crisis and Islamic banking are reduced to two components, namely 'Resilience of IFIs' and 'Risk management must be embedded institutionally'.

Furthermore, most interviewees believe that although IFIs have been more resilient to the ongoing crisis than their conventional counterparts, the shift in the environment did negatively affect some of them. Islamic finance is not an island; it has suffered from the liquidity drought, to the point where a few IFIs have defaulted, but as an industry it now has a track record of resilience (which had not been tested before). While the global crisis gave Islamic banking an opportunity to prove its resilience, it also highlighted the need to address important challenges.

Therefore, Hypothesis 7 is supported by both quantitative and qualitative analyses.

The results further confirm the findings revealed by Moody's (2011a) that while the Islamic financial industry seems to have been resilient to the crisis relative to its conventional counterpart, it is far from being a risk-free segment. The most affected line of business within the industry was undoubtedly investment banking. And yet, until 2007, *Shari'ah*-compliant investment banks were portrayed by market participants as having significant potential, benefiting from cheap funding, high liquidity, exceptional profits and robust capitalisation. At the time, the combination of these four factors led them to pursue investments in riskier markets and asset classes such as private equity, infrastructure or real estate, mostly in emerging markets ranging from the Maghreb to Southeast Asia.

When the financial crisis erupted in mid-2007, the Islamic finance industry remained relatively healthy and insulated, and recorded robust performance. Some commentators wrongly labelled Islamic finance as a 'risk-free' sector. However, the significant defaults of The Investment Dar (TID) and Gulf Finance House (GFH) since early 2009 and the growing difficulties of the rest of the Islamic investment banking community make this assessment dubious, as the structural weaknesses of the Islamic financial industry started to become more obvious. The crisis was a unique opportunity for the industry to prove that it had the capacity and ability to react to and absorb shocks, but not for all its sub-segments. While the commercial banking sector seems to have emerged from the crisis relatively unscathed, the investment banking sector could not have been more different, as it suffered a very sudden and sharp dip in performance as losses mounted (Moody's, 2011a). One of the interviewees for this research, Engel (2010), adds that the structural feature of IFIs' ALM – which was once a benefit when ample liquidity was chasing too few assets – started to turn negative when sudden massive liquidity withdrawals were backed by almost nothing but a high level of impaired assets. In addition, the crisis revealed that IFIs also had heavy concentrations across the board, by name, sector, geography and business line.

In fact, until 2007, IFIs benefited from a very favourable economic and liquidity environment, especially due to the boom in the real estate and infrastructure sectors, and supported by massive government spending within these sectors. Meanwhile, an increasing number of regional investors were attracted by the high yields that IFIs were offering through their recycling of a growing amount of oil wealth into investments that fell outside the remit of their plain-vanilla banking activities. The perception of sound capitalisation was largely artificial in the sense that it underestimated the profound impact of sector-wide concentration risks and inadequate liquidity management. Above all, IFIs registered impressive performance for one main reason: available and cheap liquidity, explains Thun (2010), one of the interviewees for this research. This element was at the heart of the business model, consisting of borrowing short to invest long on behalf of their investment constituencies, while keeping on the balance sheet a portion of the IFI's illiquid investment portfolio that was incommensurate with their liquidity and capital profile.

The interviews also indicated that by the beginning of 2009, operating revenues started to shrink for IFIs, reflecting their struggle to book new transactions (negative volume effect) and declining asset valuations (negative price effect). At the same time, their fixed charges remained stable, while funding costs and expenses escalated. This P&L scissors effect worsened in the second half of 2009, leaving the IFIs with very limited room for manoeuvre. This highlights the very weak diversification of their revenue base, their dependence on a very uncertain transaction flow rather than on an existing stock of cash-flow-generating assets, and the cyclical cost of their funding profiles. Only a few IFIs managed to mitigate this issue.

Above all, the crisis revealed weak risk management architectures among most IFIs. It had the constructive effect of focusing the minds of Islamic practitioners on their core business strategies and operating models, highlighting corporate governance and asset and liability management specifically. According to Moody's (2011a), TID, for instance, (which defaulted in May 2009) did not disclose proper risk management information. Furthermore, in 2007, most IFIs only applied Basel I, which did not make it mandatory for them to adhere to Basel II's Pillar 3 disclosure requirements. Only in the 2008 financial reporting data (released during Q1 2009, i.e. quite late in the cycle given the extreme circumstances at the time) did IFIs start to adopt more transparent approaches to risk management, Basel II guidelines and requirements. Even then, not all the information was clearly and consistently released by the IFIs. However, since 2009, disclosure practices have been improving significantly (Moody's, 2011a).

Traditionally, IFIs have not been heavily leveraged. The primary reasons for conservative financial leverage maintenance are: (i) IFIs have limited incentives to grow debt-like liabilities because their assets tend to be highly profitable; (ii) they needed to set aside extra capital buffers to prepare for expansion; (iii) funding is usually cheap, thanks to easy access to non-remunerated *qardh hasan* current account deposits; and (iv) the necessity to set aside capital charges for specific risks like displaced commercial risk (DCR), reputation risks and concentration risks as per Basel II's Pillar 2 (Moody's, 2009c). These capital and liquidity buffers, previously criticised by opponents of Islamic finance as a burden on profitability, have perhaps been one of the most important strengths of the IFIs amid the crisis because they provide a financial institution with surplus cash to use as a shock absorber. Under the recent difficult economic conditions, most IFIs have been able to seek out opportunities by using their surplus liquidity to aggressively boost deposit volumes and thus to increase their market shares by growing lending volumes, while maintaining their focus on the retail and corporate sectors. This is a strategy employed by GCC banks to de-couple their retail lending business from global markets by focusing on extending credit locally. According to another interviewee, Damak (2010), with very few exceptions (especially in Dubai), funding has been less of a constraint for IFIs because of the market's perception that these players will be more resilient than their conventional peers to the global credit turmoil.

Hasan and Dridi (2010) argue that IFIs have avoided the subprime exposure, but note that they are subject to the 'second round effect' of the global crisis. They explain that, because the global financial crisis originated from subprime mortgage portfolios which were spun off into securitised instruments subsequently offered as investments, IFIs were not affected because Islamic finance is based on a close link between financial and productive flows. However, the protracted duration of the crisis affected IFIs as well, not because these institutions have a direct exposure to derivative instruments, but simply because Islamic banking contracts are based on asset-backed transactions. With the global economic downturn, property markets have seen a decline in a number of countries where IFIs have a significant presence. This carries negative implications for these banks as a large number of contracts are backed by real estate and property as collateral. Hasan and Dridi assert that the crisis highlighted a number of sector-specific challenges that need to be addressed in order for IFIs to continue growing at a sustainable pace. Specifically, the key challenges faced by the Islamic banking industry include (i) the infrastructure and tools for liquidity risk management, which remain underdeveloped in many jurisdictions; (ii) a legal framework, which is incomplete or untested; (iii) the lack of harmonised contracts; and (iv) insufficient expertise (at the supervisory and industry levels) relative to the industry's growth.

In addition, the lack of harmonised accounting and regulatory standards was a key challenge for regulators and market participants during the crisis. This is even more acute for IFIs given the lack of standard financial contracts and products across the various institutions within the same country, as well as across jurisdictions. Local accounting standards used in the Islamic banking sector often consist of a mixture of International Financial Reporting Standards (IFRS), International Accounting Standards (IAS), AAOIFI and other specific standards, complicating the operations of Islamic banking. While full harmonisation might not be possible given the nature of the industry, mutual recognition of financial standards and products across jurisdictions would help limit this problem. It would also reduce transaction costs, help implement efficient regulatory oversight, enhance the process of compliance, and contribute to confidence and industry growth (Hasan and Dridi, 2010). Moreover, Ahmed (2009) identifies the issues and problems behind the crisis at three levels: regulatory level, organisational level and product level. "There is a real role for regulators on the national level to make regulations a fair playing field for Islamic banks" adds Asaria (2011).

In summary, Islamic banks, working within the business cycle of their respective countries, have suffered from the crisis, to the point where a few of the sector's banks have defaulted, but as an industry it now has a track record of resilience (which had not been tested before). Islamic banking is expected to emerge stronger from the crisis, provided some conditions are met: more innovation, enhanced transparency, more robust risk management architecture and culture, and above all, enhanced *Shari'ah* compliance. In theory, Islamic financial principles contribute to the stability of the financial system. Islamic modes of finance, particularly the profit-sharing principle, provide a loss absorption feature to financial institutions. However, the practice is very different from the theory. All of these deviations between theory and practice mean that the system is not functioning at its full potential and has adapted itself to limited functionality. Even if Islamic finance had been prevailing, in its current state, the crisis could have happened, but at a less severe level. Islamic finance has not yet provided a more principled mode of finance than the debunked Wall Street model because the embedded ethical foundations have not been explored yet (Asutay, 2009b).

Paradoxically, Islamic banks' reputation has generally benefited from the recent crisis. From a conceptual perspective, Islamic banks will probably be the big winners when the crisis ends. As a sub-set of ethical finance, Islamic banking is now considered not so much niche business standing at the margins, but rather as representative of a credible, viable and sustainable alternative business model for sound, ethical and socially responsible banking. Many now believe that mainstream finance has moved too far into excess leverage, meaningless innovation and value-destroying investments. The credit crunch has shaken confidence in the existing Western regulations and created the need for a better, more transparent system; this has opened the door for Islamic bankers to take up the opportunity. Indeed at the 5th World Islamic Economic Forum (WIFE) in Jakarta on 2 March 2009, Muslim leaders including Indonesian President Susilo Bambang Yudhoyono and Malaysian Prime Minister Abdullah Badawi called on the Muslim world to leverage the global financial crisis by turning "adversity into opportunity" (Parker, 2009).

According to the proceedings of the Securities Commission Malaysia (SC) and the Oxford Centre for Islamic Studies (OCIS) Roundtable and Forum (2010), after the recent financial crisis Islamic banks seem to be emerging stronger than conventional banks. According to Ken Eglinton, Director of Banking and Capital Markets at Ernest & Young, who was interviewed for this research, Ernest & Young did a comparison between the top conventional banks and the top Islamic banks. It showed that the aggregate net profits of the commercial banks dropped by USD 42 billion in 2008 from USD 116 billion in 2006. In contrast, the net profits of Islamic banks increased by 9% during the same period.

The following sub-hypotheses were developed to see if there is any significant difference in the level of perception across the different categories of respondents.

H_{7-1}: *There are no statistically significant differences among the respondents' perceptions about the credit crisis and Islamic banking according to region.*

At $\alpha = 0.05$, the null hypothesis is rejected and the alternative hypothesis is accepted, since seven out of nine statements had significant p-values. Therefore, it is concluded that there are statistically different opinions among the respondents coming from different regions.

In addition, in order to respond to this sub-hypothesis, after conducting factor analysis, further analysis was carried out using a one-way between-groups MANOVA test in order to investigate if there is any significant difference between the two component groups identified under factor analysis in relation to region as the control variable. This helped to locate the impact or significance of each control variable on the established distribution. The results signify that 32% of the variances in 'Resilience of IFIs' scores are explained by region.

H_{7-2}: *There are no statistically significant differences among the respondents' perceptions about the credit crisis and Islamic banking according to the nature of the financial institution.*

At $\alpha = 0.05$, the null hypothesis is accepted and the alternative hypothesis is rejected for all statements except Statement 3, which shows that, statistically, the nature of financial institution does not play a significant role in the difference in perceptions among respondents. This is consistent with the descriptive statistics, which show that most respondents share similar views regardless of the nature of financial institution.

Statement 3: 'Islamic finance could have solved the global crisis' produced differences among different categories of respondents. Mean rankings for Statement 3, as depicted by Table 8.36, show that fully fledged Islamic banks are far more aggressive in their belief that Islamic finance could have solved the global crisis than other categories (46.2), followed by Islamic subsidiaries (40.25), then by 'Others' and 'Conventional Banks'.

An attempt was also made to see the effect of 'Nature of financial institution' on the components identified in factor analysis through MANOVA. However, no significant results could be established.

H_{7-3}: *There are no statistically significant differences among the respondents' perceptions about the credit crisis and Islamic banking according to the nature of activities.*

As Table 8.37 depicts, at $\alpha = 0.05$ the K-W test results suggest that the null hypothesis is rejected and the alternative hypothesis is accepted. Therefore, it can be concluded that, statistically, there are significant differences in the level of perception according to the institution's 'Nature of Activities'.

H_{7-4}: *There are no statistically significant differences among the respondents' perceptions about the credit crisis and Islamic banking according to accounting standards.*

Similarly, for the accounting standards control variable, the null hypothesis is rejected in favour of the alternative hypothesis, since the p-value recorded in the testing is lower than the critical p-value limit as shown in Table 8.38. Therefore, it can be concluded that, statistically, there is a significant difference in the level of perception according to the accounting standards utilised by the institution.

H_{7-5}: *There are no statistically significant differences among the respondents' perceptions about the credit crisis and Islamic banking according to the respondent's position.*

At α = 0.05, the null hypothesis is accepted, suggesting that the alternative hypothesis is rejected since the p-value recorded in the testing is lower than the critical p-value limit. Thus, it can be concluded that, statistically, there are no significant differences according to respondent's position.

The findings from the above sub-hypotheses tests echo the findings from the descriptive statistics and from the qualitative interview analysis. However, the inferential statistical analysis provides a higher level of understanding and knowledge concerning the subject matter. Combining the results of the above five sub-hypotheses tests provides an aggregate trend that can be attributed to prevailing market conditions: retail fully fledged Islamic banks and Islamic subsidiaries, located mainly in the 'GCC' and 'Other', are more aggressive in their perceptions of the credit crisis and Islamic finance than other categories. These banks tend to use AAOIFI accounting standards or IAS and AAOIFI standards together. This trend could not be established by studying one control variable in isolation; the five control variables had to be examined together in order to see the bigger picture. This pattern is consistent with the findings of Table 7.16, which breaks down the descriptive statistics among Islamic bankers and non-Islamic bankers.

RISK MANAGEMENT AND REPORTING

This section aims to provide a discussion through further interpretation of the results on risk management and reporting issues facing IFIs by responding to the hypothesis set in advance.

Hypothesis 8: Not many Islamic banks use the more technically advanced risk measurement and reporting techniques.

Findings from quantitative analyses indicate that although IFIs are doing comparatively well in terms of their general risk management and reporting, they are still perceived to use less advanced risk management approaches. Frequency distribution in Table 7.16 shows that IFIs usually use the same risk management techniques as conventional banks for managing risks, in particular liquidity, credit and market risks. Nevertheless, the spread and frequency of utilising these techniques is lower among Islamic banks than among their conventional peers. The most widely used daily report among IFIs is the liquidity risk report, followed by the credit exposure report and the profit rate risk report. Commodity risk and equity mark-to-market reports are the least used by IFIs in this survey. Improving risk management and reporting practices represent a serious challenge to Islamic banking in order to lift itself to the next level. Interviewees also perceived IFIs to use less advanced risk management approaches. Risk management frameworks are not yet fully developed in IFIs. There is still lack of well-functioning system of controls and internal checks and balances. The findings support Hypothesis 8.

Some interviewees indicated that currently there are weaknesses and a serious lack of a robust risk culture among IFIs. However, the financial crisis has raised the profile of risk management within Islamic banks. In the current environment the painful cost of inadequate risk management is being demonstrated every day. Banks seeking to navigate the recession must put a premium on effective risk management. Also, due to limited resources, IFIs are often unable to afford high-cost management information systems or the technology to assess and monitor risk in a timely fashion. Efforts should be made to collaborate among IFIs to develop Islamic risk management systems that are customised to the industry needs. The changes required to institutionalise a strong risk culture are fundamental and far-reaching: risk must become 'everyone's business' throughout the organisation. Responsibility and accountability for risk should be intertwined among all stakeholders, from board members to business unit heads and their teams, who must be more actively committed to identifying and mitigating risks. There is a need to introduce a risk management culture among Islamic banks.

These findings contradict those by Shaikh and Jalbani (2009), whose paper optimistically concluded that the equity-based business of Islamic banks posing slightly more risk than conventional banks is well mitigated by Islamic banks through their effective and adequate distinct risk management procedures. The researcher does not agree with the research methodology and the findings of this study by Shaikh and Jalbani. Rosman and Abdul Rahman (2010) surveyed the risk management practices of 28 Islamic banks from 16 different countries. Their findings indicate that Islamic banks are doing comparatively well in terms of their general risk management and operational risk management. In terms of risk reporting, the study found that the majority of Islamic banks produced various types of risk reports and there is a significant improvement in their risk reporting over the last few years. The majority of Islamic banks they surveyed produced all the risk reports except for commodities and equities positions risk reports, and country risk reports. On the other hand, Ahmed and Khan (2007) argue that there is a need to introduce a better risk management culture in Islamic banks. Wilson (2002) also argues that IFIs can learn from conventional banks in the fields of technology and developing infrastructure, as much as conventional banks need to learn from IFIs about staff and client motivation and relationships.

The following sub-hypothesis was developed to see if there is any significant difference in the level of use of risk reporting across different regions.

H_{8-1}: *There are no statistically significant differences among respondents in the frequency of producing risk management reports according to region.*

The results from the K-W test reject the null hypothesis and accept the alternative hypothesis, since there is a significant difference among various regions in the frequency of producing risk reports (p-value < 0.05) except for commodity risk report (0.094), industry concentration risk report (0.129), credit exposure report (0.091) and large exposure report (0.071). Hence, for the rest of the reports there are significant differences in the perceptions of the participants. Thus, for most of the reports 'Region' is a significant factor. Repeating the K-W test with 'Region' as the control variable for various institutional samples provided an obvious trend: conventional banks, concentrated in Europe and the Americas, produce risk reports more frequently than Islamic banks. In addition, the results reflect the risk management culture difference between Islamic and conventional banks.

RISK MEASUREMENT

This section aims to provide a discussion through further interpretation of the results on risk measurement in IFIs by responding to the hypothesis set in advance.

Hypothesis 9: The use of risk measurement techniques is less advanced among Islamic banks than among their conventional peers.

In addition to risk management reports, financial institutions use various techniques to measure and analyse risks. Similar to Hypothesis 8, Hypothesis 9 is supported by both quantitative and qualitative analyses. Frequency distribution in Table 7.17 shows that the most common technique used by IFIs as indicated by respondents is maturity matching analysis (22 respondents), followed by reliance on external ratings provided by rating agencies (21 responses), internal-based rating and Gap analysis (19 responses each). Only 14 respondents indicated they use Value at Risk (VaR) models, while simulation techniques are used by just six IFIs in the sample. Interviewees also emphasised the fact that risk measurement techniques in Islamic banking are not as sophisticated as in the conventional banking world.

In line with this, Noraini et al. (2009) also found that more technically advanced risk measurement approaches are perceived not to be widely used by Islamic banks, except for the Internal-Based Rating System and Estimates of Worst Case. The study concluded that most IFIs did not use sophisticated risk measurement approaches as the IFIs are still new and do not have sufficient resources and systems to use the more technically advanced techniques. Supporting this argument is the study by Rosman and Abdul Rahman (2010), who concluded that IFIs are using less technically advanced risk measurement approaches.

Khan and Ahmed (2001), on the other hand, found that the overall risk management processes in IFIs to be satisfactory. They apprehended, however, that this may be because the banks that have relatively better risk management systems responded to the questionnaires. The results for risk management process showed that while Islamic banks have established a relatively good risk management environment, the measuring, mitigating and monitoring processes and internal controls need to be further upgraded. Khan and Ahmed's study also identified the problems that IFIs face in managing risks. These include lack of instruments (like short-term financial assets and derivatives) and money markets. At the regulatory level, the financial institutions apprehend that the legal system and regulatory framework is not supportive to them. Results from a survey of 17 Islamic institutions from 10 different countries revealed that while Islamic banks have established a relatively good risk management environment, the measuring, mitigating and monitoring processes and internal controls need to be further upgraded. The results indicated that the growth of the Islamic financial industry will, to a large extent, depend on how bankers, regulators and *Shari'ah* scholars understand the inherent risks arising in these institutions and create appropriate policies to cater to these needs.

Subsequently, the following sub-hypotheses were tested to identify whether there is any statistically significant difference in the frequency of producing risk measurement reports across various groups of respondents based on the selected control variables.

H_{9-1}: *There are no statistically significant differences among respondents in the use of risk measurement techniques according to region.*

H_{9-2}: *There are no statistically significant differences among respondents in the use of risk measurement techniques according to the respondent's position.*

H_{9-3}: *There are no statistically significant differences among respondents in the use of risk measurement techniques according to the nature of the financial institution.*

H_{9-4}: *There are no statistically significant differences among respondents in the use of risk measurement techniques according to the nature of activities.*

H_{9-5}: *There are no statistically significant differences among respondents in the use of risk measurement techniques according to accounting standards.*

As Table 8.56 depicts, at $\alpha = 0.05$ the five sub-hypotheses are declined. This means that statistically all the selected control variables play a role in the difference in utilising risk measurement tools. However, 'Region' and 'Nature of Financial Institution' are the control variables with the most significant results and hence these two variables are most essential to the difference in risk management techniques among banks. Mean rankings show that conventional banks in relation to their regional location, concentrated outside of the GCC and Middle East, use more advanced risk management techniques than Islamic banks. The region 'Americas' is the most advanced across all techniques, followed often by 'Other' or 'Europe'. The rest of the regional samples include mostly Islamic banks; their use of sophisticated risk measurements, however, is not as significant as in conventional banks in the Americas and Europe.

RISK MITIGATION

This section aims to provide a discussion through further interpretation of the results on risk mitigation issues facing IFIs by responding to the hypothesis set in advance.

Hypothesis 10: Islamic banks use a number of risk mitigation tools that are intended to be *Shari'ah*-compliant and that are less advanced than those utilised by conventional banks.

Both the descriptive statistics and the qualitative interview analysis clearly reflect that risk mitigation techniques in Islamic banking are less advanced than those in conventional banking. This supports Hypothesis 10.

Risk mitigation is currently one of the most contentious issues in Islamic banking. The unique nature of risks faced by Islamic banks, combined with the restrictions added by *Shari'ah*, makes risk mitigation for Islamic banks a difficult and complex process. There are risks that Islamic banks, like their conventional counterparts, can manage and control through appropriate risk policies and controls that do not conflict with the *Shari'ah* principles. However, there are other risks that banks cannot eliminate and that can be reduced only by transferring to or selling those risks in well-defined markets. These risks can generate unexpected losses that need capital insulation, and hedging can help to restrict the impact of unexpected loss. Traditionally in the conventional world risk-transfer techniques include the use of derivatives for hedging, selling or buying of financial claims, and changing borrowing terms. The challenge is, however, that most of the conventional hedging tools so far do not comply with the *Shari'ah* requirements. This causes IFIs to be faced with an additional array of risks particularly market and credit risks. As explained in Chapter 3, there have been substantial efforts in developing *Sharia'ah*-compliant hedging instruments; however, much of this progress remains localised with limited scope for cross-border application and further work is still needed.

Until recently, it had been the opinion of most *Shari'ah* scholars that hedging would fall into the category of speculation and uncertainty. In the last few years, however, the increasing sophistication in Islamic banking products has led some scholars to take the view that Islamic banks may be able to enter into hedging arrangements provided that the hedging tool is in itself structured in a *Shari'ah*-compliant manner. According to Khan (2010), "there is growing demand for hedging and *Shari'ah*-compliant derivatives, which would be used merely for hedging and not speculation". Khandelwal (2008) also asserts that there has been substantial development in finding ways to apply derivatives in Islamic finance to reduce certain risks such as currency and commodity risks. For example, some *Shari'ah*-compliant hedging instruments, such as profit rate swaps, have been introduced in Malaysia. However, much of this progress remains localised with limited scope for cross-border application and further work is still needed. The empirical study conducted by Rosman and Abdul Rahman (2010) found that IFIs are still lacking in the application of unique *Shari'ah*-compliant risk mitigation techniques, while Ahmed and Khan (2007) believe that the potential of futures, currency forwards, options and embedded options in risk management in Islamic finance is tremendous.

One of the interviewees, Chowdhury (2010), argues that derivatives are sophisticated instruments that can, if employed with care, enhance efficiency in IFIs through risk mitigation, thereby making them more competitive as well as appealing to customers. However, their application in Islamic finance is surrounded by religious dogma and is highly controversial for reasons of speculation and uncertainty, two practices banned under *Shari'ah*. There are varying scholarly opinions in the world of *fiqh* and, due to this judicial fragmentation, the final verdict on the legitimacy of derivatives varies between a total ban in some countries and actual implementation (although on a limited scale) in others (Chowdhury, 2010).

Another interviewee, Engel (2010), adds that the recent financial crisis, in the opinion of many, including *Shari'ah* scholars, is blamed on the 'speculative' use of complex derivative instruments. The economic meltdown was in fact due to a combination of several factors, primarily a lack of proper risk monitoring and quantification mechanisms. The bubble in the derivatives industry was attributed to a copycat phenomenon, whereby banks took on more risk than they could possibly cope with, exceeding their liabilities many times over and building inverted pyramid structures on their balance sheets. The consequential seizure in the market has forced financial institutions to drastically scale back their proprietary risk-taking and to revamp models, which adds to the reluctance of *Shari'ah* scholars to permit the use of derivatives. Thun (2010) agrees that despite their pivotal function, the use of derivatives in emerging countries in general, and in the Islamic banking sector in particular, has been limited, in part due to the absence of legal provisions, insufficient technical frameworks, underdeveloped capital markets, and/or inadequate accounting, regulatory and disclosure standards. Therefore, the use of derivatives in Islamic banking requires an understanding of the distinction between hedging and speculating.

As risk management and corporate governance in IFIs are already below par relative to the rest of industry, the use of securitisation and derivatives offers considerable scope for reducing IFIs' risk exposures and thus improving their overall risk profile (Smith, 2010).

Recently, highly skilled financial engineers in global conventional banks owning Islamic windows, more advanced Islamic banks, economists and a few *Shari'ah* scholars have combined efforts to develop Islamic derivative products. For this, jurists have increasingly been working on *khiar*, *arbun* and *wa'ad* concepts to turn them into contracts, as explained in Chapter 3. Although *wa'ad* is still criticised from a conceptual perspective, in practice this instrument has become a contractual promise, as it offers great flexibility, explains Thun (2010). For instance, it allows for an FX forward profile to be emulated. The writer makes a unilateral promise to buy or sell a particular amount of currency against another currency on a predetermined date and at a predetermined rate. If the promise is contractually agreed not to be binding, then the buyer chooses whether to enforce the *wa'ad* or not in exchange for a non-refundable fee, which ends up becoming equivalent to a put or call option (Thun, 2010).

Far from having a complete derivative supply, the trend in the Islamic financial industry is therefore to develop explicit Islamic derivative products. Through *Shari'ah*-compliant engineering, currency forwards, call options on *sukuk*, securities or commodities, profit rate swaps, cross-currency rate swaps, forward rate swaps and even total return swaps can be copied, at least conceptually, adds Lowe (2010), one of the interviewees for this research. On the other hand, as previously discussed, if IFIs continue to mimic conventional banking products, they will weaken the uniqueness of their value proposition and the powerful nature of their natural factors of differentiation.

Risk mitigation techniques are inherently complex by nature and require a well-thought-out regulatory framework for their management and application. For instance, in order to promote and legalise the use of derivatives, large Islamic banks in Malaysia are stepping forward in collaboration with the Malaysian Financial Market Association to establish standards in *Shari'ah*-compliant derivatives to enhance liquidity and improve balance sheet management (Moody's, 2011a). This is in addition to the progress made by supervisory bodies like IFSB, IIFM, AAOIFI and others.

It is interesting to investigate the findings further to determine whether there is any statistically significant difference in the use of mitigation techniques according to various control variables. Therefore, the following sub-hypotheses were formulated.

H_{10-1}: *There are no statistically significant differences among respondents in the use of risk mitigation techniques according to region.*

H_{10-2}: *There are no statistically significant differences among respondents in the use of risk mitigation techniques according to the respondent's position.*

H_{10-3}: *There are no statistically significant differences among respondents in the use of risk mitigation techniques according to the nature of the financial institution.*

H_{10-4}: *There are no statistically significant differences among respondents in the use of risk mitigation techniques according to the nature of activities.*

H_{10-5}: *There are no statistically significant differences among respondents in the use of risk mitigation techniques according to accounting standards.*

Table 8.59 shows that at $\alpha = 0.05$ the five sub-hypotheses are rejected in favour of the alternative hypothesis. This means that statistically all the selected control variables play a role in the difference in utilising risk mitigation techniques among financial institutions. However, 'Nature of Financial Institution' is the control variable with the most significant p-value (0.00). Mean ranking in Table 8.60 shows that with the exception of Islamic swaps and Islamic currency forwards, fully fledged Islamic banks fell behind Islamic subsidiaries in using all other risk mitigation techniques. The latter group tends to benefit from the already developed risk mitigation platforms at their conventional parents. However, of notice is that the difference in the value of mean ranking between the two groups is small, which reflects that IFIs are progressing in the use of risk mitigation, but that still the use of risk mitigation techniques in IFIs is not as developed as in conventional banking.

ISLAMIC BANKING IN PRACTICE

This section aims to provide a discussion through further interpretation of the results on practical issues in Islamic banking by responding to the hypothesis set in advance.

Hypothesis 11: Most IFIs abandoned conservative risk management *Shari'ah* principles in favour of copying conventional structures.

Descriptive statistics support Hypothesis 11 as most respondents believe that IFIs should stop simply mimicking conventional finance, as the trend seemed to be toward trying to duplicate what conventional banks did. Everyone assumed there was a single model of banking and they were copying the Wall Street model – a model that had more or less collapsed. Before the recent financial meltdown, the Islamic banking industry came under the criticism that it had not been able to match all the existing conventional products with Islamic equivalents. In hindsight, if IFIs continued on the same track as their conventional peers, they would have been prone to the same risks. Hence Islamic banks have been largely spared the subprime crisis.

Likewise, interviewees are of the view that IFIs will not achieve their objectives by simply mimicking conventional products. While the ideals of Islamic finance offer some compelling ideas, the reality is that much of Islamic finance today is focused on replicating the conventional system. This provides support for Hypothesis 11. Chowdhury (2010) argues that this reminds us that IFIs will not achieve their objectives by simply mimicking conventional products. If scholars had allowed simple mimicking without checks, IFIs would have been as exposed to subprime as the conventional banks are.

In theory, the Islamic financial system is definitely more resilient to economic shocks than the debunked Wall Street model, but unfortunately theory is a long way from fact in current financial practice. Practitioners of Islamic finance to date have been mimicking conventional products. This mimicking has resulted in a close correlation between the two systems. "People all over the world have been paying attention to Islamic finance, not necessarily because it would have solutions to all these problems; but because it is institutionalised and has embraced conservative principles" (Warde, 2009). Certainly, Islamic banks have partially ignored this conservatism by simply mimicking conventional banks, but still the fundamental principles of Islamic finance have saved Islamic banks from many of the conventional financial woes.

The crisis created a golden opportunity for Islamic finance to present itself to the world as a better, more sustainable financial system. Dr Mohammed Mahmoud Awan, a leading scholar and Dean at the Malaysia-based International Centre for Education in Islamic Finance (INCEIF), thinks that the recent global crisis has opened many windows of opportunity for Islamic finance as it has the capacity and capability to bring stability to the market (Awan, 2008). However, the defaults of *sukuk* in the Middle Eastern market, and the frauds that occurred in several IFIs, have downplayed this notion. According to the proceedings of the SC–OCIS Roundtable and Forum (2010), there were failures of credit risk assessment and over-concentration of risks in real estate assets; there was lack of transparency; there were family-owned businesses that were perceived to have government support (in some of the *sukuk*); in some areas, there was even inadequate regulation; and in a recent case there was also inappropriate use of a legal defence. The industry needs to work together to remove the negative perceptions that are seen to somewhat impact it. So, it is important to subscribe to the values of *Shari'ah*, to build robust risk management systems and IT systems, and to have greater transparency and greater practice of *Shari'ah* governance.

The following sub-hypotheses were formulated in order to identify whether there are any significant differences across various selected groups in relation to the respective control variables.

The results of the hypotheses testing can be seen in Tables 8.61 and 8.62.

H_{11-1}: *There are no statistically significant differences among respondents' perceptions about the current practices in Islamic banking according to the nature of the financial institution.*

The results suggest that the null hypothesis is rejected, which implies that 'Nature of Financial Institution' is a statistically significant determining factor. Mean rankings revealed that Islamic bankers are more critical of the current practices in the industry than their conventional peers. This could be explained by the fact that Islamic bankers are more educated about the underlying principles of Islamic finance and have a better understanding of current structures than conventional bankers.

H_{11-2}: *There are no statistically significant differences among respondents' perceptions about the current practices in Islamic banking according to region.*

The results suggest that the null hypothesis is rejected and the alternative hypothesis is accepted. There are significant 'regional' differences among respondents' views.

H_{11-3}: *There are no statistically significant differences among respondents' perceptions about the current practices in Islamic banking according to the respondent's position.*

For this sub-hypothesis, the test results were unable to reject the null hypothesis, meaning that the impact of respondent's position causes no significant difference.

THE FUTURE OF ISLAMIC BANKING

This section aims to provide a discussion through further interpretation of the results on the future of Islamic banking by responding to the hypothesis set in advance.

Hypothesis 12: Islamic banking has great potential to become a strong alternative financing system provided that it goes back to its roots.

Evidence from the questionnaire data analysis indicates that Hypothesis 12 is supported. Most respondents reckon that Islamic banking has benign potential provided that it goes back to its roots. Both Islamic and non-Islamic bankers (including Islamic subsidiaries, conventional banks and others) also consider improved risk management and mitigation practices among the top priorities IFIs should focus on in their development plans. The future of Islamic banking will highly depend on risk architecture and how the industry will develop instruments that enhance liquidity; improve ALM and risk management; and develop Islamically acceptable risk-hedging tools. This questionnaire identified the inadequacy of risk management practices by IFIs that may threaten their sustainability especially during financial crises. Adequate resources need to be devoted to risk identification and measurement, as well as risk management techniques, so as to be able to develop innovative risk mitigation and hedging instruments suitable to IFIs.

Interview findings similarly provide strong support to Hypothesis 12, as interviewees almost unanimously agree that there is now an opportunity for Islamic banking to thrive as it has the potential to contribute to a more stable economy. "We have all learnt a lot over the past few years about how to allow the Islamic finance market to mature. There's now an opportunity for Islamic finance to thrive", says Chowdhury (2010), one of the interviewees. Many interviewees, particularly consultants, researchers and *Shari'ah* scholars, revealed that in its current form Islamic banking has little to offer in terms of long-lasting solutions. The solution ultimately has to be a moral not a material one. Islamic banking needs to aim for a truly alternative vision based on the ethical and moral safeguards within authentic Islamic concepts, together with improving risk management and mitigation techniques, enhancing liquidity management and reducing concentrations.

The recommendations for the future of Islamic banking provided by both survey respondents and interviewees were numerous; however, this section focuses on the most important ones highlighted by most respondents and those that scored high mean rankings.

The continuing rapid growth of demand for Islamic financial services is clearly good news for Islamic banks. At the same time, it also presents some challenges, as the banks need to invest in upgrading their risk management capabilities in line with the more complex and larger projects into which they are entering. Given the unparalleled market conditions, the risk management process is going through fundamental and significant changes. Islamic banks need to ensure they are prepared for the constantly changing environment, and they also need to get involved in those changes to have their say.

While the Islamic banking model limited the chances of surviving the crisis unscathed, there is still strong growth potential for the industry. "After enduring the recent financial shocks, some IFIs are now conducting internal reviews and looking more deeply into ways to improve and diversify their business model", explains Engel (2010). For instance, efforts are being made to better organise professional off balance sheet asset-management activities targeting high-net-worth individuals and institutional investors who require *Shari'ah*-compliant placements, across a wider range of asset classes. Unicorn Investment Bank, for instance, typically focuses on general corporate finance, including advisory, mergers and acquisitions, debt and equity capital markets, structured finance and brokerage. First Energy Bank, an energy finance specialist, will likely follow the same path. The business evolution of Khaleeji Commercial Bank is also relevant as it is trying to consolidate its investment banking services with a more robust commercial banking platform. "Overall, I believe that the strategic move of some IFIs acquiring larger, more diversified and established Islamic banks offers the most promising potential" adds Lowe (2010).

Going forward, it is expected that lower volumes, shrinking margins and deteriorating asset quality will all weigh on IFIs' profitability and ultimately their capitalisation. However, the impact will be more manageable than for their conventional peers. Fortunately, Islamic banks have been very profitable in the past and have therefore accumulated large amounts of capital, making them capable of absorbing these sorts of shocks. As previously discussed, conventional banks have had a greater appetite for exotic asset classes than IFIs. In that sense, asset-quality deterioration at conventional banks may be more pronounced. In addition, conventional peer banks used to be less well capitalised and less liquid, and therefore will find it more difficult to book new business in the current market conditions. "To grow today, a bank must have accumulated excess liquidity and capital in the past: most Islamic banks have, some conventional peer banks haven't", says Damak (2010) during the interview for this research.

According to the latest findings (Moody's, 2011a; Fitch Ratings, 2011), IFIs are already tightening their belts and using their surplus liquidity deposits to meet their basic financing needs and to replace recent deposit withdrawals. Most IFIs have placed property-based projects on hold because of declining demand in the real estate sector and foreign direct investment. There have been financial stimulus packages supplied by governments to assist IFIs with their liquidity constraints. Those banks that are on the brink of liquidity crunch and that have been unsuccessful in attracting additional deposits will either have to issue more *sukuk* or merge with their financially stronger counterparts.

Islamic banks, organisations and regulators are working to address these challenges. The rapid developments are likely to continue. Financial institutions in countries such as Bahrain, the UAE and Malaysia have been gearing up for more

Shari'ah-compliant financial instruments and structured finance – on both the asset and liability sides. At the same time, the leading financial centres, such as London, New York and Singapore, are making significant progress in establishing the legal and prudential foundations to accommodate Islamic finance side by side with the conventional financial system. Many of the largest Western banks, through their Islamic windows, have become active and sometimes leading players in financial innovation, through new *Shari'ah*-compliant financial instruments that attempt to alleviate many of the current constraints such as a weak systemic liquidity infrastructure. More conventional banks are expected to offer Islamic products, enticed by enormous profit opportunities and also ample liquidity, especially across the Middle East.

New product innovation is also driven by domestic banks' interest in risk diversification. With a large number of new Islamic banks, especially across the Middle East and Asia, diversification of products enables banks to offer the right product mix to more sophisticated clients. A few banks are already active across different jurisdictions, and this trend is certainly going to continue in the near future, possibly with some consolidation (Moody's, 2011a).

Thun (2010) argues that just before the crisis Islamic banking was on the edge of a new era that would bring Islamic finance closer to the PLS, asset-backed and real-economy financing ideals, with innovations introduced by *Shari'ah*-compliant investment banking. Sometime before the crisis, institutions like GFH, Arcapita Bank, Unicorn Investment Bank and TID started moving away from pure banking intermediation and into more sophisticated investment/merchant banking lines of business, like private equity, asset-management, brokerage, infrastructure and structured real estate finance, as well as advisory, corporate and project finance – thereby laying the groundwork for innovation within Islamic banking. The industry was on the edge of moving beyond the focus on raising cheap *murabahah* or *wakala* deposits (so as to recycle them into safe, stable and expensive retail and corporate loans) and adopting a greater emphasis on risk-taking instead. However, the onset of the financial liquidity crisis prevented the dawning of this new era, adds Thun (2010).

On the regulatory front, whereas the growth history and forecasts are a source of optimism for the Islamic finance industry, the growing regulation in the wake of the recent credit crisis offers a newer set of challenges. There will be material, substantive change to the regulatory environment under which banks and other financial institutions operate (PWC, 2009). Regulators across the world are set to introduce a new era of tightened regulation for the financial sector in general. Central banks and financial regulatory authorities around the world are the subject of intense criticism for failure to predict and check the global financial crisis. Issues are being framed (particularly in the areas of risk management, liquidity and capital requirements), consultation papers drafted, and stakeholders' opinions sought for the introduction of a new and tougher regime of banking and financial regulations. "Islamic banks should get involved and should be proactive", asserts Lowe (2010). The IFSB has moved ahead with efforts aimed at fostering the soundness, risk management, capital standards and stability of the Islamic financial services industry through more standardised regulation.

According to Khan, S. (2009), as it stands Islamic banking regulations are framed from a conventional base and as long as the conventional yardstick is applied, certain structures, such as the *mudarabah* and *musharakah* products, will likely continue to be treated as higher risk. While some of these products may actually have a higher risk profile, concepts of risk-sharing could be ingrained further through the development of more profit- and risk-sharing *mudarabah* and *musharakah* products. This should be driven by both regulators and Islamic banking practitioners who, together, need to facilitate a transparent explanation of the risks to the customer as well as enable better risk allocation between Islamic banks and the customer. The current regulatory infrastructure for IFIs is more or less largely voluntary, such that very few penalties apply to institutions that do not follow the AAOIFI Standards, or any other set of *Shari'ah*-related rules or standards. Until a regulatory system is meaningfully enforced where penalties of non-compliance actually hurt, it is rather futile to expect IFIs to change any of their past patterns of behaviour. Such enforcement is largely dependent on both political will and vision (Khan, S., 2009).

Islamic banking will continue to grow at a faster rate than conventional banking because of the inevitable de-leveraging of the global system but also because the roots of Islamic banking are in the Gulf and South East Asia; these are regions with higher growth rates, expanding populations and abundance of natural resources especially energy (Eedle, 2009). Several IFIs are therefore in a position to gain market share at the expense of conventional peers, which have been weakened by toxic subprime assets. However, for Islamic banking to become a true global alternative to the existing Western system, there are a number of actions that must be considered, as explained earlier. The main issue is the development of products that are more in line with the spirit of *Shari'ah* and that do not just replicate conventional equivalents.

However, the political and social upheaval throughout the Middle East will undoubtedly have direct and indirect impacts on IFIs in general, and on those located in the Middle East in particular. The ability of local governments to support Islamic banking and to bail out financial institutions remains to be assessed after the scissors effect of rising oil prices and local geo-political unrest.

Subsequently, the following sub-hypotheses were formulated in order to identify whether there are any significant differences across various groups in the respective control variables. The results of the hypotheses testing are summarised in Table 8.63.

H_{12-1}: *There are no statistically significant differences among respondents' recommended growth strategies for Islamic banks according to region.*

The K-W test results suggest that the null hypothesis is accepted and the alternative hypothesis is rejected, which implies that, statistically, there are no significant differences in the respondents' views across various regions.

H_{12-2}: *There are no statistically significant differences among respondents' recommended growth strategies for Islamic banks according to respondent's position.*

Similarly, the results suggest that the null hypothesis is accepted indicating that, statistically, this control variable plays no significant role in impacting the respondents' opinions.

H_{12-3}: *There are no statistically significant differences among respondents' recommended growth strategies for Islamic banks according to the nature of the financial institution.*

For this hypothesis, the testing results decline the null hypothesis, meaning that, statistically, there are significant differences among respondents' views according to the nature of financial institution. 'Organic growth in home market' and 'Standardisation' had p-values of 0.036 and 0.015 respectively, which are lower than the critical p-value of 0.05. However, examining the mean rankings of these two strategies according to 'Nature of Financial Institution', as summarised in Table 8.64, did not identify a particular pattern.

H_{12-4}: *There are no statistically significant differences among respondents' recommended growth strategies for Islamic banks according to the nature of activities.*

The K-W results were unable to reject the null hypothesis, indicating that, statistically, the variable 'Nature of Activities' plays no significant role in impacting the respondents' opinions.

H_{12-5}: *There are no statistically significant differences among respondents' recommended growth strategies for Islamic banks according to accounting standards.*

The testing results accept the null hypothesis indicating that this control variable is, statistically, not significant in influencing the respondents' opinions.

Hypothesis 13: Perceptions of Islamic and conventional bankers differ significantly. Islamic bankers are more biased toward their business model, and vice versa.

Finally, Hypothesis 13 is a general hypothesis not linked to a specific part of the questionnaire. The researcher expected the perceptions of Islamic bankers to be biased in favour of their business model, and those of the conventional bankers to be biased against Islamic banking. Hypothesis 13 is declined as the findings from both the quantitative and qualitative analyses reflected a high degree of correlation between the responses of the two groups. However, differences generally existed between the responses of bankers and non-bankers. Non-bankers have a different risk perception than bankers; this is because bankers, whether Islamic or non-Islamic, have hands-on experience and better understanding of the Islamic banking model and its risk architecture than non-bankers, who tend to be more academic in their approach.

More specifically, the various K-W tests presented in Chapter 8 generally show that there is no significant difference in perception levels between respondents from stand-alone Islamic banks and Islamic subsidiaries. Initially it was expected that respondents from stand-alone Islamic banks would have a stronger perception compared to those from Islamic subsidiaries for two reasons: firstly, stand-alone Islamic banks have been in existence much longer than Islamic subsidiaries, and, secondly, the respondents from stand-alone Islamic banks have the advantage of dealing with only Islamic banking products and services whereas Islamic subsidiaries need to operate side by side with their respective conventional counterpart in sharing the same operating platforms and buildings. Nevertheless, the results have indicated otherwise. Some differences could be spotted between the perceptions of conventional banks and stand-alone Islamic banks, and more noticeably between the perceptions of bankers and non-bankers, represented by 'Others'. Examining the mean rankings for different questions confirmed that there is an observed pattern, which can be explained by market realities.

CONCLUSION AND SUMMARY

The current chapter is intended to combine, integrate and discuss the main results and findings from all three empirical chapters, combined with knowledge developed from the literature review, and to provide the basis for an overall conclusion.

To render the results in a more systematic manner, Table 10.1 attempts to bring together the results of the testing of all the main hypotheses.

TABLE 10.1 Summary of the hypotheses testing decisions

Hypothesis	Questionnaires Decision	Interviews Decision
The main risks facing Islamic banks are reputational risk, *Shari'ah*-non-compliance risk, asset–liability management risk, liquidity risk and concentration risk.	Accept H_0	Majority approve
Islamic bankers prefer mark-up based contracts and shy away from profit-sharing contracts.	Accept H_0	Majority approve
Profit-sharing contracts are perceived as more risky than mark-up based contracts in the Islamic finance industry.	Accept H_0	Majority approve
There is no substantial difference between risk management in Islamic banking and conventional banking.	Reject H_0	Majority disapprove
Capital requirements levels should be lower in IFIs than in conventional banks.	Reject H_0	Majority disapprove
Basel II was drafted with conventional banking very much in mind. IFIs should follow their own standards, e.g. IFSB principles on capital adequacy.	Reject H_0	Majority disapprove
Islamic banking is more resilient to economic shocks than conventional banking but not recession proof.	Accept H_0	Majority approve
Not many Islamic banks use the more technically advanced risk measurement and reporting techniques.	Accept H_0	Majority approve
The use of risk measurement techniques is less advanced among Islamic banks than among their conventional peers.	Accept H_0	Majority approve
Islamic banks use a number of risk mitigation tools that are intended to be *Shari'ah*-compliant and that are less advanced than those utilised by conventional banks.	Accept H_0	Majority approve
Most IFIs abandoned conservative risk management *Shari'ah* principles in favour of copying conventional structures.	Accept H_0	Majority approve
Islamic banking has great potential to become a strong alternative financing system provided that it goes back to its roots.	Accept H_0	Majority approve
Perceptions of Islamic and conventional bankers differ significantly. Islamic bankers are more biased toward their business model, and vice versa.	Reject H_0	Majority disapprove

As can be seen in Table 10.1, for the 13 hypotheses, nine null-hypotheses were accepted, while the alternative null-hypotheses were accepted for the remaining four hypotheses.

Based on the decisions of the hypotheses testing, the main findings and implications of this study will be presented in Chapter 11, together with recommendations for areas in which future research appears to be desirable. Chapter 11 also discusses future directions of risk management in Islamic banking.

Conclusion and Research Recommendations

This final chapter summarises the main results and presents the conclusion of the book. It brings together all the findings and ideas discussed throughout this research. To reiterate, this study was undertaken with the objective of evaluating the contemporary risk management practices in Islamic banking. In meeting this broad objective, the views and opinions of the sampled Islamic banking professionals were obtained through a survey questionnaire and in-depth interviews. The results of the survey and interviews were analysed and compared with the theoretical framework and the related literature.

This chapter briefly recapitulates the salient conclusions derived from the findings of this research. In addition, it also presents the main policy and practical recommendations for enhancing risk culture and architecture in Islamic banking. Finally, the research limitations and suggested future research topics will be presented.

SUMMARY OF THE RESEARCH

As laid down in the introductory chapter (Chapter 1), the main aim of this research was to investigate the perceptions and views of professional bankers and financiers one way or another involved in the provision of Islamic financial and banking products across different regions about risk management in Islamic banking, with the objective of mapping out the various issues related to risk through the perceptions of the participants, namely bankers, financiers and scholars.

The study, hence, consists of two major sections, namely background and empirical work. The first five chapters are the foundational chapters for the next six chapters, the latter forming the empirical part of the book. The first chapter introduces the main research questions and states the research aim and objectives as well as explaining the rationale for choosing the research topic. It also briefly discusses the research hypotheses, and the selected research methodology.

Chapter 2 covers, among other topics, the systemic importance of the Islamic banking industry and its potential growth. An overview of the various concepts of risk and the industry standards of risk management techniques are discussed in Chapter 3 along with the unique risks facing Islamic financial institutions (IFIs). This chapter represents the main chapter in the literature review part of the book. Chapter 4 looks at capital adequacy rules for IFIs in a financial world dominated by the Basel standards, while Chapter 5 analyses the roots of the recent financial crisis and its implications for Islamic banking by making reference to the risk management nature of the financial crisis.

The second part of the book is concerned with the empirical work and the findings thereof. Chapter 6, which is the first chapter of this part, deals with the research design and methodology. In essence, it is about the primary data collection and administration process, covering the different phases of that process and dwelling on its important aspects, such as the research questions, the hypotheses and the relevance of the selected research methodologies to the research questions. For the empirical part of the book, the primary data assembled through the use of the research methods of questionnaire surveys and in-depth interviews are utilised. Chapter 7 is the beginning of the statistical analysis of the survey questionnaire employing mainly descriptive analyses and Chi-Square tests as well as the more basic frequency and percentage tables. Chapter 8 is the main primary quantitative data analysis, presenting the findings from inferential statistical tests such as Kruskall-Wallis (K-W), factor analysis, MANOVA multivariate analysis of variance, and Chi-Square tests. This chapter, to a certain extent, answers the main research hypotheses and their sub-hypotheses, as the information presented in various sections of the chapter suggests. Chapter 9 is the qualitative analysis part in which the responses given by the interviewees are analysed through a coding analysis. However, more detailed discussion of the findings of both quantitative and qualitative analyses is handled in Chapter 10, which combines, integrates and discusses the main findings from all the empirical chapters, within the context of the existing literature, to provide a basis for an overall conclusion.

Finally, this chapter contains the conclusion and recommendations as already explained and also summarises the research findings and the proposed policy implications as well as the research limitations and further research topics.

REFLECTING ON THE RESEARCH FINDINGS

As discussed in Chapter 1, risk management in Islamic banking is one of the main issues as well as one of the most controversial. Although progress has been made across the industry over the past few years, Islamic banks still face significant challenges in relation to measuring and managing risks. At the same time, risk management is getting more attention all over the world due to the recent financial crisis. Within this context, it goes without saying that, for most IFIs, risk management presents specific challenges. The study therefore investigates the controversial question of whether Islamic banks are more or less risky than conventional banks. This research answers the identified research questions, not only based on conceptual research but more importantly using empirical evidence from the market place by focusing on the practical side of risk management in Islamic banking.

It should be noted that this research is practical doctoral research that fills the research gap regarding risk management in Islamic banking by investigating the perceptions and attitudes of different categories of Islamic banking practitioners toward the unique characteristics of risk management in Islamic banking from empirical evidence. This book fills the gap by taking the research one step further, by integrating theoretical concepts with the practical reality in a socially constructed manner through the opinions and perceptions of the participants.

Based on the findings in this study, it is obvious that Islamic banks face a number of challenges in terms of risk management. The entanglement of credit, market and operational risk in each contract type used by Islamic banks in their daily operations, as well as displaced commercial risks attached to the incentive to serve Profit-Sharing Investment Accounts (PSIA) holders with returns at least comparable to similar conventional deposits, are two of the main constraints IFIs need to cope with. In addition, as indicated by the findings in this research, in the absence of a wide pool of *Shari'ah*-compliant, sufficiently liquid investment vehicles (especially in fixed income), Islamic banks find it difficult to manage their balance sheet from an asset–liability management (ALM) perspective, especially liquidity and margin-rate risk.

As the findings depict, Islamic banks' funding mix tends to be imbalanced, with the dominance of deposits, PSIAs and equity making their funding profile predominantly short-term at a time when the maturity of their asset classes is widening. To mitigate nascent maturity mismatches, some IFIs have started issuing medium-term *sukuk* to lengthen the maturity profile of their funding, but *sukuk* still account for only a small portion of IFIs' total liabilities, as discussed in Chapter 3. Subordinated *sukuk* and hybrid instruments have not yet been used; these are more expensive funding sources and incentives to issue them are limited given the abundance of capital among most IFIs. The lack of liquidity and viable alternatives, combined with the competitive disadvantage, hamper IFIs and may even create a liquidity crisis. To overcome the shortcomings of the Islamic money market, many investment banks are currently designing complex new products, compliant with *Shari'ah* requirements. It remains to be seen whether these new solutions will obtain widespread *Shari'ah*-compliant status in the Islamic finance community, and generate enough demand for a functional Islamic money market to develop. To help manage their liquidity, IFIs will have to develop creative funding strategies and improve their internal capabilities to understand and forecast their liquidity needs.

In addition, the research findings identify that IFIs face other challenges from weak corporate governance practice to lack of standardisation in accounting and *Shari'ah* standards, and high concentration risk. In fact, IFIs show heavy concentrations across the board, by name, sector, geography and business lines.

Political risk was ignored by both questionnaire respondents and interviewees in this study; only a few respondents recognised it as a major risk affecting Islamic banking. However, the lesson from the recent political unrest and revolutions in the Middle East is that political risk matters. There is no doubt that the political and social upheaval throughout the Middle East will have direct and indirect impacts on IFIs in general and on those located in the Middle East in particular, as discussed in Chapter 10. The outflow of funds and exit of foreign investors, and the inability of governments to support Islamic banking and to bail out financial institutions remain to be assessed after the scissors effect of rising oil prices and local geo-political unrest.

The literature review reveals that Basel II was drafted with conventional banking largely in mind. Previous researchers also argue that Basel II is primarily for conventional banks and has limited applicability for Islamic banking. However, empirical evidence from this study found that market practitioners believe that with some adaptations Basel II could be applied to Islamic banks and that the Islamic Financial Services Board (IFSB) could play an important role in this context.

In brief, empirical findings from this study identified weaknesses and vulnerabilities among IFIs in the areas of risk management and governance. Risk management, monitoring, reporting and mitigation need to be upgraded across the whole Islamic banking industry. This study shows that the difficulties IFIs are currently faced with mostly stem from risk management failures, characterised by a very low degree of diversification, preference for illiquidity, an absence of financial flexibility and imbalanced funding strategies. This highlights the significance of risk management for the growth of the whole Islamic banking industry.

The findings in this research also show that although IFIs have shown resilience, they are not immune from economic shocks. Empirical evidence shows that Islamic banking is expected to emerge stronger from the crisis, provided some conditions are met, such as 'further innovation', 'enhanced transparency', 'more robust risk management architecture and culture', and, above all, 'enhanced *Shari'ah* compliance'. Broadly speaking, Islamic banking had a relatively 'mild crisis' in that it suffered less damage as a result of the global economic and financial turmoil of the past few years than conventional banking. Of course there were exceptions: Dubai, with its high debt and open economy, was the main regional casualty as well as the private sectors of some other Gulf countries which were bruised as their credit bubbles popped. In general IFIs have maintained relative stability despite the global financial crisis thanks to ample liquidity, safe debts and high profit margins. However, this situation will not continue for long. Islamic banks need to reform at different levels – product, operational and institutional – to be successful. They have been lucky so far, and perhaps they will learn from the difficulties faced by conventional banks.

Many studies including this one indicate that IFIs tend to shy away from equity- and partnership-based instruments for several reasons, such as the inherent riskiness and additional costs of monitoring such investments, low appetite for risk and lack of innovation. This unwillingness to take on risk reflects the lack of transparency in the Islamic banking system, which dampens confidence and trust among investors and market participants. The result is that depositors and investors become more risk averse, and so banks become even more risk averse, thus creating a vicious circle which results in severe financial and economic crises.

The original concept of Islamic financing is undoubtedly in favour of equity participation rather than creation of debt, because it is only equity that brings an equitable and balanced distribution of wealth in society. However, the practice is very different from the theory. Practitioners of Islamic finance have to date been mimicking conventional products. This mimicking has resulted in a close correlation between the two systems. These deviations between theory and practice mean that the system is not functioning at its full potential and has adapted itself to a limited functionality. In fact, due to these deviations, the Islamic banking system is exposed to additional risks that it is not supposed to be exposed to, as explained in the previous chapters. This dichotomy between the ideals of Islamic banking morals and the realities, combined with the lack of advanced risk management and mitigation techniques, render Islamic banking more risky than the debunked conventional banking model, instead of its being a safe haven. There is a growing realisation that the long term sustainable growth of Islamic banking will depend largely on the development of proper risk management architecture. Islamic banking could be a safe haven only when its broader principles on a macro-level are entirely followed by all participants. In other words, when short-term risks and longer-term stability are put together and optimised, the outlook for the Islamic banking industry looks less risky than its critics claim.

Islamic banking, so far, as it is being practised does not appear to be a genuine reflection of the aspirational expectations of *fiqh* requirements for Islamic finance. Islamic banking benefits, when measured by conventional yardsticks, do not amount to much. Therefore, IFIs and all participants in Islamic finance should strictly follow the rules of *Shari'ah*, regardless of whether the benefits of such rules are apparent or measurable. There is a particular logic and morality to *Shari'ah* principles, which Islamic banking practitioners will see only if they stop trying to shoe-horn them into conventional product structures.

Market discipline and transparency rules have been the pride of Western financial systems for decades. The irony is that those rules have consistently failed whenever tested by severe financial stress. On the other hand, more resilient and ethical rules have long existed in the roots of *Shari'ah* finance. Some of the previously criticised inherent constraints – imposed on Islamic banks by *Shari'ah* – have proved to be conservative risk management tools that enabled most Islamic banks to navigate the crisis. Limited availability of hedging tools, prohibition of derivatives and speculation, the linking of risks to assets, and extra liquidity and capital buffers are all examples of built-in principles that were criticised by opponents of Islamic banking as burdens on profitability prior to the crisis. with hindsight they proved to be important strengths that ensured stability, as explained in Chapter 5. From a risk management perspective, *Shari'ah* can provide a moral compass that guides risk takers as to which risks are acceptable and which are not.

RESEARCH IMPLICATIONS AND RECOMMENDATIONS

As mentioned in Chapter 1, the present study is motivated by an observation that there is a gap between the theoretical aspects of risk management in Islamic banking and the practical behaviour of industry practitioners – a fact that has been articulated by many in different formats. Therefore, the results of this study provide positive implications and recommendations for various stakeholders in pursuing the desired ultimate objectives of the Islamic banking system.

It should, furthermore, be stated that this research also contributes to the body of existing academic research in terms of opening up new areas of study; in addition, it renders valuable input to industry practitioners for improving current regulations and practice related to risk management, reporting, mitigation, capital adequacy and development strategies. The findings in this study may also prove very useful for promoting financial stability from a risk management perspective.

Policy Implications

The results of the research have policy implications for regulators, policy makers, *Shari'ah* scholars, practitioners, academics and institutional stakeholders. In addition, regulatory bodies such as central banks, AAOIFI, IIFM and IFSB may find the results useful for assessing the level of adequacy of risk reporting in Islamic banks and for developing new guidelines for risk management and mitigation. The findings provide evidence which enables the IFSB and regulators to pursue policies that promote transparency with regard to risk management. The general findings in this study, if combined with other studies, will have important implications for setting up risk reporting standards for IFIs.

In addition, the risk perception trends identified by this study across different countries, regions and other categories of respondents could be beneficial for marketing and growth strategies of IFIs across borders. These findings could therefore be of great help to regulators in understanding regional and institutional differences among banks.

The findings also show that IFIs are still far behind current best practice in terms of risk management methods, transparency and disclosure. This has implications particularly for PSIA holders because, as mentioned earlier, they require adequate risk information to monitor their investment due to profit-sharing arrangements.

Furthermore, the perceptions of Islamic banking professionals about Basel II and III and their applicability to Islamic banking could be useful to regional regulators and the Basel Committee on Banking Supervision (BCBS) in drafting and applying the Basel III standards, which tend to neglect the unique characteristics of Islamic banks. The failings of Basel II and the market expectations resulting from Basel III, with their wide implications for banks, regulators, consultants and researchers, were thoroughly discussed in this study.

IFIs also need to make use of the findings in this research to improve their risk management architectures and culture. By doing so, they would be able to improve their funding structures and reduce their inherent risks, and hence improve their ratings, market transactions pricing and overall profitability. Moreover, from a risk management perspective, the recommended growth strategies discussed in this book could be of great help to Islamic banks particularly during the current turbulent economic climate.

It is impossible to lay out one best strategy but various strategies can be adopted to achieve profitable growth and to enhance IFIs' competitiveness. It is worthwhile to point out that, while asset growth is important, appropriate systems and infrastructures to address risk issues need to be in place to support sustainable growth. Therefore, strategic focus needs to be timed, with risk management being implemented first, followed by growth. Finally, regulators, shareholders, management, employees and customers all have roles in shaping an organisation's strategies.

The main recommendations of the book can be summarised as follows:

(i) Consolidation:

There are far too many IFIs to serve this growing market, but none has the size necessary to compete on a global stage.

(ii) Diversification:

Consolidation will also help IFIs to gain from the benefits of diversification across different geographical territories, sectors and industries.

Currently, Islamic banks are not fully exploiting the benefits that come from both geographic and product diversification. On the asset side, diversification can reduce credit, concentration and market risks, in addition to reducing the variance in the returns that accrue to claimholders. Diversification on the liabilities side can reduce displaced commercial risk and withdrawal risk and help to improve liquidity gaps and ALM.

In addition, most IFIs need to diversify their activities from what is mostly a real estate and standard lending play, to offer a comprehensive service suite, including advanced treasury services, innovative asset management, balance sheet management and securitisation services.

(iii) **Liquidity enhancement:**

There is a growing realisation that the sustainable growth of Islamic banking will depend largely on the development of well-functioning secondary markets and the introduction of liquidity-enhancing products.

(iv) **Investing in risk management infrastructure:**

The establishment of risk assessment and measurement systems often becomes an expensive proposition as it requires sophisticated models, software packages and technologies, and skilled human resources who can understand the nature of the risks and prepare models accordingly. Given the small size of IFIs, establishing such frameworks at the organisation level may not be possible. IFIs and supervisory authorities should work together to find a reasonable solution to the problem. Risk management solutions should not be considered an extra cost but should be viewed as an investment for building a knowledge base of superior quality entrepreneurs and projects. As Islamic banks should have learnt from the crisis, the painful cost of inadequate risk management is being demonstrated every day.

(v) **Innovation:**

Islamic banking might find it difficult to innovate because it exists in a deeply-rooted conventional system. However, if the industry is not innovating authentic products according to genuine *Shari'ah* principles, it might end up with the same failures as conventional banking. At this point in time, there is no real value proposition offered by Islamic banks. While Islamic banking is considered to have a bright future, mimicking conventional banking is mostly considered as causing Islamic banking to lose opportunities to serve markets and communities around the world.

(vi) **Back to roots: a *Shari'ah*-based approach versus *Shari'ah* compliance**

Shari'ah compliance is inherently and systemically significant to Islamic banking. However, developments indicate that *Shari'ah*-based solutions should be better placed in appreciating opportunities available. It is clear through experience that any divergence from *Shari'ah* principles exposes the IFI to a wide range of additional risks at different levels, as discussed in this book, thus rendering Islamic banking more risky than the conventional model. Considering that the current practice is very much shaped by *Shari'ah* compliance, which has exposed Islamic banks and finance to further risks, it is hoped that with a *Shari'ah*-based approach such unnecessary risk areas can be avoided.

Theoretical and Empirical Implications: Significance of the Research

This research is expected to fill a gap in critically investigating risk management in Islamic banking from a practical perspective, and to be a tool to boost the growth and profitability of IFIs. It is, however, not merely another addition to the available literature. It can be distinguished for a number of reasons.

First, it focuses on the risk management aspect of Islamic banking, a highly under-researched area in Islamic finance. Second, it places theory and practice in one place by taking analysis one step further – from literature review to the market place. As explained earlier, there is a clear difference between theory and reality in Islamic banking, which subsequently leads to a distinction between conceptual formulations and actual practices of risk management in Islamic banking. The differences are discussed and analysed in depth in this study. To relate this research to the realities of banking and finance practice, the focus of this research is on the everyday aspects of risk management in Islamic banking. Moreover, this study relies on a larger sample size within the wider Islamic banking population than previous studies. The sample is well diversified as regards both the questionnaire and the interviews in order to enable the researcher to obtain better findings by conducting significance tests on the differences among the various groups. Finally, while a few have researched the practical implementation of risk management in Islamic banking, this research is the first to do so after the recent credit crisis. Thus, this research extracts empirical evidence from the perceptions of Islamic banking professionals and from the crisis to support its own views and conclusions.

LIMITATIONS OF THE STUDY

There is no perfect study and the current one is no exception. There are four limitations that need to be acknowledged and addressed regarding the present study. First, the cultural aspects of risk management and the impact of regional cultural differences on the risk perception of respondents should have been examined. Each region has its unique culture which shapes its risk management and therefore Islamic finance-related studies should also endogenise the cultural and cultural–religious dimension of risk in considering risk and risk management practices. It is hoped that such a study could be conducted in the future, perhaps as part of post-doctoral studies.

Similarly, the impact of macroeconomic factors and business cycles on risk management perceptions across different regions could be investigated. Considering that each country has a particular dynamism related to the macroeconomy with specific implications for various risk dimensions in that particular framework, such economic realities should be considered as part of risk management-related studies.

The third limitation has to do with the approach to the research process. In addition to the qualitative research methodology as utilised by this study, a quantitative methodology based on secondary data with econometric analysis to measure the 'actual' findings in literature against the 'perceptions' as studied in this research could also have been considered.

It should be noted that time and cost limitations were restricting factors for the research to address the first three limitations.

Finally, the fourth limitation has to do with literature review. The literature on risk management in Islamic banking was limited and thus the references were seriously affected.

SUGGESTIONS FOR FUTURE RESEARCH

There is still wide scope for improvement and for further research. Having mentioned the limitations that were identified and discovered throughout the research process, the researcher would like to make suggestions and recommendations which may be taken from this study for future research either to enhance the study or as a basis for new studies in the field.

Future studies may expand the scope of the sample, enlarging the coverage to include respondents from more countries and with more diversified backgrounds.

This study accessed the perception of Islamic banking professionals about risks facing IFIs. It is also possible to seek the views and perceptions of Islamic banking customers themselves. Expanding the sample in this way would allow the researcher to use probability sampling techniques. The outcome of random sampling may enable the researcher to obtain data that is more representative and would assist the researcher to make more conclusive analyses by using robust statistical tools such as parametric statistical tools.

Although the research sample for this study comprised a wide range of respondents with different backgrounds within the industry, no regulators were included. It would be useful to obtain regulators' views on the issues discussed in this book.

Including regulators in the research sample would give additional insights in relation to their role in improving risk management standards in Islamic banking.

Furthermore, the cultural aspects of risk management and the impact of regional cultural differences on the risk perception of respondents should have been examined as each region has its unique culture which shapes its risk management.

This study focused on risk management within Islamic banking. Further research may attempt to extend the study to analyse risk management among *takaful* companies, Islamic brokers and Islamic funds, and to expand the research into risk management across the whole wider Islamic finance industry.

Finally, as mentioned in the previous section, secondary data-based econometric analysis should also be considered in future research to observe and model the articulation and practice of risk and risk management in IBF. As mentioned, this could help to measure the 'actual' against the 'perceptions' as studied in the research.

Questionnaire

PHD. RESEARCH ON 'RISK MANAGEMENT IN ISLAMIC BANKING'

Part One: General and Background Information

1. Name and location of the Financial Institution: _____

_____

_____

2. Respondent's Name: _____

3. Position: _____

Department: _____

4. Nature of the financial institution:

(Please mark the appropriate boxes)

☐ Fully Fledged Islamic bank   ☐ Conventional bank with Islamic activities/windows

☐ Conventional bank   ☐ Other, please specify

5. Nature of activities: (Please mark the appropriate boxes)

☐ Commercial banking   ☐ Investment banking

☐ Retail banking   ☐ Other, please specify

6. The accounting standards used by your institution comply with:

☐ International standards   ☐ AAOIFI standards

☐ Other, please specify   ☐ Don't know

Part Two: Risk Perception

Section I Risk Issues in Islamic Banks

7. Severity of risks facing Islamic banks
Below are the main inherent risks in Islamic banking. Could you please identify the seriousness/importance of the following risks to Islamic banks according to your own personal view?
Please mark the appropriate box.

Risk	Very Important	Important	Neutral	Unimportant	Very Unimportant
Credit Risk	☐	☐	☐	☐	☐
Market Risk*	☐	☐	☐	☐	☐
Operational Risk	☐	☐	☐	☐	☐
Equity Investment Risk	☐	☐	☐	☐	☐
Liquidity Risk	☐	☐	☐	☐	☐
Asset–Liability Management Risk	☐	☐	☐	☐	☐
Displaced Commercial Risk **	☐	☐	☐	☐	☐
Shari'ah non-compliance Risk	☐	☐	☐	☐	☐
Concentration Risk	☐	☐	☐	☐	☐
Reputation Risk	☐	☐	☐	☐	☐
Fiduciary Risk	☐	☐	☐	☐	☐
Corporate Governance Risk	☐	☐	☐	☐	☐
Legal Risk	☐	☐	☐	☐	☐

*Market Risk encompasses Rate-of-Return Risk, Currency Risk, Commodity Risk, Benchmark Risk, and Mark-up; but excludes Equity Investment Risk.
**Displaced Commercial Risk is the risk of liquidity suddenly drying up as a consequence of massive withdrawals should the Islamic bank assets yield returns for Investment Account Holders lower than expected, or worse, negative rates of profits.

8. Please list below any other risks (if applicable) that you think might affect Islamic banks, in order of their seriousness/ importance.
a.
b.
c.
d.
e.

9. For institutions that use Islamic finance contracts, please rank the following Islamic finance contracts according to the intensity of use by your institution (the most used first):

Please use a scale from 1 to 7, with 1 as the most used and 7 as the least used.

Contract	Rank
Murabahah	
Mudarabah	
Wakala	
Ijarah	
Musharakah	
Istisna'a	
Salam	

10. According to your own view, please rank the following Islamic finance contracts according to their risk seriousness, starting by the most risky:

Please use a scale from 1 to 7, with 1 as the most risky and 7 as the least risky.

Contract	Rank
Murabahah	
Mudarabah	
Wakala	
Ijarah	
Musharaka	
Istisna'a	
Salam	

11. Please mark the appropriate boxes below

	Strongly Agree	Agree	Neutral	Disagree	Strongly Disagree
1. Risks for Islamic banks should be managed using same techniques used in conventional banking.	☐	☐	☐	☐	☐

(continued)

	Strongly Agree	Agree	Neutral	Disagree	Strongly Disagree
2. Islamic banking is more risky by nature than conventional banking.	☐	☐	☐	☐	☐
3. Risk management for Islamic banks is more challenging than it is for conventional banks.	☐	☐	☐	☐	☐
4. There is naturally inherent conservatism in the principles of Islamic finance.	☐	☐	☐	☐	☐
5. In an Islamic bank, a low rate of return on deposits will lead to withdrawal of funds.	☐	☐	☐	☐	☐
6. Depositors would hold the bank responsible for a lower rate of return on their deposits.	☐	☐	☐	☐	☐
7. Variation among *Shari'ah* scholars' opinions represents a major risk to Islamic banking.	☐	☐	☐	☐	☐
8. Non-*Shari'ah* compliance could severely damage the reputation of an Islamic bank.	☐	☐	☐	☐	☐
9. AAOIFI and IFSB standards should be made mandatory for Islamic banks.	☐	☐	☐	☐	☐
10. Corporate governance is generally weak in Islamic banks.	☐	☐	☐	☐	☐
11. Islamic banking in its current state is a safer option than conventional banking	☐	☐	☐	☐	☐

Section II Capital Adequacy

12. Which of the following does your bank use in calculating its minimum capital requirements?

    ☐ Basel II standards   ☐ IFSB standards
    ☐ Other, please specify   ☐ Don't know

13. If your institution is using Basel II standards, please indicate the methodology used to calculate the minimum capital requirement for:

Credit Risk

☐ Standardised approach   ☐ Foundation IRB
☐ Advanced IRB

Market Risk

☐ Standardised approach   ☐ Internal models approach

Operational Risk

☐ Basic indicator approach   ☐ Advanced measurement approach

14. Do you think that the capital requirements for Islamic banks as compared to conventional banks should be:

☐ Higher   ☐ Same   ☐ Lower   ☐ Don't know

15. Please mark the appropriate boxes in the table below

	Strongly Agree	Agree	Neutral	Disagree	Strongly Disagree
1. Basel II standards should be equally applied to Islamic banks without modification.	☐	☐	☐	☐	☐
2. IFSB standard on Capital Adequacy should be used by Islamic banks rather than Basel II.	☐	☐	☐	☐	☐
3. Basel II standards should be reviewed after failing to prevent the current crisis.	☐	☐	☐	☐	☐
4. The proposed Basel III rules would be easily applicable to Islamic banks	☐	☐	☐	☐	☐
5. Stricter capital, leverage and liquidity rules, as proposed under Basel III, are likely to prevent another financial crisis.	☐	☐	☐	☐	☐

Section III Credit Crisis and Islamic Finance

16. Please mark the appropriate boxes in the table below

	Strongly Agree	Agree	Neutral	Disagree	Strongly Disagree
1. Islamic banks are more resilient to economic shocks than their conventional peers.	□	□	□	□	□
2. The recent crisis would not have happened under a true Islamic banking system.	□	□	□	□	□
3. Islamic finance could have solved the global crisis.	□	□	□	□	□
4. Risk management must be embedded institutionally.	□	□	□	□	□
5. Banks in general used to rely heavily on rating agencies.	□	□	□	□	□
6. Islamic banks rely less on rating agencies than conventional banks.	□	□	□	□	□
7. Islamic finance industry should develop its own rating agencies.	□	□	□	□	□
8. Islamic banks will emerge stronger from the current crisis.	□	□	□	□	□
9. Consolidation is needed among smaller Islamic banks.	□	□	□	□	□

Part Three: Risk Management and Mitigation

17. How often does your bank produce the following reports, if applicable?

	Daily	Weekly	Monthly	Yearly	Never	Don't know
Capital requirement report	□	□	□	□	□	□
Operational risk report	□	□	□	□	□	□
Profit rate risk report	□	□	□	□	□	□
Foreign exchange risk report	□	□	□	□	□	□
Liquidity risk report	□	□	□	□	□	□
Commodity risk report	□	□	□	□	□	□
Country risk report	□	□	□	□	□	□
Equity mark-to-market report	□	□	□	□	□	□

	Daily	Weekly	Monthly	Yearly	Never	Don't know
Classified accounts report	☐	☐	☐	☐	☐	☐
Industry concentration risk report	☐	☐	☐	☐	☐	☐
Credit exposure report	☐	☐	☐	☐	☐	☐
Large exposure report	☐	☐	☐	☐	☐	☐
Other risk reports (please specify)	☐	☐	☐	☐	☐	☐
	☐	☐	☐	☐	☐	☐
	☐	☐	☐	☐	☐	☐

18. Which of the following techniques does your organisation use to analyse risks, if applicable?

Internal based ratings	☐
Credit ratings by rating agencies	☐
Gap analysis	☐
Duration analysis	☐
Maturity matching analysis	☐
Earnings at risk	☐
Value at risk	☐
Stress testing	☐
Simulation techniques	☐
Risk Adjusted Rate of Return on Capital (RAROC)	☐
Other (Please Specify)	

19. Risk mitigation techniques in Islamic banking compared to conventional banking are:

☐ More advanced   ☐ Less advanced
☐ Similar   ☐ Don't know

20. For institutions that use Islamic finance contracts, which of the following techniques does your organisation use to mitigate risks?

On balance sheet netting	☐
Islamic options	☐
Islamic swaps	☐
Guarantees	☐
Islamic currency forwards	☐
Parallel contracts	☐
Collateral arrangements	☐
Other (please specify)	

Part Four: Islamic Banking in Practice

21. Please mark the appropriate boxes in the table below

	Strongly Agree	Agree	Neutral	Disagree	Strongly Disagree
1. Islamic banks have been mimicking conventional models.	□	□	□	□	□
2. Islamic finance provides an ethical banking alternative.	□	□	□	□	□
3. There is difference between the current practice and principles of Islamic banking.	□	□	□	□	□
4. Islamic banks need to reform to be successful.	□	□	□	□	□

Part Five: The Next Chapter in Islamic Banking

22. According to your own view, which of the following strategies should Islamic banks focus on in order to thrive? Please rank the following strategies according to their importance, starting by the most important.

Please use a scale from 1 to 8, with 1 as the most important and 8 as the least important.

Strategy	Rank
Improved risk management	
Enhanced morality – back to roots	
Mergers and acquisitions	
Organic growth in home market	
Better risk mitigation	
Innovation	
Diversification – reduce concentration	
Standardisation	
Other (please specify)	

Thank you for your cooperation.

List of Acronyms

AAOIFI	Accounting and Auditing Organisation for Islamic Financial Institutions
ALM	Asset Liability Management
AMA	Advanced Measurement Approach
BCBS	Basel Committee on Banking Supervision
BIA	Basic Indicator Approach
BIS	Bank for International Settlements
CAR	Capital Adequacy Ratio
CDOs	Collateralised Debt Obligations
CDS	Credit Default Swaps
CEO	Chief Executive Officer
CIBAFI	(General) Council for Islamic Banks and Financial Institutions
DB	Deutsche Bank
DCR	Displaced Commercial Risk
DIB	Dubai Islamic Bank
EAD	Exposure at Default
FSA	Financial Services Authority
FX	Foreign Exchange
GCC	Gulf Co-operation Council
IAH	Investment Account Holder
IAS	International Accounting Standards
IBB	Islamic Bank of Britain Plc.
IBF	Islamic Banking and Finance
ICCS	Islamic Cross Currency Swap
ICMA	International Capital Market Association
IDB	Islamic Development Bank
IFIs	Islamic Financial Institutions
IFRS	International Financial Reporting Standards
IFS	Islamic Financial Services
IFSB	Islamic Financial Services Board
IIFM	International Islamic Financial Markets
IILM	International Islamic Liquidity Management Corporation

IIMM	Islamic Interbank Money Market
IINCEIF	International Centre for Education in Islamic Finance
IIRA	Islamic International Rating Agency
IMA	Internal Model Approach
IMF	International Monetary Fund
IPRS	Islamic Profit Rate Swap
IRB	Internal Rating Based Approach
IRR	Internal Rate of Return
IRTI	Islamic Research and Training Institute
ISDA	International Swaps and Derivatives Association
LGD	Loss Given Default
LMC	Liquidity Management Centre
LME	London Metal Exchange
NPL	Non-Performing Loan
OIC	Organisation of Islamic Cooperation
OTC	Over The Counter
PCA	Principal Component Analysis
PD	Probability of Default
PER	Profit Equalisation Reserve
PLS	Profit and Loss Sharing
PPFs	Principal Protected Funds
PSIA	Profit-Sharing Investment Accounts
RAROC	Risk-adjusted Return on Capital
REITs	Real Estate Investment Trusts
ROE	Return On Equity
RWAs	Risk Weighted Assets
SA	Standardised Approach
SIVs	Special Investment Vehicles
VaR	Value at Risk

Epilogue

This research set out to explore and analyse the perceptions and attitudes of Islamic banking professionals toward contemporary risk management issues within Islamic banking. The efforts and dedication put into this research especially during the data collection and analysis period yielded highly significant and meaningful results, which is a critical success factor. As the foundational and empirical chapters indicate, this study is considered as having fulfilled its research aims and objectives. It is hoped and expected that at least some if not all of this research will be applied by the stakeholders of Islamic banking.

A number of ideas have been discussed and analysed in this research which can be considered to constitute an agenda for further research and deliberations by researchers, practitioners, regulators and *Shari'ah* scholars. As is acknowledged by many, the Islamic banking industry is at a crossroads. The right direction can provide the required impetus for sustained growth in the long run. The only alternative is through efficient and effective risk management practices and systems within the authentic worldview of Islamic moral economy. Integrated Islamic risk management and the building of a risk-sensitive culture are needed now and for the future. Investment in better risk management systems and tools should be viewed as a strategic development rather than a situational necessity. Risk management for Islamic banking is not a destination or a project; it is rather a journey and a process – an ongoing process.

Bibliography

AAOIFI – Accounting and Auditing Organization for Islamic Financial Institutions (1999). "Statement on the purpose and calculation of the Capital Adequacy Ratio for Islamic Banks". Bahrain, March 1999.

Abbas Mirakhor, A. and Krichene, N. (2009). *Recent crisis: lessons for Islamic finance.* [Online] Available from: http://www.newhorizon-islamicbanking.com/index.

AbdelKarim, R. A. and Archer, P. S. (2005). *Islamic Finance: Innovation and Growth.* London: Euromoney Books.

Abdullah, D. (2007). "Transparency and market discipline: Basel Pillar 3", in Simon Archer and Rifaat A. Karim (eds.), *Islamic Finance: The Regulatory Challenge.* Singapore: John Wiley and Sons (Asia), pp. 366–377.

Abdul-Ghani, B. (2009). Conference Proceedings. *Understanding Sukuk – Issues, Structuring, Innovation.* London Sukuk Summit. London, 2–3 July 2009.

Abu Dawood. *Sahih Sunan Abu Dawud, Al Beyooh wa Al Egazat.* Part 3, Chapter 27, Hadith no. 3383, p. 677. [Eng. Trans 2/445 no. 1694].

Ahmed, H. (2009). Presentation. *Global financial crisis: Lessons for Islamic finance.* Durham University.

Ahmed, H. and Khan, T. (2007). "Risk management in Islamic banking", in M. Khabir Hassan and Mervyn K. Lewis (eds.), *Handbook of Islamic Banking.* Cheltenham: Edward Elgar, pp. 144–160.

Ainley, M. (2007). Summit Proceedings. *Regulating Islamic Finance in the UK Market,* Islamic Finance Summit, London, 30–31 January 2007.

Akkizidis, I. and Khandelwal, S. K. (2007). *Financial Risk Management for Islamic Banking and Finance.* London: Palgrave Macmillan.

Al-Omar, F. and Abdel-Haq, M. (1996). *Islamic Banking: Theory, Practice and Challenges.* Karachi, Pakistan: Oxford University Press.

Alsayed, A. (2008). "Risk management issues in Islamic banks", in Lori Hunt (eds.), *Islamic Finance Review 2007/08.* London: Euromoney Yearbooks.

Alvi, I. A. (2009a). *Liquidity Management in Islamic Finance.* Research Report Dow Jones Islamic Market Indexes, April 2009.

Alvi, I. A. (2009b). "Standardisation of documentation in Islamic finance: IIFM Master Agreements for Treasury Placement (MATP)", in Lisa Paul (ed.), *Islamic Finance Review 2009/10.* London: Euromoney Yearbooks.

Archer, S. and Karim, R. A. (2007). "Specific corporate governance issues in Islamic banks", in Simon Archer and Rifaat A. Karim (eds.), *Islamic Finance: The Regulatory Challenge.* Singapore: John Wiley and Sons (Asia), pp. 310–341.

Archer, S. and Haron, A. (2007). "Operational risk exposures of Islamic banks", in Simon Archer and Rifaat A. Karim (eds.), *Islamic Finance: The Regulatory Challenge*. Singapore: John Wiley and Sons (Asia), pp. 120–134.

Asaria, I (2011). Seminar Proceedings, *Eye on Islamic Finance*. Bloomberg, London, 18 March 2011.

Askari, H., Iqbal, Z. and Mirakhor, A. (2009). *New Issues in Islamic Finance and Economics: Progress and Challenges*. Singapore: John Wiley and Sons (Asia).

Asutay, M. (2007). "A political economy approach to Islamic economics: systemic understanding for an alternative economic system". *Kyoto Bulletin of Islamic Area Studies. IIUM Journal of Economics and Management*, Vol. 1, No. 2, pp. 3–18.

Asutay, M. (2009a). Seminar Proceedings, *Comparative Development of the Islamic Economic Model in the Context of Current Market Conditions: The Political Economy of Islamic Moral Economy*, London, 30 January 2009.

Asutay, M. (2009b). Seminar Proceedings, *Considering the Dichotomy between the Ideals and Realities of Islamic Finance*. Institute of Islamic Banking and Insurance (IIBI), London, 15 October 2009.

Asutay, M. (2011). *Research Workshop Handout No. 4 – Research Strategy and Design*. Durham: SGIA.

Asutay, M. and Zaman, N. (2009). "Divergence between aspirations and realities of Islamic economics: a political economy approach to bridging the divide". *IIUM Journal of Economics and Management*, Vol. 17. No. 1, pp. 73–96.

Awan, D. M. M. (2008). "Islamic finance can solve global crisis". *Arab News*, 24 April 2008.

Ayub, M. (2007). *Understanding Islamic Finance*. Chichester: John Wiley and Sons Ltd.

Babbie, E. (2010). *The Practice of Social Research*. 12th edition. Wadsworth, USA: Library of Congress.

Bartram, B. (2009). "Derivatives are not weapons of mass destruction". *Evening Standard*. 2 November 2009, p. 40.

BIS – Bank for International Settlements (2009). *79th Annual Report*, June 2009.

BCBS – Basel Committee on Banking Supervision (2006). "International convergence of capital measurement and capital standards", June 2006.

BCBS (2008). "Liquidity risk: management and supervisory challenges", February 2008.

BCBS (2009a). "Proposed enhancements to the Basel II framework", January 2009.

BCBS (2009b). "Strengthening the resilience of the banking sector – consultative document", December 2009.

Bell, J. (2005). *Doing Your Research Project: A Guide For First-Time Researchers In Education*. 4th edition. Berkshire: Open University Press.

Bessis, J. (1999). *Risk Management in Banking*. Chichester: John Wiley and Sons Ltd.

Blaikie, N. (2007). *Approaches to Social Enquiry: Advancing Knowledge*. 2nd edition. Cambridge: Polity Press.

BLME – Bank of London and the Middle East (2009). *Liquidity Risk Management under Financial Services Authority's Liquidity Policy 2009 for Islamic Financial Institutions in the United Kingdom*. February 2009.

British Bankers' Association (2009). Seminar Proceedings, *Update on Capital Requirements Directive*, London, 13 March 2009.

Brown, K., Hassan, K. and Skully, M. (2007). "Operational efficiency and performance of Islamic banks", in M. Khabir Hassan and Mervyn K. Lewis (eds.), *Handbook of Islamic Banking*. Cheltenham: Edward Elgar, pp. 96–115.

Bryman, A. (2008). *Social Research Methods*. 2nd edition. Oxford University Press.

Buffet, W. (2002). *Berkshire Hathaway Annual Report*.

Chapra, M. U. (2007). "Challenges facing Islamic financial industry", in M. Khabir Hassan and Mervyn K. Lewis (eds.), *Handbook of Islamic Banking*. Cheltenham: Edward Elgar, pp. 325–360.

Charmaz, K. (1983). "The grounded theory method: an explication and interpretation", in Robert M. Emerson (eds.), *Contemporary Field Research: A Collection of Readings*. Boston: Little, Brown and Company, pp. 109–128.

Cohen, M. P. (2005). "Sample size considerations for multilevel surveys". *Internat. Statist. Rev.* Vol. 73, No. 3, pp. 279–287.

Creswell, J. (1994). *Research Design: Qualitative, Quantitative, and Mixed Methods Approaches*. 2nd edition. London: Sage Publications.

Creswell, J. and Plano Clark, V. L. (2007). *Designing and Conducting Mixed Methods Research*. Thousand Oaks: Sage Publishing.

Dar Al Istithmar (2006). *Sukuk: An Introduction to the Underlying Principles and Structure*, June 2006.

Dar, H. and Presley, J. (2000). "Lack of profit loss sharing in Islamic banking: management and control imbalances". *International Journal of Islamic Financial Services*, Vol. 2, No. 2, July–Sept. 2000, pp. 3–18.

Das, S. (2006). *Risk Management*. 3rd edition. Singapore, John Wiley and Sons (Asia).

Davies, P. J. (2009). "Tawarruq loans split scholars". *Financial Times*, Tuesday, 8 December 2009.

Davis, E. (2009a). *The city uncovered: part 2 – tricks with risk*. BBC Two. [Online] Available from: http://www.bbc.co.uk/iplayer.

Davis, E. (2009b). *The city uncovered: part 3 – risk management*. BBC Two. [Online] Available from: http://www.bbc.co.uk/iplayer.

Denton Wilde Sapte (2009). Seminar Proceedings, *Islamic Finance*, 5 June 2009.

De Vaus, D. (2002). *Surveys in Social Research*. 5th edition, London: UCL Press.

Dey, D. and Holder, D. (2008). "Securitisation in the United Arab Emirates and Saudi Arabia – two promising markets", in Lori Hunt (eds.), *Islamic Finance Review 2007/08*. London: Euromoney Yearbooks.

Dillman, D. (2000). *Mail and Internet Surveys: The Tailored Design Method*. 2nd edition. New York: John Wiley and Sons.

Eedle, S. (2009). "A global bank's view of the evolution of Islamic finance", in Lisa Paul (eds.), *Islamic Finance Review 2009/10*. London: Euromoney Yearbooks.

EIIB – European Islamic Investment Bank Plc (2010a). *Product Programme: Dual Currency Murabaha*, February 2010.

EIIB (2010b). *Credit Risk Policy*, May 2010.

EIIB (2010c). *Implementation of Capital Requirements Directive*, June 2010.

EIIB (2010d). *Market Risk Policy*, November 2010.

Economist Intelligence Unit (2009). *Managing Risk In Perilous Times: Practical Steps To Accelerate Recovery*. April 2009.

Farook, S. (2008). "Capital adequacy ratios". *Islamic Banking & Finance*, Vol. 6, Issue 2, No. 17, pp. 18–20.

Fitch Ratings (2011). *GCC/ Middle East Outlook*. January 2011.

Foster, J. (2009). "How Sharia-compliant is Islamic banking?" BBC News, 11 December 2009. [Online] Available from: http://news.bbc.co.uk.

Freeland, C. and Friedman, S. (2007). "Risk and the need for capital", in Simon Archer and Rifaat A. Karim (eds.), *Islamic Finance: The Regulatory Challenge*. Singapore: John Wiley and Sons (Asia), pp. 215–222.

FRSGlobal (2009). *Risk Management in Islamic Banking*. Webinar, Monday, 7 December 2009.

FRSGlobal (2010). *Islamic Banks and Stress Testing*, 26 January 2010.

Funds@Work (2009). *Shariah Scholars in the GCC – A Network Analytic Perspective*. 10 October 2009.

Grais, W. and Kulathunga, A. (2007). "Capital structure and risk in Islamic financial services", in Simon Archer and Rifaat A. Karim (eds.), *Islamic Finance: The Regulatory Challenge*. Singapore: John Wiley and Sons (Asia), pp. 69–93.

Greuning, H. V. and Iqbal, Z. (2008). *Risk Analysis for Islamic Banks*. Washington D.C.: The World Bank.

Hasan, M. and Dridi, J. (2010). *The Effects of the Global Crisis on Islamic and Conventional Banks: A Comparative Study*. IMF Working Paper WP 10/201, International Monetary Fund, November 2010.

Hebel, A. (2002). Presentation. "Parametric versus nonparametric statistics – when to use them and which is more powerful?" Department of Natural Sciences, University of Maryland Eastern Shore, 5 April 2002.

Haron, A. and Hin Hock, L. (2007). "Inherent risk: credit and market risks", in Simon Archer and Rifaat A. Karim (eds.), *Islamic Finance: The Regulatory Challenge*. Singapore: John Wiley and Sons (Asia), pp. 94–119.

Heiko, H. and Cihak, M. (January 2008). *Islamic Banks and Financial Stability: An Empirical Analysis*. Research Report WP/08/16. International Monetary Fund.

HMCS – Her Majesty's Courts Service.

Howell, D. C. (1997). *Statistical Methods for Psychology*. 4th edition, Belmont, CA: Duxbury.

IFSB – Islamic Financial Service Board (2005a), "Guiding Principles of Risk Management for Institutions (other than Insurance Institutions) Offering Only Islamic Financial Services". Kuala Lumpur, Malaysia, December 2005.

IFSB (2005b). "Capital Adequacy Standard for Institutions (other than Insurance Institutions) Offering Only Islamic Financial Services". Kuala Lumpur, Malaysia, December 2005.

IFSB (2006). "Guiding Principles on Corporate Governance for Institutions Offering Only Islamic Financial Services". Kuala Lumpur, Malaysia, December 2006.

IFSB (2007). "Islamic Financial Services Industry Development: Ten-Year Framework and Strategies". Kuala Lumpur, Malaysia, May 2007.

IFSB (2008a). "Technical Note on Issues in Strengthening Liquidity Management of Institutions Offering Islamic Financial Services: The Development of Islamic Money Market". Kuala Lumpur, Malaysia, March 2008.

IFSB (2008b). "Guidance Note in Connection with the Capital Adequacy Standard: Recognition of Ratings by External Credit Assessment Institutions (ECAIs) on *Shari'ah*-Compliant Financial Instruments". Kuala Lumpur, Malaysia, March 2008.

IFSB (2009). "The IFSB membership reflects the growing interest among the Islamic financial services industry's stakeholders in the work of the IFSB". [Online] Available from: http://www.ifsb.org.

IFSB (2011). "The IFSB announces the establishment of an International Islamic Liquidity Management Corporation". [Online] Available from: http://www.ifsb.org/preess_full .php?id=149&submit=more.

IFSB (2018) *Islamic Financial Service Industry Stability Report 2018*. Kuala Lumpur: IFSB.

IIFM – International Islamic Financial Market. "International Islamic Financial Market (IIFM) holds its 20th Board of Directors Meeting". [Online] Available from: http:// www.iifm.net.

Iqbal, M. and Llewellyn, D. T. (2002) *Islamic Banking and Finance: New Perspectives on Profit-Sharing and Risk*. Cheltenham: Edward Elgar.

Iqbal, M. and Molyneux, P. (2005). *Thirty Years of Islamic Banking: History, Performance and Prospects*. Palgrave Macmillan.

Iqbal, Z. and Mirakhor, A. (2007). *An Introduction to Islamic Finance: Theory and Practice*. Singapore: John Wiley and Sons (Asia).

Ishaq, E. (2009). "Crisis a blessing in disguise". *Arab News*, 13 April 2009. [Online] Available from: http://www.securities.com.

"Islamic commodity platforms: Standing out from the crowd". *Islamic Finance News*, 8 May 2013.

Jorion, P. and Khoury, S. J. (1996). *Financial Risk Management: Domestic and International Dimensions*. Cambridge, Massachusetts: Blackwell.

Khalaf, R. (2009). "Islamic finance must resolve inner tensions". *Financial Times*, Monday, 30 March 2009.

Kamali, M. H. (2005). "Financial engineering and Islamic contracts", in M. Iqbal and T. Khan (eds.), *Fiqhi Issues in Commodity Futures*. London: Palgrave Macmillan.

Khan, B. A. and Prodhan, B. (1992). *Islamic Banking: A Survey*. Templeton College, The Oxford Centre for Management Studies, March 1992.

Khan, S. (2009). "Why tawarruq needs to go". *Islamic Finance News*, September 2009, pp. 14–22.

Khan, T. (2004). "Risk management in Islamic banking: a conceptual framework". Distance Learning Lecture. 2 November 2004.

Khan, T. and Ahmed, H. (2001). *Risk Management: An Analysis of Issues in Islamic Financial Industry*. Occasional Paper 5, Islamic Development Bank.

Khan, T. and Muljawan, D. (2006). Seminar Proceedings, *Islamic Financial Architecture: Risk Management and Financial Stability*.

Khandelwal, A. (2008). *Risk Management in Islamic Finance*. 11 March 2008. [Online] Available from: http://www.gtnews.com/article/7199.cfm.

KPMG (2006) *Making the Transition from Niche to Mainstream Islamic Banking and Finance: A Snapshot of the Industry and Its Challenges Today*.

KPMG (2007) *Basel Briefing*. July 2007.

KPMG (2009) *Basel II and Pillar III*. January 2009.

KPMG (2010) *Basel 3 Pressure is building...* December 2010.

Lee, J. (2008). "Complexities of risk outweigh Basel II". *Islamic Banking & Finance*, August–September 2008, pp. 28–29.

Lewis, M. K. and Algaoud, L. M. (2001). *Islamic Banking*. Cheltenham: Edward Elgar.

Mahlknecht, M. (2009). *Islamic Capital Markets and Risk Management: Global Market Trends and Issues.* London: Risk Books, a division of Incisive Financial Publishing Ltd.

Markowitz, H. (1959). *Portfolio Selection: Efficient Diversification of Investment.* New York: John Wiley and Sons.

McKenzie, H. (2007). "Four pillars of support". *The Banker*, September 2007, pp. 10–13.

McKinsey & Company (2009). *The Financial Crisis and the Way Forward.* The World Islamic Banking Competitiveness Report 2009/10. December 2009.

McKinsey & Company (2010). *In Search of New Opportunities.* The World Islamic Banking Competitiveness Report 2010/11. November 2010.

Miller, N. D. Conference Proceedings, *Risk Management Considerations in Sukuk Issuance & Securitisation.* London Sukuk Summit. London, 25 June 2008.

Mirakhor, A. and Krichene, N. (2009). *Recent Crisis: Lessons for Islamic Finance.* Research Report.

Mirakhor, A. and Zaidi, I. (2007). "Profit-and-loss sharing contracts in Islamic finance", in M. Khabir Hassan and Mervyn K. Lewis (eds.), *Handbook of Islamic Banking.* Cheltenham: Edward Elgar, pp. 49–63.

Moody's (2008a). *The Benefits of Ratings for Islamic Financial Institutions and What They Address.* February 2008.

Moody's (2008b). *Islamic Banks in the GCC: A Comparative Analysis.* March 2008.

Moody's (2009a). *Frequently Asked Questions: Islamic Finance, Oil Prices and the Global Crisis.* February 2009.

Moody's (2009b). *Calibrating Bank Ratings in the Context of the Global Financial Crisis.* February 2009.

Moody's (2009c). *The Liquidity/Leverage Trade-Off for Islamic Banks – and Its Impact on Their Ratings.* August 2009.

Moody's (2009d). *Global Sukuk Issuance Surges as Effects of Credit Crisis Recede: Overview and Trend Analysis.* November 2009.

Moody's (2010a). *Global Macro-Risk Scenarios 2010–2011.* January 2010.

Moody's (2010b). *Shari'ah Risk: Understanding Recent Compliance Issues in Islamic Finance.* May 2010.

Moody's (2010c). *Focus On The Middle East.* February 2010.

Moody's (2011a). Conference Proceedings. *Islamic Banking Update.* Moody's Middle East Sovereign Outlook Seminar. London, 24 March 2011.

Moody's (2011b). *Banks' Standalone Credit Strength Unlikely to Return to Pre-Crisis Levels, Even under Basel 3.* May 2011.

Moktar, H., Abdullah, N. and Al-Habshi, S. (2006). "Efficiency of Islamic banking in Malaysia: a stochastic frontier approach". *Journal of Economic Cooperation*, Vol. 27, No. 2, pp. 37–70.

Moore, E. J. (2009). *The International Handbook of Islamic Banking and Finance.* Kent: Global Professional Publishing.

Miller, N. D. Conference Proceedings, *Risk Management considerations in Sukuk Issuance & Securitisation*. ICG London Sukuk Summit. London, 25 June 2008.

Newby, A. (2009). "Islamic finance suffers from first big crisis". *Bloomberg*, 2 December 2009.

Nagaoka, S. (2007). "Beyond the theoretical dichotomy in Islamic finance: analytical reflections on *murābaḥah* contracts and Islamic debt securities". *Kyoto Bulletin of Islamic Area Studies*, Vol. 1, No. 2, pp. 72–91.

Nienhaus, V. (2007). "Governance of Islamic banks", in M. Khabir Hassan and Mervyn K. Lewis (eds.), *Handbook of Islamic Banking*. Cheltenham: Edward Elgar, pp. 144–160.

Noraini, M. A., Archer, S., and Abdel Karim, A. R. (2009). "Risks in Islamic banks: evidence from empirical research". *Journal of Banking Regulation*, Vol. 10, No. 2, March 2009, pp. 153–163.

Oakley, D. (2009). "The future of Islamic finance". *Financial Times*, Tuesday, 8 December 2009.

Oana, B. (2009). "Economist: Need for unified regulation of Islamic finance". *New Straits Times (Malaysia)*, 30 September 2009.

Obaidullah, M. (2007). "Securitization in Islam", in M. Khabir Hassan and Mervyn K. Lewis (eds.), *Handbook of Islamic Banking*. Cheltenham: Edward Elgar, pp. 191–199.

Obama, B. (2009). Speech on the economic crisis, 9 January 2009.

Oliver Wyman (2009). *The Next Chapter in Islamic Finance: Higher Rewards but Higher Risks*. February 2009.

Oppenheim, A. N. (2001). *Questionnaire Design and Attitude Measurement*. London: Printer Publishers.

Pallant, J. (2007). *SPSS Survival Manual*. Maidenhead: Open University Press.

Parker, M. (2009). "Islamic finance pushes for role in G20 agenda". *Arab News*, 30 March 2009.

Proceedings of the Securities Commission Malaysia (SC) and the Oxford Centre for Islamic Studies (OCIS) Roundtable and Forum. Kuala Lumpur, 15–16 March 2010.

PwC – PricewaterhouseCoopers (2008). *Risk appetite – How hungry are you?* Research Report.

PwC (2009). *The day after tomorrow*. Research Report, February 2009.

Robson, C. (2011). *Real World Research; A Resource For Social Scientists And Practitioner-Researchers*. Oxford: Blackwell.

Rosman, R. and Abdul Rahman, A. R. (2010) Conference Proceedings. *Risk Management Practices of Islamic Banks: International Evidence*. Durham Islamic Finance Conference, 14–15 July 2010.

Sadr, K. and Iqbal, Z. (2002). "Islamic banking and finance: new perspectives on profit-sharing and risk", in M. Iqbal and D. T. Llewellyn (eds.), *Choice Between Debt and Equity Contracts And Asymmetrical Information: Some Empirical Evidence*. Cheltenham: Edward Elgar.

Safieddine, A. (2009). "Islamic financial institutions and corporate governance: new insights for agency theory". *Corporate Governance: An International Review*, Vol. 17, No. (2), pp. 142–158.

Samad, A. (2004). "Performance of interest-free Islamic banks vis-a-vis interest-based conventional banks of Bahrain". *IIUM Journal of Economics and Management*, Vol. 12, No. 2, pp. 2–15.

Santomero, Anthony M. (1997). "Commercial bank risk management: an analysis of the process". *Journal of Financial Services Research*, 12, 83–115.

Saunders, M., Lewis, P. and Thornhill, A. (2007). *Research Methods for Business Students*. 4th edition. London: Prentice Hall.

Schroeck, G. (2002). *Risk Management and Value Creation in Financial Institutions*. New Jersey: John Wiley and Sons.

Selvam, J. (2008). "Call for more intellectual capital". *Islamic Banking & Finance*, Spring 2008, pp. 12–14.

Shaikh, S. A. and Jalbani, A. A. (2009). "Risk management in Islamic and conventional banks: a differential analysis". *Journal of Independent Studies and Research*, Vol. 7, No. 2, July 2009, pp. 67–79.

Siddiqi, M. N. (1983). *Issues in Islamic Banking: Selected Papers*. Leicester: Islamic Foundation.

Standard & Poor's (2009). *The Sukuk Market Has Continued To Progress in 2009 Despite Some Roadblocks*. September 2009.

Standard & Poor's (2010a). *The Sukuk Market Is Likely To Show Steady Growth in 2010*. January 2010.

Standard & Poor's (2010b). *GCC Outlook*. December 2010.

Standard & Poor's (2011). *Global Standards Needed to give Breadth and Depth to Growing Sukuk Market*. March 2011.

Stiglitz, J. E. (2008). "The fruit of hypocrisy". *Guardian*, 16 September 2008. [Online] Available from: http://www.guardian.co.uk/commentisfree/2008/sep/16/economics.wallstreet.

Stremme, A. (2005). Course Material, *Corporate Finance*. Warwick FTMBA 2004/2005.

Sundararajan, V. (2007). "Risk characteristics of Islamic products: implications for risk measurement and supervision", in Simon Archer and Rifaat A. Karim (eds.), *Islamic Finance: The Regulatory Challenge*. Singapore: John Wiley and Sons (Asia), pp. 40–68.

Sundararajan, V. and Errico, L. (2002). *Islamic Financial Institutions and Products in the Global Financial System: Key Issues in Risk Management and Challenges Ahead*. IMF Working Paper WP 02/192, International Monetary Fund, November 2002.

Tabachnick, G. and Fidell, L. (2006). *Using Multivariate Statistics*. 5th edition. US: Allyn & Bacon.

Taylor, M. (2010). "The devil is in the detail". *Bahrain Banker*, Winter 2010, p. 32.

Thomas, R. (2009). Conference Proceedings. *Understanding Sukuk – Issues, Structuring, Innovation*. London Sukuk Summit. London, 2–3 July 2009.

Townsend, M. (2009). "Saudi scandals lift veil on Gulf finance". *International Investor*, Wednesday, 28 October 2009.

Turen, S. (1995.) "Performance and risk analysis of Islamic banks: the case of Bahrain Islamic bank". *Journal of King Abdulaziz University: Islamic Economics*, Vol. 7, 1415/1995.

Usmani, J. M. T. (2002). *An Introduction to Islamic Finance*. The Netherlands: Kluwer Law International.

Usmani (2008). "Looking for new steps in Islamic finance", in Lori Hunt (eds.), *Islamic Finance Review 2007/08*. London: Euromoney Yearbooks.

Usmani, M. I. A. (2009) "Examining the prudence of Islamic banks: A risk management perspective", in Lisa Paul (eds.), *Islamic Finance Review 2009/10*. London: Euromoney Yearbooks.

Visser, H. (2009). *Islamic Finance: Principles and Practice*. Cheltenham: Edward Elgar.

Wan Yusuf, Wan Yusrol (2011). *The Impact of IFSB Capital Adequacy Standards on IFIs in Malaysia*. School of Government and International Affairs. Mimeo.

Warde, I. (2009). "'Pent-up demand' for Islamic finance in Egypt". *Daily News Egypt*, 29 January 2009.

Wilson, R. (2002). "Islamic banking and finance: new perspectives on profit-sharing and risk", in M. Iqbal and D. T. Llewellyn (eds.), *The Interface Between Islamic and Conventional Banking*. Cheltenham: Edward Elgar.

Wilson, R. (2005). "Are we likely to witness consolidation within the Islamic Banking Industry as we have seen with the conventional banks?" *Islamic Finance News*, August 2005.

Wilson, R. (2009). *The Development of Islamic Finance in the GCC*. Research Report/ Kuwait Programme on Development, Governance and Globalisation in the Gulf States, London School of Economics, May 2009.

Wright, C. (2008). "Islamic finance: size will matter in Islamic banking". *Euromoney*, Tuesday, 2 December 2008.

Wroughton, L. (2009). "IMF gives self an 'F' in spotting financial crisis". *International Herald Tribune*, Friday, 6 March 2009.

Y-Sing, L. (2009). "Islamic benchmark financing rate not expected in near term". *Guardian*, Monday, 16 March 2009. [Online] Available from: http://www.guardian.co.uk.

Yudistira, D. (2004). "Efficiency in Islamic banking: an empirical analysis of eighteen banks". *Islamic Economic Studies*, Vol. 12, No. 1, August 2004, pp. 1–19.

Zawya: Global Sukuk Market (2011).

Index

Page reference followed by *f* indicate an illustrated figure; and page reference followed by *t* indicate a table